'A PLACE OF GREAT IMPORTANCE'

To my wife Catherine

'A Place of Great Importance'

Scarborough in the Civil Wars, 1640–1660

JACK BINNS

Carnegie Publishing, 1996

'A Place of Great Importance'
Scarborough in the Civil Wars, 1640–1660
Dr Jack Binns

First Edition

Published by Carnegie Publishing Ltd, 18 Maynard St, Preston PR2 2AL

Copyright © Jack Binns, 1996

Typeset in 11/13 Monotype Bembo by
Carnegie Publishing Ltd, 18 Maynard St, Preston, Lancs.

Printed and bound in the UK by Cambridge University Press

British Library Cataloguing in Publication Data
Binns, J.
  A Place of Great Importance: Scarborough in the Civil Wars, 1640–1660
  I. Title
  942.84706
  ISBN 1-85936-18-1

ALL RIGHTS RESERVED

No part of this publication may be reproduced, stored in a retrieval system, or transmitted in any form or by any means mechanical, electronic, photocopying or otherwise, without the prior permission of the publisher.

Contents

Acknowledgements vii

List of Abbreviations ix

	Introduction	1
1	Decline and Recovery	7
2	Defence and War, 1600–1642	53
3	First Civil War, 1642–1645	73
4	The Great Siege, 1645	131
5	The Second Civil War, 1648	182
6	Interregnum, 1649–1660	221
7	Restoration	239
	Epilogue	263
	Notes on the Text	271
	Bibliography	292
	Index	299

Acknowledgements

A work of even this limited scope owes much to the generosity and expertise of many people, too numerous to mention here by name. However, I must record my gratitude to several special friends who collectively made possible this book, but cannot be held responsible for any errors or follies it might contain.

Mr John Rushton gave me an appetite for Scarborough's past and continues to supply me with ideas and books; Mr Gordon Forster, of Leeds University, put me on the road of historical research and gave me unfailing encouragement to follow it; Mr Bryan Berryman gave me the benefit of his unrivalled knowledge of the Scarborough Room in the town's Central Library; and, not least, the labour and enthusiasm of Mr Michael Ashcroft, chief archivist of the North Yorkshire County Record Office, furnished much of my raw material.

I am most grateful to Dr John Morrill, of Selwyn College Cambridge, who read the whole of the first draft with such care and understanding, and offered advice that only his great authority could have provided.

For the best photographic illustrations, terrestial and aerial, I am indebted to Mr Michael Marshall and Mr Michael Jaconelli respectively.

Finally, of the many hardworking staffs who have given me unstinted assistance, I should like to thank those of the libraries of Scarborough Central, Sheffield City, Whitby Literary and Philosophical Society, York City and York Minster, the universities of Cambridge, Hull, Leeds, Oxford and York, as well as those of the British Library, the Public Record Office, the Borthwick Institute of Historical Research at York and the Humberside Archives at Beverley.

List of Abbreviations

The following abbreviations are used throughout the footnotes. Full details of the works cited below and of other books and articles cited by short titles will be found in the Bibliography at the end of the book. Unless stated otherwise, place of publication is London.

APC	Acts of the Privy Council
Ashcroft	M. Y. Ashcroft (ed.), *Scarborough Records 1600–1660*, 2 vols (NYCRO, Northallerton, 1991)
Baker	J. B. Baker, *The History of Scarbrough* (1882)
BIHR, PW	Borthwick Institute of Historical Research, York, Probate Wills
BIHR	*Bulletin of the Institute of Historical Research*, London
BL	British Library
Bod. Lib.	Bodleian Library, Oxford
Chapman	J. Chapman (ed.), *Scarborough Records*, 3 vols (SRL, 1909)
CJ	*Commons Journals*
CPR	*Calendar of Patent Rolls*
CSP	*Clarendon State Papers*
CSPD	*Calendar of State Papers, Domestic*
CSPV	*Calendar of State Papers, Venetian*
CTSC	I. H. Jeayes (ed.), *Copy Translations of Scarborough's Charters* (Scarborough, 1912)
DNB	*Dictionary of National Biography*
Dugdale	J. W. Clay (ed.), *Dugdale's Visitation of Yorkshire*, 3 vols (Exeter, 1899–1917)
Edwards	M. Edwards (ed.), *Scarborough, 966–1966* (Scarborough, 1966)
EHR	*English Historical Review*
EYLHS	East Yorkshire Local History Series

Hinderwell	T. Hinderwell, *The History and Antiquities of Scarborough*, 3rd edn enlarged (Scarborough, 1832)
HMC	Historical Manuscripts Commission
HUCRO	Humberside County Record Office, Beverley
HUL	Hull University Library
Jeayes	I. H. Jeayes (ed.), *Description of Documents in the White Vellum Book of Scarborough Corporation* (Scarborough, 1914)
Leland	L. Toulmin Smith (ed.), *The Itinerary of John Leland in or about the years 1535–1543*, vol. 1 (1914)
LJ	*Lords Journal*
L & P	*Letters and Papers of Henry VIII*
MIC	microfilm edition
NH	*Northern History*
NRQS	*North Riding Quarter Sessions Records*
NRRS	*North Riding Records Series*
NYCRO	North Yorkshire County Record Office, Northallerton
Pearson	T. Pearson, *An Archaeological Survey of Scarborough* (Birmingham University Field Archaeology Unit, Birmingham, 1987)
ORN	*Oxford Royalist Newsbooks*
PRO	Public Record Office
Rowntree	A. Rowntree (ed.), *The History of Scarborough* (1931)
Scarb. Wills	E. Thompson, *Scarborough Wills*, 3 vols (SRL, c.1930)
SCL	Sheffield City Library
SRL	Scarborough Reference Library, Scarborough Room
TRHS	*Transactions of the Royal Historical Society*
TSDAS	*Transactions of the Scarborough and District Archaeological Society*
TT	*Thomason Tracts*
VCH, YNR	*The Victoria History of the Counties of England, Yorkshire, North Riding*, 2 vols (1923)
Whitby LPS	Whitby Literary and Philosophical Society Library, Whitby
YAJ	*Yorkshire Archaeological Journal*
YAS	Yorkshire Archaeological Society

YASPR	Yorkshire Archaeological Society's Parish Register Series
YASRS	Yorkshire Archaeological Society Record Series
YML	York Minster Library
YRCP	*Yorkshire Royalist Composition Papers*

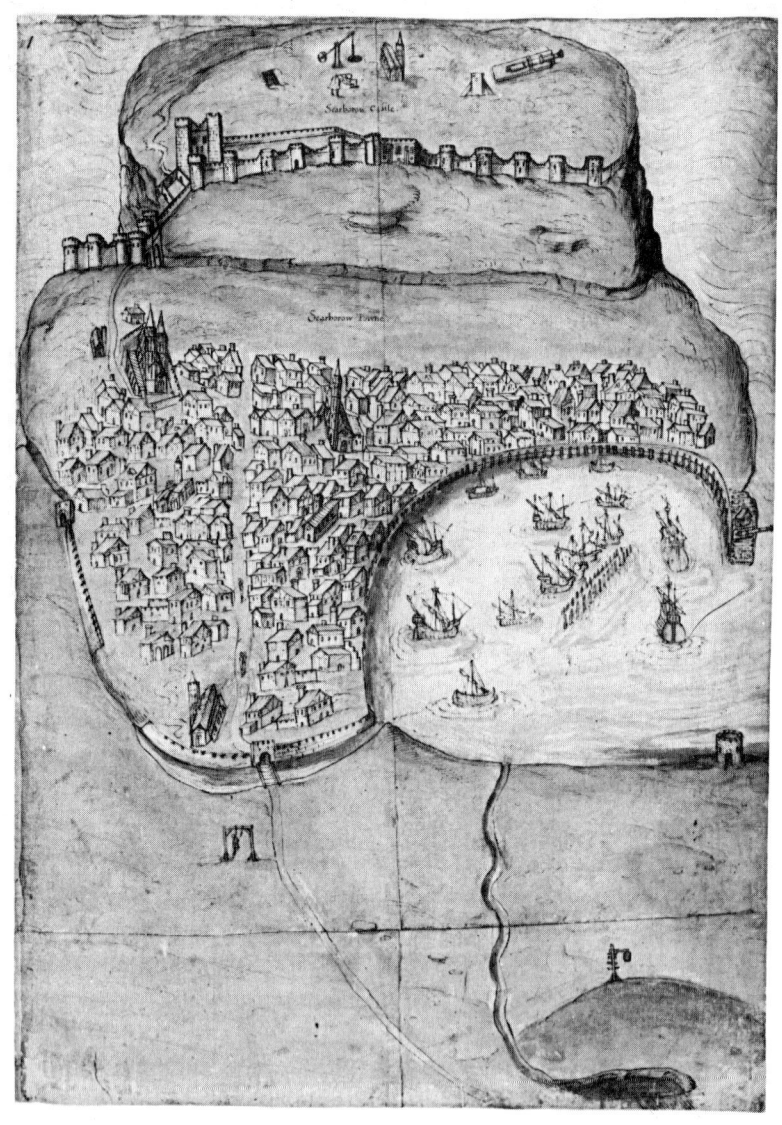

'Plat' of Scarborough, c.1538.

Introduction

THREE and a half centuries ago the kingdoms of England and Wales, Scotland and Ireland were torn apart by Civil War. Scottish Presbyterians and Irish Catholics had rebelled against English rule and the English and Welsh were divided against themselves on fundamental religious and constitutional issues. How were the kingdoms to be governed: by king or Parliament, or by king and Parliament? Who was to control the raising and spending of public taxes? Who was to authorise the recruitment and command of armed forces? What was to be the religious destiny of the British people: Catholic, Presbyterian or Anglican, or perhaps all three co-existing with and tolerating each other?

Between the summers of 1642 and 1646 nowhere in the British Isles was entirely safe from marauding troops, crushing taxation and radical upheaval. Markets closed, trade ceased, rents and bills went unpaid, women and children lost their husbands, brothers and fathers for years on end and sometimes forever. In the worst affected areas, on main land routes, in closely contested borderlands and especially larger towns and cities, civilian communities were repeatedly plundered and oppressed by soldiers on both sides. Buildings were destroyed by cannon fire. Churches were ransacked and vandalised. The loss of horses to the cavalry and waggoners was one of the most crippling grievances. The loss of trees could be almost as damaging to a community. Above all, the most widespread complaint from householders was against free quarter: soldiers rarely paid for their accommodation and food and the 'tickets' issued in place of money usually proved worthless. To add to their tribulations, the people were taxed more heavily and regularly than they had ever been before. Householders were confronted with an endless succession of levies which might be described as 'loans' or 'voluntary subscriptions' but in fact were forced collections. Parliament's new sales tax, the excise, introduced in the summer of 1643, was particularly resented.

To be at the centre of a prolonged siege was the worst fate for a community.

Yorkshire afforded no refuge from these misfortunes. On the contrary, according to the royalist historian, the Earl of Clarendon, 'there were more sharp skirmishes and more notable battles in that one county of York, than in all the kingdom besides . . .'.[1] At Marston Moor, on 2 July 1644, Parliament and its Scottish allies won a decisive victory over Prince Rupert and the king's northern army in the biggest and bloodiest encounter of the whole war. The county was repeatedly traversed by ravenous soldiers recruiting unlucky civilians, requisitioning food, demanding unlimited free billeting and sometimes taking barbarous revenge on uncooperative natives. Villagers who lived near main routes were particularly unfortunate: in some cases they evacuated their homes and abandoned their fields for the duration of the war. Several of the county's principal towns – York, Hull, Pontefract, Bradford and Skipton – were subjected to the multiple horrors of siege warfare as well as military occupation. The 'insolent' and 'exorbitant' Scots were especially feared: they terrorised many neighbourhoods in the North Riding. For instance, the farmers of Wilton, on the road between Pickering and Scarborough, had three visits from Scottish foragers in the summer of 1644. Having taken their beans, oats and barley store and their sheep, the Scots then stole the bedding they had been given free and kidnapped their hosts for ransom money.[2] One correspondent from Cleveland compared his Scottish visitors unfavourably with Mohammedan Turks.[3] General Sir John Meldrum, Parliament's commander at the first siege of Scarborough in 1645, himself a Scotsman, had to confess that he could not sustain his unpaid and hungry troops from the neighbouring countryside: 'Yorkshire and these Northerne Counties', he wrote, 'have beene soe farr exhausted both in monieyes and provisions, first by the Kings Armye, and of late by our owne, that I have no hope of any Reliefe thereby . . .'.[4] Another indication of the condition of the county was that between July 1642 and April 1645 there was only one meeting of the Quarter Sessions 'forasmuch as the said North Riding hath been sore trobled with severall armyes of soldiers . . . soe that noe sessions of the Peace cold be kept'.[5]

Whereas historians of the Civil War once researched and wrote in terms of county communities and country gentry, there is now a growing tendency amongst them to explore urban societies and measure the impact of war and revolution on them. London and most of the largest provincial towns and ports of the time, such as Newcastle, Exeter, Bristol, Norwich and York, have been well and thoroughly treated. But research has not been restricted to the most populous and wealthy: the Civil War records of Barnstaple and Boston, of Durham and Lincoln, of Bedford and even High Wycombe have been examined by professional historians in recent years. Dramatic events in Dorchester, before, during and after the Civil War, inspired one of our leading scholars of the period to write a brilliant book about them. Nevertheless, given that there were probably as many as fifty towns in England with populations of two thousand or more by the middle of the seventeenth century, there is still much more to be done. Since every borough had its own unique history, there can be no history of English boroughs generally.

As far as the political alignment of towns was concerned, it used to be thought, on both sides of the argument, that they all, or nearly all, conformed to the same pattern and persuasion. If the royalists raised their recruits from the poorer, rural communities of the North, Wales and the South West, Parliament's crucial advantage was that it could draw on the money, the industries and the concentrated population of England's commercial ports and towns, from London downwards. If the aristocracy and gentry were fairly evenly divided, the towns were overwhelmingly Parliamentarian. Such views also found favour with modern Marxists since they suggested the Civil War was about class conflict and economic differences.

However, though simplistic and misleading generalisations about the towns still find diminishing support, thanks to the work already done, it is now appreciated that there was no uniformity of political response to the challenge of civil war. Though circumstances might be similar, reactions to them were individual and unpredictable.

Apart from the smallest towns, where neighbouring gentry and nobility were usually dominant, incorporated boroughs were run by a small, self-perpetuating oligarchy which combined economic power with social superiority. Though these ruling elites were confused, challenged and strained by the competing demands and contradictory orders of King and Parliament, rarely did they break down. On the contrary, outside threats closed their ranks. They cared more about defending and retaining their privileged positions and excluding the *hoi polloi* than about the great religious and political matters that divided the two warring parties. Most of all they feared the loss of their restrictive charters which guaranteed their local hegemony. There were, of course, many exceptions, but only rarely did religious differences or ideological loyalties fracture this urban brotherhood. Generally speaking, the smaller the community, the closer and stronger the links of blood, neighbourhood and self-interest. Even when towns were in the grip of Parliament's military forces there was still extreme reluctance to expel members from the ruling council merely on grounds of so-called 'delinquency' (i.e. siding with the royalists) or even 'malignancy' (i.e. fighting on the side of the royalists). Such exclusion orders had to be delivered by outsiders, and they were resented by the inside, 'well-affected' party because they deprived the borough of some of its richest, tax-paying residents and they were regarded as unwarranted acts of foreign interference. In short, if there is an urban tendency to be seen, it is a negative, neutral and conservative response to the national conflict. Some exceptional individuals were driven by enthusiasm for wider and greater causes – Roman Catholics usually sided actively with the King, Puritans normally preferred Parliament – but they were decisively outnumbered by the political hermaphrodites and non-activists.

How did the people of Scarborough react to the upheavals of the middle of the seventeenth century? Since religious nonconformity was rare or rarely reported in the town, then, as elsewhere, the neutrals in Scarborough far outnumbered the activists on both sides. Consequently, the forty-four members of the Common Hall, Scarborough's self-elected, self-regarding oligarchy, tried to play both sides and came down on one rather than the other only when forced by circumstances. When King Charles, his court and his armed followers were no more than forty miles away at Beverley, York or Hull, then Scarborough was outwardly royalist. When the King left Yorkshire and went south and soon afterwards Parliament's governor arrived from London, Scarborough became Parliament's most northerly outpost. When the dangerous presence of the Earl of Newcastle's royalist army was massively reinforced with the money and munitions of Queen Henrietta Maria, who had landed at Bridlington, the town obediently followed its governor when he changed sides. Not a shot was fired by townsman or garrison soldier to resist this sudden turnabout. With only a handful of exceptions, the burgesses of Scarborough supported Sir Hugh Cholmley the royalist as loyally as they supported Sir Hugh Cholmley the Parliamentarian. Predictably, the notable exceptions, were religious extremists – the Harrisons, the Nesfields and John Lawson – who were already republican in sympathy.

To prove that the events of 1642–45 were not extraordinary, when Parliament's new governor, Matthew Boynton, defected to the king as Cholmley had done, the town followed him as tamely in 1648 as it had followed Cholmley five years earlier. Only when Boynton's position became untenable, did the Common Hall defy him and force its own closure. Sir Hugh had engaged the cooperation of the town until compelled to retreat to the castle, and much the same happened again in the case of Colonel Boynton. As before, town hall priority was self-preservation.

Scarborians had sound reasons to hope that they might be spared the worst horrors experienced by other urban societies. There were at least fifty towns in England with greater populations and more wealth. Even in Yorkshire, according to the ship money assessment of 1635, Scarborough ranked ninth, below York, Leeds, Hull, Doncaster, Pontefract, Beverley, Richmond and Ripon; only little Hedon was considered poorer. Scarborough had two Members in the House of Commons, but so had thirteen other boroughs in the county. Unlike many disputed towns, for example, Bradford, Sheffield, Birmingham or Northampton, Scarborough had no valuable war-supply industries producing textiles, boots and shoes, or metal wares that would have attracted military foragers and commissaries. Neither side was likely to fight over Scarborough's fish. Even as a seaport, Scarborough's status was lowly: it had long since conceded regional mercantile leadership to Hull, and recently Whitby, with its lucrative alum trade and new, great west pier, had overtaken it. Even without a pier, Bridlington's seagoing commerce equalled Scarborough's in 1640. Though Scarborough had a medieval castle, by this time it was derelict and disarmed, and certainly no stronger than a dozen or so other similar obsolete fortresses in Yorkshire alone. Above all, Scarborough's physical remoteness – its distance from London, the Midlands and the key land routes running north and south and east and west, which made such towns as Skipton, Newark, Pontefract and

Leicester so important and vulnerable – should have given it safety from garrisons and passing armies.

In these circumstances it might therefore seem astonishing that between 1642 and 1648 Scarborough changed hands no fewer than seven times; that it was twice subjected to bombardment, siege and assault; that Parliament declared a day of national thanksgiving after its forces had captured the town and harbour in February 1645; and that King Charles believed the castle so vital to his cause that he ordered it to be held 'to the last extremity'. As well as explaining how the people of Scarborough responded to the Civil Wars and their consequences, it is also the main purpose of this study to reconcile the apparent contradictions of Scarborough's geographical remoteness and its central military importance, and of the commercial insignificance and crucial strategic value of its harbour.

CHAPTER ONE

Decline and Recovery

WHEN the famous Tudor antiquarian John Leland rode to Scarborough in the summer of 1544 he came from Malton eastwards along the south side of the Vale of Pickering through the villages of Sherburn and Seamer. On his right he noted the high escarpment of the chalk Wolds and to his left the low, flat, marshy carrs. Between them, along Leland's route, now the busy A64, he saw 'champaign ground, fruitful of grass and corn'. Three miles beyond the 'great uplandishe toune' of Seamer, and after passing through a narrow valley with steep hills on either side, John Leland reached Scarborough beside the German Ocean.[1]

In fact, long before he saw the buildings of Scarborough, Leland had crossed its borough boundary. At the southern entrance to the valley he would have ridden alongside an extensive lake. This stretch of water was then known as Byward Wath, and it marked the southernmost limit of Scarborough's jurisdiction. Even as late as 1845, when the railway line from York to Scarborough was laid over it, the Mere, as it is now called, covered an area of forty acres. Today Scarborough Mere is so shallow and shrunken that many visitors are unaware of its existence. Because he was a southerner, Leland called this lake-filled valley a vale, but to local people it was Burtondale.[2]

If Leland had approached the outskirts of Scarborough town by what was then known as the borough causeway, which crossed a stream called the Washbeck, it might explain why he failed to notice and record a cluster of houses partly hidden in a hollow to his left – the village of Falsgrave. Once the heartland of a sprawling Anglo-Danish sokedom, Falsgrave, or Wallesgrave, as it was then written, had become little more than a detached suburb of big-brother Scarborough.

Anyone who came to Scarborough by Leland's landward route would have been sure to notice a prominent, steep-sided hill, rising to more than 500 feet, south of the town. For the past two centuries this flat-topped high ground has been called Oliver's Mount, but previously it was known as Weaponness and constituted Scarborough's principal common pasture. Between the town itself and Weaponness 'a rill of fresch water' ran down a ravine and across the sands into the sea south of the harbour. This overflow from Byward Wath was known locally as Millbeck and its narrow, wooded valley as Ramsdale.[3]

Leland observed that the town still retained some of its medieval defences, and a century later, though now even more neglected, they were still recognisable. According to Leland and a military engineer who drew a 'plat' of Scarborough about the same time as his visit, there were stone walls only on either side of the town's two gateways, Newborough and Oldborough Bars. Between them the gap in the town wall was filled by a wide ditch and earth bank, known for centuries as the New Dyke Bank. Leland was told that in 1484, during the time Richard III spent in Scarborough, he had begun to build a new town wall in 'quadrato saxo', squared stone; but events on Bosworth Field the following summer determined that this defensive work was never finished. More than half a century later, Leland thought that 'Newburgh gate' was still 'meately good' but 'Aldeburgh gate very base'.[4] As the name indicates, Oldborough, the original settlement, had defences which predated those of its western extension Newborough, though even by Leland's time they had almost disappeared. Nevertheless, when civil war came to Scarborough a century later, Newborough's Bar, walls, ditch and earth bank had some protective value.

Leland wrote that the oldest part of the town stood entirely 'on a slaty clife'; but though the south-facing slope down to the sandy shore is steep it is overlaid with unstable boulder clay, not stone. Since it was planted in the early twelfth century the old borough consisted of several long, man-made terraces cut east and west across the hillside and buttressed in stone. These terraces eventually became streets with names such as Paradise at the top of the slope, High and

Nether Westgate lower down, and Merchant Row and Tuthill near the foot. Connecting these long thoroughfares and at right angles to them to form a grid pattern were short flights of wooden steps with names such as Long Greece and Shilbottle, and straight, narrow, steep, stone roads called, from east to west, Eastgate, St Mary's Gate, Spreight Lane and Tollergate.

For administrative purposes the old borough was divided into two Quarters, Oldborough itself, and Undercliff, lying directly below the castle headland, and the new borough into two more, Newborough and St Mary's, the upper area around the parish church. In contrast to the bustle, noise, darkness and dirt of the densely populated old borough, St Mary's Quarter was a haven of light, clean air and ample space; much of it was open field and walled paddock and garden. Most of the land up there belonged to the parish church and included the vicarage garden, Paradise Close and Paradise Gardens, Pillory Hill, Charnel Garth and St Mary's graveyard.

Newborough Quarter was the most extensive of the four and its layout quite different from the street pattern of the older borough. Here the ground was almost level and so the long streets, formerly the boundaries of open fields, Cargate, Blackfriargate and St Thomas's Gate, ran northwards off the east–west axis of Newborough Gate as far as Richard's 'new wall'.

Leland was slightly puzzled by Scarborough's status. He knew that it was a privileged borough yet it seemed to be within the jurisdiction of the wapentake of Pickering Lythe, which extended as far as the sea coast on either side of it. An 'old mariner' of Scarborough told him that Henry I had first given the town 'grete privilege', but like any seasoned traveller he was justifiably sceptical of the tall tales of seamen.[5]

The 'old mariner' was exaggerating, but not by much. Scarborough's earliest royal charters, of 1155 and 1163, dated from the beginning of the reign of Henry II when the town had been granted the same liberties as York. In return, Scarborough's residents were required to pay an annual tax on their houses known as gablage.

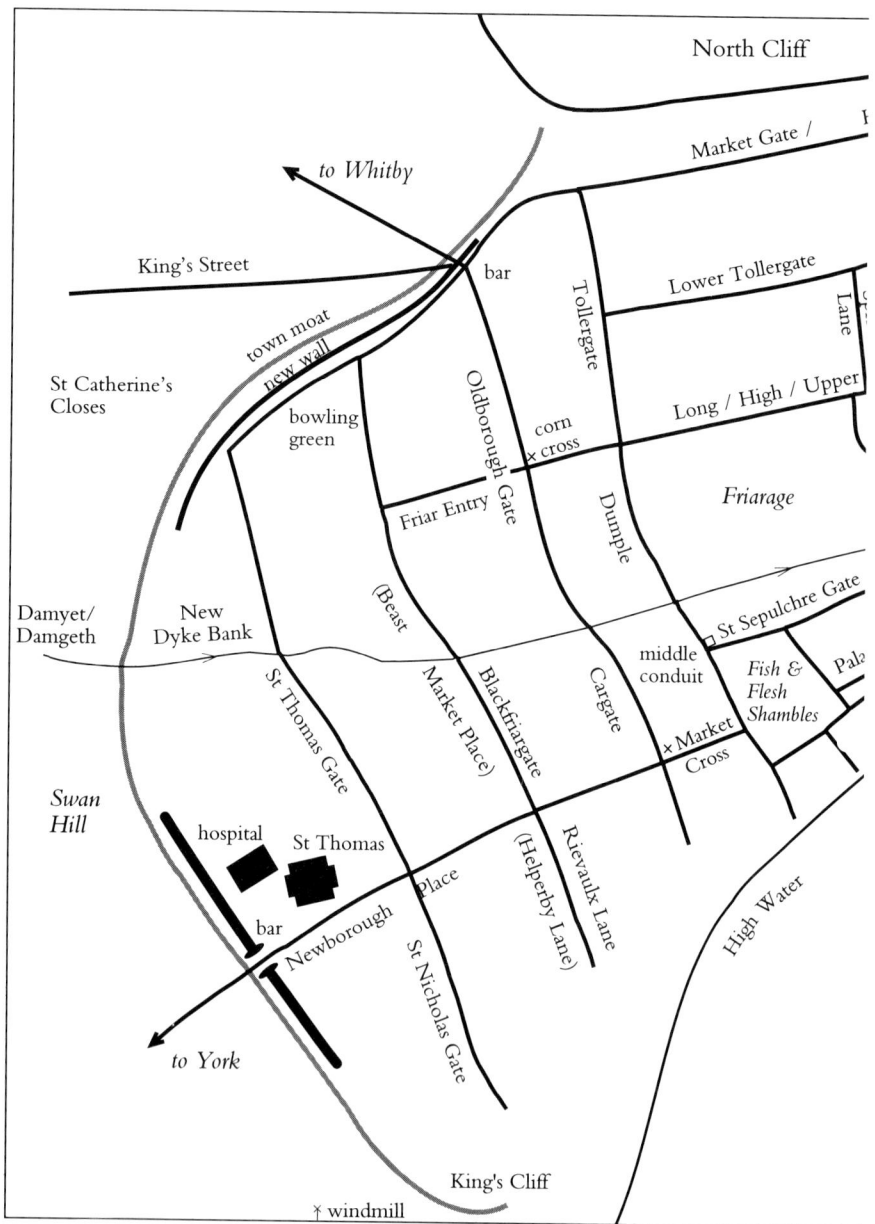

DECLINE AND RECOVERY 11

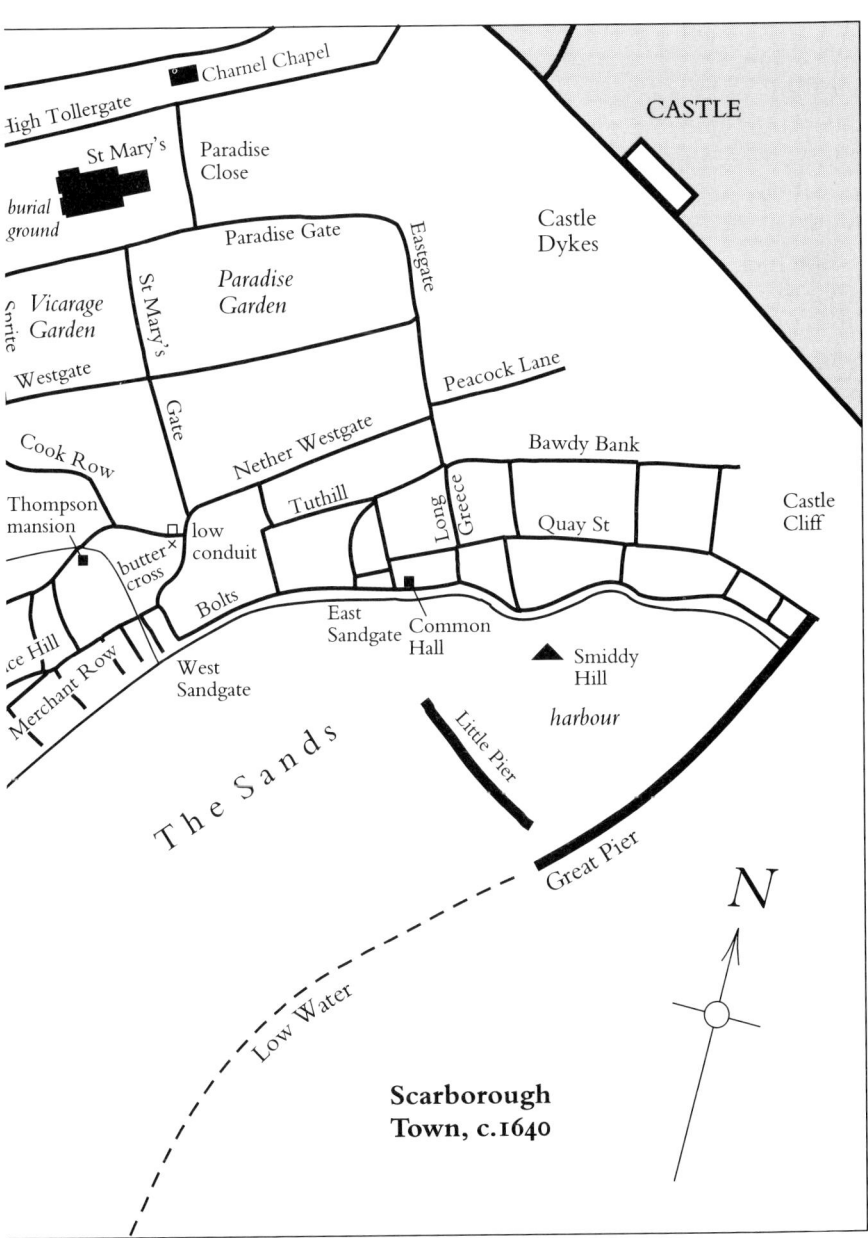

Houses built end-on to the street were assessed at four pence and those with a wider frontage lengthways along it paid six pence.[6]

The privileges of the corporation of Scarborough, like those of other royal chartered boroughs, were indeed substantial and jealously guarded. From early in the reign of Henry III, the borough was allowed to take tolls on all vessels entering or leaving by sea and on all carts entering or leaving by land. Originally this grant was intended to pay for enclosing and fortifying the town, but it was also used for building a harbour quay or pier, for paving the streets, and for establishing a system of municipal government and jurisdiction. Like the citizens of York, the burgesses of Scarborough were free to travel throughout the kingdom without having to pay taxes or tolls.[7]

At about the same time, Scarborough took permanent control of the adjacent royal manor of Falsgrave, or at least that part of it which included Ramsdale, Burtondale, common rights on Weaponness and Falsgrave Moor, and about sixty acres of arable and pasture land between Newborough Bar and Falsgrave village.[8] To compensate itself, the Crown added another £25 a year to Scarborough's fee-farm rent. Later, part of Falsgrave's fee-farm rent was given by Edward III in perpetuity to the warden and scholars of King's Hall at Cambridge; his grandson, Richard II, gave them £20 more out of Scarborough's own fee-farm, making £42 11s. in all; and finally Henry VIII confirmed this transfer in his foundation charter to Trinity College. Nearly five centuries later, Scarborough corporation still pays £42.55 a year to Trinity.[9]

One of the most valuable provisions of the royal charter of 1253 was the grant of an annual 45-day fair, to be held from the feast of the Assumption, 15 August, until Michaelmas, 29 September. The fair gave Scarborough the status of an international port: one of the longest in Europe, it was timed to coincide with the annual migration southwards of great shoals of herring which attracted fishermen from all the shores of the North Sea and Baltic and made possible an enormous fish market held mainly on the sands. To add to Scarborough's commercial strength, no ship was allowed to load or unload cargo anywhere else along the coast between Ravenscar and Flamborough, and the neighbouring markets of Brompton, Sherburn, Seamer and Filey were prohibited.[10]

As an incorporated borough Scarborough had the right to regulate its own internal affairs. Two annually-elected bailiffs sat as justices of the peace at the borough's quarter sessions and also presided over the sheriff's tourn or court leet. At the general sessions the bailiffs heard criminal cases such as assault and theft, and here they also dealt with many kinds of lesser offences, such as unlicensed brewing, neglect of sewers, fences and roads, breaches of the assize of bread and ale, and drunkenness. The court leet met twice a year, usually in April and October, to enforce the town's 'pains' or bye-laws which covered almost every activity of urban life from rounding up stray animals and cleaning pavements to checking weights and measures and preventing pollution of the water supply or the harbour. Though the name of bailiff is suggestive more of a farming foreman than a civic dignatory, Scarborough's two leading governors were men of great power and prestige. They were chosen by only twelve 'electors' of the Common Hall and usually from only its foremost members and could be re-elected any number of times. Amongst their many perquisites of office one was the sole right to take fish from the Mere; another was free pasture for their animals on Weaponness and in the town's South Field. When they died they were buried in the Bailiffs' Aisle in St Mary's.[11]

After their year as bailiffs, the two stepped down to become coroners for the next twelve months. The role of the coroners was more honorary than functional, but their responsibility for the harbour and piers was vital. Also elected annually on St Jerome's day, 30 September, were four chamberlains and thirty-six burgesses. The chamberlains kept the corporation's financial accounts: they paid officers' and workmen's salaries and wages, collected rents and taxes, secured loans, and paid the king's rent into the royal exchequer. The thirty-six remaining members of the Common Hall, as their assembly on Sandside was called, were divided by seniority into three Twelves.[12] Thus by 1640 the fate of Scarborough had been for centuries in the hands of a self-perpetuating oligarchy of forty-four men whose authority derived from a succession of royal charters.

From its original enfranchisement in 1283 Scarborough still had the right to send two members to the House of Commons and its electorate remained exclusively the forty-four burgesses of the Common Hall. By 1640, however, the borough's parliamentary importance had suffered a relative decline. In 1540, Scarborough alone had a quarter of Yorkshire's representation, but in each successive reign more of the county's boroughs were separately enfranchised: Hedon and Thirsk under Edward VI; Ripon, Knaresborough, Boroughbridge and Aldborough under Mary; Beverley and Richmond during Elizabeth's time; Pontefract in 1621; and most recently, in 1640, Malton and Northallerton. Consequently, when the Long Parliament opened, Scarborough had two of Yorkshire's thirty seats, and the whole House had swollen from 341, at the death of Henry VIII, to 507.[13]

To manage and regulate the town's internal affairs the Common Hall chose and employed many officers, usually on annual contract. Four churchwardens were responsible for the parish church of St Mary and the church of St Thomas the Martyr, now the only two places of worship in the town. Four constables, one for each Quarter, maintained street and market order. Livestock on the commons of Ramsdale and Weaponness were herded by two pasture masters. In summertime, the job of the netherd was to take cattle from Ramsdale up to Weaponness at six in the morning and bring them down twelve hours later. The town bull was also his responsibility. A warrener was employed to catch and control ground game. Highways and causeways within the boundaries of the extensive borough were looked after by four overseers. A pindar was expected to keep the streets of the town free from stray animals by locking them in his pound.[14]

Four guardians were appointed to look after Scarborough's aged paupers and infant orphans, too young to be apprenticed, who were lodged together in St Thomas's poorhouse. The piermaster and the schoolmaster, who both had greater security of tenure than other borough appointees, were each paid the same annual salary of ten pounds. As elsewhere, however, the town prison was expected to pay for itself. The gaoler had to find his living from involuntary guests; his only fee was four pence for 'every arrest of a strainger or unfreman for his gaole'.[15] The town cook had his own 'livery cloak' and was paid forty shillings a year on condition that he was always ready to provide dinners and feasts at the Common Hall and wedding breakfasts at two shillings and sixpence each.[16] Scarborough also had its own official minstrels or waits, usually two or three musicians and singers, who were expected to provide entertainment at public and private functions.[17] Finally, for almost any other task, and not merely for running messages or making public announcements, the bailiffs employed a bellman.

In 1640 the medieval assizes of bread and ale were still being strictly enforced. Two appointed breadweighers were provided with two sets of small scales, one of troy, the other of avoirdupois. The town's standard penny loaf had to be sold everywhere at the same weight which was determined by the current market price of local flour. At its cheapest, a penny wheaten loaf might be as much as two pounds in weight, but in time of scarcity and high prices, as little as six and a half ounces. Similarly, two official alefyners checked the quality, price and quantity of the other essential of life. They had to test local brews for taste and strength and they had to inspect all the measures used. Indeed, all liquids, not just beer, sold in the town were measured in the borough's own standard 'pinte pott' and 'quart potte'. There were also similar tight regulations concerning the manufacture and sale of leather goods. All leather offered for sale in the town's open markets had to be stamped with the borough's seal of approval and the corporation employed a leather searcher, a leather sealer and a leather registrar.

When Leland visited Scarborough he was favourably impressed by the castle there; according to his account, it was 'goodly larg and stronge on a stepe rok, having but one way by the stepe slaty crag to cum to it'.[18] Nature had created a fairly flat-topped promontory fanning out into the sea between two deep, wide bays. This broad-based triangle of rock, about sixteen acres in area and 300 feet above sea level at its highest point, dropped almost vertically into the sea on its eastern side and was connected to the mainland at its apex only by a narrow hogsback of a land bridge. To the north a perpendicular cliff overlooked the castle holms, and to the west a steep-sided ravine, called the castle dykes, separated the headland from the old town. The only vulnerable point in this natural fortress was strongly protected by a turreted barbican, gatehouse and two drawbridges spanning the dykes, each overlooked by towers. Inside the castle grounds, on the highest place and enclosed by an inner

Sea cliff, showing the remains of Roman signal station and the Well of Our Lady.

Aerial view of Scarborough headland and Castle between the two bays.

The Castle Keep, inner bailey and barbican.

bailey wall, stood the great keep or arx. With a basement, three upper storeys and roof-top battlements, it was almost 100 feet high. Its square walls varied in thickness from 10 to 15 feet. It dominated the headland and could be seen at a great distance both from land and sea. Running the whole length of the east side of the dykes was a curtain wall; it was 230 yards long, contained no fewer than twelve towers of various sizes and shapes, and ended at Cockhill tower on the edge of the cliff overlooking the harbour. The sea cliff was so high and precipitous that none of it had been ever guarded with walls or towers.[19]

However, even as early as 1540, the castle at Scarborough was already unoccupied, badly neglected and in an advanced state of decay. A meticulous, detailed survey conducted by Sir Marmaduke Constable and Sir Ralph Ellerker, dated Lady Day 1538, described the royal castle as dilapidated and far from impregnable. The walls and turrets of the barbican, they wrote, were 'sore decayed and shakyn'; 75 yards of the north wall had fallen down into the holms and could be restored only 'upon archis of stone'; the gates to the

Scarborough Castle Keep, showing the southern entrance by exterior staircase.

inner bailey had gone; the floors, roofs and lead of some of the curtain towers were 'decayed', 'fallend down', or 'gone'. The surveyors identified 'thre placeys . . . that men may clyme up' the sea cliff where it lacked any artificial defences. They accepted that the castle had 'a praty chapell of our lady' covered with lead and 'a fayre well' nearby, but pointed out bluntly that it had no brewhouse, bakery or horsemill. As for ordnance, the castle boasted 'a greate brasen gune, an olde serpentyne, iiij Basys and viii chambers'. However, since there was neither powder nor ammunition, all these ancient artillery pieces were useless. In conclusion, Constable and Ellerker estimated that to make Scarborough castle once more habitable and defensible they would need over a thousand tons of new stone, three hundred tons of timber, nine of iron and forty of lead.[20]

A century later, the castle at Scarborough had deteriorated even further, both in structure and status. Only at certain critical moments – during the Pilgrimage of Grace, at the time of Stafford's abortive coup in 1557, and finally in 1569 when the Northern Earls rebelled – had successive Tudor monarchs put much value on the strength and security of Scarborough castle. Henry VIII, Mary and the young Elizabeth had all spent money on its repair. As long as there was danger of a rebellion in the North, a Scottish invasion, or a foreign seaborne landing, the castle still had its royal uses.

After Sir Thomas Stafford had landed at Scarborough and taken the castle by stealth in a hopeless gesture of defiance against Queen Mary, she commanded the absentee governor, Sir Richard Cholmley, either to reside in the castle himself or to send his son to live there 'for the better garding of the same'.[21] Ten years later, when Sir Richard had still failed to renounce his Catholic faith, Queen Elizabeth deprived him of the governorship and his life tenancy of the adjacent royal manor of Northstead for being 'obstinate in religion'.[22]

Although Scarborough was described by a loyal witness as 'a very quiet place' during the rising of the Northern Earls,[23] the Queen took no risks with her castle there: she placed it and a garrison under the command of an utterly trustworthy Protestant, Sir Henry Gate of Seamer. Then, apart from the years 1579 to 1584, when Sir John Constable was governor, the castle at Scarborough remained in the safe hands of the Gate family throughout the remainder of Elizabeth's reign. After the death of Sir Henry in 1589, his eldest son, Edward, succeeded him as constable.[24]

The last time when it was reported that the castle at Scarborough was garrisoned with troops was the summer of 1602. According to a list of payments made that August by bailiff William Peacock, he had 'disbursed 30 shillings for the soldyers', and sent up to the men at the castle 'a brat & a couger' worth 14d. and wine to the value of 5s. 11d.[25]

The union of the English and Scottish crowns under James I and VI in 1603, and the end of the long war with Spain the following year, deprived Scarborough castle of what little remaining value it might have had to the government in London. Governorship of the castle had long since ceased to be an awesome and onerous responsibility. Neglected for decades, the fabric of this once-formidable fortress was now allowed to fall into utter ruin. By 1608, the castle was described as 'very ruinous and in great decay'.[26] A final inspection conducted by two local gentlemen, William St Quintin and Stephen Hutchinson, in 1619 contained a familiar catalogue of dilapidation and erosion, and led to an estimate that minimum repairs would cost at least £4,000.[27]

Probably prompted by this pessimistic appraisal, King James decided to rid himself of a worthless encumbrance: he gave the castle at Scarborough to John Ramsay, the Earl of Holderness. Just before he died childless in 1626 the earl made his chief steward, William Thompson of Humbleton, responsible for the castle, and this event marked the beginning of a long and troubled association between it and the Thompson family.[28] In 1630, William's heir, Francis, bought the castle grounds and derelict buildings from the Ramsay estate.[29] The castle at Scarborough had become by then no more than a cattle pasture, a rabbit warren, and a dangerous playground for the more adventurous youth of the town.[30] During the 1620s, when England was next at war, this time with France as well as Spain, the Crown made no attempt to recover the castle. The security of the harbour was no longer linked with the strength of the castle.

Fortunately, the people of Scarborough were not dependent on the castle for their safety or their prosperity: the most vital asset of their community was the harbour. Though the castle headland and the town itself provided adequate protection from the north and west, Sandside was openly exposed to high tide, storm and silting driven on-shore by easterly or southerly winds. Without the artificial breakwater of a lengthy and massive pier, there was no safe haven for ships at Scarborough.

Ever since Henry III had first granted the borough the right to build a 'new port with timber and stone towards the sea',[31] its burgesses had claimed that theirs was the only secure anchorage between Tyne and Humber from tempest, fog or pirates; but without a well maintained pier they knew the claim was bogus. Consequently, the condition of Scarborough's pier was always a measure of the town's well being: without its port of refuge it would be little more than a fishing village, like Filey or Robin Hood's Bay.[32]

When John Leland had passed through Scarborough he observed ominously that 'the peere wherby socour is made for shippes is now sore decayid, and that almost yn the midle of it'.[33] Soon afterwards, the pier was reported to be 'freatted and broken down, and marvellously worn away'.[34] Several Acts of Parliament and Privy Council orders granting duties on shipping and free timber from the royal forest of Pickering proved ineffective:[35] the key or quay was said to be still 'in Ruyne'.[36] In desperation, the burgesses auctioned the contents of the church of the Holy Sepulchre; and when the proceeds were found to be inadequate they sold the lead from its roof and that of the church of St Thomas. The latter's roof was re-covered with slate, but the former church was allowed to become a quarry for local builders and its burial ground a pasture for cattle.[37]

There was still no permanent remedy: all that the town could afford were temporary repairs to the pier. In 1564 a petition was drawn up and sent by the bailiffs to Queen Elizabeth. The present pier, they pleaded, was not worth mending: its timber frame and narrow base were too weak to withstand the rage of the sea. They asked for a thousand pounds to build a new pier entirely of stone which would 'contynewe forever withowte much more helpe'. It was emphasized to the Queen how much her own direct interest was at stake in this investment. Of the £91 she received annually from the corporation as its fee-farm rent, all but £14 came from the profits of fishing. Similarly, her income from the parsonage of St Mary's of £40 a year was derived largely from the fish tithe. Furthermore, Elizabeth was reminded rather bluntly that her household was supplied with four thousand fish every year from Scarborough 'at half the pryce that others payeth'. Finally, the petitioners pointed out that her income of £50 a year from former abbey, friary and chantry properties in the town would be jeopardised, as would her return from Scarborough when any Tenth or Fifteenth tax was granted to her, if the port's activity was damaged by its rotting, broken pier.[38]

Two years later, Elizabeth agreed to give Scarborough £500, a hundred tons of free timber, and six tons of iron.[39] Though the new stone pier cost at least £2,000 and took nearly twenty years to finish, it rescued the port and saved the town from further decline. Scarborough's new great east pier was a colossal structure and a feat of engineering. From Sandside, under the castle headland, it ran southwards in an almost straight line for 267 yards. Built of gigantic blocks of ashlar on the outside and filled with a core of stone rubble, the pier measured 20 yards at the base, 7½ yards at the top, and stood 10 yards high on the seaward face. At the spring tide it provided eighteen feet of water in the haven and at the neap eleven. During storms the gap between the new great pier and the old little west pier was closed by 'a greate sea-gate'. When Dover's pier had to be repaired, Scarborough responded to a request for help by sending there some of its best masons and smiths.[40]

Nevertheless, contrary to the sanguine claims made in 1564, the bailiffs had to admit that 'sometymes in great stormes some breche is made in the pere'. They reckoned that even the new pier still cost them about £40 a year in repairs and maintenance which was not covered by the 'pettie monie' raised from anchorage charges.[41] In fact, there would never be an end to work on Scarborough's piers. Built on clay, not on bedrock, and exposed to the full force of incoming sea gales from the east and south, they would be repeatedly damaged and perpetually eroded, and the town alone would never have sufficient resources to secure them indefinitely.

At the end of the Queen's reign Scarborough's tribulations prompted yet another petition and another litany of woe. The burgesses alleged that they were now having to spend more than

£100 a year on their piers and therefore they could no longer find the fee-farm rent of £91 and a double parliamentary subsidy amounting to £66 13s. 4d. Formerly, they claimed, Scarborough had been a 'Towne of great traffique by sea, as well as trade of merchandize as of fishing', but both of these sources of income and employment were now 'verie much decaied'. As a result, the town was 'greatly depopulated, 3 parts thereof to the number of 600 tenements being utterly ruinated'.[42]

Even allowing for the inevitable exaggeration in such a petition which requested exemption from taxation, it has to be conceded that when this same petition was readdressed to King James in January 1605 it carried convincing endorsements from the Earl of Nottingham and Thomas, lord Burghley. As lord high admiral, Nottingham took a particular interest in Scarborough and its harbour of refuge. Clearly he regretted that 'this pore towne' through lack of trade had 'growne to great povertie' and was 'much depopulated'. Burghley had been lord president of the Council of the North from 1599 until 1603 and he confirmed that during this time he had been 'eye-witness of the great charge whereat the towne was for the maintenance of ther peeres' and of the poverty of its people. Both men agreed that Scarborough's piers were costly but essential 'to all vessels that trade in the Northerne parts', and to the town's livelihood.[43] King James seems to have been convinced: he released Scarborough from one of the two subsidies of £33 6s. 8d. levied in 1601 but still unpaid. According to the royal exemption order, James had been 'credibilie informed' that Scarborough was 'in great p[ar]te therof depopulated and such Inhabitants as are there remayninge are much decayed and ympoverished, and very fewe of any habilitye'. Though the borough would still have to pay the fee-farm rent in full and finance its own pier maintenance, it was excused further taxation.[44]

Indirectly, it was coal that saved Scarborough, and, ironically, a great sea storm that triggered the rescue. A petition signed by Newcastle's mayor and the leading members of its corporation dated 15 December 1613 stated that Scarborough's harbour piers had suffered serious damage in a great tempest the previous month. Another petition at the end of February 1614 from the mayor and aldermen of Kingston-upon-Hull was more explicit: 'a sore and sudden storme and tempest . . . on or about the feast of all Saintes last' had 'greatlie broken' Scarborough's 'peeres and defences against the sea'. Both sets of petitioners argued that, since there was no other safe and convenient shelter for ships sailing between the Tyne and the Humber, it was vital that the harbour there should be speedily restored.[45]

From then on petitions poured in almost daily: from King's Lynn on 2 March, from Great Yarmouth five days later, from Dunwich, Ipswich, Harwich and Colchester, between 10 and 19 March, and from Deptford on 9 April. On a general petition of the shipowners, seamen and mariners 'trading for Newcastle and the north parts of England', there were 361 signatures from 14 different east coast ports, including London, the biggest, and Woodbridge in Suffolk, the smallest. Significantly, Hull was the only port in Yorkshire to support this petition; presumably, Scarborough's closest rivals, Coatham, Whitby and Bridlington, hoped to profit from its recent misfortune.[46]

This positive response to events at Scarborough was unprecedented: previously, only the Crown had reluctantly provided money and materials when the harbour needed them. Now it seemed that almost every coastal community, even old enemies such as Yarmouth and King's Lynn, was anxious to repair the haven as soon as possible. Since 1603 the union of the two kingdoms under James meant that English North Sea mariners had no longer reason to fear Scottish pirates; and since the conclusion of peace with Spain the following year there had also been relief from the unwelcome attentions of notorious Dunkirk privateers. Clearly, however, as every petition implied or explained, Scarborough harbour was now perceived to be of inestimable value in time of bad weather because it was the only safe anchorage between Tynemouth and the Humber estuary. It was not immediately obvious that what all the petitioners had in common was an immense interest in the sea-coal trade out of Newcastle and Sunderland.

By 1615 there were thought to be as many as 400 English ships engaged all-year round in the North Sea coal traffic, half of them supplying London's hearths and furnaces.[47] By far the greatest number of them were loaded from the banks of the Tyne and the Wear. Newcastle's exports of coal rose from 190,680 tons in 1603 to 452,625 tons in 1634. From Sunderland came 2,383 tons in 1609 and 11,921 tons thirty years later. In 1614, of the fourteen ports most actively engaged in this huge and rapidly growing carrying trade, eleven sent petitions in Scarborough's favour; the three exceptions were Sandwich, York and Bridlington.[48]

The massive importance of the coal trade is sufficient to explain why Scarborough's own petition to the Privy Council regarding the deplorable state of its harbour was so promptly and generously rewarded. According to the reply from Whitehall, dated 19 April 1614, over 400 owners, merchants and seamen had by then put their names to similar cries for help. The Council accepted that it was a matter of urgency that the 'uttermore peere' should be repaired and henceforth maintained intact. For this purpose Scarborough was granted the right to a levy of 4d. on every voyage of ships under 50 tons, and 8d. for every voyage of ships over 50 tons burthen from all vessels trading up and down the east coast between Newcastle and London. The duties were to be collected by the customers and all other of His Majesty's officers at the east coast ports. Foreign vessels were not entitled to exemption.[49] In practice, from now on, the money gathered at Newcastle and Sunderland was sent to the coroners at Scarborough who were directly responsible for the quay and piers. Henceforth, the harbour was paid for by the coal trade. Some smaller ports, such as those of the Cinque, seem to have secured exemption, but this privilege was never claimed by the principal carriers.[50]

After 1614 the piers at Scarborough were never again short of funds. Repairs to them were carried out quickly and fully. The great pier, so vital and yet so vulnerable, was not only carefully maintained but also much strengthened and improved by placing more heavy boulders against its 'backsyde' and extending it southwards. When the old quay house was damaged in a storm a new one was built on the same site in 1624.[51] The 'moneye ariseinge att Newcastle and Sunderland' provided such a constant and healthy surplus in the coroners' pier account that it became the town's permanent reserve, to be raided for whatever might be needed elsewhere.[52]

One of the chief beneficiaries of Scarborough's 'peare money surplus' was the parish church: during the 1630s, after almost a century of neglect and decay, St Mary's was renovated and refurnished. About 1540, on the eve of the Reformation, John Leland had described Scarborough's principal church as 'very faire'. He noted that St Mary's had aisles on both sides of its nave, two transepts and three bell towers with pyramid roofs, two at the western end and one 'yn the midle of the cross isle'.[53] About the time this was written, Henry VIII's military engineer drew a building somewhat similar enclosed by a high stone wall.[54] What both observers failed to record was the magnificent aisled choir added to the east end of the church in the middle of the previous century. Equally impressive were the four chantry chapels, built on to the south aisle of the nave between the south transept and the porch during the 1380s and 1390s. These chapels had been endowed by local men who had reason to need as many prayers as possible said for their endangered souls.[55] When Leland saw it, on its high commanding site overlooking the town, St Mary's must have looked more like a cathedral than a parish church.

By the time of Archbishop Neile's visitation of 1633, Scarborough's religious architecture had been devastated by the combined impact of Reformation and economic adversity. As everywhere else in the country, the dissolution of the monasteries and friaries marked a significant watershed in the town's history. Of least importance was the end of the connection with Bridlington Priory. Since the reign of Henry IV the Black Canons had held the advowson and patronage of St Mary's as well as a claim on its tithes. However, though the prior had appointed its vicars, in practice St Mary's remained under the day-to-day control of Scarborough's Common Hall burgesses. They presented all its many chantry priests and decided when masses were said and bells rung. After the closure of Bridlington Priory the patronage of the vicarage passed to the Crown but, for the time being, everything else, including doctrine and service, remained unaltered.[56]

The departure of the friars had much more serious consequences for Scarborough. Franciscans, Dominicans and Carmelites all had houses in the heart of the town; but their pitifully small surrender value in 1539 bore no relation to their spiritual and physical contribution to three centuries of Scarborough's history. All three had once been richly endowed in land, buildings and respect. All of them had

DECLINE AND RECOVERY

St Mary's. Exterior view from the south-west showing undamaged porch, chantry chapels, Farrer's aisle and tower.

View from Bushell's battery overlooking the ruins of the chancel of St Mary's

provided the townspeople with altars, sermons, confessors and burial grounds, so that their sudden and total disappearance left gaping holes in the life and appearance of the borough.[57] Not until well into the nineteenth century were their building sites and spacious walled gardens entirely covered with new secular structures.

Altogether the three friaries occupied an area of 7½ acres. The former Franciscan site, even today still known as Friarage, covered a three-acre square in the centre of Oldborough, astride a stream called the Damgeth. Next to each other, on adjacent land, the Dominicans and Carmelites had all the ground between the new wall at Oldborough Bar to the north, Newborough Gate to the south, Blackfriargate to the west and Cargate to the east.[58]

On the other hand, the people of Scarborough continued to benefit from two long-term legacies of the friars. Dissatisfied with the old borough well, which drew its water from the open Damgeth, the Franciscans had arranged with the burgesses to tap the springs of Gildhuscliff in Falsgrave and conduct the water from there by stone, underground conduit to their Friarage site. The town bore two-thirds of the cost and took the same proportion of supply. Sometime later, a second aqueduct was dug and lined with lead. It, too, was fed by Falsgrave's springs and ran down the long gentle slope for more than a mile underground to Scarborough where it joined the great conduit at St Thomas's Cross on the corner of St Thomas's Gate and the market place. From there the water was carried further down the hill to a middle cistern at the top of St Sepulchregate and finally to the low conduit next to the Butter Cross.[59] Falsgrave springs never ran dry and the inhabitants of Scarborough enjoyed a supply of clean drinking water that most towns in the country would have envied.

Scarborough also had a higher standard of street pavement than most other contemporary towns. Again, in both senses, the friars had led the way: all three houses had made and paved the access roads to their entrances. The Dominicans, for instance, had paved a new roadway nearly a furlong in length which came to be known as Cargate from St Helen's Cross to their main door.[60] Even before the Reformation, it was not unknown for Scarborians to leave money in their wills 'to the pavage' or 'to repair of the way';[61] and by the seventeenth century the bailiffs had taken over responsibility for all the main thoroughfares in the town, keeping them free of obstruction and refuse as well as maintaining their surfaces.

The suppression of chantries from 1547 must also have been a severe blow to Scarborough, and particularly to the income of St Mary's. Besides the south side chapels dedicated to St James, St Nicholas, St Stephen and St Mary, the parish church also had altars to St Crux, St Clement, St Christopher and Corpus Christi in the chancel and the north aisle.[62] At the same time, the nearby mortuary chapel, dedicated to St Mary Magdalene, and served by several priests, became redundant. Attached to this chapel were almshouses and a cemetery. This so-called charnel chapel, which seems to have become an overspill graveyard and ossuary for the parish, was conspicuous enough in 1538 to be drawn on Henry's plat. After the closure of the chantry and the almshouses, the chapel building became the home of Scarborough high school where the boys of the town learned their Latin grammar surrounded by the bones of their ancestors.[63]

The church of St Thomas might have met the same fate as that of the Holy Sepulchre. Leland described it as 'a great chapelle' and located it correctly 'by side by the Newborow gate'.[64] On Henry's plat it was placed on the north side of Newborough Gate just inside the Bar and given a nave, south aisle and tall tower of three storeys with a spire.[65] Fortunately, along with the poorhouse which stood next to it, St Thomas's was endowed with twenty acres of pasture and arable in Burtondale to provide it with a steady permanent income. Moreover, thanks to the puritanism and persistence of Sir Thomas Hoby, St Thomas's church appears to have gained a new lease of purpose. From as early as 1614 a weekly sermon was preached there on Thursday market day by one of his approved ministers. Twenty years later, the Common Hall ruled that the weekly lecture was to be delivered at St Mary's on Wednesdays between Michaelmas and Lady day and at St Thomas's on Thursdays between Lady day and Michaelmas. Finally, on the eve of the Civil War, the bailiffs decided that the whole town should pay for repairs to St Thomas's.[66]

By that time the restoration and modernisation of St Mary's was finished. In 1633, according to the report written for Archbishop Neile, Scarborough's parish church was in a state of advanced decay and scandalous neglect. Timbers, lead, glass and roof were all said to be in need of immediate repair or renewal. Stephen Thompson, who was rector and therefore personally responsible, was reprimanded for 'suffering the Chancell to be in decay in the roof thereof and glass'. Some of the windows of the quire had been blocked in. The church as a whole was 'not beautified with sentences of scripture', and it also lacked 'a booke of homilies, a poore mans box and a booke for the names of strange preachers'.[67]

This damning rebuke stung the burgesses into action. Immediately they assigned nearly £20 raised on leases of town land and borrowed another £20 from the coroners' pier money 'towards the repair of the church'.[68] But this was only a small beginning: what started as a minor patch-and-mend job very soon became a major refurbishment of St Mary's. The following summer of 1634 bailiffs Gregory Fysh and Timothy Thompson, together with the four churchwardens, Christopher Thompson, William Fysh, John Rosdale and Thomas Gill, drew up a contract of employment with the town's company of joiners. The pulpit and seats then in the chancel were to be dismantled. A new pulpit was to be erected on the south side of the middle of the nave or 'great allee'. New pews, modelled on those recently put up at St Mary's, Beverley, were to be made to fill the whole nave, both its aisles and all the former chantry chapels.[69]

Scarborough's carpenters agreed to work from six in the morning to six in the evening every day except Sundays until they had completed the contract. Delays were caused by lack of funds and difficulties over allocation and assessment of pews, but by 6 March 1635 all was done: 155 pews had been built, allotted and rated, and 264 parishioners named as their occupants.[70] Work on the emptied chancel came last. In March 1637 the churchwardens approved an order to repair the windows and pull down the lofts there. Presumably, Stephen Thompson had to foot the bill, though he might have recovered some of the costs by the sale of the galleries 'on the backsyde of the chancell', which raised £13 3s.[71]

If a visitor to Scarborough on Easter Sunday morning, 29 March 1635, had climbed the steep incline of St Mary's Gate and then still had the breath to walk into the parish church, he or she would have found there all, or very nearly all, of the town's self-appointed governors sitting with their families in their brand-new pews.

There were now no seats, benches or galleries in the eastern chancel or the transepts, and even St Mary's spacious nave and aisles were far too small to accommodate a parish of about 450 families, about 2,000 people in all,[72] so the new pews were for the well-to-do residents only. Yet even within this privileged number clear distinctions and gradations were discernible in the location and rating of the pews. Generally speaking, the further away from the vicar's pulpit a family sat, the lower their status in Scarborough's community.

Mr William Simpson, who had been the parish vicar since 1630, occupied the tenth place from the east end on the south side of the 'great allee'. To the east of his pew were some of the town's foremost men, all dignified with the title of 'Mister', but who aspired to that of 'Gentleman'. At £2 13s. 4d. each their pews were some of the most highly rated of all. From east to west they read: Stephen Thompson, the rector; William Thompson, his elderly grandfather; Francis Thompson, William's son and Stephen's father; Thomas Foord, a major ship and land owner; and, next to Mr Simpson, William Headley, who was married to Foord's sister Mary, and was himself a leading shipowner and resident of the Friarage, the former Franciscan property. On the other west side of the vicar sat yet another of the Thompson clan, Timothy, William's nephew, and first cousin of Francis Thompson.[73]

Opposite this formidable array, on the north side of the 'great allee', were the occupants of four more of the most costly seats – Gregory Fysh; yet another Thompson, Richard, younger brother of Francis; William Batty; and John Harrison, the elder. Mr John Harrison was in fact one of the two bailiffs that year so he and his partner, Mr William Atmar, shared the pew reserved for holders of that office. Atmar's own family pew was in the same row of town notables on the north side of the 'great allee'. Also at the far eastern end of these two 'best' rows and next to the altar under the crossing were exclusive pews for the coroners, who were then Gregory Fysh and Timothy Thompson; for the two sub-bailiffs; and the twelve aldermen, divided by seniority into the 'antient', 'midlemost' and 'youngest'.[74]

Just outside this most favoured inner group, in slightly less valuable pews, sat the remaining members of the Common Hall's First Twelve. On the north side of the 'back allee' there was Mr William Fysh, Gregory's eldest son, and Mr Christopher Thompson, the fifth of that family and younger brother of Stephen. Mr Robert Fysh sat next to his younger brother Gregory. Mr William Conyers, head of another leading Scarborough family, had a place between John Harrison and Thomas Foord's son, Mr William.[75]

Finally, among this elite of Scarborough's secular hierarchy were three widows of deceased senior townsmen. Mrs Ellinor Conyers sat opposite the bailiffs' pew. She was the mother of William and the widow of another William who had died in 1621 during his fifth term as bailiff. Mrs Thomasin 'Farroe' or Farrer was by birth a Hutchinson of Wykeham Abbey, the widow of Mr John Farrer and, arguably, Scarborough's greatest ever benefactress. Lastly, Mrs Elizabeth Peacock, sitting in a pew next to that of Timothy Thompson, was the survivor from an older generation of another of the town's richest families. The space behind St Mary's chancel altar was called Peacock's Aisle because so many of that name were buried there.[76]

Around the outer rim of this privileged inner circle were the families of men who then sat in the Second and Third Twelves but hoped one day to be promoted to the First and chosen for the highest offices. Many of them, such as William Nesfield, William Chapman, Francis Fawether, Roger Nightingale, Thomas Gill, Peter Hodgson, Henry Nicholson and Henry Coward, were master mariners with part shares in the ships they sailed. Others, such as Samuel Hodgson, the shoemaker, Peter Rosdale, the master baker, Matthew Fowler, the tanner, George Pearson, the stringlayer or ropemaker, and James Readhead, the house carpenter, were craftsmen and tradesmen with apprentices and house servants but not yet entitled to be addressed as 'Mister'.[77]

Far to the north, west and south of the well-to-do and important sat Scarborough's lesser mortals – mariners, fishermen, journeymen and market traders. Most of them had to share pews of the lowest value. In some cases as many as four families were crushed into one place whereas three of the 'gods', Robert Fysh, Richard Thompson and William Batty, appear to have had a second private pew each for their guests and relatives. Yet none of the 155 pews allocated was for poor occupants: even the cheapest, at ten or fifteen shillings each, would have been well beyond the means of nearly half the families in the town. The only free seating available was a long bench running alongside the outer north aisle wall in the Bailiffs' Aisle, so-called because since the Reformation former bailiffs were interred there. There were only two free pews: one near the font at the western end 'for children to sitt in that comes to be baptized', the other 'intended for the scollers' of the neighbouring grammar school. Those without seats, who took the trouble to come to St Mary's, presumably stood or sat on their own stools at the back of the church near the west door.[78]

If John Leland had been introduced to Scarborough's oligarchy in 1544 he would have met men with names such as Percy, Bedome, Langdale, Lacy, Cooke and Shilbottle. Sixty years later, when the town was said to be decayed and depopulated, all of these names had ceased to be prominent locally. Some, like the Percys, seem to have been the victims of the politics of the Reformation; others died out as a result of plague, influenza, drowning at sea, or simply the failure to breed male heirs. In other cases they squandered their inheritance and sank into poverty, or became so rich or ambitious that they left the town to live in Hull or London.[79]

Of Scarborough's fortunate few none was more durable and faithful to the town than the Fysh family. Guy Fysh was bailiff in 1515–16 and 1521–2; John Fysh was twice elected to that position, in 1560 and 1587; and William Fysh, grandson of Guy, described as a merchant and living in a mansion house in the Oldborough between Cargate and the Dumple, was the only townsman to represent the borough in the House of Commons during the reign of Elizabeth.[80]

This William Fysh had been one of Scarborough's bailiffs at least twice, in 1575–6 and 1589–90. At his death in 1592 he had five sons, Robert, Thomas, Gregory, Joseph and Arthur, and two daughters, Ann and Agnes.[81] All but Arthur and Agnes were named as beneficiaries in his will. Robert received the western half of the family house and shop in Cargate with the barns and coalhouse on the south side; Thomas got the eastern part of this property which included an orchard; Gregory inherited land and buildings on the west side of St Thomas Gate and the north side of the Market Place; and Joseph acquired the St Nicholas Gate part of his father's estate

The Fysh family of 17th-century Scarborough

William 'merchant'
SB 1575, 1589
died 1592
= Mary Thompson, dau. of William Thompson

Children:

- **Robert**
  JB 1608, 1616
  SB 1621, 1626, 1635
  died 1637

- **Gregory**
  JB 1615, 1618
  SB 1622, 1627, 1633
  endowed Scarborough High School
  died 1640

- **Joseph**
  'woollen draper'

- **Arthur**
  gentleman of Beverley

Children of Gregory:

- **William**
  JB 1637, 1641
  died 1644

- **Tristram** = Suzanne Foord
  JB 1644
  SB 1664, 1670, 1678
  'in arms against Parliament'
  Alderman 1684–88
  will 1696

- **Christopher** = Thomasin Headley

Cornelius
Coroner and Treasurer, 1684

Timothy
(1672–1728)

Key:
JB Junior Bailiff
SB Senior Bailiff

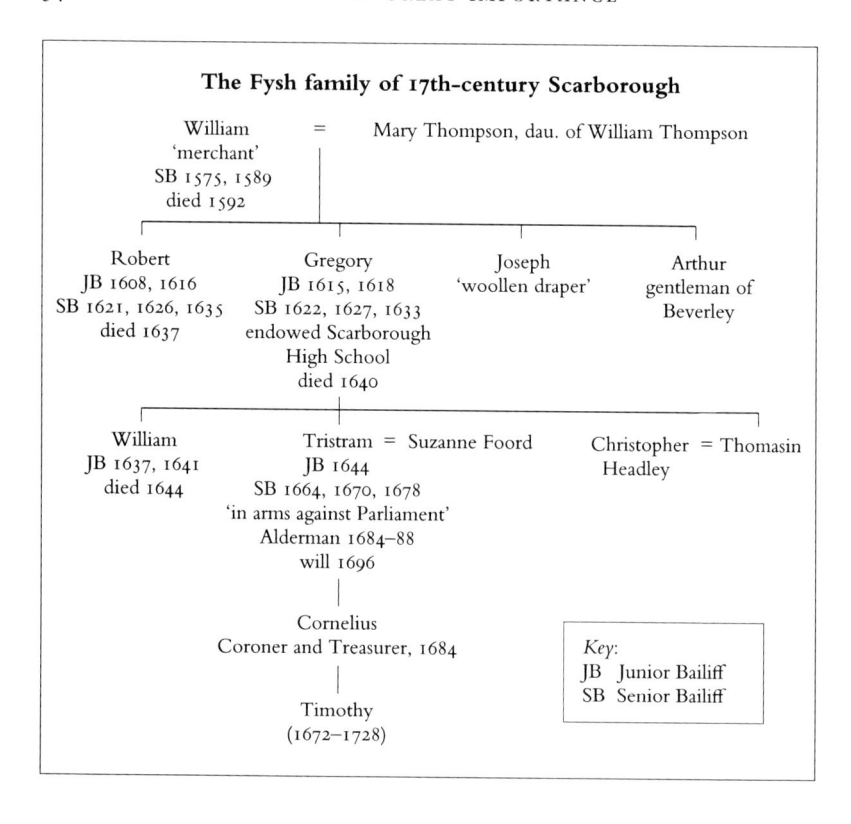

with its tenements, stables and barns. Altogether these valuable properties added up to a large block of land in the commercial heart of Newborough Quarter, from Newborough Bar down to the market cross at the end of Cargate, southwards to King's Cliff and northwards to the New Dyke Bank. Yet this was only the nucleus of the Fysh empire; beyond it, in almost every corner of the borough, William had owned or leased dozens of closes, tenements and fields, not least ten beastgates in Southfield, which he bequeathed to his widow, Mary.[82]

All but Thomas Fysh seem to have survived and prospered. Robert was chosen bailiff of Scarborough five times, in 1608, 1616, 1621, 1626 and 1635; Gregory equalled this with elections in 1615, 1618, 1622, 1627 and 1633. Robert died in 1637 and Gregory three years later. Joseph was perhaps too busy being a woollen draper to find time for local government. Arthur moved to Beverley and became a gentleman, though he retained an industrial interest in Scarborough when in 1625 he bought his brother Gregory's kiln and tannery in St Thomas Gate. About this time Gregory moved up in the world socially from 'tanner' to 'gentleman'.[83]

The Fysh family remained prominent in the next generation. Gregory's son, William, was elected junior bailiff in 1637 and again in 1641, but died young and suddenly in February 1644.[84] Tristram, his younger brother, then became paterfamilias. He had first entered the Common Hall at Michaelmas 1642 as twelfth in the last Twelve, but from then on his promotion up the local ladder was spectacular.[85]

Though the Fyshs, belying their name, were not themselves mariners or even shipowners, as principals of the hierarchy they frequently married into Scarborough's seafaring aristocracy. Tristram's wife, Suzanne, was the daughter of William Foord, an immensely rich land and shipowner, whose pew in St Mary's was directly opposite the vicar's pulpit across the 'great allee'.[86] Tristram's sister, Thomasin, married one of the Headleys, another old Scarborough family of mariners and owners. Tristram's aunt, Elizabeth, was the wife of master mariner Martin Atmar, bailiff in 1634–5 and 1638–9, and the mother of William Atmar, whom she apprenticed to another master mariner, John, later Admiral Sir John Lawson.[87]

Yet none of Scarborough's patricians – the Headleys, Foords, Battys or even the Fyshs – could compare with the Thompsons, who collectively dominated the affairs of the borough throughout much of the seventeenth century and beyond.[88] The William Thompson who died on 1 December 1637 was not the first of his family to live in Scarborough, but he could be described as the founding father of what became a ruling dynasty there. The earlier Thompsons were gentlemen farmers, with holdings at Thornton in Ryedale and on the Wolds at Langton and Lund. By William's lifetime, however, their main estates were at Humbleton in Holderness and at Kilham between Driffield and Bridlington. Nevertheless, even before 1600, they were already heavily engaged in Scarborough's commerce and had established themselves in its oligarchy.[89] William's elder brother,

Christopher, described as a 'merchant', married Isabel Hutchinson of Wykeham Abbey. Her father Edward (1543–91) and her brother Stephen (1573–1648) were both members of parliament for Scarborough. The Hutchinsons were country gentry with arms dating from 1581, and the match showed how highly regarded the Thompsons had then become.[90] Christopher himself was elected bailiff at least six times, in 1588, 1599, 1604, 1610, 1614 and 1617. He and Isabel had three sons: Robert, who became a confectioner and citizen of London; William, who settled in Hull; and Timothy, their eldest,

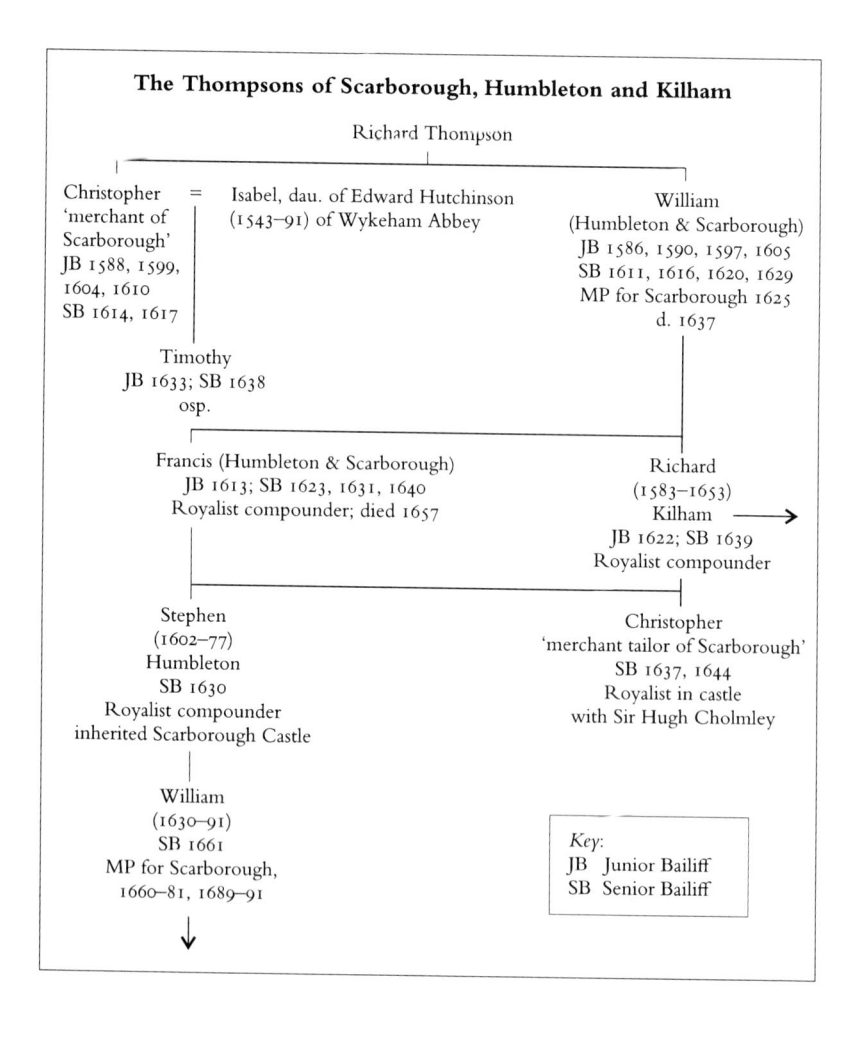

The Thompsons of Scarborough, Humbleton and Kilham

Richard Thompson

Christopher = Isabel, dau. of Edward Hutchinson (1543–91) of Wykeham Abbey
'merchant of Scarborough'
JB 1588, 1599, 1604, 1610
SB 1614, 1617

William (Humbleton & Scarborough)
JB 1586, 1590, 1597, 1605
SB 1611, 1616, 1620, 1629
MP for Scarborough 1625
d. 1637

Timothy
JB 1633; SB 1638
osp.

Francis (Humbleton & Scarborough)
JB 1613; SB 1623, 1631, 1640
Royalist compounder; died 1657

Richard
(1583–1653)
Kilham ⟶
JB 1622; SB 1639
Royalist compounder

Stephen
(1602–77)
Humbleton
SB 1630
Royalist compounder
inherited Scarborough Castle

Christopher
'merchant tailor of Scarborough'
SB 1637, 1644
Royalist in castle
with Sir Hugh Cholmley

William
(1630–91)
SB 1661
MP for Scarborough,
1660–81, 1689–91
↓

Key:
JB Junior Bailiff
SB Senior Bailiff

who stayed in Scarborough and was himself chosen bailiff in 1633, as junior to Gregory Fysh, and in 1638, as senior to Martin Atmar. Whether Timothy was married is not known, but he died without issue about 1645, thus ending this particular branch of the Thompson tree.[91]

As far as Scarborough's history was concerned, it was Christopher's brother, William Thompson, who played the leading role. His wife, Elizabeth Barker, was a Scarborough woman, and two of his daughters, Isabel and Elizabeth, married into prominent town families, the Beales and the Peacocks respectively. Though in the end William preferred to be buried with his ancestors in the church at Humbleton, his effigy there was inscribed 'Gylielmo Thompson de Scarbrough'.[92] He was elected bailiff of the borough eight times (which is probably a record), in 1586, 1590, 1597, 1605, 1611, 1616, 1620 and finally in 1629. During these years he acquired a great number of properties in and near Scarborough, notably his mansion house in St Sepulchre Gate, which became the residential headquarters of the family for the next century, and several shops on Merchant Row.[93] Under the patronage of the Earl of Holderness he bought leases of about three-quarters of the royal manor of Northstead, and eventually the freehold of Scarborough castle.[94] Along with Hugh Cholmley of Whitby, he represented Scarborough in the first parliament of Charles I in 1625, a rare distinction for a mere town merchant. When he died at the end of 1637, he left St Mary's its oldest surviving silver piece, a large chalice, and to the corporation he gave three silver cups, which are still in the Town Hall collection.[95]

William's eldest son and heir, Francis, followed in his father's footsteps. He had a legal training and for a time acted as a solicitor on behalf of Scarborough when it tried unsuccessfully to secure admiralty jurisdiction.[96] Later, he was 'collector for the farmers of the port of Scarborough', in which office he also assessed and sold prize ships during the wars with France and Spain in the 1620s.[97] Francis was first elected bailiff in 1613, and re-elected in 1623, 1631 and 1640. From his father he inherited the Northstead estate and ownership of the castle at Scarborough.[98]

William's younger son, Richard, does not seem to have been as directly or closely involved in Scarborough's trade and politics as his brother. Though he had a house in St Mary's Quarter, his chief

Bushells, Cholmleys, Hothams and Legards

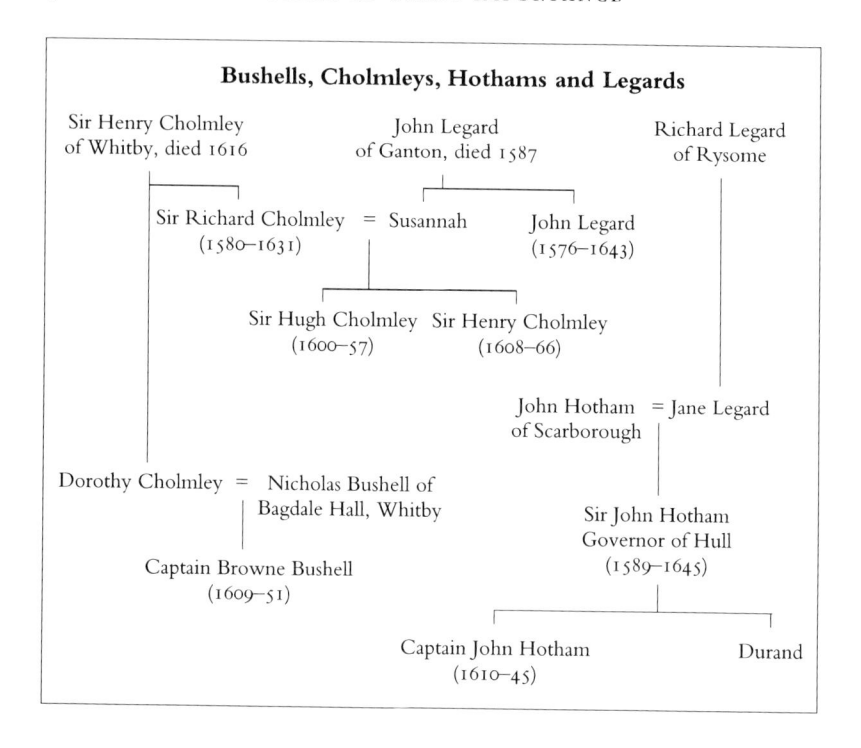

```
Sir Henry Cholmley            John Legard              Richard Legard
of Whitby, died 1616          of Ganton, died 1587     of Rysome
         |                             |                       |
  Sir Richard Cholmley  =  Susannah    John Legard
      (1580–1631)            |         (1576–1643)
                             |
              Sir Hugh Cholmley    Sir Henry Cholmley
                 (1600–57)            (1608–66)

                                    John Hotham      = Jane Legard
                                    of Scarborough
  Dorothy Cholmley  =  Nicholas Bushell of
                    |  Bagdale Hall, Whitby     Sir John Hotham
                    |                           Governor of Hull
          Captain Browne Bushell                   (1589–1645)
              (1609–51)
                                    Captain John Hotham        Durand
                                        (1610–45)
```

residence was at Kilham. Nevertheless, he served two terms as bailiff, in 1622–3, as junior to Gregory Fysh, and in 1639–40, as senior of the pair. When his Scarborough properties were valued in 1646, he had half-shares in two ships and one-eighth shares in two more, estimated to be worth £150, and his lands and tenements in Scarborough, Falsgrave and nearby Scalby brought in a clear annual income of £78.[99]

The next generation of Scarborough Thompsons, Stephen and Christopher, sons of Francis, were already well established there by 1640. Each had taken one term as bailiff, Stephen in 1630–1 and Christopher in 1637–8. Stephen was the principal heir, both in Humbleton and in Scarborough. By hereditary entailment he had Scarborough castle, a major part of St Mary's rectory, and valuable leases in Northstead and Peasholm. According to his testimony of 1647 to the Committee for Compounding with Delinquents, he had a household of twenty-one members, including ten children, to support. Christopher's resources and responsibilities were more modest.

He also had a house in St Mary's Quarter and was described as a 'merchant tailor' of Scarborough. His lands were widely scattered as far away as Whitby, Settrington and Scagglethorpe, but in value they amounted only to £64 13s. 4d. Whereas Stephen's rectory at Scarborough was worth £270 annually, Christopher's share of the rectory at Scalby had a clear value of only £7 a year. Christopher's shipping interests in Scarborough were also smaller than those of his uncle Richard's: altogether they were said to be worth no more than £95.[100]

The dominance of the Thompson family in the business and politics of Scarborough during the first four and a half decades of the seventeenth century was extraordinary. For example, of the original thirty-five founding owners of the town's most powerful and wealthy 'trade union', the Society of Owners, Masters and Mariners, set up in December 1602, five were Thompsons. More strikingly, between 1597 and 1644 at least one Thompson was either bailiff or coroner in all but fifteen years. Most revealing of all is the new royal charter of 1626 granted by King Charles to Scarborough soon after his accession. Instead of forty-four burgesses, consisting of two bailiffs, two coroners, four chamberlains and three Twelves, the borough was to be governed by a radically reduced corporation of a mayor, a coroner and twelve aldermen. According to the terms of the charter, Stephen Hutchinson was appointed to be the first mayor and John Farrer the first coroner. Both of these men were closely related to the Thompsons by business partnership, and both were related to each other and the Thompsons by marriage. Christopher Thompson and John Farrer had taken sisters of Stephen Hutchinson, Isabel and Thomasin, as their wives. Of the twelve men who were named as the new ruling council of aldermen, no fewer than five were Thompsons – Christopher the elder, William, Timothy, Francis and Richard. It would be hard to find a more blatant illustration of political nepotism. The other seven aldermen were to be Paul and Richard Peacock, Robert and Gregory Fysh, William Conyers, Thomas Foord and William Headley, who were all related to each other and hand in glove with the Thompsons. Since all twelve were to continue 'in that office during their natural lives' and future mayors and coroners were to be chosen annually only by them and from amongst their number, Scarborough's oligarchy of forty-four would have become an exclusive, self-perpetuating cabinet of a dozen members run by one extended family.[101]

For reasons which are not known, the Crown failed to issue letters patent and the new charter was never put into practice. In May 1632 Scarborough's old charters and form of government were confirmed.[102] There was only one local man who had the will and the means to challenge the Thompson take-over, and although direct evidence for it has not been found, it seems that Sir Thomas Posthumous Hoby of Hackness had successfully intervened.

In 1596 Thomas Hoby of Bisham in Berkshire had become the third husband of Margaret Dakins, the heiress of the Hackness estate, five miles inland from Scarborough. For the next forty years he meddled incessantly in the town's internal affairs and clashed repeatedly and fiercely with its rulers. Hoby was a small man with a short temper and a long memory. He always took offence and was never known to forgive it. He enjoyed making enemies and then defeating and humiliating them. Throughout the North and East Ridings, where he was a justice of the peace, he was bitterly resented and resisted as a carpet-bagging southerner and puritan spy for the government in London. In return, Hoby despised his neighbours for their uncouth northern manners and their 'backwardness' in religion. By 'backwardness' Hoby meant Catholic recusancy; he was a relentless hunter of papists. His father, who had died before he was born, hence the name 'Posthumous', had been Queen Elizabeth's ambassador in Paris and a most distinguished scholar and linguist as well as diplomat. Through his mother's family and second marriage, Hoby was related to some of the most powerful people in the kingdom – the Cecils, the Bacons and the Russells.[103]

Trained and profoundly learned in the law, Sir Thomas was a perpetual litigant who made himself feared and hated by almost everyone in the locality. Apart from the puritan Gates of Seamer, he soon quarrelled with all his gentry neighbours – the Eures of Malton, the Dawneys of Ayton, the Hutchinsons of Wykeham, the Legards of Ganton and, worst of all, in what became a lifelong vendetta, the

Cholmleys of Whitby. As one hostile witness in Star Chamber said of him, he was 'the busyest sawcie little Jacke in all the Contrie, and wolld have an ore in eny bodies bote'.[104] Another biased, but not unrepresentative observer, Sir Hugh Cholmley, later wrote that he was 'a troblesome vexatious neighbour . . . who haveing married a widow ye inheritor of all Hackness Lordship, haveing a full purse and noe children (& as it was thought not able to get one) delighted to spend his mony & tyme in sutes'.[105]

Hoby's overbearing self-importance and Scarborough's acute sensitivity about its ancient rights soon brought the two into head-on conflict. In 1597, when Sir Thomas failed to secure a Yorkshire county seat in the Commons and had to settle for one of Scarborough's instead, he had the ungrateful impertinence to object to the Common Hall's choice of his partner. When next elected in 1604, Hoby still did not like his new colleague, Francis Eure, though on this occasion he did condescend to be feasted by the bailiffs before he left for London.[106]

Scarborough's Common Hall burgesses must have heaved a collective sigh of relief when they heard that Sir Thomas did not propose to offer himself for re-election to the parliament of 1614. Indeed, Hoby never represented Scarborough again after he had secured one of Ripon's safe seats from 1621 onwards.[107] However, the town was still far from free of him: at many different points and on numerous occasions there was direct conflict between Hoby's conception of his rights and the corporation's jealously guarded privileges.

Only when Sir Thomas was himself bailiff in 1610–11 did he seem satisfied with the town's trained band, or homeguard militia. As both justice of the peace and deputy lieutenant of the North Riding, Hoby never accepted the long-standing claim of the bailiffs that they alone had the responsibility of inspecting musters of the town's armed men. The most serious confrontation with him over the view of arms came in the summer of 1629. At first Sir Thomas ordered the bailiffs to muster their men for his inspection 'at nyne of the clocke . . . on the sandes' in a week's time. Five days later he changed his mind. Now he asked for the trained band to be paraded in St Mary's churchyard since he did not have time to go down the hill 'soe lowe as the sande'. Finally, only hours before the inspection was due to take place, the bailiffs received a third imperative from Hackness:

now he would view the men 'upon the sandes at tenn of the clocke & not before', and he would bring Lady Margaret with him to dine with the burgesses afterwards. A half buck sent with this last order was not sufficient to placate Scarborough's governors: the day after the review the Common Hall decided that the first of them who next visited York would complain about Hoby's behaviour to Thomas Wentworth, lord president of the Council of the North.[108]

For the next two and a half years there was open warfare between Hoby and Scarborough corporation. As usual, Sir Thomas brought an action in Star Chamber and, as he had done previously, he tried to win his case by driving a wedge into the oligarchy. His suit was aimed at the Thompsons – all five of them, William, Francis, Stephen, Richard and Timothy – and William Foord, junior bailiff to Stephen Thompson in 1630–1. In a letter to Wentworth at York written in September 1631, Hoby assured the lord president that his action in Star Chamber was 'only againste the Thompsons, & not against the whole corporacon of Skarbrogh'.[109] But the Common Hall stood united behind the Thompsons: in July they had already agreed that the suit was 'a townes busines', not a private matter, and the town would pay all the defence costs.[110]

As the case dragged on, Hoby concentrated his attack on the corporation's conduct of recent elections. He alleged that the Thompsons had altered the old rules by excluding non-residents from the corporate body. When, in their defence, the Thompsons invoked the borough's ancient charters, Hoby insisted that a new exemplification of the charter of Edward III should be paid for by the town and brought from London to Hackness for his examination.[111] Finally, in August 1632, bailiff John Harrison, Mr Richard Thompson and the town clerk carried the town's own copy of the charter to Hackness for Sir Thomas to compare it with the new exemplification.[112] Since after this meeting nothing more is heard of Hoby's suit in Star Chamber, presumably he must have been convinced, though certainly not pleased, that he had no legal case against the Thompsons.

In the meantime, Hoby had committed another blunder and had been reprimanded by Wentworth for it. Although he had signed a settlement with Francis and Richard Thompson, acting for themselves and on behalf of their father William, to accept the arbitration of the lord president in the dispute over the review of Scarborough's trained band, within three months Hoby had wilfully broken it. In July 1632 he summoned the town's militia to a general muster of the area at Hutton Buscel, six miles inland, and demanded that thirty-six instead of the customary thirty armed men should be sent. Bailiffs Harrison and Gregory Fysh went out to Hackness to protest and plead with him, but Hoby would not budge.[113] When the lord president received another petition against Sir Thomas from Scarborough, this time his response was immediate, decisive and crushing: as long as he remained lord lieutenant of the county, Scarborough, 'a sea towne . . . of greate importance', would remain exempt from general musters beyond its borough boundaries. As for the number of its trained band, the traditional limit of thirty should be observed.[114]

The Thompsons had won. Hoby had exceeded his authority and annoyed Wentworth, and the oligarchy had stood by the family. When William Thompson had the nerve to threaten to sue the corporation for failure to pay his legal costs, the burgesses in the Common Hall secretly consented to foot his heavy bill of £80 in full.[115]

On other matters, regarded by the burgesses as less vital to their corporate authority, Sir Thomas was allowed to have his own way. He made it his business to ensure that Scarborough had licensed ministers to preach weekly sermons in the town, and that these lecturers met with his approval.[116] However, if Hoby frequently interfered in the civil affairs of the borough, he seems to have been satisfied with the way the bailiffs regulated the religious life of the town. Compared with many other urban communities at this time, Scarborough was a model of conformity. Absentees from St Mary's Sunday and holy day services were almost invariably too old, too busy, too poor, too sick, too idle or just too far away, to attend them. Only a handful of recusants stayed away on principle, and they were suitably persecuted by the town authorities. Given the extent of the parish and the location of and lack of space inside St Mary's, it would have been impossible to check and compel attendance there of the whole population. Nevertheless, most bailiffs and churchwardens seem to have tried honestly to enforce the religious laws of the kingdom. The construction of pews to seat more than 250 families no doubt had the purpose of making it much easier for the churchwardens to identify persistent absentees, just as it was also intended to improve the behaviour of those who attended. Though as a non-resident Hoby himself had no claim to a private place, significantly his approval was sought of the allocation and rating of St Mary's new pews.[117]

Hoby would have been pleased to note that sabbatarian laws were strictly enforced in Scarborough. During the 1620s and 1630s the bailiffs punished residents and non-residents alike for playing 'att coit[s] in sermon tyme', 'playing football upon the Sabbath day', 'playing at knacks', or even 'playinge on the sand in time of devine service'.[118] Indoor entertainments were also forbidden on Sundays, particularly if they involved drinking, gambling or keeping company with guests.[119] Nor was it safe to be seen working on a Sunday, whether it was carrying coals, twisting ropes or just going out in a rowing boat to ships in the harbour.[120]

The fasting laws of Fridays and Lent were also officially respected in Scarborough. Butchers and victuallers were obliged to enter bonds of £10 each against killing, selling or even eating meat at home during Lent, and they were forbidden to provide Friday suppers throughout the year. Every year, from 1623 onwards, the corporation minute book records the names of tradesmen, including taverners and brewers, who had to enter recognizances of £10. Usually only one butcher in the town was permitted to kill calves during Lent 'for sicke & weake persons'.[121]

Finally, as further evidence of Scarborough's official conformity, Common Hall minutes of 1624 and 1628 show that serious attempts were made to exclude from the communion table adult residents who failed to pay their penny Easter dues for bread and wine. Any householders who refused to pay their pennies to the churchwardens were threatened with presentment at the next bailiffs' sessions.[122]

Not surprisingly, therefore, the archbishop's visitors who reported on Scarborough in 1633 expressed more concern about the fabric of St Mary's than the conduct of its parishioners. John Wolfe was the only identified recusant; Robert and Ellinor Weatherill were the only two named as habitual absentees from services; Edward and Jane Hickson had been unable to wait until they were married; according to rumour, Robert Fysh had been 'solliciting the chastity of Frances Bolton, servant to William Batty'; and John Newton had fornicated with a woman who had since died. And that, apart from some few cases of unruly behaviour during church services which would be deterred by the new seating arrangements, was all.[123] It seemed that Scarborians were not just outwardly orthodox, they were also well-disciplined.

Hoby also took a particular interest in Scarborough's own grammar school. Indeed, if one usually reliable authority is right, he and his puritan neighbour, Henry Darley of Buttercrambe, were responsible for saving or re-founding the boys' school with a new and generous endowment.[124] Since the school had a monopoly of the education of local boys in English and Latin from the age of seven upwards, Sir Thomas was concerned that the schoolmaster should be suitable in every way. In August 1619, for instance, we find him recommending Mr Ogle for the post. From Hoby's letter to the bailiffs, who were to make the appointment, it is clear that Mr Ogle was one of the many clergymen he and his pious wife had taken under their wings. He assured the bailiffs that not only was Mr Ogle's 'learneinge very sufficient for that place' but from personal experience he could testify to his 'gift in prechinge'.[125] However, if Ogle did get the job he did not last long in it. In 1623, the Common Hall ordered that 'Gregory Dickenson should be head mayster & have the oversyght & chardge of the high schoole so long as he behaved him self well in that place'.[126] Eventually, in 1627, the town got better than it deserved: Mr William Penston, a Scotsman by birth and education, agreed to become headmaster. In its typically miserly and over-cautious manner, the Common Hall allowed him to take over the school for a trial period of six months 'upon the good likyng of the towne'.[127] Penston remained headmaster of Scarborough high school for the next fifty years.

Hoby's last recorded brush with Scarborough took place in October 1636. He had presented the corporation with a great silver mace for which the two newly-elected bailiffs, Roger Wyvill and William Foord, thanked him by letter. The reply from Hackness was characteristically curt and uncivil. Sir Thomas addressed his letter to 'Mr Bailiff Foord' alone 'because by your charters Mr Wyvell ys not legally elected'.[128] This was a nice irony. In his lengthy, legal battle with the Thompsons Hoby had claimed that they had no right to exclude non-resident gentlemen, like himself, from the Common Hall. The old charters had been summoned as evidence and Hoby had lost the argument. Now he was indignant that a non-resident,

Roger Wyvill of Osgodby, had been elected to the corporation's highest office. Sir Thomas enjoyed making trouble for its own sake, but in this case his real objection to Wyvill's election was probably religious. Though Sir Roger himself might not have been a practising Catholic, it was well known that in 1632 he had sent his eldest son William to be educated abroad at Douai College.[129] In other words, in Hoby's eyes, the Wyvills were damned as papists.

The next assembly on Sandside of the Common Hall agreed that bailiff Foord should write to Hoby pointing out that Sir Roger had been legally elected 'by our charters . . . as you were chosen'.[130] Decoded, the message to Hackness was that Scarborough corporation's rules of election did not disqualify a candidate for his religious affiliations, and if Hoby's objection to Wyvill was his non-residence then this would have invalidated his own election as senior bailiff in 1610. This response might not have satisfied Sir Thomas but it seems to have silenced him, at last.

Hoby was in his seventy-fifth year when he finally succumbed, in the words of Hackness parish register, to 'a fit of cold palsy' in December 1640.[131] In life he had lost to the Thompsons and to his other old enemies the Cholmleys. When be died Francis Thompson was again senior bailiff of Scarborough and his brother Richard senior coroner. Sir Hugh Cholmley had rescued his Whitby estate from bankruptcy and now held all the offices – justice of the peace, deputy lieutenant, colonel of the trained bands and member of parliament for Scarborough [132] – which Hoby himself had once used to intimidate the locality.

In the longer term, however, Hoby's legacy was more important than that of all the Thompsons. True, he had no children to succeed him at Hackness and so his name disappeared with him from the local records, whereas the Thompsons, after the setbacks of the Civil Wars and Interregnum, recovered their prosperity and re-established their influence in Scarborough until the middle of the next century. Yet William Thompson's graceless and battered tumblers, now hidden away amongst the Town Hall silver, compare unfavourably with Hoby's magnificent mace, which is still carried proudly and prominently before Scarborough's rulers. According to a local tradition, when the mace of the City of London was destroyed in the Great Fire of 1666, Scarborough's mace was borrowed to serve as a model for a new replacement. Secondly, if Sir Thomas did rescue Scarborough high school from extinction then he did the town a very great service since in many different forms and locations the school survived until 1973. Finally, Hoby achieved a disguised immortality denied to any of the Thompsons or the Cholmleys. When William Shakespeare was writing *Twelfth Night* he could find no better real-life example for his character of Malvolio than Sir Thomas Posthumous Hoby, then in London pursuing one of his many Star Chamber actions against his neighbours.

When John Leland had passed through Scarborough in 1544 he saw a town that had been in decline for the past two centuries and was about to be hit by the destructiveness of the Reformation. Measured by the lay subsidy assessments of 1334, Scarborough would then have been placed equal to Hull as the twenty-sixth richest provincial town in England; and measured by the returns of 1377, when Scarborough had 1,393 poll-tax payers, it was then the thirtieth most populous.[133] However, by the reign of Henry VIII, in terms of lay subsidy assessment, Scarborough had dropped down and out of the wealthiest fifty towns, whereas, ominously, all of its main east coast rivals – Newcastle, King's Lynn, Great Yarmouth, Hull, Boston and Ipswich – were still among the top twenty-two.[134] Nearly all of England's urban communities, with the outstanding exception of London, suffered loss of population and commercial contraction caused by plague and war during the fifteenth and early sixteenth centuries, but Scarborough's decay during this prolonged period was relative as well as absolute.[135]

By 1600 Scarborough's position had deteriorated even further. When the bailiffs petitioned Queen Elizabeth to ask for the closure of Seamer market, they contended that it was directly and mainly responsible for Scarborough's loss of population and trade. In reply, however, Sir Henry Gate argued strongly and convincingly that the town's sad decay preceded the re-opening of his weekly Monday market in 1577. Sixty years previously Scarborough had about 700 householders, but during the next thirty years their number had fallen by 400 or to 400. During this same catastrophic period, the town's fishing fleet had declined from fifty to only six, and its merchant shipping from twenty to four. Where once there had been buildings there were now waste spaces in the town, and grass grew in the market place.[136]

Even after some allowance has been made for the inevitable exaggeration in these figures, it is clear that the loss of endowment, employment and benefactors caused by the dissolution of the religious houses and the chantries had severely damaged Scarborough, as it did other urban communities. Further damage was caused by the disruption of trade following wars with the Scots and the French; currency debasement which produced inflation; and, perhaps worst of all, repeated visitations of plague and other diseases, which are known to have brought about high mortality in other towns in the 1550s such as York.[137]

A visitor to Scarborough in 1640, coming to take its newly-discovered spa waters, would have been certain to notice its unfinished and neglected stone walls, its dilapidated gateways, its derelict and abandoned castle and its many open areas where chapels, churches, hospitals and friaries had stood a century before. Such a visitor might well have concluded that Scarborough had once known more prosperous and populous times and that its decline had not been halted; but such a pessimistic conclusion would have been mistaken. By 1640 the town's population had begun to recover. In the absence of parish registers and depending entirely on fragmentary bishops' transcripts, any estimate of Scarborough's resident population is necessarily tentative and at best approximate. Nevertheless, all the surviving evidence points in the same direction. During the years 1602 to 1606 the average number of annual baptisms at St Mary's was 54; in the years 1626 to 1629, it was 73; and for the period 1632 to 1639 it was 87. During the first four decades of the century the average number of marriages annually performed at St Mary's rose from 10 to 23. In only one year of plague, 1635-6, did recorded burials exceed official baptisms. On the basis of these figures, Scarborough's population seems to have grown from about 1,700 at the beginning of the century to about 2,800 by 1640.[138]

On the other hand, different kinds of evidence yield lower population totals than those derived from registered baptisms. According

Population of Scarborough in the 17th Century

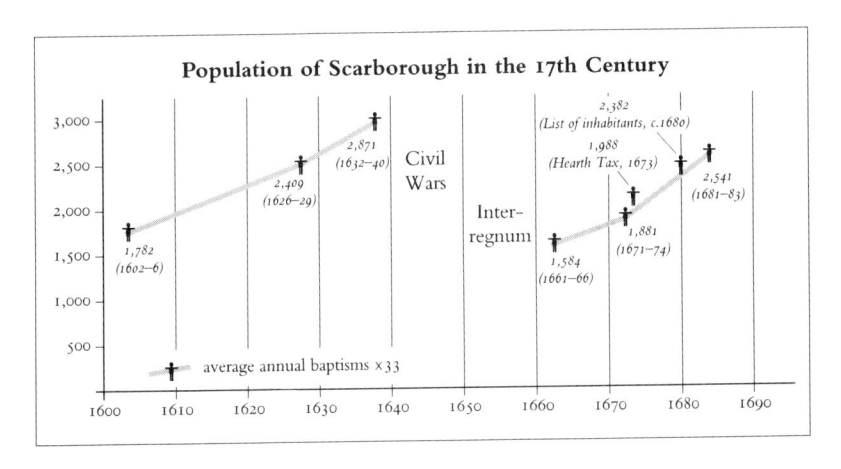

Year range	Population
1602–6	1,782
1626–29	2,409
1632–40	2,871
1661–66	1,584
1671–74	1,881
Hearth Tax, 1673	1,988
List of inhabitants, c.1680	2,382
1681–83	2,541

Periods marked: Civil Wars, Interregnum.
average annual baptisms × 33

to bailiffs John Harrison and Martin Atmar, both men with considerable knowledge of the town and without motive to mislead, in 1635 Scarborough had 'about fower hundreth & fifty familyes'.[139] Though there are no extant records of family size in Scarborough at this time, between 1674 and 1680 lists of the inhabitants of the community were drawn up, Quarter by Quarter. Only the lists for Newborough and Undercliff have survived among the corporation papers, but they appear to be complete and include the names of masters and mistresses and the numbers of their children, servants, apprentices and other dependants living in each household. In Newborough, 502 residents lived in 131 families and in Undercliff 689 belonged to 171 households.[140] These figures suggest, therefore, that Scarborough had a rather low average household size of about four, and if this average pertained to 1635 it would result in a total town population of only 1,800.[141] Nevertheless, the general point remains valid: even if the baptism-derived numbers are inflated, the more modest estimate for the mid 1630s still indicates that the population had increased since the beginning of the century.

Scarborough's growth in population reflected an expansion of its economy. The great and growing coal trade down the east coast not only saved Scarborough's pier and therefore its harbour, it also gave impetus to Scarborough's own commerce, shipping and eventually shipbuilding industry. In 1600 no Scarborough ship was engaged in the coal traffic; in 1612 its own vessels were said to have carried 25 cargoes of coal out of Newcastle; in 1625, 75, and in 1636, 50.[142] Unfortunately, the only year during this period for which there is a full official record of Scarborough's coastal trade is 1639, but it shows how dominant coal-carrying had become. During that year Scarborough imported 3,323 chaldrons of coal, only 368 from Newcastle and nearly all the rest from Sunderland. Of the 154 cargoes this required, 138 were carried in Scarborough's own colliers.[143] Much of this coal was re-exported down the coast to London and across the North Sea to continental ports. In 1634 of the 28 voyages made to the continent, 26 carried only coal, mainly to Rotterdam and Calais, and 24 of them were in Scarborough ships.[144] The re-export of coal from Sunderland had become the chief concern of Scarborough's merchants selling at home and abroad, and by 1640 this profitable commerce had stimulated a flourishing shipbuilding industry there.[145]

Unlike Whitby harbour, Scarborough's had no local alum industry to promote its commercial activity, yet it still managed to increase the value of its foreign as well as its coastal trade. In 1609 its exports abroad were said to be worth £124; in 1634 they had risen in value to £400.[146] Though coal dominated Scarborough's cargoes by the 1630s, the port was still sending out cloth, malt, beer and barley, mainly to Scotland, and importing deals and tar from Norway, raisins, prunes and iron from Rotterdam, apples from Ostend and Dunkirk, and yarn from Scotland.[147]

The coal trade had several other profitable industrial by-products. For example, plentiful supplies of cheap fuel made possible two new large-scale industries at Scarborough. The earliest reference to 'the makynge of trayn oyle' in the town is contained in a petition of 1597.[148] Train oil was the name given to the melted down blubber of whales and seals which was then used to make soap, candles and fuel for domestic and ships' lamps. By 1602 the bailiffs had secured control of the local industry, and from then on they leased monopolies of manufacture and sale to enterprising business men.[149] The old 'oyle house' was built at the far south end of St Nicholas Gate, on the site of the present Town Hall, no doubt in consideration of the sensitive noses of Scarborians.

Boiling sea water to make salt was probably not a new industry at Scarborough, but the earliest reference to it there is in 1600 when eight leading townsmen, who included John Farrer and Francis Thompson, bought a bailiffs' licence which secured them a monopoly for the next seven years. The initial 'fine' of £60 and the annual rent of £20 indicate how lucrative salt-making was expected to become.[150] When a new licence was granted in 1616 for 21 years it was bought by outsiders, a London alderman and two Hull merchants. The licensees were permitted to build staithes and steps on the beach to bring in their 'salte sea coles'.[151]

Coal had its domestic as well as industrial uses. As early as 1603, writing from his home at Roxby, Sir Henry Cholmley complained to Scarborough's bailiffs that his 'cole carriers' were being charged tolls contrary to the 'priviledge and charter of Pickeringe lithe'.[152] At least town residents knew that the price they paid for their hearth and furnace fuel was strictly controlled. In 1625 the bailiffs licensed a dozen 'horse porters for coales' and laid down regulations on measures and tariffs. Since all Scarborough's coal came in by sea and the town was built on a hillside, the further a customer lived from the harbour the more he had to pay for his coal. As a result, the cost of a chaldron varied from 8d. on Sandside to 2s. at Newborough Gate – a differential which probably encouraged shipbuilding at the former but not tanning and brewing near the latter.[153]

Another event since 1600 which had favoured Scarborough was the final closure of Seamer market. A protracted war had begun in 1577 when Sir Henry Gate, lord of Seamer, constable of Scarborough castle and one of Scarborough's members of parliament, had broken a 200-year-old tradition and revived Seamer's weekly Monday market and annual fair. Seamer was only three miles inland from Scarborough and perfectly positioned as an exchange between the Vale of Pickering, Blackmoor (North York Moors) and the Yorkshire Wolds. Scarborough's burgesses tried every method, legal and underhand, petition, intimidation and bribery; Scarborians were forbidden to travel to Seamer on Mondays; the dispute went before the Exchequer, the Council of the North, the Court of Queen's Bench, the Privy Council and even a jury of twenty-four local gentry. The borough's legal fees and expenses eventually came to £2,000. In the end, but not until 1612, Scarborough won: a new royal charter finally put a stop to Seamer market.[154]

Seamer's annual fair, running for several days from the feast of St

Martin (4 July) survived, but it presented no competition to Scarborough's own famous fair. As long as the herring migrated southwards down the east coast every summer in enormous numbers, Scarborough would remain a major centre for their sale – fresh, salted, smoked or dried. As a town petition had reminded Queen Elizabeth: 'The inhabitauntes there [Scarborough] is [sic] most mayteyned by fishinge and by the dryenge and makeinge thereof into salt fish'.[155] Scarborough fishermen drew a distinction between 'winter herring', which they took in April and May off Shetland and Scotland, and 'land herring', which were brought ashore between June and October, mainly in Dutch and Fleming boats. Yet herring were not the only fish in the North Sea. Cod, haddock, ling and skate were to be found all the year round and were taken in coastal waters or off the further banks of the Dogger. The five-man fishing boat or *farcosta* was often laid up during the winter months and only at Lent taken out to the Dogger for cod and haddock or northwards for the herring. Most of Scarborough's fishermen, however, went to sea at any time of the year in their cobles, smaller craft with three pairs of short oars and a single mast. Still, whatever the craft or the catch, and whoever the catcher, in 1640 fish and fishing were Scarborough's standby and staple.[156]

The appearance of Scarborough in 1640 might have deceived a casual but not a perceptive stranger. The decayed, privatised castle mattered little compared with the bustling, safe harbour inside its well-maintained and massive stone piers. The neglected walls and gateway of Newborough indicated only that the residents had no longer any fear of an invasion from the landward. A visitor with commercial acumen might even have appreciated the money-making potential of Mrs Farrer's discovery of medicinal spa springs under South Cliff. One day, Scarborough could become an Epsom or a Buxton by the sea. What no one, traveller or townsman, could have foreseen was that within a short time Scarborough would become a bloody battleground.

CHAPTER TWO

Defence and War, 1600–1642

THE destruction of Scarborough's pier by the great storm of November 1613, and the flood of petitions that followed from nearly every East coast port, focused the attention of the central government on Scarborough's harbour. The following year King James ordered a search to be made in the Tower of London for documents concerning the town of Scarborough and its privileges. According to a letter sent by Ralph, third Lord Eure, to bailiffs Farrer and Francis Thompson in August 1614, in London it was believed that 'in Queene Mary's tymes or before or since' Scarborough had exercised a right to grant off-shore fishing licences to 'strangers [such] as those of Flaunders or France or any forreyners'. Eure asked the bailiffs to look into their corporation records. If they found any papers concerning this licence they were to send them to him in London. If no relevant documents could be found in Scarborough's archive, then the bailiffs were to pass on Eure's inquiry to Edward Gate at Seamer. Perhaps amongst the papers of the late Sir Henry Gate there might be something 'materiall in that kind'. Failing that, the bailiffs were asked to take the testimonies of 'such auntient men' of Scarborough who might remember a time when foreigners paid for such a licence in money or fish.[1]

Accordingly, the bailiffs ordered a 'diligent seartch' to be made in the town's records, but could find nothing except reference to the old custom whereby all fish brought into Scarborough had to be offered for sale in the open market and not forestalled at sea or on the beach. However, the bailiffs did possess 'a booke in Inglish intituled Hytchcoks New Years Gyft to the Parliament' which stated that the Flemings, who set out from Flanders, Holland and Zealand at Bartholomew Tide (24 August) in four or five hundred busses to catch herring off the east coast of England, first asked leave 'befoar they fysh' at Scarbrough 'as evermoare they have done'.[2]

Nevertheless, though Robert Hitchcock's book had been published

King Charles I, by Mytens.

as recently as 1580, by 1614 there was no recollection in Scarborough of any such licence being requested or granted. The bailiffs accepted that in Hitchcock's time and before 'infinite numbers both of Flemming and Frenchmen have yearly repayred unto this towne befoar ther fyshing and ther remayned a certen tyme as ther staple for netts, lynes, hooks and vittayles', but not for the past twenty years. If any records concerning foreign fishermen existed, the bailiffs suggested that they would have been kept at the castle by Sir Henry Gate when he was constable there.[3]

Nothing further is recorded at Scarborough on this subject. As the bailiffs sensibly pointed out to Eure, even if Hitchcock had been right, there was no means whereby foreign fishermen could be compelled to pay for a licence. The unwelcome truth was that the Dutch and the Flemings in their fleets of busses dominated the annual herring fishing; they were at liberty to catch and land whatever and wherever they wanted along England's North-Sea shore. Unless and until the English had warships stationed off these shores, foreigners could do as they pleased.

All the kingdom's shores, it seems, were undefended. As late as 1619, the Privy Council was most concerned about the robberies and kidnappings at sea of the pirates operating out of Algiers and Tunis. Early that year, they sent out an appeal to ports as far north as Scarborough to contribute to the building of royal warships. Such ships, it was claimed, would 'extorpate' the pirates 'utterlie'.[4] However, as the government soon discovered, from 1624 when England went to war with Spain, the main threat came not to the south coast from North Africa but to the East coast ports and their ships from Dunkirk privateers. Scarborough men soon found themselves in the thick of this North-Sea war.

Despite repeated and expensive attempts to secure it, Scarborough had failed to acquire admiralty jurisdiction in its own courts. Christopher and Francis Thompson had almost succeeded only to see, at the last moment, the lord chancellor refuse to pass a measure which diminished the authority of the lord admiral.[5] Not surprisingly, therefore, when admiralty deputies acted in Scarborough without the consent of the bailiffs, the Common Hall burgesses were displeased. In the summer of 1624, Alexander Jacobson from Flushing and Peter Browne, a Dutchman, were arrested by admiralty officers 'within the libertyes of the towne' when they bought fish 'of[f] the boat'. Since buying fish straight from the fishing boats was strictly forbidden by long-standing Scarborough bye-law, the bailiffs protested; but to no avail. Both admiralty men and aliens ignored the town's governors. Browne paid a fine of 40s. to the admiralty and 'sayd he cared nott for the bailiffs nor never a man in the towne'.[6] It was the first of many insults and humiliations to come.

The bailiffs, then Francis Thompson and William Batty, were already irritated and alarmed by the peremptory summons they had recently received from the lord admiral. They were commanded to report to Bridlington Quay on 6 July 1624 along with all the owners and part owners of Scarborough's vessels and their crews. From later correspondence, it is clear that the bailiffs ignored the admiral's summons and as a result were fined £10 in the admiral's court. When they appealed to Lord Sheffield, vice-admiral and formerly lord president of the Council of the North (1603–19), whom they regarded as their special friend and guardian, they were sharply reprimanded for their impertinence and told bluntly that the admiral 'hath a jurisdiction to preserve'. On this occasion, 'Mr Baylif Tompson' was singled out for special condemnation. However, since Scarborough by this time was infected with plague, it seems unlikely that the admiralty insisted on the attendance of men from the town.[7] After the death of King James in March 1625, the bailiffs, now Paul Peacock and Thomas Foord, tried to make amends with the lord admiral, the Duke of Buckingham, by offering him one of Scarborough's parliamentary seats for his nomination. However, if the duke did use his 'blank' it is not recorded in the bailiffs' correspondence. Perhaps Sir Guilford Slingsby, Controller of His Majesty's ships, was Buckingham's man, but he was nominated by Edward Cayley of Brompton, and he was not elected. Sir Edward Waterhouse, Lord Sheffield's choice, was also rejected by the Common Hall. Lord Scrope, Sheffield's successor as lord president of the Northern Council, exercised his 'blank' by proposing Sir William Alford of Meaux, only to see him accept a seat from his neighbours at Beverley. In the end, the Common Hall elected William Thompson, who was his own man as well as the Earl of Holderness's, and re-elected Hugh Cholmley. In neither choice were they likely to find favour with the Duke of Buckingham or Lord Scrope, the two men whose protection they needed most, especially in time of war.[8]

Meanwhile, the Dutch and Dunkirkers were fighting a fierce battle in the North Sea. In October 1625, the mayor of Newcastle reported that fifteen Dunkirker warships had been sighted off Scarborough. They had sunk two out of eight Dutch escorts and plundered seventy Hollander fishing boats. The following March, three Dunkirkers were seen off Scarborough. They had already taken a ship carrying alum and a dozen other vessels and constituted a direct threat to people living on the Yorkshire coast. These Dunkirkers were probably the same as those reported by Scarborough's bailiffs to the Council at York. They were thought to be waiting off Scarborough for a fleet of Newcastle colliers which had to pass that way.[9] So serious was the Dunkirker menace to alum shipments that early in 1627 the farmers of the industry in north Yorkshire were provided with an admiralty warship to escort their loaded vessels between Whitby and London.[10]

The presence of so many hostile warships off the Yorkshire coast, and the inability of its inhabitants to defend themselves or their property against off-shore piracy or even invasion prompted the government to insist that military preparations should be made at all points and especially unprotected harbours. In September 1625, Paul Peacock and Thomas Foord were instructed by lord president Scrope to make sure that their warning beacons were in good repair and attended by a permanent watch. They were also to lay up military stores and appoint guards for them.[11]

A fortnight later, a more urgent and detailed order was received at Scarborough from the Council at York. The town's trained band had to be mustered immediately and 'be in redines at an howers warninge'. Every foot soldier, common and private, had to be furnished with three pounds of gunpowder and six of match and bullet. Deficiences in this issue would be made good by an allowance at the rate of twelve pence for every pound of powder and sixpence for every pound of match. However, though the situation was grave, there were to be no panic, false alarms. The watchers must not light their beacons to signal invasion 'unlesse they shall see a fleete of shipps above an usuall nomber & that it shall appeare to them that they have longe boates or others fitt for the landing of men & that they shall see then goe about to make use of them to that purpose'.[12] What the authorities meant by an unusual number of enemy ships they failed to explain, but their order must have caused some consternation on the coast.

Scarborough seems to have responded quickly and fully to these official warnings, though no doubt the proximity of Sir Matthew Boynton of Barmston and Sir Thomas Hoby at Hackness, two highly conscientious justices, as well as that of Dunkirk warships, spurred the action of the bailiffs. Only a day after the naval battle off Scarborough, when fifteen Dunkirkers routed eight Hollanders, Captain Phillips reviewed the town's trained band. All fifteen of the common and the same number of private men mustered, altogether nineteen of them carrying muskets. But there must have been a shortage of ammunition since a few days later the Common Hall approved an assessment of £30 'for powder & shott & other needfull provisions for his majesties service'. However, since by this time the emergency had passed, and the Dutchmen and Dunkirkers had gone home for the winter, the bailiffs now met resistance to the assessment. On 28 November 1625 they had to issue warrants to the town constables to collect debts from 'partyes [who] have obstinately refused payment'.[13]

At the same time as one of Scarborough's Members of Parliament, Hugh Cholmley, was chiefly concerned to build a new pier for his home town of Whitby, the other, now Stephen Hutchinson of Wykeham Abbey, had the welfare of his constituents at the forefront of his endeavours. From his 'chamber at a habrdasher shop next the thre cranes over agaynst Burley house in the Strand', Hutchinson wrote to his brother-in-law, Christopher Thompson at Scarborough, at the end of January 1626. He was pleased to report that the Privy Council had sent two warships northwards 'to gard your costes from the Dunkerks', though this was of limited comfort to Scarborough, which he had heard was the most 'ill provided' of all the North Sea ports. He hoped to present a petition on behalf of the town and that the House of Commons would 'press the king for defenc of his realm, and to make himselfe master of the Narow Seases'.[14]

As a view of arms in the town revealed a month later, Scarborough was indeed poorly defended. Only ten of the private men appeared: William and Francis Thompson and Gregory Fysh were conspicuous absentees, and most of the ten lacked powder and shot for their muskets. The same applied to most of the common men who turned out at the end of February. Since Scarborough suffered from a double threat of plague and Dunkirker, bailiffs John Farrer and Richard Peacock made a direct appeal for help to the Duke of Buckingham. In their letter of 8 August 1626 they claimed that sixty of the town's seamen had been taken into the king's service and that they were required to maintain a permanent watch of thirty or forty men 'agaynst thattemts of the Dunkerk[ers]'. They were particularly worried by the information that the Dunkirker men-of-war in the vicinity had 'earnestly examined mariners [of captured ships] of the state of our castle & the towne'. If the enemy should try to come ashore at Scarborough there would be little there to deter them. They therefore asked the Duke to strengthen the defences of the castle and the town 'with some furniture of ordinance shott and powder so as we may be the better able to withstand the threatned attempts of the enimye'.[15]

Whether Scarborough ever received 'furniture of ordinance shott and powder' is not recorded, but it seems highly unlikely since more than a year later the Common Hall had to ask its own members to pay for their gunpowder. The First Twelve were asked for fifteen shillings each, the Second for twelve, and the Third for five, making £18 in all. The rest of the town was assessed for £6 13s. 4d. Soon afterwards, when Buckingham nominated two candidates for the Scarborough seats in the Parliament of 1628, the Common Hall defied him by rejecting both. They preferred Sir William Constable and John Harrison. Neither Hugh Cholmley nor Stephen Hutchinson offered themselves for re-election.[16]

Though England made peace with Spain and France in 1630, there was no peace between Spain and Holland. After a temporary lull in the early 1630s, Scarborough was threatened by Dutchmen and Dunkirkers as never before. During the lull the town lost whatever artillery it might have gained during the recent wars. In October 1632 the bailiffs received a letter from Malton asking them to send their cannon 'with convenient bulletts and shotts for the service' and an 'enginier or master gunner for plantation of the same'. Since Lord Eure had refused to quit his fortified manor house at Malton, he was to be blasted out with artillery and Scarborough was thought to be the nearest place with such weaponry. Two days later, the newly elected bailiffs, William Batty and William Tennant, wrote to the high sheriff of the county, Sir Thomas Langton, who was in charge of the siege at Malton. There was only one piece of ordnance in the castle 'fitt for the service intended' and they were sending it down the road to Malton in the hope that it would be restored to its 'accustomed place after the execution of the service required'.[17]

But the sheriff was not satisfied and neither was lord president Wentworth at York. The latter dismissed the castle's 'peece' as 'of very lyttle or no use' and demanded Scarborough's other cannon 'which lyeth upon your peere'. Reluctantly, and very tardily, the Common Hall agreed to part with their 'peace of old ordinance lyeinge uppon the peere'. That Wentworth of all people should have seen fit to rob them of all their defences must have seemed astonishing to Scarborough's governors. After all, less than four months previously, the lord president had emphatically overruled Hoby's direction for the town's trained band to muster several miles inland at Hutton Buscel. As he had then explained in words that would have sounded sweetly on Sandside: 'Scarborough is a sea towne and the Castle their a place of strength, and of greate importance'; in case of 'some suddaine and unexpected danger' it must not be deprived, even briefly, of its defenders.[18]

From now on Scarborough's corporation records refer frequently to battles fought in local waters between Dutchmen and Dunkirkers. In November 1633 a Dunkirk man-of-war had taken a Hollander called the *Blackhound*, late of Henlopen, and then brought it into Scarborough harbour. It seems, however, that the ship and its cargo had already been bought by Captain Luke Foxe of Whitby and his business associates, William Bellwood of Mulgrave and George Lane of Lythe, who were also engaged in the alum trade. Altogether, ship and cargo were said to be worth £700. By long-established custom, the two bailiffs and burgesses of the Common Hall had the right to first refusal of purchase, and on this occasion Gregory Fysh and Timothy Thompson believed that they had a bargain. The great ship was subsequently offered to Launcelot Alured of Rudston for £320 and some of the oak timbers in its cargo given to William Simpson, St Mary's vicar, for the new pews then being built. But the Common Hall had sold what it had not yet paid for, and Foxe, Bellwood and Lane entered a bill of complaint with the Council at York for payment of a £400 bond which was nearly a year overdue. From the minutes of the Common Hall it is obvious that the burgesses had no intention of paying a penny a moment earlier than was absolutely necessary. Captain Alured, it seems, was also unwilling or unable to fulfil his side of the transaction. In the end, the Captain promised to deliver £170 to the bailiffs in three instalments.[19]

On 24 April 1635 the Lord Mayor of York received £100 from Scarborough, its heavy contribution towards a ship of 800 tons for His Majesty's new fleet of warships. Since the town had received the high sheriff's demand only a few days previously, the unusual alacrity of Scarborough's response was probably caused by the alarming increase in Dunkirker and Dutch naval activity off the East coast.[20]

The worst of all the incidents arising out of the Thirty Years' War took place in July 1635. On the thirteenth of that month, a Dunkirker, towing a captured Dutch fishing boat, came into Scarborough harbour without invitation. Within less than an hour, it was followed in by the *Post* of Amsterdam, which drew alongside and boarded it. Both ships were soon engaged in close cannon and musket combat. About a dozen men on the Dunkirker were killed, more wounded, and the rest swam ashore. Some over-curious spectators on the sands and piers were hit by stray bullets. The Dutch ship, under Captain Browne, sailed away, towing the Dunkirker and its prize, and refusing even to allow its surgeon to come ashore and help the wounded. Two of the Dunkirker crew, 'slaine in the fight', were buried in St Mary's, 19 and 24 July.[21]

As bailiff Martin Atmar explained ruefully to Sir Edward Osborne, vice-president of the Council at York, there was nothing the town could do to defend itself: 'The harbour is of great importance to his Majesty, being the refuge of Newcastle ships in their way to London, and for all the fishers on the coast . . . [but] the ordnance in the castle are old, dismounted and of no use as they are now.'[22]

Twelve days later, before anything had been done about Atmar's plea for assistance, another 'insolence' was committed at Scarborough by foreigners. Again, a frigate of the King of Spain had been chased into the harbour by a Dutch man-of-war, this time the *Prince Henry* of Amsterdam under Captain Cornelius Clauson. On this second occasion, however, the Dutch were determined that none of their enemies should swim to safety, so they sent 'three or fower score men ashore with musketts and pikes' to prevent their escape. The bailiffs, Atmar and Harrison, pleaded with the Dutch officer in command of the landing party to return to his ship and not to start a fight either in the town or the harbour. Eventually, after 'manye perswaysions', Clauson agreed to sail away on condition that no Dunkirker should be allowed ashore and the Dutch fishermen imprisoned on board the Spanish frigate be released. After more 'parleys', Henry Jespers, the Dunkirker captain, accepted Clauson's terms.[23]

Only after the second incident had ended peacefully, thanks to the skilful diplomacy of Atmar and Harrison, did they receive instructions from the Privy Council in response to the first: 'If the lyke shall happen againe, and any of the parties that make the assault, either come ashore or within commande', they were to use their 'best endevors to apprehend and make stay of them, until farther order from this Board'![24]

Fortunately and wisely, the bailiffs did not even call out the local home guard on either occasion; had they done so it would have been no match for Hollanders or Dunkirkers, who might well have trained their guns on the town instead of one another.

The 'insolencies' at Scarborough, which might have been so hurtful, in fact brought long-term benefits to the town. The second writ for the collection of Ship Money, dated 4 August 1635, was this time addressed to the whole of Yorkshire, not just to its ports, and Scarborough's own assessment was reduced from £100 to £30. From then on, year after year, it remained at £30. Needless to say, whatever might happen elsewhere in England, particularly in the depths of Buckinghamshire, there was no resistance to Ship Money in Scarborough. No place in the kingdom had greater need of a strong Royal Navy.[25]

Secondly, what happened at Scarborough in July 1635 drew London's attention to the defenceless of the harbour there, and finally forced a positive reaction from the central government. As early as 26 July, writing from York, Sir Edward Osborne informed the Privy Council of 'the decay of the castle at Scarbrough', which was no longer Crown property, and 'the nakedness of the harbour for want of ordnance and other provisions of defence'. Since the port of Scarborough, he continued, was 'a place of great importance for the safety of these northern parts', it followed that more than the welfare of one town was at stake.[26]

The Privy Council agreed: two days later they wrote to Scarborough's bailiffs to reassure them that they were well aware of 'the wants that are in the castle, which wee understand is disfournished of ordinance', and that they would soon give consideration to what should be done 'for the safety of the towne and harbour'. On Monday, 10 August, Scarborough had a visit from Sir Edward Osborne who had instructions from the Privy Council to inspect the town's defences. Since Captain Alured was 'a gentleman of good experience in matters of fortification', Osborne asked the bailiffs to make sure he was present and 'any other expert that way'.[27]

Whether Scarborough did subsequently receive some artillery for its defence is not recorded, but in other ways the Privy Council reacted speedily, strongly and decisively to what it called 'that insolency at Scarborough'. What had occurred at Scarborough in July 1635 was nothing less than a foreign invasion. The honour as well as the security of the kingdom had been jeopardised. A strongly-worded protest was delivered to the Dutch ambassador in London and two warships were sent northwards to Scarborough at the beginning of August. Their orders were to seize any Dutch vessel in English waters, bring it into the nearest home port, and hold it there as hostage until the guilty Hollanders were delivered up by their own government for trial. In fact, however, the *Rainbow* and the *Royal Exchange* never ventured beyond Hull. They took a Dutch man-of-war off the mouth of the Humber and conveyed it into Hull. Captain Povey on the *Rainbow* was clearly relieved that he had been spared a voyage even further north. Since few of his officers were 'accustomed to the north coast', he had been obliged to take pilots on board as early as Yarmouth! Whatever other mariners might say about the safety of Scarborough harbour, Captain Povey believed that it was 'not a place . . . to ride in'. By the end of August he had rejoined the main fleet in the Downs.[28]

Nevertheless, by the following summer, as the shoals of herring once again came southwards down the East coast of England, the situation had improved radically. In May the Dutch were so impressed by the growing strength of the Royal Navy that the States of Holland agreed to pay £30,000 a year for permission to fish unmolested in

English and Scottish waters.[29] From now on there were regular patrols of English warships off the Yorkshire coast issuing licences to Dutch herring busses which guaranteed them protection from Dunkirk predators. The lord high admiral himself, the Earl of Northumberland, took station off Scarborough aboard the *Triumph* in August 1636. Two hundred fishing licences, worth £500, were granted by him that summer.[30]

A year later, Captain Richard Fielding was on guard duty off Scarborough in the *Unicorn*. He reported a fishing fleet of between six and seven hundred sail escorted by twenty-three Dutch warships. Thirteen Dunkirkers had picked off one of the Hollanders and sunk it. The *Unicorn* had taken five men out of the sea but they were all dead. Yet Fielding was no more than a powerless observer. After Northumberland's modest success the previous summer, not a single licence was sold in 1637. For whatever reason, the English attempt to assert sovereignty in their own off-shore fishing waters was abandoned. Perhaps the Dutch were considered just too strong to challenge. Fortunately, Scarborough had no more unwelcome visits from Dunkirkers and Hollanders.[31]

As the threat from the North Sea subsided, a new one from Scotland took its place. By the beginning of 1639, when war with the Scots seemed unavoidable, Scarborough was called upon to make extraordinary military preparations. Sir Thomas Posthumous Hoby was now too old to bully the town into conformity, but his successor as leading local gentleman, Sir Hugh Cholmley of Whitby, was even more demanding. When King Charles began to make plans to form an army by calling out the Northern trained bands for field service, as deputy lieutenant in the North Riding and colonel of the militias of Whitby Strand, Pickering Lythe, Ryedale and Scarborough town, Cholmley was one of his more assiduous servants. Some deputies, such as Cholmley's cousin, Sir John Hotham, governor of Hull, were most reluctant to muster their men when called, but not Cholmley. There was therefore no escape for Scarborians.[32]

Previously, Scarborough had been required to equip and muster a select band of thirty men, but on 21 and 28 January 1639 Sir Hugh inspected an unusual number. Twenty-three men from Falsgrave turned out; at least a dozen of them with muskets and the others with bills. The muster roll for Undercliff Quarter listed 21 names, that for St Mary's Quarter, 16, for Newborough, 24, and for Oldborough, 29. The last time a force of this size had been mustered was probably as long ago as 1542, on the eve of a previous Scottish war, when Scarborough was then said to have had 28 archers, 80 bill men, harness or armour for 40 soldiers, and 40 horses.[33]

Hoby had failed to bring Scarborough's trained band six miles inland to Hutton Buscel, yet Cholmley expected some of it at least to march much further for training. On 11 February 1639, bailiffs Timothy Thompson and Martin Atmar asked Sir Hugh not to insist that the townsmen muster on Seamer Moor and that instead he should see them exercise in Scarborough; but only a week later, Scarborough's musketeers were training on 'Scallowmore', north of Pickering, a full fifteen miles inland from their homes.[34] According to his own account of these events, Sir Hugh was reviewing and training his 'whole Regem[en]t together on Pexton Moore neare Thornton' at about this time. By his whole regiment presumably Cholmley meant the combined force drawn from the four companies of Whitby Strand, Pickering Lythe, Ryedale and Scarborough town. Scalla Moor and Pexton Moor are very close to one another.[35]

Sir Hugh 'caught cold & a dangerous sickness' as a result of being out on the moors in winter weather and was therefore unable later to command his troops in the field.[36] However, in Scarborough and Falsgrave his place was ably filled by Captain Launcelot Alured. In May 1639 Alured wrote to the bailiffs reminding them that their 'shoulgers' had to be kitted out with cassocks and hose and blue capes lined with red. Scarborough's trained band had to be ready to march northwards towards Durham 'in fowerteene daies'. Sir Ferdinando Fairfax, Sir John Hotham and Sir Thomas Metham had already received orders to lead their Yorkshire militia men in the direction of Berwick. Three days later, the captain wrote to the bailiffs from Muston, a village seven miles south of Scarborough, on behalf of the bearer of the letter, Will Robinson of 'Phaulsgrave' [Falsgrave]. Robinson was only 'a poore man & a tradesman, whose hands next under gods providence is [his] only means of subsisting'. Therefore, during his time of employment in the king's service, his wife should be allowed a shilling a week in his absence. Falsgrave would have to foot the bill.[37]

Since the town had to pay coat and conduct money for its own militia, it was reluctant to add allowances to dependants to this heavy bill. When, in June 1639, Cholmley discharged four of Scarborough's 'common men' for unexplained reasons, the bailiffs objected on the grounds that three of them had no infant or other dependants: one had 'noe children as yett', another had 'but one child and in a manner able to gitt her owne liveings', and the third was a bachelor. Whether these men would make competent soldiers mattered less to the bailiffs than how much more money their replacements might cost the town.[38] In the event, none of Scarborough's trained band was called upon to join the king's army. The day after the bailiffs complained to Sir Hugh, Charles signed a truce with the Scots at Berwick in which he agreed to disband his rabble of an army.

Still, as a fragment of a corporation receipt book for 1638–39 shows, Scarborough had already paid a high price for the First Bishops' War without making a direct military contribution to it. During that year, £8 11s. 10d. had been spent on a long list of items which included officers' cloaks, wages, girdles, scabbards for swords, knapsacks, bandoliers, primers, musket rests, 'scowers' and 'worms', and expenses for the training sessions on Scalla Moor. Yet even this account tells only part of the story. To add to the bill there must have been the cost of powder, match and ammunition, not to mention the cassocks and hose which Cholmley expected his men to wear.[39] Sir John Hotham was probably not exaggerating too much when in Parliament the following spring he complained that whereas Yorkshire had to pay £12,000 in Ship Money, the military charges laid upon the county during the recent Scottish war had amounted to £40,000.[40]

During the First Bishops' War there occurred another event to illustrate Scarborough's value as a port of refuge. In April 1639, lord admiral of the fleet, the Marquess of Hamilton, was forced by 'evil weather' to find shelter there with eight warships and twenty colliers.[41]

The King's humiliating failure to subdue the Scottish rebellion, and increasing resistance in England to payment of Ship Money, forced him to call a new Parliament, the first for eleven years, in the spring of 1640. The earliest letter of recommendation for one of Scarborough's seats came from Sir Edward Osborne, Lord Wentworth's right-hand man in Yorkshire. Osborne nominated himself and was supported by Wentworth, who had lately returned to London from Dublin. On the same day, 12 December 1639, that Wentworth's letter of endorsement arrived in Scarborough, Sir John Melton, another Yorkshire knight without Scarborough connections, recommended himself for the second place. Melton had the backing of the Earl of Northumberland, now restored to the office of lord admiral.[42]

In normal circumstances this might have been the end of the 'election'. The custom whereby Scarborough's two seats were filled by the nominees of the lord president of the Council of the North and the lord high admiral was by now long established and it was rare, though not unknown, for the Common Hall to prefer other candidates. But these were not normal circumstances. Wentworth and Northumberland were now seen as the king's chief advisers and supporters in the late war against the Scots; should their will prevail, in Westminster and Whitehall, then the war would soon be resumed, Ship Money would continue indefinitely, and the extraordinary burdens of the past year increase. Moreover, two powerful, respected, local gentlemen, Sir John Hotham and Sir Hugh Cholmley, were now known to oppose Ship Money and to question its legality, despite the judgement in Hampden's Case. Also, both men had spoken out in public against the unfairly heavy charges laid on their fellow countrymen as a result of the king's vain and disastrous Scottish policies.[43]

As early as January 1639, Hotham had refused to collect or pay another penny of Ship Money and as a result was dismissed from his post as governor of Hull and replaced by Captain William Legge. Cholmley's position is more difficult to pin-point, though before the Short Parliament opened he was one of the county's deputy lieutenants who had refused to raise any militia for service unless there was a promise of coat and conduct money from the government.[44]

Consequently, when the bailiffs opened a letter from Sir John Hotham recommending his cousin, Sir Hugh, to be their next

Member of Parliament, along with Wentworth's own nominee, this was probably well received. The embarrassment might be solved by a diplomatic compromise: Scarborough would be represented by both parties if it was represented by Cholmley and Osborne. On Boxing Day, Sir Edward wrote to the bailiffs from York thanking them for making him 'the prime burgesse for your Corporacion'. However, there was to be a final, unexpected twist to the story. On 24 February 1640 Osborne again wrote to Scarborough asking its electors to delay their choice of Members. He enclosed a request from Wentworth, now the Earl of Strafford and lord lieutenant of Ireland, to nominate Mr George Butler as Osborne's replacement should the latter accept one of the seats of the city of York.[45]

Perhaps the bailiffs and burgesses of the Common Hall now resented this latest attempt to gerrymander and delay their election; whatever their reasons they proceeded to defy the king's most powerful minister. As Cholmley's partner they chose Hotham's eldest son, Captain John, even though Sir John had asked them to give Strafford's nominee preference to his son. Northumberland's candidate was also ignored.[46]

In Cholmley's absence at Westminster, Roger Wyvill, who was a former bailiff, an active North-Riding magistrate, and a deputy lieutenant, took Scarborough's next review of arms 17 April 1640. On this occasion only the 'common armes' are recorded, but the list shows that Cholmley's expectations remained unfulfilled. Fifteen men turned out for inspection. Only ten of them had muskets. Of these ten, one lacked three bandolier boxes for his cartridges, one a knapsack, one a rest, one a firing pin for his weapon, one a scourer to clean out the barrel, and one a rest and scourer. Two of the men Cholmley had discharged were back in the ranks. William Robinson, however, who had cost Falsgrave dearly, was a fully-furnished musketeer.[47]

If Scarborough's forty-four electors had wanted their representatives at Westminster to stand up to the great Lord Strafford and speak out plainly against Ship Money and the burden of coat and conduct money, they would not have been disappointed with Sir Hugh Cholmley's performance in the Short Parliament. Twice he openly questioned the legality of imposing Ship Money on the whole country, and on the second occasion was rebuked by Mr Solicitor for his 'boldness'. When King Charles agreed to discontinue Ship

Money if the Commons granted him twelve subsidies during the next three years, Cholmley's impertinent reply was that if Ship Money was illegal then the king was making no concession by giving it up. Finally, he infuriated all the king's ministers, not just Strafford, by declaring that if Charles wanted more subsidies from Parliament and the people he should first promise to reimburse all those subjects who had suffered so grievously from the intolerable militia charges of the past two years.[48]

Three days after the dissolution of the Short Parliament, on Friday, 8 May 1640, Cholmley was summoned to appear before the Privy Council to answer for his words in the Commons. Three other Yorkshire Members of Parliament, including Sir John Hotham, who represented Beverley, were also ordered to attend. All four were accused of making disloyal and improper speeches. Hotham was so stubbornly defiant that he was sent immediately to the Fleet Prison. Cholmley was more circumspect, if perhaps less honest. He denied the charges, which he said could not be proved against him. Since there was no written proof of what Sir Hugh had said, and only one fellow Yorkshireman, Francis Nevile of Chevet, was prepared to inform against him, he was let off lightly. He was commanded not to leave the capital but to report to the Privy Council every day for the next four weeks. At about the same time, however, Cholmley was deprived of all his offices and commissions, principally justice of the peace and deputy lieutenant in the North Riding and colonel of the trained bands in his neighbourhood. A similar punishment was inflicted on his cousin Hotham. Sir John was soon released from prison and Cholmley was back home in Whitby by 11 June, but neither could now be reconciled with Strafford whom they regarded as the chief cause of their disgrace and the greatest threat to their safety.[49]

The truce of Berwick soon expired and the so-called Second Bishops' war with the Scots began in August 1640. Scarborough, however, seems to have been spared its worst effects. Many other Yorkshire towns and villages on or near the main roads running north and south were soon complaining of unpaid, forced billeting, mutinous militia and innumerable outrages committed by the king's ill-disciplined army. At York, Hotham and Cholmley were the authors of a series of petitions addressed to the king against his unruly soldiers and his impositions on their countrymen of coat and conduct money. Even when Charles in person asked Sir Hugh to resume his commission as colonel of his regiment of trained bands he refused. Bluntly, he told the king that he could never again serve under Strafford, who had been made General when the Earl of Northumberland fell ill. On the other hand, Sir Hugh recommended his younger brother Henry to take his place, and even consented to accompany the regiment as far as Northallerton, where the king had his headquarters. Consequently, when the Scots crossed the Tyne southwards after their rout of the English at Newburn at the end of August, Cholmley's 'Bluecoats' were standing guard over the king at Northallerton.[50]

It seems most unlikely that there were any men from Scarborough amongst these Bluecoats. Cholmley's militia were probably from Ryedale and perhaps a few from Whitby. The Scarborough company was expected to stay at home and, if necessary, defend the harbour against a Scottish seaborne attack. Fortunately, though only for the time being, Scarborough escaped a Scottish invasion. The humiliating treaty forced upon the king by the Scots at Ripon in October 1640 kept them at bay north of the Tees, while much of the county of Yorkshire remained the victim of even more ravenous predators, 'foreign' English militiamen.[51]

Under bombardment from the merchants of the City of London and the Council of Peers at York, and having agreed to pay the Scots £850 a day for the pleasure of camping in his northern counties, King Charles was compelled to call a new Parliament for November 1640. As before, Strafford was first off the mark. As early as 24 September, long before the writs had been issued, the lord president wrote to the bailiffs of Scarborough to recommend his cousin, Sir George Wentworth of Woolley, as one of their burgesses in the forthcoming Parliament. However, the electors who had cocked a snook at him the previous March when he was riding high were not now likely to show deference to a man who was fast running out of credit and authority. Woolley was passed over. He had to settle for one of the family's pocket-borough seats at Pontefract. Sir William Sheffield, son of the Earl of Mulgrave, offered himself as a candidate and was also rebuffed. This time there was little hesitation or delay on Sandside: on 9 October Sir Hugh Cholmley and John Hotham were again chosen to represent the borough at Westminster. A similar story ran across the county. All four of Strafford's nominees for the city and county of York were defeated. Of Yorkshire's thirty seats only five were won by his candidates. When New Malton was enfranchised the following year, Sir Hugh's brother Henry won the seat.[52]

The Bishops' Wars were over but, much to the dismay of its people, the king's army continued to occupy Yorkshire. Until Charles persuaded his new Parliament to grant him subsidies, he could not pay off his troops. The longer they remained idle, unpaid and away from home, the greater threat they posed to their unwilling hosts. Yet Parliament relished and exploited the king's embarrassment: until he had satisfied their many grievances it would not give him more money. Not until August 1641 were warrants issued to bailiffs Francis Thompson and William Foord to collect money in Scarborough 'for disbanding the army'.[53]

By that time many local people would have said that it was far too late: the damage had already been done by the royal army. Colonel Fielding had a regiment billeted at Pocklington, Colonel William Vavasour's men were quartered about Crayke castle, the Marquess of Hamilton's regiment were at Wetherby and Colonel Wentworth's at Ripon, but it was Lord Carnarvon's cavalry, camped at Hutton Buscel and Ayton, which aroused the greatest indignation. On 20 February 1641, Justice Roger Wyvill of Osgodby wrote a lengthy letter to General Sir John Conyers at York demanding 'exemplary punishment' and 'plenary satisfaction' for 'insufferable offences' and 'evil behaviour and grand abuses' perpetrated by the troopers in his neighbourhood. He accused them in general terms of highway robbery, attempts to violate women, threats to burn down houses and 'frequent riding forth of their quarters to drink themselves drunk etcetera'. In particular, he himself had been the victim of a most outrageous assault. When he had intervened to try to stop four troopers mauling two villagers in the main street of Seamer, they had turned on him viciously. Not content to wound him six times to the head and three times to the right hand, the troopers had chased him into a nearby house where he had tried to find shelter. When he climbed a ladder to an upper chamber they pursued him. To escape he had to break through the back wall of the house. He was fortunate not to lose his life as well as his dignity. For confirmation of the truth of these many serious incidents, Wyvill referred the General to his neighbouring justices, John Legard of Ganton and William Cayley of Brompton.[54]

The four murderous troopers were arrested by their own lieutenant, conveyed to York, and there imprisoned. Conyers had to confess to his commander-in-chief, the Earl of Northumberland, that 'by report of all men it is a foul fact'. He had also received so many protests and petitions from the people in and around Pocklington that he had instructed the Quarter Master General to transfer some of the most ill-disciplined men there to new billets in Pickering Lythe. It seems that no one wanted to be hosts, or even neighbours, to such guests as these. Significantly, when the House of Commons finally agreed to allow eight pence to every soldier for every fifteen miles he had to travel back to his home county, the notorious regiments in east Yorkshire were ordered to be disbanded first.[55]

CHAPTER THREE

First Civil War, 1642–1645

CIVIL WAR came to Scarborough by degrees, not suddenly or unexpectedly; the town had a long time to prepare for it. The earliest indication that Scarborough might soon have to defend itself came in a Common Hall minute of 22 February 1642: 'The placeinge of the brasse peece now lyeinge on the peer is by the wholl Commons now assembled refarred to the discreesion of Mr Bailiffs and three or fower of their bretheren.'[1] Perhaps the 'brasse peece' on the pier was the fruit of Sir Edward Osborne's inspection and report on the harbour defences made in 1635,[2] but since there is no further reference to it in the corporation records its value could hardly have been great. One possibility is that this cannon was eventually drawn up the hill through the town to Newborough Bar to guard the main gateway there. By 1642, the threat to Scarborough came from the land rather than from the North Sea.

That no threat from any direction was yet taken too seriously is demonstrated by the next item in the Common Hall minute book. The four churchwardens, then Robert Salton, Thomas Gill, John Powell and Matthew Fowler, were required to present their accounts to the bailiffs, in particular those concerning the rents collected and due from the town lands belonging to St Thomas's, 'thatt further order may be taken for the repaire of St Thomas church'. When it was soon appreciated, however, that the income from St Thomas's churchyard and St Thomas's fields in Burtondale was quite inadequate to cover the anticipated costs, in April 1642 the Common Hall ruled that the church should be repaired by a levy on the whole town.[3] So while the country was sliding quickly and inexorably towards outright civil conflict, Parliament was raising trained bands, and the King was already at York trying to recruit his own army from there, Scarborough was about to tax its householders for church repairs!

As far as Scarborough's governors were concerned, the King's presence only forty miles away at York since 18 March was the most significant political development. The Common Hall did not know what to do, except that they did not want to be seen to take sides until it became absolutely unavoidable. In the meantime, the best course was to play safe. It was decided, therefore, that bailiff William Fysh, representing the borough, and Francis Thompson, owner of the castle, should write to the high sheriff at York asking for his advice. This would be interpreted by the King as a loyal gesture without alienating Parliament. Should they take steps to fortify the town or the castle? No hint was given of the identity of the enemy that might threaten them; and, as a token of their friendship, 'a horsse load of fyshe' was sent to York along with the letter.[4]

Nevertheless, by mid-summer 1642, the King's continued presence in the locality had begun to make itself felt in Scarborough. On 7 July thirty of the town's armed men were mustered and reviewed by Captain William Wyvill, 'by vertue of warantt' from the Earl of Lindsey, the King's commanding general. If notice of Parliament's militia ordinance had been received in Scarborough, the bailiffs ignored it. As long as the borough's two Members stayed in London, 250 miles away, they could exercise no influence on Common Hall policy. However, it was perhaps significant that none of the thirty men who paraded before their Catholic officer, Captain Wyvill, were civic leaders: even all the fourteen 'privaite men' were substitutes provided by the wealthy but cautious rulers of the town. Four Thompsons, Francis, Timothy, Richard and Christopher, two Foords, Thomas and William, John Harrison, William Batty, William Conyers, and Martin Atmar, as yet preferred to keep their options open.[5] No doubt they all hoped that bloodshed would be avoided.

Only two days later, Scarborough's bailiffs received a warrant from King Charles, then at Beverley, addressed to them and the Wyvills, father and son, Roger and William. They were informed that 'a barque from London' carrying munitions was 'near Scarborough', and they were instructed to call out their armed men to guard the ship and its cargo until further orders.[6]

Either Charles was misinformed or he was deliberately trying to deceive the governors of Scarborough, or, most probably, both. The 'barque' in question was almost certainly the *Providence*, which had come from Holland, not London; a fact well known to the King since his wife had loaded and sent it from there. Secondly, though the *Providence* was indeed carrying a munitions cargo and might have intended to bring it into Scarborough, it had been intercepted off Spurn Point by Parliament's *Mayflower* and forced to seek refuge in a shallow creek at Keyingham in Holderness. In the event, though the *Providence* itself was lost, its precious arms were rescued by the trained bands of Holderness and safely conveyed to Charles at Beverley. There is no indication that Scarborough's militia even turned out for what would have been a wild-goose chase.[7]

Nevertheless, there is plenty of evidence that the King and his followers regarded Scarborough as one of the very few friendly ports in the country. Nearly all the Royal Navy had by now belied its name and gone over to Parliament, but the one warship Charles thought he could rely on, the 40-gun *Lion*, he ordered northwards from the Downs to Scarborough.[8] But it was too late: Parliament's admiral, the Earl of Warwick, had already seized its royalist captain and secured the ship for his own fleet.[9]

At first, the King's nephews, the Princes Rupert and his brother Maurice had tried to cross from Holland to England in the *Lion*, but soon after they set sail a violent storm from the south-west drove them back up the coast. The two Princes were so ill that they came ashore at Texel and the *Lion* carried on to the Downs without them. Consequently, when they did finally arrive off Flamborough Head some weeks later, they were on board one of the warships of the Prince of Orange. There they were challenged by one of Parliament's patrol ships, the *London*, and took flight towards Scarborough. A galliot they were escorting, loaded with powder, shot and small arms, they sent into Scarborough while the rest of the royalist party reached Tynemouth and came ashore safely there. Why Rupert and Maurice themselves did not land at Scarborough is not explained; perhaps the tide and wind were wrong for a larger vessel. Nevertheless, these new arrivals from Holland were far more valuable than guns and ammunition. Prince Rupert was soon to join the King at Nottingham and take command of his cavalry. The two military experts he brought with him were Bernard de Gomme, the brilliant engineer and authority on fortifications, and Bartholomew de la Roche, the 'fireworker', famous for his unrivalled knowledge of explosives and artillery.[10]

Royalist dependence on Scarborough was understandable. Since March 1642 the Queen, Henrietta Maria, had been at the Hague, raising colossal sums of money on the crown jewels and persuading her son-in-law, the Prince of Orange, to assist her husband's cause. The Dutch connection was essential to a royalist victory. Only the Dutch fleet could deny Parliament's command of the Channel and the North Sea; only the bankers and merchants of Amsterdam could raise the money and offer the credit Charles needed. The Queen's recruitment of mercenaries and purchase of arms in Holland had been extraordinarily successful, but Parliament's capture of the Royal Navy and its control of all the ports facing the Continent, from Portsmouth to Hull, posed an acute problem for the King.

Hull would have served the King's purposes perfectly, yet twice, in April and July, he had tried to take it and twice he had been rebuffed by Parliament's governor there Sir John Hotham. Newcastle was loyal but far from satisfactory: it was too far north, too easily blockaded at the mouth of the Tyne, and too vulnerable to the Scots. If Charles was denied Hull, with its port, fortifications and arsenal, he would have to make do with Scarborough. Though second best, Scarborough still had a strong castle to defend its harbour, which offered refuge from even the worst seas. Scarborough was also only forty miles by a good road from the King's northern headquarters at York, and it was too open to the North Sea to be closely and permanently blockaded, especially in bad weather. Above all, unlike most of his seaports, Scarborough seemed to be genuinely sympathetic to the royalist cause.

When the eldest of Charles's nephews, Elector Charles Louis, passed through Scarborough on his way back to Holland, the town had provided him with as many muskets as it could spare, out of its 'duties & good affections to his highnes'.[11] Also, at about the same time, in late July or early August, when the purser and six seamen from Parliament's *London* had carelessly come ashore at Scarborough, they were promptly arrested and sent in irons to the King's prison at York for refusing to serve his majesty.[12]

Parliament was soon receiving intelligence of royalist activity at Scarborough. On 4 August Captain Trenchfield on the *Unicorn*, stationed in Bridlington Bay, reported that the *London* had recently intercepted and taken the *Mary* of Scarborough. Master of the *Mary*, William 'Hixson' [Hickson], carried a safe conduct pass from Queen Henrietta Maria and horses which belonged to Prince Rupert.[13]

Also according to the watchful Captain Trenchfield, the King's newly-appointed admiral of the fleet, Sir John Pennington, transparently disguised as 'Sir John Porter', had lately visited Scarborough. Accompanied by two royalist sea captains, Scudimore and Carteret, the admiral had been making inquiries there about the port, its ships and seamen.[14]

Reference to Sir John Pennington is also to be found in an order from General Lindsey at Beverley to Lieutenant-Colonel William Wyvill dated 5 August 1642. Wyvill was instructed to march immediately to Scarborough with what remained of the regiment of Henry Bellasis and to take command of all his majesty's forces there. Presumably, Lindsey assumed that Scarborough's trained band was loyal to the King. Wyvill was to remain at Scarborough until he received orders to march out from Lindsey, Sir John Pennington or King Charles.[15]

General Lindsey's assumption, like that of the King's, that Scarborough could be relied upon was, however, no more than an assumption derived, at least in part, from wishful thinking. Just because the town's dominant burgesses were ' royalist' it did not follow that they would remain constant, or that they could always carry the whole community with them if they did.

Only 16 of the Common Hall of 44 voted to send the horse-load of fish as a gift to the King's sheriff at York the previous April.[16] Captain Trenchfield on Parliament's *Unicorn* might have better understood the political situation in Scarborough in the summer of 1642 when he wrote: 'The people of this town are very kind and faithful to us . . . and, as they profess, are for the parliament, although forced to the contrary'.[17] On the other hand, whatever 'the people' of Scarborough might prefer, as long as the town was effectively in the hands of the Wyvills, Thompsons and Fyshs, they would determine its 'loyalties', Secondly, as long as King Charles, his court and his army were at York and at Beverley, they and not Parliament, 250 miles distant, would continue to exercise decisive influence in Scarborough.

The King raised his battle standard at Nottingham on 22 August 1642. The following morning the bailiffs of Scarborough received notice of a warrant issued by the King's high sheriff of Yorkshire to local justices, John Legard of Ganton, Roger Wyvill of Osgodby and

Stephen Hutchinson of Wykeham Abbey. They were authorised to search every house in Scarborough 'for all such armes as are not of the trayned band and the same to seiz & send' to York. By the next day, Wednesday, 24 August, the search had been made and a list drawn up of 22 men who had 25 muskets. But the arms were not sent to York. Politely but firmly, the sheriff was reminded that Scarborough was 'a sea towne' and that 'by reason of the disquietnes of the times as well at sea as on land' it was vital that its mariners should be armed when they put to sea. Scarborough, the bailiffs continued, was now particularly short of weapons because it had recently provided the Prince Elector with muskets for his voyage to Holland. Finally, all the arms listed were private property: none had been 'embezilled from his ma[jesties] magazine or bought of any soyldiers as is supposed'. Though the town was ready 'att all times to do his majestie the best service' it could, clearly there were limits to that service when the security of its inhabitants was at risk. Service was one thing, self-sacrifice was more than could be asked. What the bailiffs did not add to their diplomatic letter was that, since the King and his army were now a hundred miles away in Nottingham, the sheriff lacked the means to enforce his warrant.[18]

Perhaps the most revealing entry in Scarborough's own record of this time of national crisis and dark uncertainty is to be found for 11 July at the general sessions. After fourteen jurors had been sworn in, there were no presentments for them to hear. The court clerk wrote simply 'Omne bene'![19] This had never happened during the past forty years; that it should have been written on the eve of the most violent and painful era in Scarborough's history was the richest of ironies. In retrospect, mariners would have recognised it as the dead calm before the most terrifying storm.

Contemporary royalists were convinced that English towns in general, and those with strong mercantile interests in particular, were prejudiced in Parliament's favour. Lord Clarendon later wrote of 'the natural malignity' which 'poisoned the affections' of townsmen.[20] Thomas Hobbes argued, even more unconvincingly, that 'the city of London and other great towns of trade' had noted the success of the Dutch cities and ports in the wars against Spain and believed that they could also profit from rebellion.[21]

From the opposite political standpoint and three centuries later, Christopher Hill and his protégé, Brian Manning, have contended that Parliament drew its main strength from the mercantile 'middling sort', whereas the King's followers were aristocratic, feudal, rural and lumpen proletarian.[22]

These attractively simple but grossly misleading generalisations have now been so often repeated that they have become the orthodoxy of superficial explanations of the English Civil War that began in 1642.[23]

Detailed examination of many individual cases eventually reveals a multitude of different urban responses to civil war divisions. For example, Newcastle, one of the largest of provincial mercantile communities, was a royalist stronghold until it fell to the Scots in 1644; both Bristol and Exeter ultimately took Parliament's side, but not immediately and with some evident reluctance; York was never Parliamentarian by choice, and neither was Worcester; nor was the manufacturing town of Wolverhampton; even Hull and Bradford, usually regarded as solidly for Parliament, were not so.[24]

One factor which sometimes exercised a decisive influence on the course taken by an urban oligarchy was the presence of a particularly powerful individual. Edmund Prideaux turned the scales at Exeter; Sir John Marley turned them the other way at Newcastle. Sir John Hotham played a crucial role at Hull in April 1642, and so did his cousin, Sir Hugh Cholmley, at Scarborough five months later.[25]

The arrival of Sir Hugh Cholmley in Scarborough in September 1642 transformed the situation there. According to his own account, he brought only a commission from the Earl of Essex, lord lieutenant of Yorkshire, to be colonel of the foot regiment of local trained bands – the commission which he had lost in 1640 after his fall-out with Strafford. He was to travel from London to Yorkshire, raise the regiment, and then bring it into the town of Scarborough. When Parliament's Committee of Safety also required him to occupy the castle at Scarborough, he replied bluntly that the castle there was private, not state, property, and that it belonged to a leading burgess called Thompson. As Sir Hugh explained later in his 'Memorialls

Tuching Scarbrough', written in 1647, since Parliament 'att that time' was 'nice to take any man's inheritance from him by force', the Committee accepted that he should try to persuade Thompson to hand over his castle 'for service of King and Parliament'.[26]

Cholmley might have expected more than verbal resistance to his Parliamentary take-over of Scarborough. Other than being one of the borough's two Members of Parliament, he had little claim on the loyalty of its people. He had no property in the town and had spent little time there. On the contrary, his home and interests were in Whitby, twenty miles away, and as that town's lord and patron he would have been regarded with some suspicion, even hostility, by Scarborough's mercantile oligarchy. There was no love between Whitby and Scarborough, particularly since Whitby's recent and spectacular growth as an alum, coal and ship-building port which had intensified their rivalry. Despite Scarborough's unconcealed opposition to it, thanks to Sir Hugh, Whitby had got its great west pier. Though he had been elected to be the borough's Member no fewer than five times, he had done nothing comparable for Scarborough. At Westminster, he had been absorbed wholly in national and personal, not local, issues.

In contrast, all of the Thompsons, who, in Cholmley's words, were 'verie much affected to the King's cause', had been running the town's affairs, more or less, for the past half century.[27] After the death of William in 1637, the family's influence seems to have grown even greater. From that year until 1641, four Thompsons in succession, Christopher, Timothy, Richard and Francis, held the highest office of senior bailiff. The political power of the Thompsons in the Common Hall reflected their wealth in the town. Of Scarborough's ten richest residents who were assessed for the Parliamentary subsidy of £24 in April 1641, four of the Thompsons contributed £14 between them. When later, in July 1643, the whole town was assessed at £60, five Thompsons, including Stephen, owner of the castle and St Mary's rectory, were to be found amongst the top dozen contributors. Altogether, their share was £4 11s. 8d., or nearly 8 per cent. Francis Thompson, elder brother of Richard, cousin of Timothy, father of Stephen and Christopher, and now head of the Thompson clan, was by far the richest man in Scarborough.[28]

Surprisingly, then, there is no evidence of confrontation between

Cholmley and the Thompsons. When the Common Hall held its annual elections soon after Sir Hugh's arrival in the town, no purge of the Thompsons, as might have been expected, took place. All five of them retained their positions in the First Twelve. In accordance with time-honoured tradition, the two bailiffs of the past year, William Fysh and William Headley, both of whom had royalist leanings, became coroners for the next year. The two new bailiffs, John Harrison and William Chapman, could have been chosen at any time. Both were senior men of substance. This was Harrison's fourth term as bailiff. He had served briefly as Scarborough's Member of Parliament in 1628–1629 and has been described as a wealthy financier and customs farmer. Chapman had not been bailiff before, but he had houses in Nether Westgate and Merchant Row, and in these terms his election was unremarkable.[29]

All this might suggest that the town, and particularly the Thompsons, were bullied into submission by Sir Hugh Cholmley; but this was not so. Lieutenant-Colonel William Wyvill, with whatever force he could raise, had already left Scarborough and moved south to join the King's army in the Midlands leaving behind a military vacuum in north-east Yorkshire, yet Cholmley brought with him no more than a small party of Parliamentary cavalry. According to his own version of events, and the only one that has survived, Sir Hugh had been promised two companies of infantry out of the garrison at Hull under Sir John Hotham. However, it was decided that they could not be spared, and so Cholmley rode into Scarborough accompanied by only 'a troope of horse fro[m] London'.[30]

Parliament's Committee of the Two Houses had restored Sir Hugh to his former commission as colonel of the trained bands of Ryedale, Pickering Lythe and Whitby Strand, as well as Scarborough town. That was in August 1642. However, by September, when he reached Scarborough from London, his younger brother, Sir Henry, already had many of these men under his command in the Midlands. Early in August, Sir Henry, now Member of the Commons for the newly enfranchised borough of Malton, had been named as one of Parliament's colonels of Yorkshire infantry regiments in the army of the Earl of Essex. Three weeks later, Colonel Cholmley's regiment of Bluecoats was reported to be marching towards Coventry via Buckingham. By mid-September, when Sir Hugh had arrived in

Scarborough, his brother's Bluecoats were in Northampton. There, according to Nehemiah Wharton, a sergeant in the London trained bands, the Yorkshiremen plundered a local justice called Edmonds and 'bereaved [him] of his beds', only to be compelled by their own cavalry to return the loot.[31]

Perhaps Sir Hugh was better off without his Bluecoats: at their first battle at Edgehill on 23 October they disgraced themselves. In the words of one eyewitness, all of Cholmley's regiment except one company of eighty men, 'used their heeles'.[32] Many of them ran much further than was necessary to save their necks. Before the battle, the regiment had numbered 1,200; a month later, after many more desertions than combat casualties, only 552 were left. What happened to the deserters can only be guessed; some must have eventually found their way back to Ryedale, Pickering and Whitby. One survivor of Edgehill who did return to Scarborough was Sir Henry's Lieutenant-Colonel Launcelot Alured. Sir Hugh must have been very pleased to accept his service.[33]

The first entry in the Common Hall's minute book recording Sir Hugh's presence in the town was made on 16 October. On that day the bailiffs and burgesses agreed 'with a mutuall and unanimus consentt' that 'in his proceedings for the protection of the towne' Cholmley should have the assistance of the trained band and of private men carrying arms, on condition that he, and not the town, paid for their services. In other ways, however, Scarborough was soon paying a heavy price to improve its defences. On 28 October the burgesses decided that the town should have two new gates made, one pair at Newborough Bar and another at Auborough Bar. Three days later, they set up a permanent night watch of eighteen men under the command of two of the Common Hall, one of the First Twelve and one of the Third. Every household was required to provide a watchman, or pay a penalty of twelve pence. Common Hall members who neglected their watch duty would be liable to a fine of five shillings for each offence. With the fines the bailiffs would buy powder and shot. To pay for the new gates, for scouring the New Dyke and building a wall at Newborough Bar near the house of coroner Fysh, the whole town was assessed at £50.[34]

Meanwhile, Sir Hugh had been busy. During October he claimed to have spent £200 on the castle. Guns had been mounted there;

breaches in the walls filled; and platforms for artillery and musketeers built. Yet, according to his estimates, it would cost another two or three hundred pounds to make the castle ready for siege. It still lacked sufficient store of food, ammunition and powder. Nevertheless, by his captains he was assured that if garrisoned with three or four hundred men and fully provisioned it could withstand an attack by any number. Sir Hugh told his masters in London in the same letter that he did not trust the Thompsons. Recently, Francis had shown interest in selling the castle for £600, but now he would accept nothing less than £800 for it from Cholmley. Sir Hugh described him as a 'malignant man' who was said to have 'sent a horse to the King against Parliament'. His son, Christopher, was no better: just before Sir Hugh's arrival there he had helped to send a ship carrying arms from Scarborough to Newcastle.[35] Sir Hugh would have preferred the Thompsons out of his way, but they were too powerful and he was too weak locally to challenge them directly.

Parliament's purpose in dispatching Cholmley north to Scarborough was to deny its harbour to the King, and within a few weeks he had done that and much more. Though his regiment had been depleted by Wyvill's recruitment, royalist foraging for arms in the locality and, not least, by his brother's commission in Essex's army, by the end of October Sir Hugh had gathered together about 400 militia men. Parliament was well pleased with his performance. On 2 November the House of Commons passed a resolution complimenting Cholmley on his 'acceptable and good service to the Commonwealth' in securing the castle at Scarborough. The commander of Parliament's most northerly outpost was promised its full support.[36]

Sir Hugh was not content merely to sit in the comfort and safety of the town and castle of Scarborough and allow the war to happen elsewhere, or wait for it to come to him. Early in November he left 112 men behind to garrison the castle and led the rest of his regiment, 40 cavalry and 300 foot, down the road to royalist York. The day after he was congratulated for securing Scarborough castle he arrived at Stamford Bridge, forty miles from the coast and only six from York. There he was joined by two companies of infantry, 220 men altogether, under Captains Mildmay and Alured, who had been sent out from Hull by Sir John Hotham.[37]

From Stamford Bridge Cholmley wrote to John Pym in London.

He was in an optimistic and belligerent mood. Soon he expected to receive a further reinforcement of 200 infantrymen under Colonel Boynton. Though he was short of artillery and cavalry, he intended to close in on York. He had sent back to Scarborough for 'a great ordnance' and asked for more horse. He had only one troop of cavalry though he could find employment for six.[38]

Whatever John Pym's reaction to it, none of this could have been welcome news in Scarborough. Even according to Cholmley's own admission, his captains had tried jointly and individually in writing to dissuade him from leaving Scarborough in the first place. With good sense they argued that the town was weakly held, the castle still far from defensible, and the enemy too strong, especially in cavalry, in the vicinity of York. They must have been appalled by Cholmley's proposal to besiege the city. The longer and further Cholmley's 'home guard' were away from their homes and families the more nervous they became. Those left behind in Scarborough also were not pleased to see Sir Hugh march away and leave only a token force in the castle. They were probably alarmed when they heard that from faraway Stamford Bridge he was asking for dragoons and artillery.[39] Nevertheless, when asked to raise a company of dragoons, the Common Hall responded on 21 November by voting 28 to none in favour. Of the First Twelve, only Stephen and Timothy Thompson were absent. All the other senior burgesses made generous contributions. The two bailiffs, Harrison and Chapman, coroner William Fysh and Francis Thompson each gave a man and a horse; Tristram Fysh, a mare; and Richard and Christopher Thompson, Thomas Foord and William Batty, each £5. Altogether, the Common Hall offered Cholmley four men, five horses and £55 15s. 4d. in money. Only nine of the forty-four members appear to have been absent or unwilling to contribute. Of the nine, apart from Stephen and Timothy Thompson, only one other, Francis Fawether, is known to have been a royalist sympathiser.[40]

However, just as the situation in east Yorkshire had been transformed by the departure of the King and his army in August, so now, at the beginning of December, the invasion from the north of a royalist army of 8,000 men, a quarter of them cavalry, turned the tables once again. Brushing aside Captain John Hotham's feeble force at Piercebridge on the Tees, the Earl of Newcastle's army entered

York soon afterwards. The Parliamentary militias of Richmondshire and Cleveland, under Sir Edward Loftus and Sir Henry Anderson, broke up and went home. The whole of the North Riding, apart from Scarborough, was now wide open to the royalist army.[41] As Parliament's general in Yorkshire, Lord Fairfax, put it, 'the enemy is mighty and master of the field'.[42]

Cholmley had no choice but to retreat from his exposed position, first to Malton, to cover the main route to Scarborough, then all the way back to the safety of the coast. In doing this he deliberately disobeyed the explicit order of Lord Fairfax to bring his men westwards to Tadcaster, and thereby took a decision which had momentous consequences for all the people of Scarborough as well as himself.

Cholmley's retreat from Stamford Bridge back to Scarborough was surely the wisest course. Even if he had been able to cross a swollen river Ouse below York and join Fairfax at Tadcaster, there was nothing certain to be gained by it and everything to be risked. Fairfax had only 1,000 men; the addition of 700 infantry under Cholmley and Boynton would still not make them a match for Newcastle's army. Besides, how was Cholmley ever to return to his base, the source of his manpower and his money? Royalist cavalry would have barred his way back to the east coast and Scarborough would soon have fallen to them.

When Sir Hugh was severely rebuked for his disobedience by Fairfax and his masters in London, he and his officers wrote a masterly explanation of why it was their duty, and in Parliament's best interest, to return to Scarborough. John Pym and the House were reminded that Scarborough was 'a place of very great consequence' for four reasons. Firstly, the castle there was of major strategical value: not only did it command the harbour and the town but it also had 'a great power over the adjacent parts of this country'. Secondly, they continued, Scarborough was now the only port where the enemy could conveniently and safely land men and munitions from the continent: 'it lies so opposite to Holland, or Denmarke, that he [the King] might take opportunities to send men or provisions from thence thither in despite of any Navy on the sea'. Thirdly, though the port of Newcastle was still royalist, the King would prefer to have Scarborough because it was much nearer York: 'ordnance or cariages may passe in the depth of winter to Yorke' from Scarborough, but not from Newcastle. Finally, they argued that if Parliament continued to hold the harbour at Scarborough from there the King's supplies from Holland or Denmark could be intercepted by pinnaces 'upon every occasion'. Among Sir Hugh's officers who signed this letter were Lieutenant-Colonel Launcelot Alured and Captain Browne Bushell.[43]

Heavily outnumbered, Fairfax was forced to abandon Tadcaster, but instead of blaming Cholmley, as a lesser man might have done, he accepted the logic of his case. Before the end of the year he agreed that without Sir Hugh at Scarborough the whole of the North Riding coast would soon fall to the royalists; he no longer demanded Cholmley's assistance in the West Riding.[44] Eventually, the House of Commons also changed its tune: it authorised a grant of £500 to Sir Hugh to help him 'to employ his best Endeavours in the charge and custody of the Castle of Scarborough'.[45] Cholmley had won the argument and the civil-war fate of Scarborough was sealed.

Meanwhile the town continued to strengthen its defences. On 5 December the prison at Newborough Bar was converted into a sentry house. What happened to its inmates, if there were any at the time, is not recorded. Both sides of the gateway were to be reinforced with a stone wall and the town ditch in front scoured and deepened. At the same time the £50 assessment laid on the town to pay for this work was being collected. Unfortunately, the lists for only two Quarters, Oldborough and St Mary's, have survived. They show that the highest levy of £1 2s. was on Thomas Foord, closely followed by £1 1s. 8d. paid by Francis Thompson. Richard Thompson was expected to find £1, and his two sons, Stephen and Christopher, 15s. and 18s. each respectively.[46]

Furthermore, the town ditch was lengthened and deepened at the head of St Nicholas Gate on the south side of Newborough Bar and a new ditch dug in Ramsdale. Since these earthworks were 'for the goodd and saifftye of the towne', every adult inhabitant was required to give his or her free labour or pay for a substitute 'stronge man or strong woman'. Failure to contribute to these 'common not[es]' incurred a penalty fine of sixpence.[47]

The town soon began to train more musketeers. George Boyes, a veteran of Scarborough's trained band, who had three muskets of his own, was considered best qualified to take over the instruction. The town paid him 2s. 6d. a day.[48] A fortnight later, at the beginning of

February 1643, the Common Hall passed an order that when Captain John Legard, one of Cholmley's officers, commandeered horses from townspeople they should be compensated at the rate of 'a penny a mile forward and halfe a penny a mile backward'. Why the charge for return journeys should be only half of that for outward ones was not explained. Again, the town was to pay for the hire of horses.[49]

These additional charges were expensive. The first extra assessment on the residents of £50 was soon spent. Another £50 were borrowed in December 1642, probably from the funds of the Society of Shipowners, £30 more a month later, and then, when the town watch was increased to sixty every night, a further assessment of £60 was made on the whole community 'dureinge this presentt time of danger'. Some indication of resistance to the last measure is given by the entry in the minute book that it was agreed 'by the greater part of the Bailiffs, Burgesses and Commons'.[50] The days of Common Hall unanimity had passed.

Nevertheless, Sir Hugh and his officers and men were still welcome in the town. As the war came closer to Scarborough their presence was increasingly valued. At Christmas 1642 Cholmley and his officers were treated by the corporation to a traditional venison feast. Altogether, including the vintner's account and the money paid to 'the bringers of the venison', the bill came to £3 2s. 4d.[51] No doubt everyone who took part thought it was a good investment.

Though Cholmley was sharply aware of the strategical importance of Scarborough, his preference was to mount sorties deep inland rather than to wait inertly for the enemy to come to him. Consequently, soon after the Christmas festivities were over, he again took the road westwards. On 29 December 1642 Fairfax reported to London that Sir Hugh's troopers had been active in the area around Malton, where they had taken money from royalist recruiters. A little later, the Earl of Newport's royalist cavalry were driven off in a skirmish with Cholmley's horsemen outside the same town.[52]

Sir Hugh was still at Malton when he was warned that a royalist force, led by Colonels Robert Strickland of Thornton Bridge and Guilford Slingsby of Hemlington, were at Guisborough and intended to move down to the coast at Whitby. Leaving a small company under Captain Browne Bushell at Malton to guard the main road from York to Scarborough, Sir Hugh took two troops of horse and

Captain Browne Bushell (1609–51), aged 23, dated 1633, by unknown artist.

a regiment of 130 foot northwards in the direction of the enemy. A week later, Strickland and Slingsby were cornered and routed at Guisborough. Cholmley's men took more than a hundred prisoners, including Colonel Slingsby.[53]

Cholmley's decisive victory at the battle of Guisborough on 16 January 1643 ought to have given him much encouragement and personal satisfaction. This was his first experience of command in combat. His Scarborough dragoons and musketeers had behaved with exemplary discipline and bravery. A superior force had been very thoroughly beaten and taken heavy losses in officers, men and equipment. Whitby and Cholmley's estate had been saved from occupation and plunder. The north-east corner of Yorkshire from Cleveland down to the north Wolds remained firmly under Parliament's control. If Queen Henrietta Maria, who was now known to be preparing her own crossing from Holland, had any thought of landing in the neighbourhood of Whitby, she would have to think again. Indeed, when Lord Goring, one of the King's senior commanders, crossed the North Sea from Holland at the end of January he was obliged to sail all the way north to Newcastle before he could come ashore safely.

However, what had happened at Guisborough tormented Cholmley's conscience and undermined his weakening resolve. He was physically sickened by the sight of so many dead and mutilated. Both of Sir Guilford's legs had to be amputated above the knees and he was in agony for three days before he died. No doubt Sir Hugh had the cries of the wounded in his ears when he wrote the following to Speaker Lenthall at Westminster: 'I confess it grieves my heart to see how these calamities increase and how I am forced to draw my sword not onely against my countrymen but many near friends and allies'. Even at this late hour he still deluded himself with the thought that all-out civil war could be prevented if only Parliament would make some concessions to the King.[54] Cholmley returned to Scarborough with a sad heart, not as a triumphant hero.

The disastrous events of the next few weeks finally persuaded Sir Hugh that he had been fighting on the wrong side. In February a company he had sent north under Captain Medley to prevent Lord Goring's crossing of the Tees was cut to pieces at Yarm. Most of Medley's men were killed, wounded or taken prisoner: very few of

Admiral Sir John Lawson (c.1615–65), painted by Sir Peter Lely for James, Duke of York, in 1666 to hang in the Admirals' Gallery at Greenwich. It belongs to Queen Elizabeth II and hands in the National Maritime Museum at Greenwich.

them returned to Scarborough. Soon afterwards *Mercurius Aulicus*, the Oxford royalist newspaper, announced Goring's arrival in York with 120 waggons carrying ammunition, 140 horses laden with muskets and 16 pieces of artillery.[55]

Queen Henrietta Maria came ashore at Bridlington Quay less than a week later. Like Goring, she had intended to sail as far as Newcastle because it was thought to be the only friendly port on the east coast. However, off Scarborough, the wind turned round to the north-west and her fleet had to find shelter in Bridlington Bay in the lee of Flamborough Head. Finding that the natives were amicable and there was not a Roundhead soldier to be seen, the Queen decided to land there and wait for the Earl of Newcastle to escort her priceless cargo to York.[56] It required 500 carts to carry everything she had brought from Holland; they were said to contain arms for 10,000 men. The Queen herself had £80,000 in ready money and was accompanied by 1,000 foreign mercenaries.[57]

Whatever Sir Hugh's personal thoughts about these momentous events, he was powerless to intervene. By comparison, the forces at his disposal were puny. The Earl of Newcastle alone had 2,500 horsemen to guard the Queen's convoy as it made its ponderous way via Burton Fleming and Malton to York. After the slaughter at Yarm, Cholmley had recalled Browne Bushell from Malton, where he was in danger of being swamped or outflanked by overwhelming numbers of enemy cavalry.[58] Given the military situation elsewhere in the country, no reinforcements could be expected to reach Scarborough.

The consequences of Goring's and the Queen's triumphant arrival in Yorkshire soon made themselves felt in the county's north-east corner: the royalists were now able to go over to the offensive. On 11 March Sir Hugh sent out armed parties from Scarborough to secure Pickering castle and to destroy the bridges over the rivers Derwent and Rye at Yedingham and Howebridge; but they were too late. General Mackworth had already occupied Pickering town and its undefended castle and put his musketeers at Howebridge to secure the main road to Pickering from Malton. Most alarming of all, and especially to Cholmley, a troop of Cavalier cavalry rode north from Pickering over the moors and plundered Fyling Old Hall. The Hall and its deer park now belonged to Sir John Hotham, but they had been sold to him by Sir Hugh. The Hall had been the

Queen Henrietta Maria, by van Dyck.

North and East Yorkshire in the Civil War

Route of Queen Henrietta Maria February–March 1643

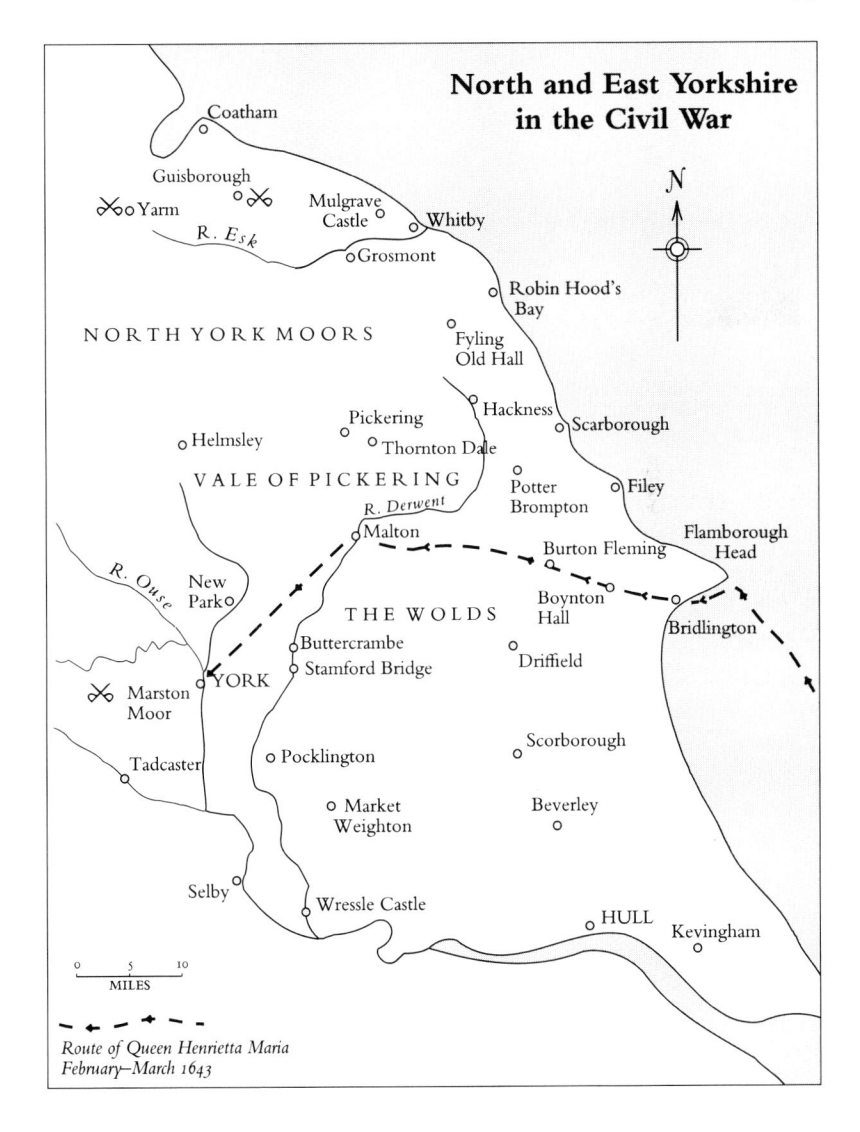

Cholmley home for five years. It must have been small consolation to him that an advanced royalist party had been repulsed briefly in the main street of Thornton, since that village too, including the former Cholmley castle at Roxby, was now overrun by Mackworth's cavalry. Thornton was only a dozen miles from Scarborough.[59]

Cholmley's motives for transferring his allegiance from Parliament to King were complex and remain controversial; but there can be no doubt that his sudden and unexpected action had woeful results for Scarborough. His decision was private and secret: he seems not to have consulted either close colleagues or relatives. Very early in the morning of Monday, 20 March, with only a French servant as companion and wearing 'a blacke patch upon one eye' to disguise his identity, Sir Hugh sneaked out of Scarborough. He had obtained a safe conduct pass from Lord Newcastle to see the Queen at York. The following day, after promising to change sides, he returned alone to Scarborough. He lied to his officers that he had been to Beverley to see the Hothams; they suspected nothing. Not until Saturday, 25 March, did he break the news to John Legard, captain of the castle guard, and his other officers.[60]

Amazingly, there was no more than verbal resistance to Cholmley's bombshell. Captain Legard first thought of assassinating his colonel, rejected the notion because Sir Hugh's soul would then be certain to go straight to hell, and finally settled for a ship to Hull for himself and his family. Two Dutch captains, Frome and Vanderhurst, both experienced military campaigners, Sir Thomas Norcliffe of Nunnington Hall and Lieutenant Thomas Strangways of Ugglebarnby, also preferred Parliament's Hull and took there the men who would follow them. On the other hand, Launcelot Alured, Cholmley's second-in-command, stuck with his colonel, and so did Browne Bushell, Cholmley's cousin, after some last-minute hesitation.[61]

The passive acceptance of Cholmley's change of loyalties by Scarborough's civilian population was therefore less surprising. According to Sir Hugh's partisan, but not unsupported, judgement, there were 'not above 4 families' who refused to stay in a royalist town.[62] One of these families was certainly that of John Lawson, master and part owner of one of Scarborough's merchant ships. With his young wife and child, he too left his native town and promptly offered himself and his vessel to Parliament's service. For a Puritan such as Lawson, even exile in Hull was better than living under a royalist regime in Scarborough.[63]

Later, Cholmley acknowledged that one of Scarborough's bailiffs favoured Parliament, but otherwise he could depend upon the full backing of the town. When he came back from York a second time, now openly with the King's commission, the 'townesmen upon the guarde . . . expressed great joy to see Sir Hugh and to have him amongst them'.[64] To some extent this report is confirmed by Captain Legard who at the time wrote that 'the Inhabytants of the Towne were extreme malignant', and gave this as one of the reasons why he advised his fellow officers not to resist Cholmley.[65] Both Cholmley and Legard contended that the reaction of the rank and file soldiers, particularly those in the castle, largely determined civilian response. As Sir Hugh put it, 'the townes men [were] over awed with the Castle'.[66] Legard was more precise: he counselled caution because they, the officers, 'had not felt the pulse of the Soldiers, nor knew how they stood affected, nor what the Gunners intended to do, who were the men [who] must do much of the business if it came to action'.[67]

In the end blood ties proved stronger than anything else. Cholmley's relatives – his cousin James Cholmley, and his Bushell cousins, brothers Browne and Henry – stood by him and carried the day. Apart from Alured, they were the only senior officers not to quit Scarborough. As events proved, Sir Hugh was wise to refuse the Queen's offer of an armed escort of 1,500 cavalry when he returned to Scarborough the second time on 30 March.[68] Though this time he brought with him a troop of Newcastle's horsemen, he left them behind at Falsgrave and came down to Newborough Bar the following morning with only three servants. Outside the town gates he met Browne Bushell face to face and reminded him of 'the relations between them, and the favours hee had donn him'. Bushell, a man 'of a rash but flexible and good nature', responded by opening the gates and handing over to his cousin the keys of the castle.[69]

Sir Hugh had intended that the people of Scarborough should regard him as their friend and protector, not as their martial conqueror, and by securing both town and castle 'without one drop of bloud spilt on either side' he had been brilliantly and entirely successful. The next entry in the corporation record for 11 April 1643 reads 'Omne bene'!.[70]

One of Parliament's news-sheets, *Certain Informations*, reported that Cholmley had retaken Scarborough for the King without opposition because its inhabitants were 'such Malevolents';[71] but this is a misleading and biased explanation of what happened. Though some leading burgesses, notably the Thompsons, the Fysh family and John Hickson, were royalist by preference, there were at least as many prominent members of the Common Hall who did not leave Scarborough after March 1643 yet were just as strongly inclined in the opposite direction. John Lawson was an exception because he was, or soon became, a convinced anabaptist and republican. John Harrison seems to have shared similar views and suffered imprisonment in York castle because of them. Much more representative of the oligarchy, however, were the majority of senior burgesses, such as William Foord, William Conyers, William Batty, Mathew Fowler, Peter Rosdale and Nicholas Saunders, who remained in Scarborough, and even held office in a royalist regime despite their partisanship. Later, when Scarborough was restored to Parliament, they would all accept senior posts in the corporation.[72]

Perhaps the great majority of Scarborians tolerated Sir Hugh Cholmley whether he was the King's man or Parliament's. They could judge the military situation well enough. Most of the garrison soldiers had gone to Hull or returned home; royalist troops were sweeping across the county towards the coast in overwhelming strength; the town could not hope to defend itself against them. If they had resisted Cholmley's change they would have invited invasion, plunder and mayhem, followed by a permanent occupation of foreign, hostile soldiery. Sir Hugh alone had the power to save them from this fate, and most must have felt grateful to him for using it so benevolently.

Both sides soon appreciated the significance and seriousness of Cholmley's change-over. Among the letters captured in the King's baggage after his defeat at Naseby were two from his wife written at York and telling him of Cholmley's defection. She had never liked or trusted the man, but she understood the value of Scarborough harbour to her husband's cause, more so after her terrifying experience at Bridlington Quay.[73] The royalist mouthpiece, *Mercurius Aulicus*, welcomed Sir Hugh's 'coming over', not because he brought with him '80 horse and 400 foote' (which was untrue), but 'in respect of his authority in that county, and his being privy to the counsells and designs of the chief actors of this rebellion'.[74] In other words,

Cholmley's reputation and status far outweighed any material assistance, however exaggerated, he might bring to the King's side. Whatever the Queen might think of Cholmley personally, his importance to the King was demonstrated by the many important commissions now granted to him. He was to be governor of the town and castle of Scarborough, colonel of horse and dragoons in the royal army, and responsible for 'all marine affayres within all the ports from Tease to Bridlington, & to iudge of all marine matters that fell within that extent'.[75]

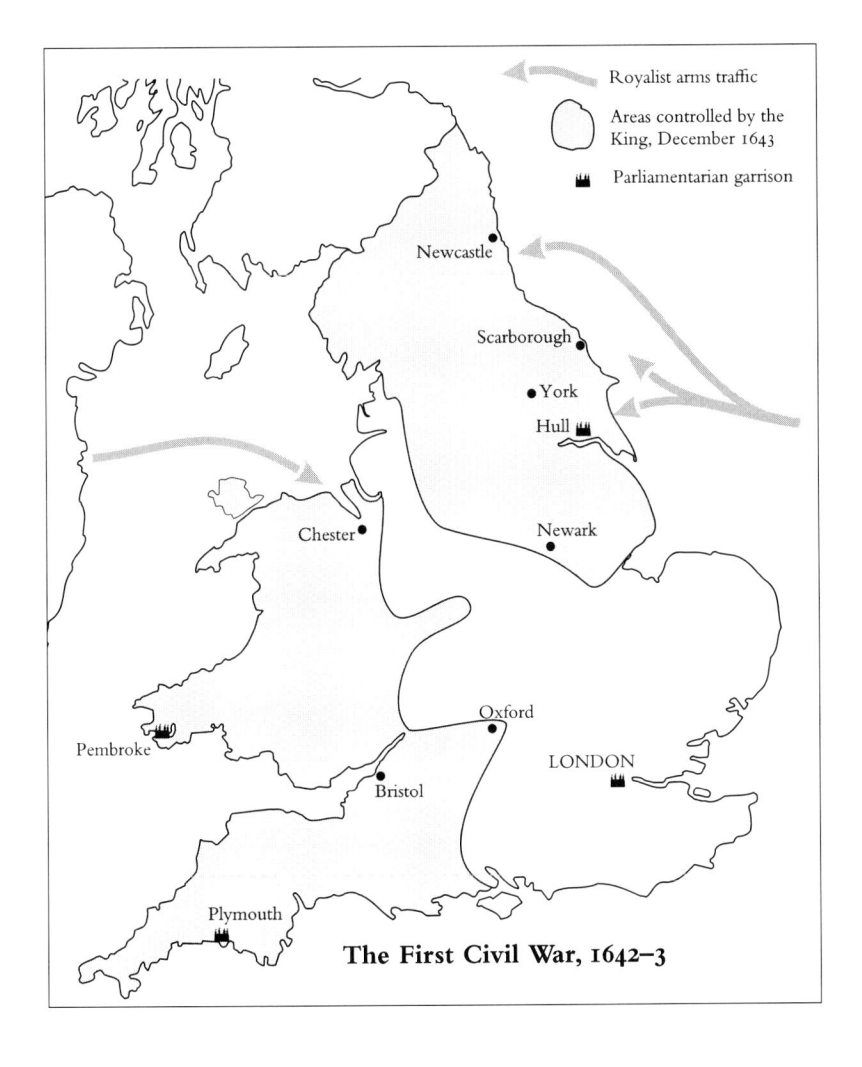

The First Civil War, 1642–3

Parliament's reaction to Cholmley's desertion was predictably strong. He was disabled from ever again sitting in the House of Commons and impeached on a charge of high treason.[76] The Venetian ambassador in London thought that Cholmley's action and Parliament's sentence on him were worth reporting to his superiors.[77] As for the London press, from now on it referred to Sir Hugh as 'traitor', or 'apostate', or 'Judas Cholmley'.[78]

Sir John Hotham's response was more practical than name-calling: from Hull he sent expeditionary forces by land and by sea to recapture Scarborough. While his son, General John Hotham, marched north by land, two pinnaces carrying ten cannon were dispatched by sea. The ships arrived in Scarborough harbour first, Sir Hugh lured their crews ashore by pretending that he was still loyal to Parliament, seized their two vessels, landed their cannon, and positioned them on Ramshill south of the town to command the road from Hull. Hotham's men ran into a well-prepared ambush. Twenty of them were killed by artillery and musket fire, thirty surrendered, and the rest, with Hotham, were put to flight.[79]

Cholmley's defection, or 'bad action', as Sir John called it, had damaging repercussions for Parliament's fortunes in Yorkshire. The cooperation between the Fairfaxes in the West Riding and the Hothams at Hull, which had never been better than fitful and grudging, now broke down completely. Starved of supplies which had to pass through Hull, Lord Fairfax had to abandon Selby, the vital link between East and West Ridings, and retreat all the way back to Leeds. It was during this defeat that his son, Sir Thomas, received a mauling on Seacroft Moor on 30 March.[80]

As for the Hothams, their morale was now shattered. Both father and son had long since been in secret correspondence with Lord Newcastle, yet both were afraid of jumping too soon or too suddenly into the King's camp. Cholmley's successful coup at Scarborough helped to convince them that a royalist victory in Yorkshire was now inevitable and that their change-over might be effected without suicidal consequences. In the event, both were betrayed by their own folly before their plan matured, but neither might even have attempted such a dangerous course without the example of Cholmley's bold initiative.

In fact, the effects of Scarborough's change of sides went far beyond the boundaries of Yorkshire. As Parliament's most northerly and exposed outpost, Scarborough had only negative value: Cholmley's commission had been merely to prevent the royalists from using its harbour. As long as it held Hull and controlled the Humber estuary, Parliament had no use of its own for Scarborough. Once Scarborough became royalist, however, it assumed a positive, vital function as the King's most secure and convenient entry port for his continental supplies. Henrietta Maria's convoy of soldiers and munitions was by far the largest but by no means the last of its kind. Denied Scarborough by Sir Hugh Cholmley, as well as Hull by Sir John Hotham, the royalists had been compelled to use Newcastle, which was always their third choice. In September and October 1643 the Marquess of Newcastle made yet another attempt to capture Hull, and failed. Early the following year, when the Scots entered the war and England on Parliament's side, their first objective was to neutralise the port of Newcastle. Though the town itself did not fall to them until October 1644, as early as the previous February the lower Tyne was so effectively blockaded that it ceased to be available to the King's ships. In short, for a full year before it was overrun by General Sir John Meldrum's troops in February 1645, Scarborough was the only English port on the North Sea coast of any value to King Charles.

As a Parliamentarian colonel, Cholmley had never been content to play the passive role of a garrison commander; now as a royalist he continued to be just as active, mobile and audacious. Scarborough became a base of military operations on land as well as at sea which Parliament soon found embarrassing and sometimes even alarming. Within a range of thirty miles almost every Roundhead gentleman was plundered, expelled, suborned or, in one case, even kidnapped.

At the end of May 1643 it was reported to the House of Lords that one of its members, the Earl of Mulgrave, a steady Parliamentarian, had had his house and estate north of Whitby pillaged.[81] The culprits were almost certainly Cholmley's long-range cavalry. In June, Sir Hugh was at Market Weighton threatening Captain William Goodricke's garrison in Wressle castle. Though Goodricke bravely refused to be intimidated, Hull had to bolster his defiance with a supply of powder, muskets and shot.[82] By this time Sir Hugh was the only senior royalist officer operating in east Yorkshire. The Queen had finally left York with a hugh retinue to re-join her husband at his Oxford headquarters, and General Newcastle had gathered up his considerable army to advance deep into the West Riding. He was determined to settle with the Fairfaxes once and for all. At Adwalton Moor, near Bradford, Yorkshire's Roundheads, greatly outnumbered, suffered a crushing defeat. With only a few hundred men the Fairfaxes were forced to flee to Hull which was now the only safe Parliamentarian stronghold in the North. Consequently, the Marquess of Newcastle was able to take most of his army southwards into Lincolnshire; and he did not return to Yorkshire until the end of August 1643.[83]

In these favourable circumstances and since Scarborough now seemed absolutely secure, Cholmley felt able to venture well beyond the locality with most of his soldiers. *Mercurius Aulicus* reported on 7 July that Sir Hugh had led his men as far south as Beverley. He had captured the market place there after a skirmish and then driven the town garrison back to the gates of Hull.[84]

Cholmley was also present throughout the second siege of Hull which lasted from 2 September to 11 October 1643. The Marquess of Newcastle, who commanded the royalist siege, promoted him to brigadier of horse and put him in charge of a third of his cavalry which included Sir Hugh's own regiment of 350 horsemen. Also out of Scarborough's garrison came 400 infantry led by Alured and Browne Bushell. But this second siege of Hull was a most miserable and frustrating experience for Cholmley's soldiers. His own cavalry were useless against redoubts, dykes, trenches and flooded fields; they waited for a breakthrough that never came. As for the foot soldiers, the only success recorded was Bushell's capture of Colonel Thomas Rainsborough. He was ransomed back to his wife on her payment of £500.[85]

Once again Hull had stood stubbornly in the way of a royalist victory. Just as Parliament's Plymouth prevented General Hopton from bringing his royalist Cornish and Devon men out of the south-west, and Parliament's Gloucester pinned down the King's Welsh army, Hull had distracted and preoccupied Newcastle's 12,000 foot and 4,000 horse in a futile, wasting engagement. The summer of 1643 was the King's last, best chance of inflicting a decisive defeat on Parliament's disorganised field army; by 1644 it was too late, the opportunity had gone forever. During 1643 a series of royalist successes in Yorkshire and elsewhere had fallen short of decisive victory. During the following year the tide turned irreversibly against the King's cause until on Marston Moor it suffered a crushing injury from which there was to be no recovery. What had seemed in March 1643 to Cholmley and most Scarborians as a likely winner became a certain and disastrous loser within little more than a year.

The entry of the Scots on the side of Parliament early in 1644 was the first event of the new year to tip the military balance in the north of England. In February, as General Leslie's army closed in on the port of Newcastle, the Marquess of Newcastle was obliged to march northwards out of York to relieve it. His absence from Yorkshire now allowed Sir William Constable to lead a Roundhead army up the east coast from Hull. First he captured the town and quay of Bridlington. Then, showing a healthy respect for Cholmley's strength at Scarborough, from Filey he came inland to Potter Brompton before striking north again through Everley and Hackness to Whitby. Cholmley was taken by surprise: contrary to the wild inventions of Parliament's propagandist press, Whitby was undefended. But Constable had over-reached himself: within days he was driven out of Whitby by Sir Hugh's counter-attack. For sometime yet the Yorkshire coast from Scarborough northwards remained royalist.[86]

From now on, however, there were to be no more royalist victories: the King's cause in Yorkshire deteriorated rapidly and then collapsed entirely. In April Sir John Bellasis was routed at Selby, thereby opening the way for Parliament's three forces under the Fairfaxes from Hull, the Earl of Manchester from the Eastern Association and the Scots under the Earl of Leven to link up and enclose York. The Marquess of Newcastle had no choice but to abandon the far north, retreat to York, and prepare to meet a siege there. The tables had been turned: the royalists were now on the defensive and outnumbered. The siege of York lasted a month until broken by the arrival of Prince Rupert's army, but the brilliance and speed of his manoeuvres were thrown away on the battlefield of Marston Moor on 2 July.

The battle of Marston Moor ended in a royalist débâcle: it was the biggest, bloodiest and arguably the most decisive engagement of the whole war. Though it did not bring the war to an end, effectively it brought an end to the war for Yorkshire. The city of York fell almost at once to Parliament. Lord Newcastle and all his staff officers rode pell-mell to Scarborough and from there sailed to Hamburg and permanent exile. Rupert crossed the Pennines back into Lancashire. The only significant royalist force now left in the county was Cholmley's at Scarborough.

As the area of royalist territory in Yorkshire shrank, Cholmley's cavalry, which he declared immodestly were the best in the North, continued to make sorties deep inland behind enemy 'lines'.[87] For instance, early in June 1644 Major Crompton with 'fiftie of his best horse and choicest men' rode out of Scarborough on a long-range night-time mission. Their purpose was to surprise and kidnap Henry Darley, one of Parliament's commissioners to the Scots, who was then staying at his father's house at Buttercrambe. At that moment the three Roundhead armies were about to complete the encirclement of York and Darley, only twelve miles from the city and nearly thirty from Scarborough, felt safe enough not to raise the drawbridge over the river Derwent even at night. The daring mission was a total success. Darley was brought back to Scarborough as a prisoner. Later Sir Hugh was to make good use of him.[88]

When Whitby and Mulgrave castle were taken for Parliament by Sir Matthew Boynton in July 1644, Scarborough was effectively cut off from all landward communication.[89] Nevertheless, Sir Hugh refused to withdraw his depleted garrison into the security of the castle; his 'Scarborough horse' continued their sorties into the surrounding countryside until the town was closely besieged. At the beginning of October, *Mercurius Aulicus* was delighted to announce that 'the gallant knight', as it called Cholmley, had scored another audacious success. He had sent out a 'Party of horse to visit the Rebells at Pickering Lithe (14 miles from Scarborough) and there found some Rebell Dragooners, 37 whereof were brought prisoners into Scarbrough'.[90] Thornton Dale, Sir Hugh's birthplace and the original Yorkshire home of his family, is exactly fourteen miles west of Scarborough in the wapentake of Pickering Lythe.

As late as December 1644, with Parliament's soldiers now quartered in all the villages around Scarborough, some of Cholmley's cavalry broke through the tightening ring, rode as far as Cleveland more than twenty miles away, and captured a party of Scotsmen and their horses. Later Sir Hugh was proud to recall that, though he now had only two hundred cavalry, they were 'verie good men and perpetually in action'. With some natural exaggeration, he alleged that their reputation had become so fearsome that 'the enemie durst not stand to looke them in the face, under treble the number'. Again according to Sir Hugh's memory, a certain 'Collonel [sic] Foulthrop and most of his troope' were the last Roundheads to be brought back to Scarborough as prisoners by the 'Scarborough horse'.[91]

Whatever the quality of Sir Hugh's cavalry might have been, they were never more than a mild irritant to Parliament; but Scarborough harbour in royalist hands was an entirely different matter. As Cholmley and his officers had once explained so cogently and perceptively, Scarborough might serve two vital war purposes: positively, it could be a port of entry for men and munitions from the continent; and negatively, it could become a safe refuge for privateer pinnaces which preyed upon enemy shipping as it passed close by up and down the North Sea coast. Sir Hugh's chief commission for the King had been to hold the port of Scarborough for his reinforcements and supplies from Holland. This was a service he had performed, in the words of Lord Clarendon, 'with courage and singular fidelity'; but there soon came a time when the second of Scarborough's functions would become far more important than the first.[92]

As long as the royalists held York and the way to it from the east coast remained open, Scarborough harbour's main function was as an arms entrepôt. This traffic was not always one way. Soon after the town had passed into the hands of the King, a Scotsman called sergeant-major Ross brought 200 muskets, 20 barrels of powder and a quantity of match down the road from York. Ross also carried a letter from Henry, later Lord, Jermyn, the Queen's trusted secretary, instructing Cholmley to provide a ship for these munitions; they were to be sent to Ireland and Scotland. Half of them were intended for the Earl of Antrim, and the other half for Viscount Aboyne. However, Sir Hugh argued so persuasively that he was dangerously short of weapons for the defence of Scarborough that Jermyn agreed that they should stay there.[93]

Usually, however, royalist arms came into Scarborough by sea from the continent and were then distributed throughout the country, normally via York. Sir Hugh worked closely with suppliers and carriers in Amsterdam and Dunkirk and the commander of the magazine at York. Throughout 1643 the traffic flowed freely and in considerable volume, despite a so-called blockade mounted by Parliament's warships. For instance, in November, Cholmley signed an order to deliver 62 muskets and bandoliers to a Captain Jones at York.[94] The following day an enormous shipment of firearms arrived by sea at Scarborough. It was delivered by Jacob Williamson, a Dutchman from Amsterdam, master of the *Mary* of that port. His cargo consisted of 46 chests containing 1390 muskets and bandoliers, 884 pair of pistols, 100 carbines, 100 pair of holsters, 100 barrels of gunpowder and 50 bundles of match. Of the pistols, a Mr Robson received 540 pair, Major Jackson 200 pair, Lieutenant Markenfield 37 pair, Captain Markenfield 25 pair, Captain Dunwell 24 pair, Captain Norton 15 pair and Lieutenant-Colonel Mason 6 pair. Twenty-seven pair of pistols stayed in Scarborough's own arsenal, along with 218 muskets. Thirty-eight more muskets were dispatched to York 'for Captaine Jones to make his 62 upp [to] 100'.[95] Instead of being concentrated dangerously in one magazine, Scarborough's arms and ammunition were stored in several places – Mr Woolfe's chamber, Francis Fawether's cellar, and the cellar of the Common Hall are all referred to in the corporation records. At this time it was probably thought unnecessary to carry munitions up to the castle.[96]

Simultaneously, 'ends of iron' were being taken out of the King's stores at the Manor House at York and carried to Scarborough 'for the use of Sir Hugh Cholmley'. According to an order dated 17 November 1643, no fewer than thirty loads of iron, weighing altogether more than fifteen tons, were delivered to Scarborough. Carriers were hired from all over the vale of Pickering and villages near Scarborough.[97]

The last official customs book recording the foreign trade of Scarborough ended on 24 March 1643. During the previous quarter, while the port was still Parliament's, Scarborough's maritime commerce seems to have been unaffected by the war. Apples and sack came in regularly from Ostend and Dunkirk, iron, timber and tar from Norway, raisins and prunes from Rotterdam, and textiles from Scotland. In return, Scarborough continued to export beer, barley and malt to Scotland and Norway.[98]

After the port at Scarborough became royalist no official record of its trade was kept, or has survived. Cholmley broke off contact with Hull and London, and in the name of the King he took over the management and receipts of the harbour. From April 1643 onwards the only description of Scarborough's maritime commerce is to be found in a carelessly written and certainly incomplete account book kept by Cholmley's port agents. For most of 1644 there is no record at all. Not until July 1645, when Cholmley finally surrendered the castle to Parliament, is there a resumption of customs accounts.[99]

At least until the spring of 1644, when the Scots had sealed off Newcastle and taken Sunderland, Scarborough's seaborne trade continued without serious impediment. Soon after Captain Williamson brought in his shipment of arms, another, more typical, cargo from Rotterdam arrived in William Lawson's ship, the *Isabel* of Scarborough. Lawson carried hogsheads of sack and Newfoundland trainoil, hundredweights of raisins from Malaga and Smyrna, iron and barrels of tar from Sweden.[100] That such goods found their way into the heart of Yorkshire and that inland merchants were still using Scarborough to export their wares abroad is attested by a list of twenty-three men who paid £313 4s. 3d. in duty to the port between 10 October and 30 December 1643. Three of them were said to be of Leeds, and six of York.[101] Clearly, Scarborough was profiting from the misfortunes of Hull, which in peacetime took most of Yorkshire's outgoing and incoming trade.

The letters that passed from Sir William Sandys, the King's chief agent at Dunkirk, to Cholmley in May 1644 indicate how the situation had deteriorated for them by that date. The Dutch had become less reliable; Parliament's warships were more active and effective; and the advance of the Scottish army southwards had sealed off the mouths of the Tyne, Wear and Tees. Merchants were no longer willing to take the increasing risks of running guns to Scarborough across the North Sea. The previous February Sandys had sent a shipment of arms to Newcastle, but it was taken by Zealanders. Two Danish ships with similar cargoes and the same destination had also been lost to privateers. Sir William claimed that he had sent 100 barrels of gunpowder to York via Scarborough and received no payment for them. Two days later he sent to Cholmley a list of arms he was about to dispatch in the *Sunflower*, a ship of Colchester with Giles Wigginer of Whitby as its master. King Charles was now so concerned about the security of Scarborough that he had instructed Sandys to reinforce and arm its garrison. The *Sunflower* would bring Sir Hugh 182 rapiers, 142 ammunition belts, and 320 muskets with bandoliers. The King was paying a guinea for every second-hand musket, which Sandys thought was a fair price. To protect his merchant ships Sandys advised Cholmley to raise two or three thousand pounds to buy some frigates. The following day Sandys wrote to the Dutch Admiral Tromp asking him not to interrupt the passage of the *Sunflower* to Scarborough, but there is no record of its fate.[102]

Towards the end of June 1644 Cholmley received bad news from Amsterdam: Captain Percy, in command of Sir Hugh's 'catch', the *Charles*, had betrayed his trust, sold an arms cargo he was carrying worth £4,257 14s. 8d. and even the *Charles* as well! John Webster, Cholmley's agent in Amsterdam, complained that he could find no one willing to insure another Scarborough ship, the *Minikin*, for £600, 'these people being very fearful to insure from that port'.[103]

Agostini, the Venetian secretary in London, was not the most accurate or trustworthy witness of events at this time. In his correspondence he wrote Cholmley as 'Sciomle' and Hull appeared as 'Uls'. Moreover, when he said that Prince Rupert had gone 'towards Scarbrough' after his defeat at Marston Moor, he was clearly misinformed. Rupert never came further east than York and it was the Marquess of Newcastle who fled to Scarborough after the battle. Nevertheless, it is worth a passing mention that, according to Agostini, Lord Craven, a 'very rich, devoted servant of the Palatinate House', had 'arrived at Scarboro from France with money, arms and officers' early in July 1644.[104]

If Lord Craven did come safely ashore at Scarborough he was a lucky exception. As Parliament's blockade tightened in the summer of 1644, it became increasingly difficult for royalist ships to cross the North Sea. The fate of the Dutch frigate *Utrecht* was typical. In July 1644 it was intercepted by Parliament's *Sampson* under captain Brown as it tried to make its way to Scarborough with a royalist colonel and 70 barrels of powder aboard. The *Utrecht* was probably the last of its kind: after their defeat on Marston Moor, the royalists ran out of money, credit and credibility.[105] If there were any optimistic royalists still coming into Scarborough after the fall of York, they were greatly outnumbered by realists leaving the country by this route. From July 1644 onwards Scarborough became a bolthole into continental exile.

The most distinguished party of royalist escapees to pass through Scarborough was that of Lord Newcastle and his staff. The experience of Marston Moor convinced the marquess, who was now bankrupt in morale as well as money, that the war was lost and his only honourable course was to quit the country. With a retinue of about seventy officers, he rode to Scarborough on the morning of 3 July and sailed from there to Hamburg in the evening of the next day. Cholmley supplied two ships, one for Newcastle, his two sons 'and other of his special friends', the other for General King and his associates. Sir Hugh acted as host but refused the invitation to go with them. He said he would not surrender his commission or abandon Scarborough until he had 'heard from the King or was forced to it'.[106] Cholmley's stubborn loyalty to King Charles was to cause his fellow countrymen, his family and especially the people of Scarborough much pain and poverty.

Shortly after Newcastle's hasty departure, Sir Hugh did indeed hear from Charles. Cholmley had written to him for advice and support on 19 July and the reply, from faraway Trevarrick in Cornwall, was dated 2 August. Naturally, the King was keen to raise Cholmley's spirits by praising his service and promising him reward 'when God shall enable us' . Furthermore, he wanted to convince him of the vital importance of holding Scarborough castle 'to the last extremity'. But the reason Charles gave why Sir Hugh should stay at Scarborough as long as it was physically possible must have seemed rather curious to its governor. No reference was made in the King's letter to the value of Scarborough's harbour either as a place of refuge or as a base for offensive operations. No mention was made of more help that might come that way from the continent. Instead, the King believed that Cholmley's prolonged defence of Scarborough would draw away and divert Parliament's forces 'to give our Nephew Rupert time to make head again'. How the Prince could 'make head again' in the North or anywhere else without new supplies and reinforcements was not explained by the King.[107]

Either Charles was badly misinformed or he was trying to flatter Sir Hugh, or both. After York fell to Parliament on 16 July 1644, the Roundheads almost ignored Cholmley and Scarborough. The Scots went back north to end Newcastle's resistance; the army of the Eastern Association under Manchester and Cromwell returned south; and the Fairfaxes mounted sieges of the other royalist castles in Yorkshire at Pontefract, Knaresborough and Helmsley.

Sir Hugh convinced himself that it was his bogus offer of surrender terms, 'meerly to gaine time and accomodations', that deceived Fairfax, sent Lord Manchester into Lincolnshire and Lord Leven into Durham. In fact their decisions were taken weeks before Cholmley's terms were broadcast, and they were taken for reasons which had nothing to do with Scarborough. The port of Newcastle was considered, quite rightly, by Parliament to be far more important than Scarborough's because its capture would release vast stocks of coal on Tyneside which Londoners had been deprived of for the past two winters. Moreover, once the King's army in Yorkshire had been defeated and scattered, Scarborough became isolated and of little use to the King or threat to Parliament.[108]

Fairfax kept well clear of Scarborough in the summer and autumn of 1644, not because he believed Cholmley was about to surrender it without a fight, but because he did not have the strength to take it. He knew the castle there was stronger than any in the county and he dare not commit forces to the coast when there were still several enemy garrisons in the heart of Yorkshire. As he told the Committee in London, the best he could hope for was 'to restrain their incursions upon the country'.[109] Sir Hugh's repeated claim that Sir Thomas Fairfax had 1,000 horse and 3,000 foot only six miles from Scarborough was retrospective fantasy.[110] In truth he had 300 cavalry and 700 infantry, badly clothed and unpaid, besieging Helmsley castle more than thirty miles away. The siege lasted three months until November, tested Fairfax's powers to the limit, and almost cost him his life.[111]

Whether Sir Hugh really intended to surrender Scarborough in August 1644 remains arguable, but the main point is that Parliament, knowing how costly and time-consuming it might be, was concerned to avoid a siege. Though the Committee of Both Kingdoms at Westminster doubted Cholmley's sincerity, it had nothing to lose by offering him a truce and examining his nineteen propositions. Fairfax was urged to come to an agreement with Sir Hugh as quickly as possible. Even Cholmley had to admit later that London had been willing to make generous concessions to him.[112]

Of Cholmley's nineteen propositions, the Committee was able to accept or negotiate all but four. Sir Hugh's request that Scarborough itself should not be punished for harbouring him was agreed: the townspeople would retain their ancient privileges and not be deprived of their private property. His request that the soldiers of the garrison and any of the civilian population who wanted to should be allowed to leave the town freely was also accepted. What the Committee found absolutely unacceptable was the governor's proposal that clergymen in the town, including the notoriously anti-Parliamentarian vicar of St Mary's, William Simpson, should keep their livings; this concession would be made only to Robert Remmington, who had been vicar at Whitby until 1638 and was now rector at Walkington, one of Hotham's parishes in the East Riding. Remmington was a close personal friend of the Cholmleys, but he had been in trouble with the High Commission for his puritanical tendencies which no doubt recommended him to the London Committee. Parliament would allow no exceptions when it came to the subject of oath-taking, and Cholmley must have known this would invalidate his tenth proposition. Even more outrageous in the eyes of the Committee would have been Sir Hugh's twelfth proposal that he should not be disabled from sitting in the Commons or charged with treason. Finally, in answer to his fifteenth suggestion that he should be followed by his brother, Sir Henry, as governor of the town and castle, the Committee's restrained reply was that it 'thinkes itt not reasonable Sir Hugh Cholmeley name his successor'.[113]

If Cholmley was only playing for time, as he later claimed in his 'Memorialls Tuching Scarbrough', then Parliament was content, as yet, to let him have it. Even after the truce had expired and all negotiations ceased, London had many other more pressing concerns than Scarborough. Early in September the King had won a crushing victory at Lostwithiel in Cornwall. He still held the whole of the south-west of England except Plymouth. As winter approached Parliament was anxious to remodel its army before the spring campaigns. Furthermore, even when Helmsley castle finally surrendered on 22 November there were still several royalist strongholds in Yorkshire – Knaresborough, Pontefract, Sandal and Skipton, to name the principal ones – besides Scarborough. Only when Scarborough presented a new and alarming threat in the winter of 1644–5 did its capture become an urgent priority.

***

In the middle of the tenth century Scarborough had been re-founded or fortified as a Viking pirate's nest, and named after him, Skarthi's burg. For a short time in 1644–5, but to great effect, the harbour again became a pirates' base.

Even when Cholmley had held Parliament's commission, Scarborough ships were used to rob and seize merchant vessels off the coast that were believed to be serving the King. Between piracy and privateering the line was almost invisibly thin. For instance, the *Commons Journal* for 4 April 1643 recorded that a ship bound for Newcastle and loaded with corn had fallen into the hands of three Scarborough men – John Legard, John Lawson and William Nesfield. Subsequently, all three were to prove their loyalty to Parliament. In this case they were authorised by the Commons to sell their prize ship and its cargo to pay for Scarborough's Parliamentarian garrison, since at that moment the House was still unaware of Cholmley's defection.[114]

What had once been done in Parliament's name could now be practised legitimately in the King's cause. In June 1643, *Mercurius Aulicus* applauded Sir Hugh's recent success in bringing into Scarborough harbour 'two ships laden with corn and other provisions for the rebels sustenance, which honester men will now make use of'.[115]

The Scarborough port book referred to above was mainly a record of provisions bought for, stored and put on board Cholmley's privateer pinnaces in 1643 and 1644. Of eight ships that can be identified, two were Dutch or captained by Dutchmen, Peter Anderson and Jacob Williamson, who were engaged in carrying arms from Amsterdam and Dunkirk, and the others were fitted out to prey on Parliament's vessels. One of these was under the command of the most infamous of all the many privateers then operating in the North Sea – Browne Bushell.[116]

Captain Browne Bushell, a native of Whitby, had served the king of Spain for nearly ten years at sea and in the Low Countries. He was a most experienced soldier and sea captain and undoubtedly Sir Hugh's most valuable and valued officer. Without his support in March 1643 Cholmley could not have taken Scarborough over to the King's side. After the abortive siege of Hull, Bushell returned to Scarborough and there Sir Hugh gave him command of the 12-gun *Cavendish*, referred to in the port book as 'the Great Catch'. By 1645 of all the 'sea rovers' and 'pyrates' who preyed on Parliament's shipping passing up and down the east coast none had greater success and was more hated and feared than 'the Bushell'.[117]

Early in 1644 Bushell was recognised at Newcastle by one of Parliament's informers. He had been there for six or seven weeks, probably advising Sir John Marley, its royalist mayor, on the town's fortifications. No arms had reached Newcastle for ten weeks other than 500 muskets which had arrived from Scarborough. According to this same source, Bushell had seized the *Ipswich Sarah*, loaded it with coal and sent it off to Holland to exchange for arms and ammunition for the King.[118]

Other privateer captains who used Scarborough at this time as a supply base and refuge were John Denton, Browne Thomas and possibly Ralph Hogg, who was master of the *Blessing of Scarborough*. Regularly they took onboard provisions of coal, candles, butter, salted beef, vinegar and 'soft bread' from Cholmley's Sandside stores and, presumably, they received their gunpowder and ammunition from the same source. Later, when there were no more royalist ports to run to, like Bushell, Denton and Thomas became notorious pirates.[119]

During 1644, as the traffic in royalist arms petered out, Scarborough's captains took to plundering the coastal coal trade. In 1642 and 1643, when the King had controlled Newcastle and Sunderland, very few colliers sailed past Scarborough with cargoes for London and the south. Scottish pits could not make good Parliament's deficiency. Exports of sea-coal from the Tyne, which in peacetime had averaged half a million tons annually, dropped to a tenth of that figure in the year ending Michaelmas 1643, and to a trickle of three thousand tons in the year ending Michaelmas 1644.[120] Parliament forbade ships to sail to Newcastle and Sunderland for coal and salt as long as they were in the King's hands. Consequently, attempts to control the price of fuel in London failed: in the winter of 1642–3 the cost of coal and firewood in the capital soared.[121] In July 1644 Agostini predicted that there would be riots in the streets of London if there was no radical improvement in coal supplies during the next winter: 'the miss of [coal] . . . will be unbearable . . . as they have felled most of the trees in the neighbourhood', he explained.[122] Nearly all Londoners now burned coal in their domestic hearths and depended on it to keep warm and cook their food. Brewers, bakers, brickmakers, iron masters and many other craftsmen were utterly dependent on coal as a fuel. Everyone in the capital dreaded the prospect of another winter without cheap sea-coal.[123]

As soon as Sunderland was captured by the Scots in April 1644 and the river Wear cleared for lighter traffic, Parliament encouraged the east coast ports to resume their trade in coal.[124] There were said to be as many as 120 colliers riding in Sunderland harbour waiting to load coal from the vast stocks which had accumulated up river in the Durham coalfield.[125] Similarly, when the Tyne was at last opened up the following October there were huge piles of unsold coal on the riverside ready to be bought and shipped to the south of England. Only Scarborough's 'pyrates' now impeded the resumption of full winter supply of fuel to London.

Coal, then, was the principal reason why Parliament became concerned to recover Scarborough harbour as quickly as possible and why it now regarded Cholmley as a serious nuisance. *Mercurius Aulicus* did not exaggerate, apparently, when in October it announced gleefully that 'the gallant knight' [Sir Hugh] had 'taken 22 London coal ships': Parliament's own propaganda Northern news-sheet, the *Scottish Dove*, had already admitted the loss of '20 saile and upwards . . . laden with coals to London'.[126] It was in response to this damaging attack on the capital's coal imports that the London Committee wrote to Lord Fairfax early in November 'about finding some way to trade to Newcastle for coals without danger of interruption from Scarbrough'.[127]

Since Parliament's navy seemed incapable of maintaining a close blockade on the port of Scarborough, particularly in winter weather, and did not have enough warships to protect all the colliers, there was no alternative but to storm the town and seize its harbour by attack from the land. Parliament would have preferred to wait until the spring or the summer of 1645 before mounting such an assault, but the matter had become too critical to be delayed.

Hardly a week passed without the London news-sheets deploring some further outrage committed by 'Scarborough pyrates'. Collier masters were too afraid of them to put to sea. Early in February 1645, as Sir John Meldrum moved his Scottish army up to Falsgrave, the *London Post* reported yet another loss: a cargo of coals worth £10,000 had been seized by Cholmley's pinnaces, not off the Yorkshire coast, but somewhere between King's Lynn and the mouth of the Thames.[128] Soon afterwards, another London paper, *An Exact Journal*, rejoiced that Scarborough was about to be stormed by Meldrum's men, and added: 'Indeed the reducing of that place would be a work of great importance, there is almost no day but brings in one complaint or other concerning the pyracies committed by rovers there.'[129] When Scarborough was finally captured by Parliament's forces a few days later, there were said to be 120 ships in the harbour, most of them prizes.[130]

Characteristically, Sir Hugh never admitted to promoting piracy. He attributed Scarborough's miraculous supply of 'coales, salt and corne' to 'Devine power and providence'. By providing him with so many rich windfalls God was not only showing him special favour, He was actually encouraging and helping him to hold out longer. As Sir Hugh wrote later in his 'Memorialls Tuching Scarbrough', 'God having soe plentifully furnished them [provisions for the town and castle] that there were more prises brought into the Harbour in one mounth past, then ever had beene in all the time Scarbrough was a Garrison'.[131] A similar claim, with the same doubtful theological and moral reasoning, was made a decade later by Cholmley in his memoirs: '. . . my wants was [sic] supplyed most miraculously with all necessaryes as if they had bene dropped downe fro[m] heaven'.[132]

Whether the inhabitants of Scarborough appreciated that they were the beneficiaries of 'Devine power and providence' seems doubtful:

some of them might have profited from piracy but the majority must have seen their condition and prospects deteriorate during the previous six months. As Parliament's forces moved steadily closer in greater numbers and the royalist cause collapsed in Yorkshire, Scarborough became increasingly isolated and imperilled.

Soon after the town had passed into royalist control further demands were made on the pockets of its people. Though the danger of a landward attack on Scarborough had, for the time being, receded, Parliament's overwhelming superiority at sea meant that the harbour could be invaded with impunity, as it had been a decade earlier by Dutchmen and Dunkirkers. Consequently, on 12 April 1643, the Common Hall agreed without dissension that 'the battrye maid and builded att the southstile shalbe maid and builded att the townes chardge, and likewise the sentrye house'.[133]

South Steel battery, as it is still called, was radically improved and 'modernised' in 1746–8 to prepare Scarborough for a Jacobite invasion that never happened, and since then heavy erosion into the sea has worn away the cliff it stands on.[134] It is therefore not possible to describe with confidence what was built there in 1643 under Sir Hugh Cholmley's directions. However, it seems that steps were cut and laid in stone to lead down from the sally port in the curtain wall to a flat promontory which overlooked the inner harbour. On the castle-dyke side of this flight of steps a stone wall with musket loopholes was also constructed and the promontory itself was enclosed with an earth rampart.

South Steel battery was a perfect artillery site from which to protect the harbour below and a hitherto vulnerable part of the curtain wall above it. On its seaward, northern side the cliff was virtually perpendicular and unstable, and above and behind it Cockhill or Charles's tower, the last in the curtain wall, provided further cover. Another gain was that from the protection of the covered steps musketeers could direct crossfire on anyone attempting to negotiate the castle dykes to attack the curtain wall. Nothing more on South Steel battery is to be found in the corporation minutes, but it is clear from later Parliamentary news-sheets that Sir John Meldrum regarded its capture as his first priority.[135]

About the same time that South Steel battery was being built, Captain Browne Bushell was strengthening another point of the

Interior view of sally port steps and gate built by Cholmley in 1643 to give access to South Steel battery.

Flight of stone steps running down from sally port to South Steel battery, protected by wall with loopholes for musketeers enfilading the Castle dykes.

View from South Steel battery overlooking Scarborough's great pier and harbour.

castle's defences. A doorway was cut through the outer wall of the barbican to lead on to another flat promontory, this one overlooking the approach to the main entrance. Though the site has long since lost its artillery and ramparts, it is still called Bushell's battery. According to James Schofield, author of the earliest guidebook to Scarborough, published in 1787, Bushell had no professional 'artillerists' to man his guns and so had to rely on 'such volunteers as would turn out for that service'. When one of the cannon exploded in the breech, killing seven of Bushell's 'volunteers', it so 'intimidated the unpracticed and . . . undisciplined garrison, that however strange to tell . . . eleven weeks elapsed before they could be brought to attend to the great guns.'[136] 'Bushell's Fort', or 'Bishop's Fort', as Parliament's press sometimes called it, was soon to figure prominently and bloodily in the siege of Scarborough castle.

As the weeks passed Scarborians were called upon to make greater contributions towards their own defences as well as those of the castle. For example, in October 1643, a brief Common Hall memorandum ordered the outgoing and newly-elected chamberlains 'to gitt the house for the court of gaurd maid ready and . . . to provide fewell for the watch every neight'. Several sentry houses had already been set up around the perimeter of the town and at the Newborough gateway and these, along with the candles and coals needed by the nightwatchmen, were all paid for out of the chamberlains' chest.[137]

Not only had the town lost its prison, which had been converted into a blockhouse next to Newborough gates, but even the cellar of the Common Hall on Sandside had been requisitioned by Cholmley to serve as a storeroom for the harbour. Scarborough's grammar schoolhouse, the former charnel chapel, had also been taken over by Sir Hugh because it stood at a vital point next to the main road to the castle and opposite St Mary's church. There is no record of what happened to the scholars during this time, but the school must have continued elsewhere since Mr Penston, the headmaster, was paid £5, the second half of his annual salary, as late as September 1644.[138]

The previous October, when it might have appeared that Scarborough was in no danger of attack from any quarter, the newly-elected bailiffs, Roger Wyvill and John Hickson, were 'intreated by the commons to moue Sir Hugh for halff of the hall sceller to make a prison on and likewise to moue him to gitt the scholehouse againe'. But there is no evidence that Cholmley could be moved on either count.[139]

Only one ill-written fragment of the chamberlains' accounts, dealing entirely with defence works for the borough for the year ending October 1643, survived long enough for a copy to be made from it about a century ago. This account adds up to £6 17s. 8d. and appears to deal mostly, if not exclusively, with the defensive works, weapons and guards at 'Newborough Gatts'. Christopher Gilson, the town plumber, whose peacetime preoccupation was repairing St Mary's windows and maintaining the water conduit, was paid 11s. 8d. for 56 pounds of bullets at 2½ pence a pound. Presumably the extra ten pence were to cover carriage costs. Mr Moone, one of the First Twelve, received 7s. 6d. for supplying a hundred yards of match. Twenty pounds of gunpowder cost the town just twenty shillings. It appears that several artillery pieces were positioned at or near the main entrance to Scarborough. The chamberlains paid 4d. to bring up 'the great murderer chamber' and another 10d. for the carriage of '2 murderers 2 pees of wood and chambers to Newborough Gatts' from ships in the harbour. When these guns were mounted their crews had to be paid attendance money. In view of what happened at Bushell's battery they ought also to have been given danger money. The largest single item of expenditure on the chamberlains' list was £2 10s. 6d. paid to Henry Swaine and Matthew Sharps 'for attending the gunns'. Captain Ruddock's gunner, probably a veteran naval artillerist, got 6s. 8d. 'for standing by the ordinance and plying then when the shipps shott'. Presumably the guards and gun crews were alerted and summoned to their posts by the sound of a drum. If so, this would explain why Sam Burton was given five shillings 'for drumming 16 dayes for the towne'.[140]

Another fragment of the chamberlains' accounts, from 6 April 1644 until the end of that calendar year, itemised an expenditure by them of just under £100. Here the extra costs of war-time defence were mostly of whins and coals for warming the nightwatchmen and sentries. Londoners might be starved of coal but there was no shortage of fuel in Scarborough at this time. Over a period of eight months, that was more summer then winter, the watch was provided with nearly thirteen tons of coal at 7s. 6d. a hundredweight. Other larger items of exceptional expenditure recorded were on fourteen yards of cloth at 7s. 6d. a yard for sergeants' cloaks, and a bill 'for candles and other things' put at £6 14s. 6d. The candles were also for the benefit of the town's nightwatch. Among the smaller bills paid by the chamberlains there was one for 2s. 6d. for 'a lark for towne pickes', one for 3s. for 'tow woole skines for spundyers [sponges] for gunes', and one of 1s 6d. for 'a drumb head for Cap[tain] Turner'.[141]

Most of the chamberlains' disbursements were wages paid for work that might, or might not have been, concerned with Scarborough's attempts to defend itself. What did Robert Minithrop, the blacksmith, do for two payments of £1 3s. 4d. and £1? What services did the town receive in return for paying Christopher Gilson two wages of £1 each? However, most payments to workmen were still for routine maintenance to fences, ditches, pipes, doors and locks, or as regular salaries to officers and servants of the Common Hall. George Merry, the netherd, got £2 for making up cattle fences; William Sanderson was paid £2 5s. a year for looking after the town bull; and Paul Neighall did odd jobs such as repairing fences on Weaponness common. Philip Benson no longer had a gaol but as one of the two sub-bailiffs he was still salaried. Mr Penston had lost his schoolroom but not his £10 annual salary.[142]

The heaviest single burden on the borough's finances in 1644 was £19 16s. 'for lone monye'.[143] Assuming an interest rate of eight per cent this indicates a debt of nearly £250. In these exceptional times, when the community was under severe financial stress, it is rather surprising that it continued to honour its debts; but there is a simple explanation. The town's chief creditors were themselves the members of the Common Hall and the more senior the burgess the greater his credit was likely to be. There was a long-standing tradition that when the borough borrowed money it did so in the ratio of three, two and one from the First, Second and Third Twelve respectively. Lending out money and then making sure it was repaid with interest must have been one of the few profitable certainties in an increasingly insecure business world.

More surprising in these straitened times was the Common Hall's success in fulfilling its obligations to the town's poorest inhabitants. The inmates of St Thomas's poor house received their £2 10s. annual allowance from 'Mr Conyers mony' at the head of the list of the chamberlains' payments, and a further dole of 16s. 8d. at the foot of it.[144]

Nevertheless, the borough's financial accounts provide a misleadingly 'normal' picture of Scarborough in 1643–4: they convey no hint of the unusual and onerous demands made by Sir Hugh Cholmley and his garrison on the civilian population of the town. Irregular and infrequent parliamentary subsidies were never more than £40, and sometimes as little as £10; even then they fell only on the richest men in Scarborough. Ship Money had become an annual levy yet the town was assessed at only £30. Even the king's fee-farm rent, which had not been paid since 1642, by this time was only £40.[145] Civil war taxation, in contrast, was on an entirely different scale and bore down on virtually the whole community, not just the well-to-do.

In November 1642 the Common Hall had approved a special levy on the town of £50 to pay for improvements to its defences. The money was soon spent. Three months later another £60 levy was authorised, and in July 1643 a further £60 raised 'for the use of the town's affairs'. As the war came closer to Scarborough Cholmley asked for and got still more. In August 1643 the burgesses agreed to take £30 from the landstock 'for the present affaires and use of the towne', part of which was needed 'to pay the gunners that stood within the townes batteries, vidzt Captain Ruddocks men'. Finally, in February 1644, acting on behalf of Sir Hugh, Captain Richard Legard came down to the Common Hall to ask the burgesses to find £30 a week to maintain three hundred soldiers in the castle and to choose one hundred more men of the town to defend it who would be provided with 'neither billitt nor pay'.[146]

Throughout the remainder of 1644 the town seems to have kept its promises of payment to Cholmley. About three hundred households, approximately half the total number, contributed to the weekly tax of £30, though it must have been increasingly difficult to raise this unprecedented amount when incomes were so depressed and depleted. The loss of the coastal coal trade meant that pier dues from Newcastle and Sunderland had dried up. Consequently, in July 1643, when the great pier needed to be repaired, the charge could not be met 'with the moneyes ariseinge att Newcastle and Sunderland'.[147] Even when the coal trade resumed in the summer of 1644 Parliament was hardly likely to allow money from it to go to a royalist port harbouring pirates and enemies. As long as Scarborough remained royalist it would have to find the money for pier maintenance out of its own resources.

The town might be in royalist hands but there was no question of paying the king his annual fee-farm rent, even though the money for it had been set aside by the coroners. Forty pounds should have been paid into the Exchequer during the Michaelmas term of 1643; instead the cash was 'imployed for the townes use in payeinge workemens wages, for building the works without Newbroughgait and other works'. Since the rent was to be spent in the king's cause, the burgesses believed that they were acting loyally and honourably. By April 1644 the burgesses in the Common Hall had convinced themselves that they had merely borrowed £40 of the king's rent, though they must have known that there was no prospect in the foreseeable future of paying off the debt. In fact, by this date there was not even the pretence made of putting aside £40 in the coroners' accounts: the money collected for 'the Kings rentt' went straight to the chamberlains. When the vote was taken in the Common Hall to 'borrow' £40 of the fee-farm rent, nineteen of the members were in favour and only one against.[148]

A month later, in May 1644, the town's funds were again so severely stretched that the Common Hall had to be asked for another loan. According to the old custom, the members were asked to contribute at the rate of three, two and one, depending on their seniority, and on this occasion the sums borrowed were 12s., 8s. and 4s. from the First, Second and Third Twelves respectively. But now the strain was beginning to show: only fifteen members voted in favour of the loan and as many as ten or eleven against it.[149]

The Common Hall elected at the end of September 1643 naturally reflected to some extent, the political change that had been brought about by Cholmley's defection to the King the previous March. The two new bailiffs were in effect 'outsiders' called in to give a sound royalist leadership to the corporation. Roger Wyvill of Osgodby had been bailiff only once previously in 1636–7 and he was not a regular member of Scarborough's Common Hall. The Committee for Compounding with Delinquents later assessed the annual value of his lands in Osgodby, Cayton and Deepdale at £160, which in terms of income placed him amongst the lesser gentry. Until his last appearance on the Bench in July 1642 Roger had been a senior and active member of the North Riding commission of justices of the peace. During that summer of 1642 his eldest son and heir, William, had been commissioned lieutenant-colonel in the King's northern army and was chiefly responsible for royalist recruitment in the Scarborough area. Unlike his son, Roger was not a Catholic, but his royalist credentials were good enough. Indeed, given Sir Hugh's strong antipathy to papists, he would probably have prevented one becoming Scarborough's senior bailiff at this time.[150]

John Hickson, the new junior bailiff, came from a leading Scarborough family of master mariners and shipowners which had been divided by the war. John's grandfather, William senior, had been bailiff in 1602, 1606 and 1609. John and his cousin Edward had married daughters and heiresses of Robert Harthropp and were principal beneficiaries of that rich man's will. Edward's father, William junior, was the William 'Hixson', master of the *Mary*, who was caught carrying horses for Prince Rupert and taken into Hull as Parliament's prisoner (see above, p. 76). However, whereas John Hickson stood by Cholmley as bailiff and then coroner in 1643–5, and was said to have taken up arms against Parliament, his cousin Edward preferred Parliament. Though John was the only Hickson to be called 'gentleman', before 1643 he had never held a corporation post.[151]

It was customary for retiring bailiffs to serve as coroners the following year. William Chapman, who had been junior bailiff in 1642–3, therefore became coroner for 1643–4; but his senior partner, John Harrison, who had been elected bailiff for the fourth time in September 1642, disappeared entirely from the Common Hall attendance lists before his term expired. According to a sworn statement he made in 1650, John Harrison, the elder, refused to sign a letter sent to him by Sir Hugh and was thereupon 'carried up to the castle & made a prisoner'. Soon afterwards he was 'sent away prisoner to Yorke'. When Parliament had recovered control of Scarborough in September 1645, Harrison became senior bailiff. There can be no doubt that when Cholmley referred in his 'Memorialls' to 'the Bailiff of the Towne beeing a person favouring that party'[Parliament], he meant John Harrison.[152] For how long Harrison was imprisoned at York is not known. In July 1643 'Mr Bayliffe Harrison' was assessed at £1, the third highest on the list, but it is almost certain that he was not then in Scarborough to pay it.[153]

Another conspicuous victim of Cholmley's change was William Headley, gentleman. He had been bailiff in 1641–2 and coroner the year after. However, from April 1643, like John Harrison, his name disappeared from the Common Hall minute book. Corporation orders henceforth were issued in the names of bailiff William Chapman and coroner William Fysh. When the new Hall was elected in September 1643 William Headley had plummeted to the foot of the Third Twelve. This must have been regarded as a profound insult to a gentleman of Headley's standing in the local community. In 1641 he was one of the town's ten subsidy men. In November 1642 he had given £2 towards Cholmley's troop of dragoons. The Headleys lived at and owned the Friarage site where the Franciscans had once been. No man in Scarborough was better connected than

William. His sister Dorothy was the wife of master mariner and future bailiff and Parliamentarian captain, William Nesfield; one of his daughters was married to William Batty; another was the wife of Robert Rogers, one of the chamberlains of 1642–3. The supervisors of his will made in May 1643, though not proved until 1649, were Francis Thompson and another brother-in-law, William Foord.[154]

With Wyvill, Hickson and Chapman in the lead, Harrison and Headley out of the way, and five Thompsons in the First Twelve, Sir Hugh Cholmley might have expected to receive the full and active cooperation of the Common Hall. When he summoned them on 5 February 1644 to agree to raise one hundred soldiers at their own expense and pay him £30 a week to maintain his garrison at the castle, twenty-seven members voted in favour of raising and paying, one in favour of raising but not paying, but none against both proposals. Of the remaining sixteen burgesses, two, William Fysh, the coroner, and Thomas Foord, had recently died, and the other fourteen were absent from the meeting. Absence should not be read necessarily as opposition: on the contrary, Richard, Timothy and Christopher Thompson were all absent that day probably because they were engaged in the King's business. The same explanation might have applied to Tristram Fysh, William's younger brother, who was later named as being 'in arms against the Parliament'. On the other hand, some doubtful burgesses, particularly William Foord and William Lawson, might have stayed away deliberately to avoid the vote.[155]

The next critical test of the loyalty of Scarborough's leaders to Cholmley came at the beginning of July with news of the disaster at Marston Moor, the headlong flight of the Marquess of Newcastle and his entourage, and the fall of York to Parliament. The sudden appearance in the town on 3 July of the commander of the King's northern army and about seventy other royalist officers and servants and then their almost immediate departure by sea into exile must have had a most demoralising effect in Scarborough. In Cholmley's own words, 'the gentlemen and strangers then with in Scarbrough . . . quitt itt, procuring passes either to goe to Prince Rupert or to live att there owne houses'. As for 'the common soldiers' in his garrison, 'they ranne away dayly', so that it was 'reduced to 300 foote and 200 horse, and many of those wavering'.[156]

Most of the townspeople stayed put: by running away they had far more to lose than 'common soldiers'. Soon after the news of York's surrender reached Scarborough, on 20 July the Common Hall was assembled to decide whether it would continue to support Cholmley and King Charles. Most of the twenty-seven members present said that they would stand by Sir Hugh as long as possible. Two who would not, William Foord and Thomas Gill, and a third, non-member, John Woodall, were then 'licensed to departe' from the town. Amongst the absentees there were several with known royalist sympathies including Richard Thompson and Francis Fawether.[157]

William Foord, currently ranked number six or seven in the First Twelve, was a senior member of Scarborough's oligarchy. He had been bailiff three times, in 1630–1, 1636–7 and 1640–1, and would hold the highest local office again in 1653–4 and 1656–7. He died a very rich man in 1663. In his will he left many closes of pasture and arable in Falsgrave and Scarborough fields, several tenements and shops in the town, and shares in a number of ships. His decision to leave Scarborough must have been a difficult one to make, and not just because of his property and commercial interests there. His two sons, Timothy and Daniel, were still too young to manage his business affairs; they probably left Scarborough with him. However, one of his daughters, Suzanne, had married the royalist Tristram Fysh, so she probably stayed behind with her husband and their young family.[158]

Thomas Gill was a senior master mariner and leading member of the Society of Owners, Masters and Mariners. In July 1644 he was placed fourth in the Second Twelve. Like many of his status in Scarborough he had interest in landed property as well as shipping. As late as April 1642, for example, he took out a seven-year lease from the corporation on a parcel of ground called Tonge close for which he paid an entry fine of ten shillings and an annual rent of the same amount. At the time when he left the town as a political exile he is also known to have been the lessee of Driple Cotes, the site of the spa springs and the meadow on South Cliff above it.[159]

William Foord might well have had second thoughts and soon returned to Scarborough, since his name appears in its customary place among the First Twelve in October 1644.[160] However, it seems unlikely that he gave any support to Sir Hugh during the next six months, otherwise he would not have been chosen coroner in September 1645 by the new Parliamentary regime. At the same time Thomas Gill was first elected to be one of the two bailiffs. Since he had never been higher than the Second Twelve, this accelerated promotion indicates that he had recently done outstanding service to Parliament. From then on, until his death in 1656, Gill was scarcely ever out of office. Here was at least one Scarborian who profited from civil war.[161]

Apart from the few Scarborians who voluntarily chose to exile themselves in Hull rather than live under a royalist regime, notably seafaring Puritans, such as John Lawson and William Nesfield, and these three others who went in July 1644, the town's ruling body, though depleted, remained steadfast. Despite the potentially dangerous consequences, all but a small minority of the Common Hall allowed themselves to be re-elected at Michaelmas 1644. The two new bailiffs were Christopher Thompson and Tristram Fysh.[162]

Christopher was the youngest of the Thompsons and a permanent resident in the town. His elder brother Stephen inherited the Humbleton estate in Holderness from their father Francis, whereas Christopher is described as a merchant tailor or draper of Scarborough. Though both Stephen Thompson of Humbleton and Richard Thompson, his uncle, of Kilham, near Bridlington, were listed in the First Twelve in 1643–4, they seem to have left Scarborough during this time, probably to manage and guard their East Riding properties. Before the Committee for Compounding Richard later claimed that when the Queen's army came through Kilham in February 1643 it had ransacked his house there to the value of £300. Richard was re-elected to Scarborough's First Twelve in September 1644 but marked absent at all subsequent meetings. Stephen had not attended any of the sessions of the Common Hall since October 1643 and a year later even his name was taken off the membership list. Later, Stephen told the Committee for Compounding that in July 1644 after 'his abode there was accounted a fault' he had left Scarborough and returned to 'his house in Parliament's quarter'. So apart from Christopher the only Thompson still living in Scarborough was his second cousin Timothy, who was duly elected to the First Twelve in September 1644.[163] For his loyalty to Cholmley, Timothy was proscribed from office by order of the House of Commons in April 1646.[164]

The rise of Tristram Fysh was meteoric. During the previous year he had been a member of the Third Twelve, but the death of his father Gregory in 1640 and then of his elder brother William in 1643 left him as the senior member of the family and the heir of a considerable estate in Scarborough. Yet, whatever his local standing and influence, Tristram would not have been placed in the highest office unless he had shown strong royalist convictions. Eventually, he was named in a list of Scarborough men who 'had beene in armes against the Parliament'.[165]

John Hickson stayed on as coroner, but Roger Wyvill stood down. Roger was now nearly sixty-years-old and not in good health. Furthermore, he was probably concerned to protect his home and estate at Osgodby which were now threatened by Parliament's troops.[166] His place as coroner was taken by William Chapman who seems to have had the knack of accommodating himself to whatever regime was in power on Sandside. This was to be Chapman's second year as a coroner.

To fill the vacancy left by Stephen Thompson's exit, Francis Fawether was promoted from the Second to the First Twelve. Fawether was a master mariner who had already proved himself a loyal servant of the Cholmleys. His cellar on the harbour front was used to store gunpowder. In November 1643 James Cholmley, Sir Hugh's cousin, gave Henry Swaine a note to collect forty barrels of powder for the use of the castle out of 'Fran Fouthers seller'.[167] Fawether's spacious and convenient cellar also stored firkins of butter and other provisions when they came into Scarborough from Whitby, and before they were delivered to sea and land captains in Cholmley's service.[168] When the town was taxed at £30 a week in February 1644, Francis was named as one of the assessors.[169] Later, in April 1646, when the House of Commons listed Scarborough's 'delinquents', Francis Fawether was named as one of them along with the Thompsons and William Cooper.[170] William Cooper was also a master mariner and shipowner. His name appeared in the custom book when in March 1643 in his ship the *Margery* he brought into Scarborough from Rotterdam a cargo of iron, prunes and raisins. His first appearance in the Common Hall as a lowly member of the Third Twelve took place in September 1644.[171]

So, despite the radical change of circumstances during the past year, the First Twelve was virtually unaltered. In September 1643 the war situation seemed entirely favourable to the King. The defeat of the Fairfaxes on Adwalton moor near Bradford at the end of June, the fall of Bristol to Prince Rupert a month later, and the siege of Hull, Parliament's last stronghold in Yorkshire, which had not yet failed – all pointed towards a royalist victory. No one then could have predicted that within four months a Scottish army in alliance with Parliament would be advancing on Newcastle. By September 1644, when the Common Hall was renewed, all had changed. Rupert and Newcastle had been routed on Marston Moor; the King's northern capital, York, was Parliament's. The once-triumphant Marquess of Newcastle and his staff had run away humiliated and defeated. The King no longer had an army in the north of England and he could never again threaten Hull. Scarborough, formerly basking in the security of a royalist sea, had become an isolated, helpless outpost in Parliament's ocean. The essential continuity of the membership of the town's governing body was therefore quite remarkable.

Senior burgesses, such as William Batty, William Conyers and Thomas Moone, all dignified with the title of 'mister', were still in the First Twelve as they had been in 1642 and 1643. Their durability and adaptability were extraordinary. Samuel Hodgson was another member of the First Twelve who kept his place there throughout every political vicissitude. If he had any personal political view he must have kept it to himself. The same description would apply to other veterans in the Second Twelve, such as Robert Rogers, John Rosdale, Henry Coward and William and Christopher Poskitt, who seem to have confined their activities to commerce and eschewed politics.[172]

Down in the Third Twelve there were a number of interesting newcomers in September 1644; Francis Sollitt was one of them. He first appeared in the corporation records in March 1634 as a fifteen-year-old servant of Francis Thompson. Thompson suspected that some of his beans had been stolen from the parsonage barn and set the young Sollitt to keep watch there during the night. Sure enough, at two or three o'clock in the morning, Sollitt caught the widow Elizabeth Taylor and her son red-handed taking about a peck of his master's beans.[173] Eight years later it is not clear whether 'Fracis

Sollyte' was in business on his own account or still working for the Thompsons, but in October 1642 he was presented at the sheriff's tourn 'for not bringing in his watter measures'.[174] However, the following year, when William Lawson, master of the *Isabel* of Scarborough, came into port from Rotterdam, he carried a cargo of sack, prunes, raisins, train-oil, tar and Swedish iron for Francis Sollitt.[175] Sollitt's name also figured in the harbour account book for 1643-4 from which it appears that he was one of Cholmley's principal suppliers of iron, timber and victuals for his privateer frigates.[176] Like Francis Fawether, Sollitt was doing well out of the war.

Other new names, besides William Cooper, amongst the last Twelve first elected in September 1644 included John Denton, the privateer sea captain and William Lawson, gentleman. Since there were several William Lawsons or Lowsons in Scarborough about this time this particular one cannot be identified for certain. He was definitely not William Lawson, master of the *Isabel* and senior member of the Society of Owners and Mariners. This particular William Lawson 'naut' had been one of the Third Twelve since September 1643 but rarely attended the Common Hall assemblies. There was a William Lawson who had a tavern on Sandside next to the Bolts. During the 1640s and 1650s he held one of Scarborough's two vintner's licences and was still supplying the vicar of St Mary's with communion wine in the 1660s.[177] Alternatively, he might have been the William Lawson who served as bailiff four times after the Restoration, in 1660, 1664, 1669 and 1674.[178]

Only two meetings of the newly elected Common Hall were recorded in the minute book. On 23 October 1644 a motion to raise another £50 for purposes unspecified was only just carried by 22 votes to 16. The same clerk also noted seven absentees on that day: Richard Thompson in the First Twelve, Peter Hodgson, Robert Rogers and William Monkman in the Second, and William Lawson, sailor, William Headley and William Hickson in the Third. Since this would give a total membership of forty-five, the clerk had miscounted the votes by one or marked someone absent who was not. Nevertheless, whatever the exact figures, the Common Hall was now more evenly divided than it had ever been.[179]

A month later, on 25 November, when the Common Hall was faced with Sir Hugh's motion that the town should continue to maintain a guard of one hundred at its own expense, the vote was 19 in favour and none against. On this final occasion only three absentees were marked, all in the lower Twelves – William Monkman, William Lawson sailor and William Headley. So if the clerk was correct this time the abstentions outnumbered the supporters by 22 to 19.[180]

However, by now, Sir Hugh knew that he could no longer control Scarborough merely through majorities of votes in the Common Hall: two days earlier he had broken all precedent by calling a meeting of the entire township community.[181] Unfortunately, no account of this extraordinary assembly has survived. If it did take place then it would have been held inside St Mary's church, the only building in the town large enough to accommodate several hundred people. What Sir Hugh might have said to the residents of Scarborough at this moment of crisis can only be surmised.

On 8 July, less than a week after the battle of Marston Moor, the clerk of the general sessions at Scarborough had entered 'omnia bene' when the jurors found there were no presentments to hear.[182] As far as Scarborough's prospects were concerned, no comment could have been more ironical: everything was far from well. Even as early as 29 April, long before Marston Moor and the loss of York, every resident of the town had been ordered to lay in three months' provisions.[183] After the breakneck flight of the Marquess of Newcastle it must have been obvious to everyone in Scarborough that the town could not escape the war for much longer: a siege was inevitable. In the light of what actually happened when the attack finally came the following February, at the general meeting on 23 November Cholmley probably assured Scarborians that if the town was closely besieged and there was no hope of relief by land or sea he would not submit them to the horrors of artillery bombardment, street fighting, plunder and rapine. Rather than attempt to defend the indefensible, he would retire to the castle. Only those who wished to do so might follow him there; as in March 1643, when he had changed sides, no one would be forced to fight.

CHAPTER FOUR

The Great Siege, 1645

AT ten o'clock in the morning of Shrove Tuesday, 18 February 1645, Scarborough was attacked from the sea and at four points from the land. Under the command of General Sir John Meldrum, a mixed force of twelve hundred Scottish infantry and five hundred Englishmen from the garrisons of Hull and Whitby captured the harbour and overran the town within a few hours. The two hundred landsmen and mariners from Sir Hugh Cholmley's home town of Whitby were led by Captain Isaac Newton, Browne Bushell's brother-in-law.

No more than twenty, and possibly as few as ten, of Meldrum's men lost their lives. Of the defenders, perhaps half a dozen were killed. Parliament took 80 prisoners, 32 pieces of ordnance and, in the harbour, 120 ships carrying 200 guns. Among the captured was Sir Jordan Crosland, formerly governor of Helmsley castle, who had been allowed by Fairfax to join Cholmley at Scarborough after his surrender. Crosland, and most of the other royalist prisoners, had been taken after heavy hand-to-hand fighting in and around St Mary's church, near the main entrance to the castle.

Scarborough castle, however, did not fall to Parliament. Sir Hugh had tried to flee abroad in a little pinnace which he called his *Running Horse*, but Meldrum's swift advance along the sands of South Bay had cut off his retreat to the harbour. Consequently, he was forced to retire to the castle which was now entirely surrounded and closely besieged.

Such was the news of the capture of Scarborough as reported in Parliament's London press. *Mercurius Britanicus* declared triumphantly that this victory proved that 'God was visible at Scarborough'.[1]

Cholmley's own accounts of the events of this day differed at several points from that of Parliament's news-sheets. In his 'Memorialls Tuching Scarbrough', written in 1647, he gave Meldrum's strength as '2000 foot and one thousand horse' when, in the late

January frost and snow, it moved up to Falsgrave village, 'not 2 fleete shotts from Scarbrough Towne'. To this figure Cholmley added another 'thousand Scotts' under 'Collonel Steward' who reinforced Meldrum with his Galloway regiment just before the assault.[2] However, in a letter written from the besieged castle only six days after he had lost the town and harbour, Sir Hugh gave a more modest and realistic estimate of enemy troops opposing him: 'Heer are 10 colours of Scots, as I imagine, though not above 800 of them: but Meldrum (who commands in cheif and is the most active man here) had 6 or 700 more of the Lord Fairfaxes Foot'.[3] Presumably, after the successful attack on the town, Meldrum's cavalry were drawn away from Scarborough.

As for the battle for Scarborough, Sir Hugh wanted his readers to accept that he had never intended to fight it. As he explained in the 'Memorialls', though he 'understood well of what consequence the place was', he did not have enough men to defend it. In his own words, '2 thousand men ware scarce sufficient to maintain the towne and there was not 700 in itt with the Townesmen, most of which verie wavering'. Consequently, in the face of Meldrum's overwhelming superiority, Cholmley held the walls and ditches for only three weeks, during which time the castle was provisioned with munitions and food. The defenders were so short of guards 'that for 10 days together not any soldier stirred from his poast'. When he received advanced warning of Meldrum's allout assault, Sir Hugh withdrew all his cannon, 'except those in the sunke shipp which could not be moved', the night before. The next morning he summoned 'all his men into the Castle without making the least shew of opposition'.[4]

Cholmley's memory was characteristically selective. The loss of Crosland and 80 men after the bloody skirmish at St Mary's was conveniently omitted from his account, and so was the loss of 32 cannon in the town and all the ordnance in the harbour. If Sir Hugh had been so well informed of Meldrum's intentions then royalist casualties might have been even lighter. Indeed it was the seizure of Scarborough harbour and all the ships in it which gave the London news-sheets most pleasure. The *Weekly Account*, for instance, reported first the taking of 'a fort [South Steel battery] . . . which was on the east side of Scarbrough between that last and the sea', then 'the haven' with its prizes, and finally, almost as an afterthought, the town itself.[5] The same order of importance was given by *Perfect Passages*, which emphasized that the capture of 'one of the Forts' was 'very material' because it commanded the harbour.[6] Parliament too seemed far more interested in Scarborough port than in Scarborough town. With some satisfaction it was noted that a merchantman, the *Blessing of Cramond*, which in April 1644 had been intercepted on its way to Scotland, was one of the many ships re-taken at Scarborough.[7]

Substantially, however, Cholmley's version of events makes sense.

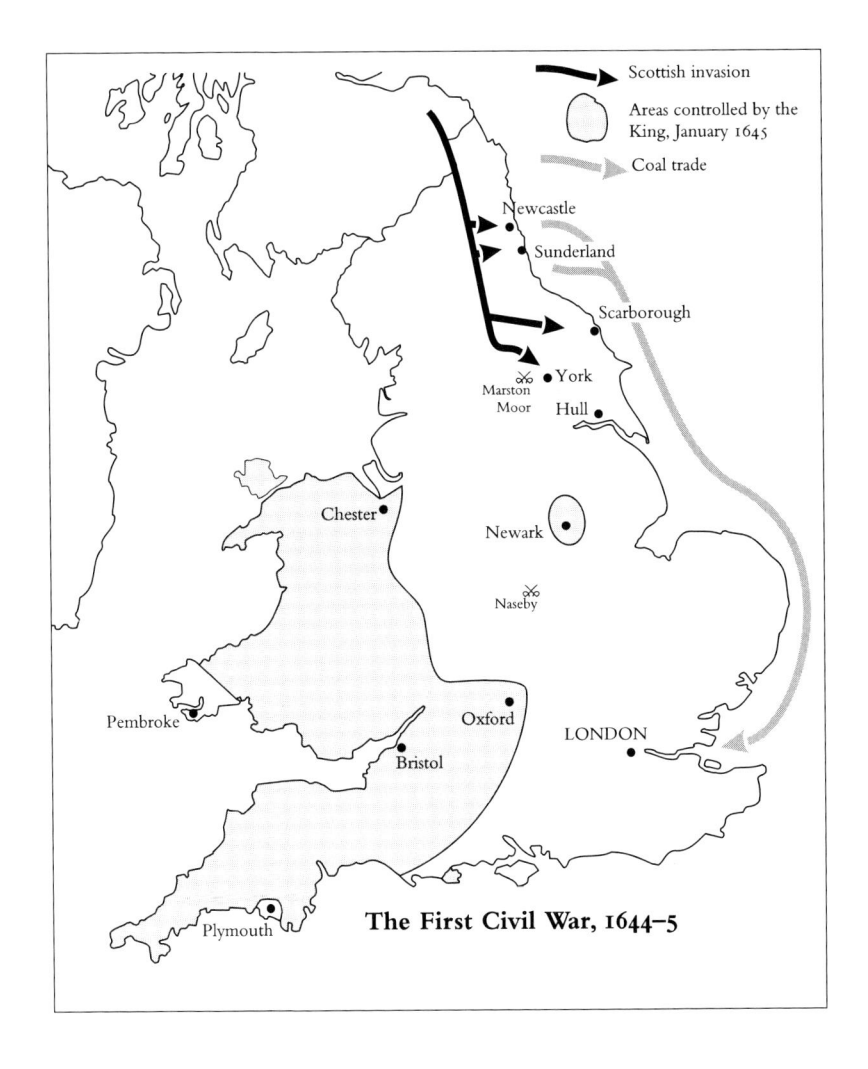

The First Civil War, 1644–5

Scarborough's incomplete walls and shallow ditches could not halt a determined sustained infantry assault. Both to the north and the south, the town's defences could be outflanked by approaches along the sands at low-tide. Even if Sir Hugh did have as many as 700 soldiers to defend the two gateways and the lengthy perimeter of wall and ditch, that number would have been inadequate. From the vantage point of Windmill Hill, Meldrum overlooked the town and haven and could bombard them at close range with his artillery. His troops also had supporting fire from Parliament's warships in South Bay which sank two Dunkirkers and chased away another three. Cholmley was surely right: the town and harbour were untenable.[8] Furthermore, if by the afternoon of 18 February there were 500 men safely inside the castle, 'three score gentlemen and officers, 250 foot, and the rest troopers', out of an original garrison of 700, then this indicates that a planned, orderly retreat not a runaway rout, had taken place.[9]

Crosland's valiant rearguard action at St Mary's might have been forced by the surprising speed of Meldrum's pincer movement, one arm advancing directly towards the castle gateway up High Tollergate while another came up the castle dykes from the harbour and South Steel battery. Alternatively, Sir Jordan might simply have disobeyed Cholmley's order by refusing to retire into the castle without at least a gesture of defiance. Sir Hugh's failure to mention Crosland's action and capture suggests that the second explanation might be nearer the truth.[10]

Cholmley was now a deeply-detested enemy: worse than an ordinary 'malignant', in London he was regarded as a dishonourable, cowardly traitor. For example, *Mercurius Britanicus* recommended that he should suffer the same fate as the Hothams who had both been executed the previous month for betraying their commissions and trust.[11] All reports of Sir Hugh in the Parliamentary news-sheets ought, therefore, to be treated with caution and suspicion. There is no corroboration elsewhere of their allegation that he was prevented from taking flight by ship. On the contrary, evidence and logic point in the opposite direction: Cholmley was resolved to withstand a siege of the castle. Long before 18 February he had received several invitations and turned down many opportunities to run away or surrender; it would be another five months yet before he finally abandoned the struggle. If he had planned to escape by sea himself,

Sir Hugh Cholmley (1600–57), artist and date unknown.

he would not have sent his two daughters, ten-year-old Ann and six-year-old Elizabeth, to Holland at the beginning of February. If he had secretly intended to leave Scarborough he would have departed with his wife, Lady Elizabeth, when Meldrum moved up to Falsgrave; he would not have risked a last-minute getaway three weeks later. As for another Parliamentary calumny, that he had brought soldiers out of the castle to intimidate the townspeople 'when they would have yielded the town', this is in direct conflict with what is known about Sir Hugh's relations with Scarborians since he arrived amongst them in September 1642.[12]

According to Cholmley's 'Memorialls Tuching Scarbrough': 'At the entring into the Castle most of the Townes men quitt the Governor, except one of the Bailiffes and fower or five others which retyred thither with there familyes'.[13] The bailiff in question might have been either Christopher Thompson or Tristram Fysh, but the latter seems the more likely candidate. Christopher was named as a delinquent and permanently disenfranchised, along with others in the Thompson family, by the House of Commons in April 1646.[14] Yet there was no suggestion in the report of the Committee for Compounding that Christopher had fought against Parliament or actively assisted Cholmley. On the contrary, Christopher's claim that Sir Hugh had robbed him of £4,000 worth of credits, goods and wares seems to have been accepted by the committee who let him off with a fine of only £150.[15] On the other hand, in 1659 the captain of the garrison of Scarborough castle named Tristram Fysh as first on a list of leading townsmen who 'had beene in armes against the Parliament'.[16] The 'fower or five others' who followed Cholmley into the castle with their families are more difficult to identify. Francis Fawether and William Cooper were two other Scarborians disenfranchised by the Commons in 1646, but by 18 February they were probably at sea with Browne Bushell, Browne Thomas and John Denton, the other privateer captains.[17] Three other burgesses who appeared on the same list of royalist belligerents as Tristram Fysh were John Hickson, Francis Sollitt and Richard Bilbrough. John Hickson had served as coroner since September 1644 after his year's term as bailiff, so his loyalty to Cholmley is well documented. So is that of Francis Sollitt.[18] Richard Bilbrough, however, is more elusive. Unlike other local men of his status he does not appear as a member of the Common Hall; he held no civic office; and his name is strangely absent from assessment lists. We know only that he shared a preferential pew in St Mary's, between Mrs Conyers and Mrs Farrer, with Steven Walker for which they paid £2 6s. 8d.[19]

One of Cholmley's most faithful followers, whom he never referred to by name, was William Simpson, the vicar of St Mary's since 1630. According to a letter from bailiffs John Harrison and Thomas Gill written in June 1646, 'for our burgesses', Simpson had been 'an inveterate enemye to the Parliament' who 'att the tyme when Sir Hu Cholmley revolted . . . became his chaplaine domesticke, and read comon prayers in his hous'. From his pulpit in St Mary's Simpson had denounced all who fought against the King as 'caterpillers, canker wormes & cursed Achitophells, and that they were like unto Korah, Dathan & Abiram which rebelled against Moses'. When Sir Hugh had retaken Whitby from Sir William Constable, Simpson had invited his congregation to 'give thanks for that great victorye god hath given us over the rebells'. Also from the pulpit he had declared that whereas once he had believed that 'the papists were a bloody minded people . . . he did now see that the Anabaptists, Brownists, Separatists and Schismaticks were worse than papists, and bloody minded'. Afterwards he had repeated this opinion and announced that he would hold it 'till his death'. Whether Simpson actually went into the castle with Sir Hugh is not explicit in this forthright denunciation. However, the same draft letter also stated that Simpson had two sons who were with Cholmley in Scarborough castle during the siege 'untill it was reduced and after they came forth one of them . . . went immediately to sea in a pyrates shipp haveing beene formerly in that service'.[20] Not surprisingly, Simpson paid a painful price for his outspoken views: he was deprived of his vicarage and had to wait until 1660 before it was restored to him.

The London press was delighted by the news from Scarborough. Every paper, from the *London Post* to the *Scottish Dove*, reported the capture of the town and harbour. The latter regretted that Sir Hugh was not one of the prisoners taken, but it still looked forward to the day when 'Judas Cholmley' was brought to the capital 'and rewarded as some other of those destroying apostates have been'.[21] *A Perfect Diurnall* similarly wished that 'the liver-hearted Cholmley' might eventually 'have his just reward at Tiburne'.[22] Meanwhile, other rewards were granted, if not always paid out promptly. The messenger who brought Meldrum's news from Scarborough to London was given £20 and on the General himself Parliament bestowed a gift of £1,000. Later, when he suffered grave injuries gallantly trying to capture the castle, the old Scottish veteran was awarded another £500, though unfortunately for him he did not live long enough to receive it.[23] According to the royalist version of *Mercurius Aulicus*, when the House of Commons gave thanks to God on 12 March 1645 for its latest victories, the fall of Scarborough was put at the head of the list.[24]

Parliament's joy soon turned into disappointment when Meldrum failed either to persuade Cholmley to surrender the castle or to take it immediately by storm. The *London Post* announced that some royalist gentlemen, 'Sir Thomas Ingram, Mr Bellasis and three more' had deserted Cholmley and come to York to submit themselves to Lord Fairfax, but it was soon ominously clear that there had been no collapse of morale amongst the castle defenders.[25] As *Perfect Passages* had to admit reluctantly, Meldrum might be 'within a stones throw of the castle', yet he was having to raise 'mounts' and 'pieces' to 'batter the castle about their eares if they will not yield'.[26]

In fact, Meldrum was too conscious of his own weaknesses to attempt a direct attack on the castle. Even before the assault on the town, from Falsgrave he had complained to his political masters in London that he was short 'of men, money, victuals, ammunition and arms' and warned them that he feared a 'mutiny of the soldiers for want of supplies'.[27] Now that he was face to face with the castle's walls, redoubts and vertical cliffs he knew that he had not the weight of artillery to batter Cholmley into submission, whatever *Perfect Passages* might claim. Besides, he also knew that the Committee of Both Kingdoms, upon which he depended for supplies, did not give to the castle the same high priority that it had given to Scarborough harbour. As the Committee had already explained to him:

> We received the good news of your taking Scarborough town and harbour, which being in your hands we hope the castle will not be of much concernment to the enemy nor the harbour be any more a den of thieves, either to interrupt the coasting trade of our small vessels, or a refuge for them to escape the pursuit of our ships or the dangers of an Eastern storm, for they have now no place left them on our whole eastern shore. In which regard we conceive the place to be of very great concernment and future influence.[28]

Consequently, the Scot at first tried to bully his way into the castle: on 25 February he wrote a haughty letter to Sir Hugh demanding his immediate surrender. Though he lacked the weight of ordnance to make a breach in the walls and sufficient infantry for an assault on them, he also appreciated that Cholmley's position was hopeless. He had no hope of relief or even reinforcement by land or by sea.[29]

Sharply aware of his predicament, Sir Hugh had already written twice to the King's headquarters at Oxford, on 23 and 24 February, explaining his position. 'If we have not timely help', he wrote, 'the king will lose his interest there [Scarborough]'. He was afraid that if taken prisoner his life would be forfeit and this would deter other gentlemen, like himself, from continuing with the struggle or taking his majesty's side. Even if Cholmley had not read recent issues of *Mercurius Britanicus*, he must still have known about the fate of his old friends, comrades in arms and blood relatives, the Hothams. In the second letter, Sir Hugh admitted that he was 'now blockt up close in the castle'; that many of his soldiers had run away or surrendered; and that more were bound to desert on account of 'the ill accommodation' and shortage of food and supplies in the castle. He asked to be given hope of relief 'from the Queen, or Ireland, or probability of a good issue from the Treaty'.[30]

Nevertheless, despite or possibly because of the odds against him, Cholmley's mood was defiant. He told his superiors in Oxford that even if they could not promise him 'speedy supply', he would not 'quitt this trust otherwise than becomes a gentleman, and a good subject'.[31] To prove that this was no empty gesture of bravado, on 26 February Meldrum received a sharp answer to his demands of the previous day. Cholmley rebuked the Scotsman for what he called 'the stile of conquerors alone'. He then reminded Meldrum that he had always 'abhorred whatsoever tended towards tirranie', though every day he heard of 'impositions upon men's consciences and personall liberties by your partie'. In his letter Meldrum had referred to 'the Grace of the Kingdom', and Sir Hugh now gave him a brief lesson in English constitutional law by pointing out that 'all acts of Grace' were 'inseparable from the sovereigne power, of which you cannot be ignorante, though perhaps unwilling to name the Kinge'.[32]

As a Member of several past Parliaments, Cholmley knew that Meldrum was one of the notorious patentees of the Dungeness lighthouse which had been the subject of seamen's petitions to Westminster for more than twenty years. All ships passing Dungeness were required to pay a toll to the patentees, but instead of maintaining a proper lighthouse with their takings they provided one candle! Not surprisingly, there had been many avoidable shipwrecks on this part of the coast of Kent. When Meldrum's summons to capitulate contained the phrase 'the dazeling lights of Reformation', Sir Hugh, in reply, could not resist reminding him that his lights were less than dazzling: instead they were like 'ignis fatui' which had misled him out of obedience to the King. Finally, Meldrum was rebuked for the damage he had done to St Mary's church by turning it into a forward strongpoint, and warned that he would find only the graveyard useful for burying his dead.[33]

Sir John's immediate reply to what he called a 'lofty and impertinent answer' pointed out the utter futility of Cholmley's beleaguered position. Revealing that he had intercepted and read Cholmley's letters to Oxford, Meldrum then informed him that he could expect no outside help 'from the Queen, out of France, from Oxford, or from Newark, or from the issue of the treaty'. By his reference to Meldrum's lights Sir Hugh had touched a sore spot, and in retaliation he was told that 'those lights have done more service to the Kingdoms . . . than the breaking down of many fair bridges'. Which bridges Meldrum had in mind is not exactly clear, but it is known that Cholmley had destroyed the bridge over the river Derwent at Stamford Bridge, and that he had tried and failed to destroy those at Yedingham and Howe. What Meldrum did not know, or conveniently overlooked, was that

Sir Hugh had given these orders in the name of Parliament before defecting to the King.[34]

Finally, with a clever argument that was designed to have maximum cutting effect on Sir Hugh's political certainties, Meldrum drew a distinction between what he called 'a moderate and well tempered monarchy' and 'a Straffordian . . . that is at least cousin german [to], if not worse than, anarchy itself'. The wily Scot then assured Cholmley that his quarrel was not with King Charles, but only with the 'viperous brood' of 'pernicious counsellors who have brought him and his posterity to so low an ebb'. As a postscript came Meldrum's threat: if Sir Hugh was so foolish as to reject his terms of surrender and 'the kingdome be put to the trouble of bringing great ordnance', the royalists could expect no further mercy. Meldrum promised that he would 'endeavour to make your strong walls spue you out at the broadside'. This was to be Sir Hugh's last summons: Meldrum did not intend to trouble him again with his pen.[35]

The walls of Scarborough castle were indeed 'strong' and it would require 'great ordnance' to breach them. During the past two and a half years Cholmley had converted a dilapidated, redundant, medieval castle into a formidable, modern fortress. He had foraged over a wide area for timber, lead and iron. For example, Newtondale forest, north of Pickering and fifteen miles inland from Scarborough, had lost thirty trees, 'by the instruction of Sir Hu Cholmley for the repair of Scarborough castle'.[36] Pickering castle, the nearest to Scarborough's, had not escaped his attention: the lead, wood and iron of its Diate tower 'was by Sir Hugh Chomley (as we are informed) carryed to Scarborough castle'.[37] Perhaps Cholmley was aware of a precedent for this: his great-grandfather, Sir Richard, 'the great black knight of the North', had pillaged Pickering castle of its stone and slate to improve his own fortified manor house at Roxby.[38]

Meldrum had been quick to appreciate the significance of South Steel battery and had taken it at the first assault; but Bushell's battery, dominating the main approach to the castle, remained intact; its guns had forced the Scots to retire to the shelter of the thick walls of

St Mary's church. Behind Bushell's battery, the barbican, towers and curtain walls had been heavily reinforced on the interior with earth and stones, to buttress the masonry against cannon fire and to provide more artillery and musketry platforms. Since the castle was everywhere founded on solid rock and almost surrounded by precipitous, high cliffs, it could not be undermined and it would be perilous to scale. Even if Meldrum had enough men and ships to seal off the castle night and day by land and sea, inside the garrison had a good supply of food and ammunition, and a reliable, invulnerable supply of drinking water. Moreover, by the time the siege began, the worst of the winter weather had passed: Cholmley's men could stand guard and live out in the open without too much discomfort.[39]

So Meldrum had to send to the magazines at Hull and York for his 'great ordnance'. During the next fortnight there was a lull as both sides prepared for the next encounter. From Hull, by sea, came several demi-cannon and demi-culverin. Some of these had originally belonged to Newcastle's siege-train and had been captured by Parliament in October 1643.[40] From York, by land, came the heaviest pieces of artillery in the whole kingdom. The 'Queen's pocket-pistol', which weighed 2½ tons and fired a 36-pound shot, had been taken by Meldrum himself when he sallied out of Hull on the day before the royalists raised the second siege.[41] After that it was re-christened 'Sweet Lips' in honour of a well-known Hull whore and carried to the siege of Newark by Meldrum. Prince Rupert re-captured it from Parliament at Newark in March 1644 only to lose it again in July after Marston Moor. The Earl of Manchester used it to batter Sheffield castle the following month and now this iron demi-cannon was called to Scarborough for further service.[42]

Meldrum would have been pleased to see 'Sweet Lips' again, and overjoyed to receive from York its bigger sister, the cannon-royal or whole cannon. What Sir Henry Vane had once called 'the best battering piece' fired a huge ball of more than sixty pounds.[43] It had last been employed by Parliament in the siege of York with devastating effects: at least two church steeples in the city were victims of its long-range fire.[44] However, since it weighed as much as 3½ tons, it took eight pairs of horses or ninety men to pull it even when the ground was firm and level. According to a contemporary artillery manual, when the way was 'foule, morish and dirty, then for a whole

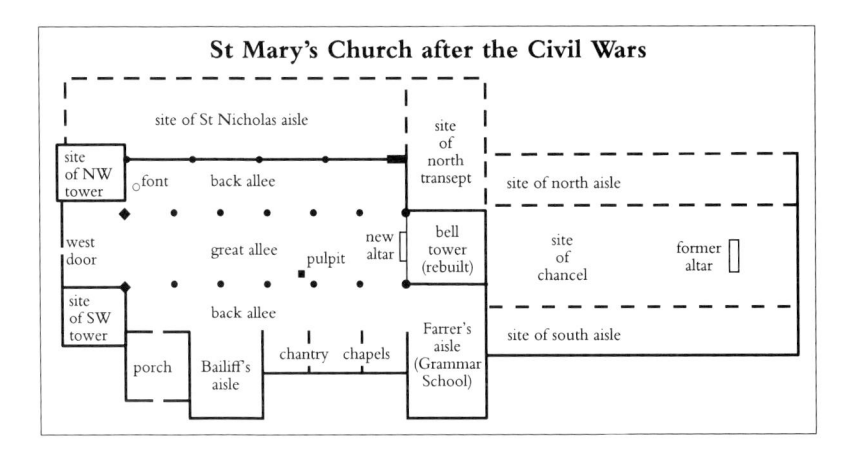

```
                St Mary's Church after the Civil Wars
    ┌─────────────────────────────────────────┐
    │       site of St Nicholas aisle    site │
    │                                     of  │
    │ site                               north│
    │ of NW  ○font   back allee         transept   site of north aisle
    │ tower                                   │
    │                              new   bell │
    │ west                         altar tower│          former
    │ door          great allee  pulpit (rebuilt)   site   altar
    │                                          of
    │ site                                   chancel
    │ of SW         back allee                │
    │ tower                           Farrer's│   site of south aisle
    │         porch Bailiff's chantry chapels  aisle
    │                 aisle                  (Grammar
    │                                         School)
    └─────────────────────────────────────────┘
```

cannon . . . you must spanne in 15 couple of horse'.[45] Nevertheless, despite these difficulties, in the middle of March, under cover of darkness, this monster arrived in Scarborough and was brought through the west door of St Mary's, down the long central nave, and mounted in the chancel. From there it was fired over the altar through the great east window at point-blank range at the castle keep.[46]

The royalists too attached great importance to the harbour and castle at Scarborough, and they made many recorded attempts by sea to relieve Cholmley, or at least keep him supplied with essential munitions. In April 1645 a Dunkirker, carrying gunpowder and arms, was intercepted and seized by Vice-Admiral Zachary's frigates which were operating a permanent sea blockade.[47] In June there was a report that one of the King's few remaining warships, the *John*, under Captain Mucknell, was sailing northwards up the English coast in the direction of Scarborough. Zachary was warned that 'Captain Mucknell may be disposed to relieve Scarborough Castle' and ordered to keep a sharp look out for him.[48]

Moreover, Meldrum had failed to capture all of Scarborough's privateers and their captains: indeed, the most successful and infamous, John Denton, Browne Thomas and Browne Bushell, were still actively at sea. One 'ship of Scarborough' was reported in June to have been driven by storm into Hartlepool Bay and there taken by Parliament's forces. It was said to be carrying two brass and four iron guns and a store of arms.[49] But this was Parliament's only success at sea: Browne Bushell, especially, was more impudent and more dangerous than ever. Though now deprived of a safe anchorage and supply base at Scarborough, he had begun to operate out of Dunkirk and Ostend. In the same issue in which it recorded the fall of Scarborough to Meldrum, *Perfect Diurnall* revealed that it had received letters from Holland relating that the 'perfidious apostate', Captain Browne Bushell, was at sea again in command of a small fleet of pirate warships.[50] Three months later, *Exchange Intelligencer* announced that Bushell had lately come out of Dunkirk with fifteen ships and that he was 'now a robbing up and down our coasts'. With more indignation than wit, it concluded: 'the Bushell is almost heap't up: and he is likely to be measured according to his deserts'.[51] There was some alarm expressed in the London press that Bushell might even try to break through Zachary's sea blockade at Scarborough to relieve or rescue his cousin, Sir Hugh Cholmley. In the words of *Mercurius Veridicus*, published at the beginning of July 1645, 'Brown Bushell looks big, and threatens much with his little squadron, if he comes we have four stout ships in the harbour [Scarborough] to welcome him'.[52]

Wisely, Bushell never returned to Scarborough, but every East coast sailor, merchant and shipowner had good reason to fear an encounter with him. In a letter dated 22 June and sent from Ostend, Yarmouth, in particular, was threatened by 'the Bushell' and his associates. Addressed to the town bailiffs, the letter says much about the conditions then prevailing in the North Sea:

> We hereby give you to understand, that those seamen of ours, which your men of war have lately taken . . . be not imprisoned. And that you set at liberty all those that are confined; otherwise you shall not have that usage you formerly have had from us . . . Now we can, if you compel us, make a hundred suffer for one. Our pleasures are commended to you, by just and due observation, not to make suffer the innocent for the nocent. Therefore we do daily set at liberty yours, supposing that upon receipt of these you will do the same by ours; otherwise we shall soon make known to you our intentions.

The letter was signed by Browne Bushell and eleven other privateer captains who included 'Francis Fowther' and 'William Coope'.[53] Since Francis Fawether and William Cooper of Scarborough were subsequently named in April 1646 as delinquents who should be disenfranchised and permanently excluded from office, their signatures would explain why they were so condemned.[54]

The real threat from privateers like Bushell and the potential menace of a Scarborough harbour that might fall back into royalist hands were employed by Meldrum to raise money and materials for his siege of the castle. As a lighthouse patentee who had also spent many months in Hull, Sir John knew how important Scarborough harbour was to all East coast mariners and shipowners, and how much they looked forward to its restoration as a place of refuge. However, as long as Cholmley held the castle and from there could direct cannon fire down upon the harbour and at passing ships, Scarborough could hardly be regarded as a safe haven for colliers and merchantmen.

Consequently, in early March 1645, before his 'great ordnance' arrived, Meldrum addressed letters to several of the major East coast ports, namely Hull, Boston, King's Lynn, Yarmouth and Ipswich. In his letter to the governors of Ipswich, he warned them that though he had possession of 'the Towne and Peere' of Scarborough, his position there was by no means secure. He commanded 1,600 soldiers yet did not have provision for them beyond six days. The mayor of Hull had already sent him £240 and he owed that town £300 more for 'victualls and amunicon'. For the present, Whitby was also providing him with supplies. However, he continued, after nearly three years of war, Yorkshire had been 'exhausted, both in monieyes and provisions', first by the King's army and of late by Parliament's, so that he had no hope of raising enough of his needs locally. If he did not soon receive money and supplies he would be forced to abandon the siege and leave Scarborough 'as a Receptacle for the Enemyes of the Kingdome, and an obstruccon to the Northerne Trade'. Meldrum therefore appealed to their 'perticuler interests' in their 'Comon Trade', and asked them to send money or 'victualls and powder' raised by voluntary collection. In a postscript Meldrum added that he was sending Richard Dighton to carry the letter and 'to fallicite the suddeine dispatch' of their gifts.[55]

A second letter from Meldrum at the end of April also to Ipswich revealed that in the meantime King's Lynn had sent him £391 12s. 10d. in provisions, Yarmouth, £234 10s. in ready money, and Ipswich had collected, but not yet delivered, £140. Even so, Sir John was still far from certain that all his needs could be satisfied. Unless his troops soon received a month's back pay, which they were promised when they captured the town, he could not expect them to storm the castle.[56] In the event, Meldrum died before Ipswich's money reached him via Hull, but his correspondence with the East coast ports and their generous response to his requests for help give further proof of the high value placed on Scarborough port at this time.[57]

On the other side, royalists went on believing, against the odds and the facts, that Scarborough might be retaken or the defenders of the castle rescued by help from the continent. Writing to Lord Digby, the King's secretary of state, Lord Jermyn, with the Queen at Paris, explained that she now placed her faith in aid from the King of Denmark: 'If he could be prevailed on to give us an army, its descent on Scarbrough or Burlington [Bridlington] would give a new turn to all'.[58] Jermyn did not know that Sir Hugh Cholmley had surrendered Scarborough castle the day before he wrote these wishful words; yet even after the loss of the castle was known everywhere, the Yorkshire coast was still thought by both sides to be the most suitable point of entry for royalist agents and arms. As late as 9 August, Lord Digby implored Jermyn, 'For God's sake hasten gunpowder and match in plenty to the northern coast, and what muskets and pistols you can, but ammunition in the first place; let these be directed to Burlington or Whitby, for Scarborough is lost.'[59] Lord Digby was at Bridgnorth when he wrote this letter, but his ignorance of the true situation 150 miles away on the Yorkshire coast was still inexcusable for one so highly positioned in the King's counsels. Nevertheless, Digby's ill-informed desperation was not untypical of royalist reaction to defeat in an area of such prime importance to both sides in the Civil War. On the other hand, there is some evidence that royalist agents, though not royalist arms, were coming ashore at Bridlington, if not Scarborough, as late as the summer of 1646. An unsigned letter from Newcastle to Scarborough's bailiffs warned them to 'examine strictly what persons land at your port from foraine parts', and added that 'some persons of noate' had recently come ashore at Bridlington and 'passed away without interuption'.[60]

Scarborough's potential value to its enemies was not lost on Parliament. Though some of Meldrum's Scots were drawn away to Cheshire during the stalemate that followed the fall of the town,

THE GREAT SIEGE, 1645

London soon came to realise that of all the sieges then taking place in Yorkshire, principally at Pontefract, Sandal and Skipton, that of Scarborough castle ought to be given the highest priority. As a result, on 1 May 1645, Lord Fairfax was ordered by the Committee of Both Kingdoms 'to send a sufficient force to take in Scarborough'. As the Committee explained in a covering note, a copy of which also went to Meldrum:

> ... Scarborough Castle is not so effectively besieged as were necessary for the carrying of a place of so great concernment to the public. All the ports on the east and south sides of the kingdom from Berwick to Topsham [near Exeter], with the sole exception of Scarborough, are already in the power of Parliament. If this also could be taken there would be no place left along all the coast for the enemy to retire unto and from whence they may be able to interrupt and hinder the whole trade of the coast wherein the City is deeply concerned. We consider the taking in of that Castle to be of greater consequence than any inland fort whatsoever can be, and therefore especially recommend to you that the siege may be carried on with effect. Send thither what foot forces you can spare, as they could nowhere be employed to greater advantage.[61]

The London and Oxford presses showed the same keen interest in events at Scarborough during the spring and summer of 1645. However, because their reports were written at second-hand and at some distance, they lacked knowledge and understanding of what was actually happening there. For example, in its account of the capture of Scarborough town, Parliament's *Perfect Occurrences* tried lamely to explain the location of the castle to its readers in the capital: 'The Castle stands in Scarborough upon the Sea, as the tower of London stands in London upon the Thames . . . but something more butting into the water, standing as a point into the sea'.[62]

At least *Perfect Occurrences* made an effort to inform its readers about a remote place few of them, if any, might have visited; the other London news-sheets never even made the attempt to describe the topography of Scarborough. None of them seem to have discovered that the variously named 'fort', 'battery' or even 'sconce' overlooking

Scarborough harbour was in fact called South Steel battery. As late as 13 May, when the siege was nearly three months old, *Perfect Passages*, one of the principal sources of news from the North, was still referring to the 'Bishops Fort' when it meant Bushell's battery.[63]

If Parliament's reporters exposed their ignorance and confusion, on the other side the royalist *Mercurius Aulicus* actually invented its propaganda about events in Scarborough. On 8 March it declared boldly that Meldrum had been ordered to break off the siege of the castle and was then marching away 'with bagge and baggage to patch up with Lord Fairfax'.[64]

A month later, without explaining why or when Meldrum had returned to Scarborough, it reported that he had died of wounds there![65] This was a message Mark Twain would have appreciated though not Sir John Meldrum. It was left to *Mercurius Rusticus*, which listed 'the Murthers, Robberies, Plunderings and other outrages committed by the Rebells on His Majesties faithfull subjects', to announce that Meldrum had died on 11 May.[66]

Unfortunately, Scarborough's local historians, in particular, Schofield, Hinderwell and Baker, relied too heavily and exclusively on these contemporary but unsatisfactory news reports and consequently their accounts of the siege are incomplete and sometimes misleading. None of them made use, or were aware, of the existence of Sir Hugh's 'Memorialls Tuching Scarbrough' which he had written in 1647. Cholmley was then an exile living in Rouen when he received from Sir Edward Hyde, the future Earl of Clarendon, a request to provide him with information about the civil war in Yorkshire. Hyde knew very little about events in the north of England, but he was aware of the key and courageous part that Sir Hugh had played in them, and he was anxious to construct a royalist version of what had happened. Since Cholmley was also concerned to put the record straight and thereby vindicate his own conduct and that of his friends who had also changed sides, he was happy to oblige. As a result he wrote three papers for Hyde to include in what he later called his *History of the Rebellion and Civil Wars in England*. One paper related the tragic story of the Hothams; another described and attempted to analyse the disaster on Marston Moor; and the third recounted Sir Hugh's own experiences in Scarborough from his arrival there in September 1642 until his surrender and departure in July 1645. The first two were brief, mostly second-hand pieces; 'Memorialls Tuching Scarbrough', however, was lengthy, personal, graphic and uniquely informative.[67]

When his *History* was finally published posthumously in 1702–4 it was clear that Clarendon had made small use of Cholmley's work. After acknowledging that Scarborough castle was 'a place of great importance to the King', and that Sir Hugh had discharged his royal commission there 'with courage and singular fidelity', the earl had nothing more to say about either after March 1643.[68] Moreover, when some of Clarendon's rich manuscript sources were published in the 1770s, the paper on the Hothams alone was judged worthy of print; at the end of it the editors noted: 'It is accompanied by "Memorials touching the Battle of York and the siege of Scarborough" too immaterial to be published'![69]

When James Schofield, the Scarborough bookseller, wrote the resort's first *Historical and Descriptive Guide* in 1787, he knew that Cholmley had kept 'an exact journal of the siege' in his own hand. He also knew, however, that, 'with a view to gratify the curious public', a descendant of his, Nathaniel Cholmley, had taken the manuscript with him to London to have it published there. That was in 1751. Unfortunately, before the manuscript could be converted into print it was 'entirely consumed' by 'a great fire' which occurred in Nathaniel's 'inn'. Schofield's story of the destruction of Cholmley's 'Memorialls Tuching Scarbrough' was slightly garbled but essentially correct. What he did not know was that a fair copy of Sir Hugh's holograph was then sitting in the Bodleian Library at Oxford amongst Clarendon's papers.[70]

What Schofield did not know, neither Hinderwell nor Baker his successors ever discovered. They accepted Schofield's sad story of an all-consuming fire and assumed that the only surviving work of Sir Hugh was his memoirs, which had been written at the end of his life in 1656–7.[71] Since Cholmley had already written an account of his part in the Civil War ten years earlier, when he reached this point in his life he noted:

> . . . how I deported myselfe in these imploym[en]t[s] & when how & for what causes I quit it & the Parla[men]t, I shall forbeare to speake now but referre the Reader to the Account I have given booth of that & the seage of Scarbrough together, in w[hic]h it will appeare

I did not forsake them/Parla[men]t till they did faile in performeing those perticulers they made the ground of the warre when I was first ingaidged vidz. the preservation of Relegion, protection of the Kings person, and liberties of the subiect . . .[72]

Consequently, when Nathaniel Cholmley published Sir Hugh's *Memoirs* in a very limited edition in 1787, the same year as Schofield's *Guide*, they conveyed nothing of what had occurred in Scarborough between 1642 and 1645.[73]

Even after Sir Charles Firth had recognised their value and had Cholmley's 'Memorialls Tuching Scarbrough' printed in 1917 in the *English Historical Review*, they remained widely unknown and rarely exploited.[74] Professor A. J. Grant, who wrote a chapter in Rowntree's *History of Scarborough*, published in 1931, was the first and the last historian to quote extensively from Sir Hugh's 'Memorialls', and even he failed to explain his source or refer to it in footnotes. Furthermore, Grant's account of the siege at Scarborough in 1645 was seriously weakened by his failure to consult either the contemporary newspaper literature or the corporation records. Apart from the 'Memorialls', he drew his evidence only from official state papers.[75]

The siege of Scarborough castle lasted twenty-two weeks, from 18 February to 25 July 1645. Other Civil-War 'leaguers' lasted longer, but they were usually little more than prolonged blockades, punctuated by outbursts of bloodshed. At Scarborough, it was different: there were no truces and no cease-fires. As in 1914–18 trench warfare, the fighting was almost continuous and always destructive. Losses on both sides, in men and materials were heavy. Until the final surrender, no quarter was asked for and none given.

According to Cholmley's 'Memorialls', after he had rejected Meldrum's summons to surrender, the veteran Scot tried to undermine the loyalty and resolution of the garrison's officers by writing letters to them; but again he failed. Then he shot messages attached to arrows into the castle yard offering generous conditions of treatment to the common soldiers, but these had no more success. After the first three of four days, when as many as forty of Cholmley's soldiers ran away, there were no more desertions to reduce his strength.[76]

Once Parliament's ordnance from the magazines at Hull and York began to arrive in Scarborough, Meldrum was busy determining gun positions around the castle perimeter. On Monday 24 March, as he was giving directions on the sea cliff, probably at South Steel battery, a strong gust of wind blew him clean off the rock. Meldrum was severly bruised by the fall but not mortally injured. Such was the bald and brief account given by Parliament's *Perfect Diurnall*. Presumably, this dramatic event was also the basis on which *Mercurius Aulicus* alleged that Sir John had died of wounds.[77] Neither Parliament nor royalist versions compare favourably with Sir Hugh's own vivid and colloquial description of Meldrum's accident:

> Beeing to plant these ordnance neere to the sea cliff for more advantage to batter, Meldrum there in person giving directions about them, his hatt blowes of his head, and hee catching to save that, the winde beeing verie great blowes his cloake over his face, and hee falls over the cliff amongst the rockes and stones att least steeple height; itt was a miracle his braines were not beaten out and all his bones broaken, but itt seemed the winde together with the cloke did in some sorte beare him up, and lessen the fall; yet hee is taken up for dead, lyes 3 dayes speachless, his head opened and the bruised blood taken out, though a man above threescore yeare old, recovered this soe perfectlie that with in six weekes hee is on foote againe, and beginns to batter the Castle.[78]

Sir Hugh was never one to sit and wait for the enemy to take the initiative. Sensing that something was wrong with Meldrum, but at the time not knowing exactly what had happened to him, he sent out Captain Wickham with fifty men to make a surprise attack on the Scots manning South Steel battery. Though it was midday the Scotsmen were taken off guard. Many jumped off the rock into the sea, 'whoe thincking thereby to esscaipe fire died by water'. Wickham returned triumphantly. He had left a hundred dead and wounded and taken as many as twenty prisoners. It was from these prisoners that Cholmley learned the details of Meldrum's recent misfortune.[79]

Meldrum's fall might have killed many younger men but within six weeks he led an allout assault on the castle. The cannon-royal inside St Mary's chancel directed its fire through the east window at

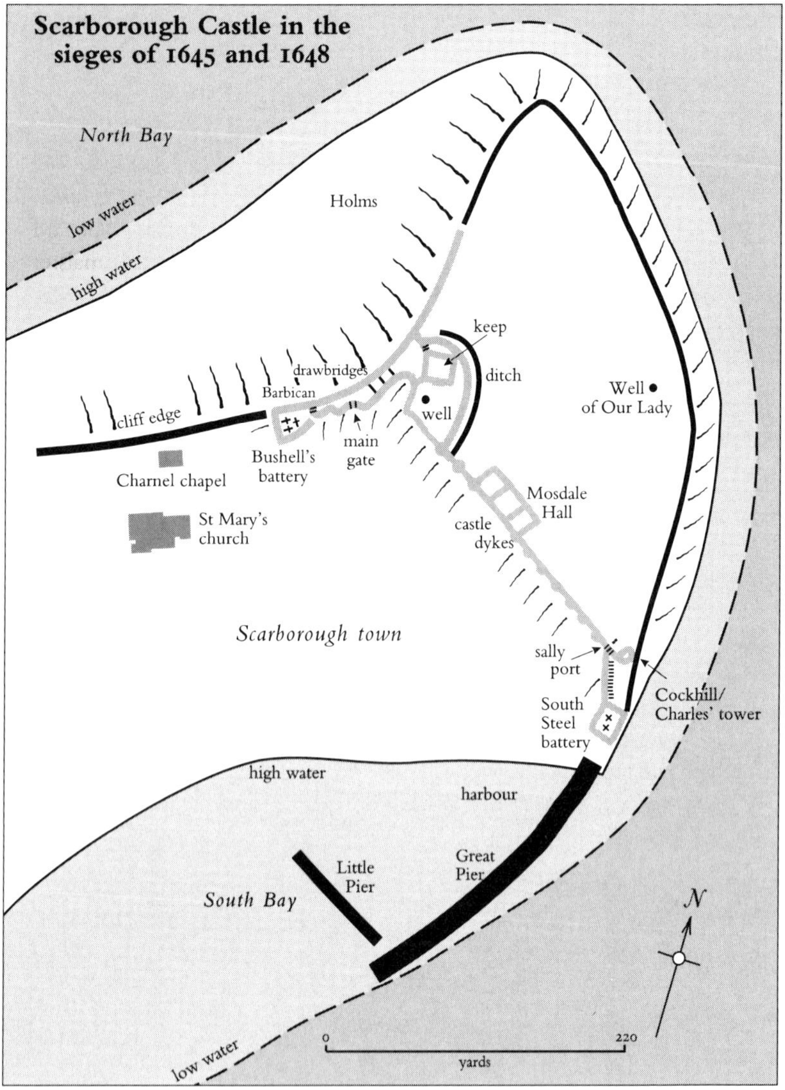
Scarborough Castle in the sieges of 1645 and 1648
North Bay
low water
high water
Holms
keep
ditch
drawbridges
Barbican
cliff edge
well
Well
of Our Lady
main
gate
Bushell's
battery
Charnel chapel
Mosdale
Hall
St Mary's
church
castle
dykes
Scarborough town
sally
port
South
Steel
battery
Cockhill/
Charles' tower
high water
harbour
Great
Pier
Little
Pier
South Bay
N
low water
0
220
yards

the great Angevin keep. Time and time again its 65-pound shot hit the masonry of the west wall less than two hundred yards away. Though above its deep battering plinth this west wall was fifteen-feet thick and contained a central newel stairway and mural chambers, after three days of continual pounding it suddenly collapsed. Again the only detailed description of this event is to be found in Cholmley's 'Memorialls':

> . . . in 3 dayes the great Tower splitt in two, and that side which was battered falls to the ground, the other standing firme beeing supported by an arch of stone that went through the midst; there were neere 20 personns upon the topp of the tower when itt cleft, yett all gott into the standing parte, except 2 of Captaine Richard Ledgard's servants which were in the turrett where there maister lodged . . . The fall of the Tower was a verry terrible spectacle . . .[80]

The collapse of the keep was indeed so spectacular and unexpected that both sides were stunned by it. After a moment of silence the attackers shouted in triumph and the dismayed defenders prepared for the expected infantry assault. But Meldrum was now so confident of victory that instead of overrunning the barbican, which was temporarily cut off from the main body of the castle by heaps of rubble, he sent Sir Hugh another peremptory demand for his surrender. If Cholmley should again refuse it, Meldrum promised that no one person in the castle would have quarter.[81]

While Meldrum waited for a reply, Cholmley's men were breaking through the debris of the fallen keep to reinforce the gatehouse and barbican beyond it. When three hours later, at nine in the evening, Meldrum realised his mistake and ordered an infantry attack, it was too late. Though Bushell's battery was taken at the first charge, none of the outer walls was breached or scaled. The west wall of the keep had been one hundred feet high with corner turrets and up to fifteen feet thick and it had collapsed outwards and downwards on to the narrow approach road below. The defenders now had a huge arsenal of ready-made missiles. As Cholmley explained: 'the stones of the falne Tower were throwne freelie amongst them and did the greatest execution'. In this encounter alone, Sir Hugh reckoned that his men killed or wounded two hundred of the attackers.[82] Later, even after the gatehouse beyond the drawbridge was lost to the Roundheads, the road up to the castle yard was 'so barracadoed' with masonry rubble from the keep that attackers could not break through it and the besieged were unable to come out, even to surrender. To allow the defenders to pass out of the castle a passage had to be cut through the curtain wall into the dykes.[83]

The three-storey tower was no longer habitable. The governor,

The western wall of the Keep destroyed by cannon fire in May 1645.

Lady Elizabeth and 'most of the gentlemen and officers of quality . . . were forced to betake themselves to poore Cabbins raised against the walls and banckes in the Castle yeard'. Nevertheless, this was only a minor inconvenience in summer time compared with the fortuitous bonus to the castle's defences. The mountain of debris from the west wall of the keep provided both cover and ammunition for the defenders throughout the remainder of the siege.[84]

At this point the reports of the London news-sheets become more than usually confused about both time and place. However, it seems that Meldrum now directed a furious cannonade at the barbican and gatehouse. The royalists had no answer to Parliament's heavier artillery, which soon levelled the walls and brought down the towers, and were obliged to retreat back across the bridges to the debris of the keep.[85] This allowed Meldrum to bring up two demi-cannon, each firing 34-pound balls, on to Bushell's battery and from there bombard the exposed castle yard. Cholmley's reply was an infantry counter-attack. With sixty picked men, Major Crompton, one of his most senior and experienced officers, led a desperate sally against the battery. According to the 'Memorialls', the operation was a brilliant success. The Roundheads ran from their earthworks and abandoned their guns. The two demi-cannon were dismounted and their carriages smashed.[86]

Even Parliament's one-sided reporters had to concede the success of Crompton's ferocious sortie which occurred on the night of Saturday, 10 May.[87] The high proportion of officers killed and wounded on Parliament's side suggests that Sir Hugh was probably not exaggerating much when he claimed that Meldrum's soldiers took flight and had to be rallied by their leaders. 'Crompton had soe maulled and frighted those upon the guard as the rest with in the towne were readie to run away, probable if itt had beene a little darker they had donn soe, and as itt was the officers had much to doe to keepe the soldiors together'.[88] *A Perfect Diurnall* and *Mercurius Civicus* put the courage of Crompton's men down to their drunkenness.[89] *Perfect Passages* said that 'the pangs of death' were upon the royalists and they were 'desperately mad', as well as drunk.[90]

Cholmley now ordered Crompton to fall back from his forward position. The battle that took place the next day, Sunday, 11 May, was the bloodiest of the whole siege. For several hours the two sides fought in and for the ruins of the barbican. As usual, Meldrum was in the thick of it. Casualties on both sides were heavy. There was savage hand-to-hand fighting in the rubble while musket and cannon-fire rained down from opposite sides. No mercy was shown.

According to *Perfect Passages*, after he had killed Lieutenant John Gower, one of the king's officers, Lieutenant-Colonel Stanley, himself wounded in the thigh, was taken by the royalists when his sword had broken. Inside the castle Stanley was 'basely slaine by a Blackamore' who stabbed him to the heart. After the battle, their corpses were exchanged. Besides Colonel Stanley, Parliament lost Colonel Cockerman, 'one that Sir John Meldrum loved dearly', Major Dent, Captain Pearcie, and perhaps as many as fifty more dead. In addition to Lieutenant John Gower, Cholmley lost half a dozen junior officers and perhaps a dozen soldiers. Parliamentary reports of the death of John's brother, Sir Thomas Gower, were untrue.[91]

Though the two sides differed about the number of casualties they had inflicted and received, both announced that Sir John Meldrum himself had been severely wounded in the close fighting. In what Sir Hugh described euphemistically as a 'scuffle', the old General had taken a musket ball 'in att the bellie and out of the backe'.[92] Naturally, the London news-sheets offered an optimistic prognosis. *A Perfect Diurnall* said that the wound was definitely 'not mortall'.[93] *Mercurius Civicus* reported that the valiant knight had received only 'a brush neere his belly with a bullet, a shot in the thigh, and another flech wound with a sword, but his hurts [were] not mortall'![94] *Perfect Occurrences* assured its readers that 'none of his guts [was] touched'.[95]

The attackers might have re-taken the barbican, gatehouse and perhaps even the bridges over the castle dykes, but their casualties were much heavier than those suffered by Cholmley's men. The death of Meldrum a few days later was a terrible blow to the strength and the morale of the besiegers, which the London press failed to conceal. Even before the news of Meldrum's death reached the capital, *The Moderate Intelligencer* suggested that perhaps it might now be better to starve rather than storm a garrison of '300 souldiers and well nigh 100 officers', who were 'stout and resolute' and had a 'great store of Corn and wine within'.[96] Several of Parliament's newspapers admitted that it had been necessary to summon reinforcements to Scarborough from York.[97] *Mercurius Veridicus* took an uncharacteristically pessimistic line. The garrison, it pointed out, had enough ammunition as well as bread and wine; they lacked only water and fresh meat. Should they run out of shot, they still had penty of stones to annoy and hurt the besiegers.[98]

It is clear that the death of Meldrum, who had been a brave example and an inspiration to all around him, changed the character of the siege from infantry assault and counter-assault to attrition. Cholmley had to concede that Sir John had been a formidable opponent: 'hee [Meldrum] had often both in woords and letters protested hee would either take the Castle or lay his bones before itt, and though he dyed with in six dayes of this wound, hee before had esscaiped verie great dangers, for beside that of his fall hee had beene shott through the codds and perfectlie recovered'.[99] The 'bones' of the old and gallant knight were in fact carried from Scarborough to Hull, where they were given 'honourable interrement' in the parish church.[100]

After Meldrum's death the siege of the castle lasted another ten weeks.[101] Sir Matthew Boynton, Meldrum's replacement, tried no more direct infantry attacks: instead, the castle was now closely and continuously harassed by cannon fire, both from land and sea. Vice-Admiral Zachary's warships drew so near to the headland shore that it became too hazardous for Cholmley's men to fetch water from the springs at the base of the cliff. Even the Well of Our Lady, on the top of the sea cliff, was brought under fire. The castle was completely sealed off from the outside world. Boynton put up a new battery on the north side of Peasholm Gap to prevent any approach or escape by way of North Bay. The besieged had no hope of relief from any direction. Perhaps even worse they had no news of what was happening elsewhere, except by way of their besiegers.[102] Both Oxford and London seemed to have lost interest in Scarborough. As *Mercurius Veridicus* reported towards the end of June, 'little is said of Scarbrough but onely that it is besieged, the Enemy not makeing many sallyes forth, nor the besiegers any late attempts'.[103]

The complete silence of the royalist press and the general indifference of Parliament's news-sheets mean that we are almost totally dependent on Sir Hugh's 'Memorialls' for an account of the second half and conclusion of the castle siege. Fortunately, Cholmley provided his readers with a lengthy and vivid description of the last days and also explained why the royalist surrender came so abruptly and unexpectedly on 25 July 1645. Without any previous warning, *Mercurius Civicus* announced that on Tuesday, 22 July, there was 'a confident report of the surrender of Scarborough castle to Colonel Boynton'.[104] A day later, *The Scottish Dove* confirmed this news from Scarborough and, by way of explanation, added briefly that the royalist garrison was 'sick of the scurvie . . . and manie of Cholmley's officers are dead of it, himselfe sick'. Sir Henry Cholmley, who had just received the surrender of Pontefract castle, was said to be on his way to Scarborough to treat with his brother.[105] Further references in the London papers related no more than a summary of the terms of Scarborough's surrender and the stock of arms taken by Boynton.[106]

In marked contrast to these laconic reports from Parliament's press, Sir Hugh's own account of his capitulation ran to nearly three pages. Naturally, he was anxious to justify his conduct so that some allowance has to be made for his exaggeration of the plight of the garrison. The reader is meant to believe that the castle had indeed been held 'to the last extremity', as King Charles had requested.[107] Cholmley denied that news of the royalist defeat at Naseby on 14 June had undermined the morale of his men. When the Roundheads outside the castle celebrated their victory with bonfires, cannon fire and 'huge acclamations of joy', those inside replied with trumpets, drums and muskets, and 'such cryes and hollowing as they caused the enemie to decist from there jolletie'. After that the garrison held out for another six (not eight, as Cholmley wrote) weeks in the hope of relief, or at least better news. Since they had no means of knowing 'how affaires went with the King', they were reluctant to accept the decision at Naseby.[108]

Cholmley gave three main reasons why he and his officers finally agreed to accept Boynton's terms. For once, *The Scottish Dove* was right: of the many miseries endured by the besieged, the worst was scurvy. As Sir Hugh himself put it: '. . . halfe of the soldiers were either slaine or dead of the scurvy, of which disease neare the other halfe laid soe miserable handled they were scarce able to stirr hand or foot . . . there dyed tenn in a night, and manie layed two dayes unburied for want of helpe to carrie them to the grave'.[109] Only about sixty defenders, mostly officers, were fit enough to walk out of the castle unaided; most of the remaining 180 survivors had to be carried over and through the rubble in blankets, and some of them died before they reached the town.[110] So, by Cholmley's reckoning, of the five hundred who had taken refuge in the castle in mid-February, five months later fewer than half of them came out of it alive.

Some confirmation of the toll of scurvy came from two of Parliament's news-sheets. Quoting an unsigned letter from Hull, dated Saturday, 26 July, the day after the surrender took place, *An Exact Relation* declared that 'scurvey [had] made such a mortality among the souldiers . . . that Sir Hugh hastened to make conditions'.[111] *Parliament's Post*, one of the more reliable sources, reported that Cholmley had gone to Newark or Holland and had left behind in Scarborough '100 sicke of the scurvy'.[112] Finally, when Dr William Simpson came to write his glowing tribute to Scarborough spa water more than thirty years later, he related what must have become by then a part of the town's folklore. In Simpson's words, when many of 'the Garrison which was kept by Sir Hugh Chomly in the Castle were fallen into scurvy', they were 'perfectly and speedily cured' by drinking the local spring water.[113]

Another 'miserie' of the beleaguered royalists, according to Cholmley, was lack of water. Scarborough castle had two wells: a very deep one in the inner bailey near the keep, which by 1645 had already failed, and a shallow Well of Our Lady, near the edge of the sea cliff. The latter was barely adequate in winter and by July must have been almost dry. At first, the garrison had taken water from the springs at the foot of the sea cliff, 'though with much paines, difficulty and perrill'. However, as the enemy's cannon-fire intensified and the defenders grew weaker, this supply became increasingly inaccessible. There was barely sufficient drinking water for the men and women and none at all to spare for the animals so that 'manie horses had beene with out water for seaven dayes together, which occasioned contagion amongst them alsoe'. Grain was still plentiful, but there was no one strong enough 'to make the mills goe' and grind it into flour. To get himself bread Cholmley had 'often in person turned the mills'. By the time of the surrender, 'most in the Garrison had not eaten a bitt of bread for divers dayes'. Those who suffered severely from scurvy and thirst would not have been able to eat the bread had it been available.[114]

A 'reign' of scurvy, 'which grew to be as contagious as the plague', and 'a want of water' would have been quite enough to justify surrender. The men were so sick and weakened by hunger, disease and thirst that there were not sufficient to stand guard on the walls and cliffs. As Sir Hugh expressed it: 'in lieu of guards there were not persons with in the walls able to stand sentynells, and in a weeke longer probable there would scarce have been one able to looke over the walls'. Only twenty-five of the common soldiers were fit for duty and the officers who 'were glad to undertake it in there roome were almost tierd out of there skinns'.[115]

The presence of scurvy and the shortage of water in the besieged castle are both corroborated by sources other than the 'Memorialls'. For example, as early as 14 May, one London newspaper claimed, perhaps rather prematurely: 'All supplies of water are stopt from Scarborough [castle] except a well which is called our Ladyes well that affords but little'.[116] On the other hand, Cholmley's third 'miserie', 'want of poother [powder]', is challenged by some Parliamentary reports.

More than once in his account Cholmley referred to his shortage of gunpowder; clearly, he considered it a serious handicap to the defenders. After the death of Meldrum, 'the want of poother' meant that the royalists could not make use of their cannon and this allowed 'the enemy to make there approaches verie neare'.[117] Without fear of retaliation from the castle, Zachary was able to bring his ships close into the headland and thereby cut off the garrison's water supply from under the sea cliff. By the time of the surrender, Sir Hugh claimed that he had only half a barrel of gunpowder left and that during the previous eight weeks he had used only one and a half barrels.[118]

However, when Major-General Poyntz, governor of York and Parliament's commander in the North, sent his report of the fall of

Scarborough castle to London, it stated that Colonel Boynton had taken five brass and thirty iron pieces of artillery, a thousand small arms, and 'a great quantitie of Powder, Match, Bullets, and other Ammunition'.[119] This official list was soon repeated, word for word, in several London news-sheets, such as *An Exact Journal* and *Mercurius Civicus*.[120] On the other hand, almost simultaneously, two other Parliamentary sources, usually less partisan and therefore more trustworthy, *The Weekly Account* and *Parliament's Post*, reduced the number of cannon captured at Scarborough to twenty-five and referred only to arms and ammunition, not specifically to powder.[121]

In all probability, Poyntz was merely parroting a conventional formula and Cholmley, as usual, was exaggerating his predicament to justify his conduct. All that can be said for certain is that if the garrison was really as desperate for gunpowder in June and July as Sir Hugh wrote then the siege might have ended six weeks earlier. Had Boynton mounted an allout infantry assault the castle would have been overrun. Meldrum would not have been so cautious and patient.

Finally, Cholmley and his officers conceded defeat because they were offered terms too generous to refuse. *Mercurius Britanicus* was sure that Sir Hugh would not be permitted to go free and leave the country: 'Treachery hath shackled him to another destiny in England', it declared.[122] *The Scottish Dove* did not disguise its displeasure when it heard of Cholmley's escape to Holland; it would have much preferred him to 'cut a caper on an English tree' and to be 'drawn on an English oak rather than a Low Country waggon'.[123]

Why Parliament's Northern Committee granted such easy conditions to Cholmley is not clear, particularly in the light of what he subsequently admitted in the 'Memorialls'. Perhaps there was an unfounded fear of a royalist rescue by sea; probably there were pressures from London to settle the matter quickly, since possession of the castle far outweighed the fate of its garrison. Certainly, Parliament overestimated Cholmley's powers of resistance. The bloodbath in the barbican on 10 and 11 May, and the demise of the 'indestructible' Meldrum, gave the castle's defenders a terrible notoriety. Parliament seemed unwilling to risk another repulse. Boynton was allowed to wait for a surrender and not ordered to force one by storm. Also, and not for the first time, Cholmley bluffed his enemies. He asked for even better terms to give the false impression that he was negotiating from a strength he did not in fact possess.[124] Given Cholmley's record and in the circumstances of the surrender, the royalists were treated very charitably.

What further concessions could have been made to Cholmley are hard to imagine. The articles were agreed and signed on 22 July, Sir Hugh's forty-fifth birthday, but the garrison was given until midday on the 25th to begin evacuation. Article 3 allowed Sir Hugh and all his officers and men to go peacefully to the nearest royalist garrison at Newark or to Holland by sea from Scarborough, Bridlington or Hull. Article 4 protected all the inmates of the castle from interference, theft or intimidation. Article 5 permitted Lady Elizabeth to return to the Cholmley home, Abbey House at Whitby, to 'enjoy such of [the] estate as is allowed by ordinance of Parliament'. After what he had done to betray Parliament in March 1643, and in consideration of all the trouble, cost and casualties he had caused Parliament since then, Sir Hugh could hardly expect his property to be exempted from sequestration. He was lucky to avoid the fate of the two Hothams. In Parliament's eyes, all three were traitors. If Meldrum had lived to dictate terms to Cholmley, they would have been harsher. In the event, Sir Hugh's fellow Yorkshiremen, Sir Matthew Boynton, Colonel Francis Lascelles and Colonel Simon Needham, not only conceded magnanimous conditions, afterwards they made sure that they, in Cholmley's words, 'were verie justlie observed'.[125]

Accordingly, at noon on Friday, 25 July 1645, the siege of Scarborough castle came to an end. The main gateway was so blocked with rubble and the debris of battle that a new exit had to be cut through the curtain wall into the dykes to allow the defenders to be brought out. Sir Hugh was the last to emerge. According to some of the London news-sheets, a hundred of Cholmley's men 'came into Parliament', but these were probably the sick and wounded who were not fit to travel and had to be carried down into the town.[126] A more reliable report was that a hundred and sixty men and women had gone to Newark with Sir Hugh.[127]

Cholmley himself put no figure on the size of the sad company that followed him on the road to Selby the next day. At Selby, however, he changed his mind. He had intended to join the royalists holding out at Newark, but he was now told that the King was in the remotest part of Wales, a Scottish army blocked the way there, and he felt too weak to continue the journey. From Selby, Colonel Crosland led the dispirited group on to Newark, while Sir Hugh and his faithful aide Major Crompton turned back to Bridlington. From there they soon took a ship to Holland.[128] Cholmley was ruined and practically penniless. When he came out of the castle his brother Henry was there to lend him £200, but he had distributed this 'amongst the officers and souldiours to relieve their necessityes'. When they parted, Lady Elizabeth had 'not a bove £10 in her purse', and after he had paid for his sea passage he had only £10 of his own left.[129]

At Selby, Cholmley had decided that he had done as much for the King as anyone had the right to expect; his first duty now was to his own family. His eldest son and heir, William, was twenty years old and living as an exile in Italy. When Sir Hugh moved on from Holland to Paris he learned there that William's state was desperate: unless he soon received money he would be 'forced to turne souldier & traile a picke in Catelonia for his subustance'. Had he stayed in England, Cholmley believed that his 'poore boy' would have been put to great danger and hardship.[130] As for his younger son, Hugh, he had been left behind as a boarder at St Paul's school in London when his mother came north in 1643. Though he had not suffered ill-treatment from his father's enemies, Sir Hugh was naturally concerned for his welfare.[131] Finally, there were the two girls, Ann and Elizabeth, who were already in Holland with the Remmington family. It took Sir Hugh another two years to rescue and re-unite his whole family at Rouen in France.[132]

Lady Cholmley had stayed with her husband throughout the siege. According to Sir Hugh's memoirs which were intended as a tribute to her, she would not forsake him for any danger, and 'though by nature according to her sex tymerous', she 'indured much hardshippe & yet with little shew of troble'. When the keep collapsed she was forced to live in a little cabin on the ground for several months. Sir Hugh was convinced that this had caused 'a defluction of rume upon one of her eies which trobled her ever after'. Also, in his opinion, she never quite recovered from 'a tuch of the scurvie then riffe in the Castle'. Nevertheless, despite these hardships and illnesses, she would not be daunted and 'shewd a courridge even above her sex'.

When one of her maids tried to desert and was returned to the castle by the besiegers, Lady Cholmley accepted her back because there were 'not persons in health to attend the sicke'.[133]

Article 5 had allowed Lady Cholmley to go back to her Whitby home and re-possess it, but that was easier to write than do. Abbey House was occupied by one of Parliament's captains who had no desire to quit such spacious and comfortable quarters. So Elizabeth was obliged to lodge with Christopher Percehay, one of her husband's friends, who lived at Ryton, north of Malton. However, as soon as she heard that the captain had abandoned her house when his servant had died there of the plague, regardless of the risks, she resolved to reclaim her property. Though it was mid-winter and the way was deep in snow, with only a maidservant and a male cook as companions, she travelled the thirty miles home over vale and high moor. Abbey House had been ransacked and she spent a very cold, miserable time there – the saddest and worst of her life – but, in the words of her admiring husband, ' her sperret would not submit to make complaint & application to the Parliament's Committee at Yorke, as most others did . . .'[134]

Apart from disappointment at Cholmley's escape into exile, the news of Scarborough castle's surrender was received in London with delight and relief. The House of Commons declared 22 August would be a day of thanksgiving for 'the gaining of the towns of Bath and Bridgwater, and of Scarborough Castle, and Sherborne Castle, and for the dispersing of the Clubmen, and the good success in Pembrokeshire'.[135] Scarborough was no longer head of the list of Parliament's concerns, though to both sides it was still a place of some importance.

If one Parliamentary account is to be believed, Sir Hugh needed physical protection when he came last out of the castle ruins: in the words of *An Exact Relation*: 'The women of Scarborough could hardly be kept from stoning of Sir Hugh Cholmley'.[136] Though there is no need to take seriously the report of *Mercurius Civicus* that 'the women in the castle' could scarcely be restrained from assaulting him, the women of the town certainly had sufficient reason for revenge.[137] The damage to Scarborough town had indeed been colossal, and by refusing to yield the castle for the past five months Cholmley had inflicted severe hardship on the townspeople.

That there are no Common Hall records at all for the period 25 November 1644 to 19 August 1645 indicates that, even before the close siege of the town had begun, its normal government had broken down. Then, from the day Meldrum's men stormed Scarborough in the middle of February until the election of a new corporation at the end of September, the town was effectively under martial law.

Scarborough's parish church of St Mary's, one of the country's finest and largest, was now an utter ruin: its chancel, north transept and north aisle were windowless and roofless; its two western towers were shattered; and the great central tower over the crossing had been so undermined by direct hit and vibration that it collapsed entirely in 1659. Despite a national appeal in 1660, much of old St Mary's was never restored: it remained truncated and towerless.

Meldrum had used the church as an artillery platform, an observation post and a forward redoubt, yet surprisingly the Restoration church brief of December 1660 seemed to place the blame for the destruction of St Mary's on Cholmley's royalist cannon:

> . . . That in one day there were three-score pieces of ordnance discharged against the steeple of the upper church, there called St Maries, and the Quire thereof beaten down, and the steeple thereof so shaken, that notwithstanding the endeavours of the Inhabitants to repair the same, the Steeple and Bells upon the tenth day of October last [1659] fell and brought down with it most part of the body of the same Church.[138]

This version of how St Mary's was devastated by cannon-fire from the castle is still the widely accepted explanation;[139] but an alternative view, provided by Sir Hugh in his 'Memorialls', makes much more sense. The castle was so high above and so close to the parish church that the royalist gunners could not depress their cannon far enough to hit more than its upper parts, in particular its three towers. As Cholmley subsequently wrote: '. . . though the Castle could make shotts into the Church and the workes about itt, yett they laid soe lowe the execution was not much, nor the prejudice answerable to the expence of powder'.[140] In other words, Sir Hugh had no more scruples about bombarding a church than Meldrum had in using it as a fortification and battery; in this case St Mary's was not a worthwhile target. Neither side showed any respect for the building and its contents, but the responsibility for causing the greatest structural damage was probably Meldrum's three-and-a-half-ton cannon-royal planted at the east end of the chancel and firing repeatedly through its windows.

As for the interior fittings and furniture of St Mary's, they too had been carried away or destroyed beyond repair. A year after the siege ended the assessment on Scarborough and Falsgrave to pay for 'repair of the roofe, leads, windowes, and sole trees laid for the pewes' was put at £110, of which Falsgrave was to find £10. When these repairs had been accomplished 'then every p[ar]ticular man' was to build his own pew at his own expense. To save the town some of the cost, the timber frame at the east end of St Mary's, known as Peacock's aisle, was to be taken down and used as framework for the new pews in the nave.[141] In November 1645 the total cost of renovating the parish church was estimated at £600;[142] but after the fall of the central tower this figure had risen to £2,500 'at the least'.[143] In fact, the Scarborough appeal of 1660–1 raised £247 7s. 6½ d.![144]

St Mary's nearly-new pews, more than 150 of them, had been consumed as firewood and presumably, since none has survived, the registers of baptisms, marriages and burials were also misused at the same time by the same Roundhead occupants. The earliest extant register dates from 1682; prior to that there are only incomplete bishops' transcripts from 1602. As late as 1787, James Schofield referred to 'the parish registers', which he said recorded the burials of 'divers persons slain by chance cannon shot, while firing was continued against, or in defence of the Castle'.[145] Regrettably, however, these so-called registers have long since disappeared.

St Mary's plate was also never recovered. If William Simpson took it with him into the castle then he did not put it back after the siege. Perhaps some of the church silver was used to pay wages to the garrison. Sir Hugh described how he continued to give his men '12 pence a weeke besides dyett' and 'sixpence for everie dayes labour' with 'plaits which belonged to some persons hee had perticuler interest in'. The silver was cut up into crude shapes which were stamped according to their weight and value. All of them carried a rough inscription of the keep and some a motto such as 'Caroli fortuna resurgam' or 'OBS Scarborough 1645'.[146] The only pre-war plate still belonging to St Mary's now is a large cup given by William Thompson's heirs after his death in 1637.[147]

If Meldrum and Boynton had employed St Mary's as a forward bastion, they had also done nearly as much disfavour to its sister church of St Thomas. This 'great Chapelle', as Leland had called it, had become a stable and a magazine. As late as April 1642 the bailiffs had ordered a general assessment for its repair, but it is doubtful that any of the money raised was spent on it.[148] Significantly, no reference was made to St Thomas's in the bailiffs' list of town property damage drawn up in November 1645. Perhaps it was by then obvious that the church was beyond salvation.

Another building that suffered severely before and during the siege was the former charnel chapel in charnel garth which for nearly a century past had housed Scarborough's grammar school. Standing below Bushell's battery and close to St Mary's, the schoolhouse was right in the line of fire. Cholmley had made it into a guardhouse. Meldrum had used it as a front-line post from which to storm Bushell's battery. During the year ending Michaelmas 1647, the chamberlains' accounts show that the town spent £17 10s. 6d. on the 'scolehouse'. Most of the money was for timber: £3 16s. 6d. was the price paid for 90 fir deals, and another £3 13s. 6d. for a further 74 deals. The joiners used nearly a pound's worth of nails. Re-glazing the schoolhouse windows cost the town £1 18s. 0d. The two masters, presumably carpenters and glaziers, were given £4 11s. 0d. for seven weeks' work.[149]

The only two properties mentioned specifically in the catalogue of damages drawn up for the borough's two new Members of Parliament in November 1645 were conduit pipes and mills. The conduit, 'which brought water in leaden pipes to the towne' from Falsgrave springs 'a mile from thence', had been pulled up, broken up and carried off. No doubt the lead was converted into ammunition. The cost of replacing the pipes was put at £200, a suspiciously high and rounded figure. Six months later a Common Hall assessment on the town 'for defraying the charges for repaireing the conduit and pipes and cisterne' was put at only £30. The following month the same assessment was said to be 'for bringinge water to the towne of Scarbrough' and also for 'puttinge the clock [in St Mary's] into frayme'.[150] Throughout 1647 the town continued to spend money digging out, mending and maintaining its water conduit in addition to the contractual payments made to Christopher Gilson, the plumber.[151]

The town claimed that all four of their mills, three water and one wind, had been 'totally puld downe'. This tale of total loss was slightly altered in the memorandum addressed to Lord Fairfax, Sir William Constable, Sir William Strickland, Sir Philip Stapleton and 'the rest of the Northerne gentlemen with our burgesses in Parliament'. Here the cost of 'the new building of 3 mills & 1 quite gone' was assessed at £300. Yet only a month before this claim was lodged, the three water corn mills in Ramsdale, the upper, middle and nether, had been leased for seven years at a rent of £60 per annum. As usual with such leases, the tenants were to bear the costs of repairs and the town would pay for new millstones when they were needed. There is no hint in the lease that the mills were not in working order. On the contrary, the annual rent of £60 for the three Ramsdale mills compares with the pre-war rent of £72 for all four. Moreover, of the six millers who took out the last pre-war lease in February 1641, five of them had survived to renew it in October 1645.[152] It seems therefore that the Common Hall's damage claim for all four mills in the autumn of 1645 was grossly inflated and downright dishonest: only the windmill had been put out of use during the siege. There is no doubt that the windmill had been in working order before the war. Indeed in 1641, its miller, Ralph Gibson, got himself into trouble for working it overtime. In May of that year he was presented at the general sessions 'for grindinge upon the sabboth day 21 Mar beinge warnned to the contrarye'.[153]

Other claims made for losses incurred during the years 1642–5 are not so easy to check. Ever since Scarborough had become a garrison town 'the soldiers horses of both partyes' had taken free herbage from its pastures which was valued at £600.[154] If, as was claimed, ground had been spoiled then such pastures might be expected to have fallen in value by 1645. Also, given the general impoverishment of townsmen, we should assume a fall in rents. However, with one possible exception, there appears to have been no depression in land values as a result of the war.

Weaponness was the town's most extensive and valuable pasture. Its seven-year lease was much sought after not only for its grass but also for its whins and bracken which were sold to the townspeople for kindling and animal bedding. Traditionally, the lessee, invariably a leading burgess, such as Robert Harthropp in 1624, Gregory Fysh in 1631 and Thomas Foord in 1638, paid a rent of about £20 a year. Fifteen pounds of this were set aside at Michaelmas for the king's fee-farm rent; £4 6s. 8d. went to the netherd for his wages; and the rest went towards 'keeping the common bull at the usual times'.[155] When the seven-year leases were granted anew in February 1646, Peter Rosdale got Weaponness pasture for an annual rent of £21 10s.[156] So much for the Common Hall's claim that the 'herbage' had been 'totally eaten up'.[157]

The most distant pastures from the town, though still within the borough boundary, were the three Marr or Mere closes, altogether twenty acres on the east side of the 'king's road' to Seamer. In 1623 Robert Harthropp had leased them for £9 10s. a year; in 1631 Thomas Woodall, the butcher, took out the same lease at a slightly reduced rent of £9. When Matthew Fowler became the new tenant of Marr closes in 1646 his rent for them was also £9.[158] The same story applied to St Thomas's fields, also in Burtondale. Part of the rent for these town pastures supported the poor inmates of St Thomas's house. Richard Thompson paid £15 a year for them from 1631, and Robert Woodall's rent from 1646 was only £1 less. Similarly, Francis Thompson in 1634, William Foord in 1641 and Captain John Lawson in 1646, all paid exactly the same rent of £7 annually for their leases of the Garlands, on the northern slope of Weaponness.[159]

All these grazing grounds were some distance from the town and the battle zone so perhaps this explains why they seem to have escaped the alleged spoil. However, even the smaller town fields and closes which must have been used by both armies did not suffer a significant loss of rental value. St Catherine's closes on the New Dyke bank were leased to John Hickson in 1624 for £2 6s. a year and to Matthew Fowler, in October 1645, for £2 3s. 4d.[160] Bull Lane, which ran northwards to the Common from outside Newborough Bar, was let out by the town at ten shillings a year in 1647 as it had been in 1639.[161] In the same area, Swan Hill close was leased at eight shillings in 1624, ten shillings in 1647, and twelve shillings in 1668.[162] When George Pearson, the stringlayer, took out a lease on Greengate, alongside the road northwards to Whitby, his rent was a pound a year in 1639. Eight years later, Nicholas Saunders secured exactly the same terms.[163]

The one outstanding exception to this continuity is the town Common. This rather indeterminate area astride the main road to and from the castle and St Mary's must have witnessed the passage of many soldiers, horses and vehicles between 1642 and 1645. Probably this is sufficient explanation for its apparent decline in value. Robert Harthropp was tenant of the Common in 1622, paying an annual rent of £6. He was succeeded by William Batty in 1629 and he in turn by John Rosdale in 1637; they paid £5 and £6 respectively.[164] However, when the Common Hall granted new leases in October 1645, Richard Farthing was named as the tenant of the Common at an annual rent of only £3 16s. 8d. Richard was still the tenant in 1648, by which time, after the second siege, the rent had been lowered to £1 6s. 2d. Thereafter, the value of the Common increased. Christopher Jarratt paid £3 14s. for it in 1651, John Rosdale, £4 15s. in 1662, and Francis Sollitt, £6 10s. from 1664.[165] In short, it took twenty years for the rental value of the Common to recover its pre-war level.

Fortunately for the town and its inhabitants the principal battleground, St Mary's Quarter, was the most sparsely populated area of Scarborough: in 1645 it was still mostly garden, paddock, pasture and graveyard. The physical damage to domestic and commercial buildings was probably less serious, therefore, than might be assumed. Except for an hour or two after 10 a.m. on the morning of 18 February there was no street fighting; even then it was largely confined to the vicinity of St Mary's and the approaches to the castle. Meldrum's preliminary cannonade before the infantry assault had much greater psychological than physical impact. During the siege of the castle the weight of artillery fire was directed at very short range from St Mary's church and the earthworks around it, and from Parliament's ships in the harbour and off the headland. Civilian casualties were the result of chance misdirected shots, usually from the castle or the ships. There was no looting of domestic property: Meldrum and Boynton maintained a strict discipline over their soldiers.

Nevertheless, there is evidence enough that Scarborians who stayed in the town did suffer grievously from the effects of the prolonged siege of the castle. Most buildings survived intact, but many needed repairs and some disappeared altogether. Though Spital House, on the site of the former hospital of St Nicholas, was still there in 1645, Philip Benson's rent of 2s. 8d. suggests that it was in a poor state. In July 1647 the lease was extended to thirty-one years and the rent reduced further to only 2s.[166] The old pinfold had gone completely: in October 1645 its ground was sold to Robert Salton for £7. A new common fold was made outside Auborough Bar, where West House, another civil-war casualty, had once stood. The swinefold was still there, but it needed repairs; in the meantime, the bellman was to charge the owners of stray pigs four pence a foot.[167]

※

In the absence of court or Common Hall records there is no extant evidence of conditions in the town during the siege of 1645. For what it is worth, however, Schofield's first *Guide* of 1787 contained some anecdotal information. According to this source, many cannon shot weighing 36 pounds were found in and about the town as well as the castle.[168] Most of these were probably the result of Meldrum's preliminary bombardment of the town in January and February 1645. When the foundations of the Cliff footbridge were dug in 1827 several cannon balls were found embedded in both sides of the Ravine in the banks of Ramshill and St Nicholas Cliff opposite.[169] Again according to Hinderwell, 'several persons were killed . . . by cannon balls from a battery on Ramsdel mount';[170] but all Schofield's stories are of miraculous escapes from, not death by, cannon-fire. A lady who was busy with her needle and thread had just moved from the darkening east window of her house to the lighter western one when 'a glancing shot' from the castle aimed at St Mary's came through her east window 'and tore every thing in its way to atoms'. Another local female had an even narrower deliverance. She was at her spinning wheel in an upper room of the Old Globe inn in Fleshergate. As she stooped down to pick up the spindle a cannon ball fired from a ship's gun in the harbour passed directly over her and smashed the distaff to pieces.[171]

Also according to Schofield, since no markets were permitted in the streets of the town or on the sands, residents had to walk to Peasholm to buy their food supplies. Even then every householder was obliged to carry and produce 'an authenticated ticket signifying of how many the family they purchased for consisted'. These food ration cards entitled the bearers 'to a bare subsistence'.[172]

The town's official damage report claimed that ships were rotting on the beach since their cables, sails, anchors and furniture had been taken by Meldrum's soldiers as prizes. To recover their own vessels owners had had to pay a quarter of their value, but many would never be fit to go to sea again. Altogether shipping losses were put at £3,000.[173] Yet even before Cholmley surrendered the castle, Scarborough's trade with other east coast ports had restarted. By 25 July 1645, William Lawson, master of the *Isabel*, had already completed four voyages to Sunderland and back carrying cargoes of coal; William Robinson in the *Unity*, another Scarborough merchantman, had brought in codfish and salt from Newcastle; and three loads of strong beer and malt had arrived in the harbour from King's Lynn and Yarmouth.[174] Nevertheless, though the official report no doubt exaggerated the damage sustained, it would be a long time before pre-war volumes of trade, particularly with foreign ports, returned to Scarborough.

Some of the town's losses, however, were entirely genuine and serious. For the past two or three years no money had been received by Scarborough's coroners from the customers at Newcastle and Sunderland, the main source of revenue for pier maintenance. The first payment, brought by master William Robinson, did not arrive from Sunderland until March 1646. Even then it amounted to only £20 13s. According to Sunderland's collector, during the last quarter, 1,049 ships had paid 8d. or 4d. each, but in a letter of explanation to bailiff John Harrison it was implied that many colliers had evaded the duty. The collector had deducted only two shillings in the pound to cover his costs which he thought too little on account of the great trouble he had 'bringing the masters to pay'.[175] Again, the disruption of war would take some time to repair and during that time the pier at Scarborough would be neglected.

To add to the town's trading difficulties, King's Lynn had imposed a charge of four pence on every chalder of coal brought in by

Scarborough ships. For this King's Lynn had, in the words of the bailiffs, 'neither compos[ition] nor prescription', and by ancient custom and charter Scarborough men had liberty to trade freely and exemption from all duties throughout the kingdom.[176] The corporation of King's Lynn might still value Scarborough harbour as a potential refuge for its own vessels, but it seems that it was now trying to take advantage from the town's recent misfortunes. Finally, there were the new excise duties which Parliament had levied in all ports under its control since July 1643. In November 1645 the bailiffs requested the government in London that they might have 'the benefit' of this money 'towards the reparation of the losses of the well affected'.[177] Not surprisingly, there was no response to this impertinent suggestion.

The last item on the list of losses drawn up by Scarborough's bailiffs towards the end of 1645 was 'the charges of works' which were estimated at £300. By 'works' the bailiffs explained that they meant wooden platforms, candles and fuel, and other military services rendered at the town's expense 'before Sir Hugh Cholmley revolted' and 'ever since the town was reduced'. Naturally no claim could be made for the impoverishment of the town 'by the oppression of Sir Hugh Cholmley while it was under his power'.[178] The town's new leaders had no wish to prejudice their own case for compensation by reminding Parliament that Scarborough had cooperated willingly with a royalist Cholmley for nearly two years. Consequently, they frequently referred to themselves as 'the well affected party' and distanced themselves from the 'delinquents' who had been ousted from local control. As a result, no claim for 'works' was made for the period beginning March 1643 and ending February 1645.

No householders' vouchers or promissory notes for billeting expenses have survived in the corporation records at the time of the first Civil War, but it cannot therefore be assumed that they were all honoured. Given the experience of other communities oppressed by unwelcome and uninvited military garrisons, it seems probable that Scarborough's residents were never paid for providing bed and board.

To add to the burdens of Scarborough's inhabitants, the chamberlains' accounts for 1646 and 1647 show that significant sums were being spent by them on military defences and repairs. For Scarborough the war was still not over. The gates at Newborough and Oldborough entrances had been renewed in 1642–3. However, the latter, in particular, seem to have been yet another Civil-War victim.[179] In the year ending Michaelmas 1647, the town spent altogether £6 13s. in 'mending the ould barr at Aubrough gates'. An 'Ingeneere' was hired and paid wages of 13s. 6d., and James Ellis, the blacksmith, got £2 5s. 8d. for making a new gate and 'for loups and staples to set it on'. The rest of the bill covered labourers' wages. A new lock for the door cost 1s. 4d.[180]

From one of the first entries in the Common Hall minute book after the resumption of local government it is clear that Scarborough was still expected to pay for its own security. More expensive than the repairs to Oldborough Bar was the cost of constructing or re-building a court of guard or sentry house. Unfortunately, the chamberlains' accounts do not reveal the location of this work, but according to a Common Hall minute of December 1646 'a guard house for the soldjers' was to be built 'att the townes charge upon the cliffe neare the oyle house'.[181] The oil-house, where whale blubber was melted down, was then at the south end of St Nicholas Gate, overlooking King's Cliff, on or very near the site of the present town hall.[182] It cost the town £8 13s. 2d. to put up a walled enclosure, a wooden house and provide it with beds for the guards. The workmen were given 4s. 8d. worth of drink to lubricate the job.[183]

Another entry in the minute book of the Common Hall records that the guardhouse at Newborough Bar, which had been converted from a private house belonging to Mrs Wright, was to be maintained and manned by the town. For allowing her property to be used in this way Mrs Wright was to receive thirty shillings compensation from the chamberlains, who were also instructed to negotiate terms of rent with her for the future.[184]

In addition to these perimeter sentry houses the town operated a street watch every night. Two members of the Common Hall, beginning with one of the First Twelve and one of the Third, 'till they all have gone there corses respectively', were to walk the rounds to make sure that the watch was being properly kept. At the same meeting the town's ruling body ordered that 'severall peices of ordnance' should be planted in and around Scarborough; the town would pay for them. A fortnight later, on 26 November 1645, the new bailiffs, John Harrison senior and Thomas Gill, asked the North Riding Committee to hasten 'the dispatch of the ordnance'.[185]

As for the military garrison still in the castle and town and now under Colonel Matthew Boynton, the new commanding officer and governor, Parliament's failure to pay their wages had provoked a mutiny amongst some of them. From letters which passed between the bailiffs and the borough's new representatives at Westminster, Sir Matthew Boynton and Luke Robinson, in March 1646, it appears that the town had been 'forced to lend' the governor £100 'towards the quelling of the mutinous soldiers'. In view of this recent loyal service to Parliament, the bailiffs pleaded with Sir Matthew and Robinson to persuade the government in London not to insist on Scarborough's payment of the arrears of its fee-farm rent.[186]

The Civil War had also deprived Scarborough of its vicar, William Simpson. After he had served Sir Hugh and the King so persistently and impenitently, there was no question of his reinstatement. The town quickly washed its hands of him, or tried to do so. Out of the seven pounds Robert Salton had paid for the ground of the old pinfold, Mr Simpson was paid five, 'in liew and full satisfaction of all stypend & wages due'.[187] But Simpson would not go quietly. He refused to give up his vicarage, denied the slanders on his name, and said he was owed £58 in unpaid stipend. In an abject petition to the bailiffs, Simpson claimed that in both 'life and conversation' he had been 'honest, innocent and justifiable', that his doctrine had always been sound, but that now he was penniless. He had neither money nor credit or even horse 'to go about his occasions'. Mr Francis Thompson, he wrote, was behind £48 and the town still owed him another £10.[188]

Two years later, Simpson was neither reconciled nor repentant. From Cloughton, a village four miles north of Scarborough, he wrote to Luke Robinson at Seamer. He was still without a horse and now too ill to walk. He had sent one of his sons (presumably the one who was not a pirate!) with a letter from his patron Lord Bridgwater, who had agreed to release Simpson from his vicarage 'if it were voyd'. However, Simpson was still 'loath to part with itt', even though he had been promised another living at Lythe, a parish north of Whitby. He was afraid of forfeiting a bond of £200. Besides he had yet to see any Parliamentary order depriving him of his 'inheritance' at Scarborough. If such an order did reach him he would 'submitt to the divine providence' and obey it. In the meantime he hoped that Mr Robinson would let him have 'libertie serenity [to?] disharg a good conscienc'.[189]

Simpson had written his incoherent letter to the wrong man: Luke Robinson was not one to sympathise with 'disaffected malignant ministers'. The previous March he assured bailiffs Harrison and Nesfield that if Simpson did not relinquish the vicarage of Scarborough he would make sure that he was deprived of the living at Lythe.[190]

The expulsion of William Simpson from St Mary's was probably well received by many townspeople, even though he had convinced himself that he still had 'the hearts of most in the parish'.[191] However, the sequestration of the £28 a year, which Stephen Thompson, as impropriator, had paid to the vicar out of the profits of his share in the rectory, was a serious and embarrassing blow to the parish.[192] Scarborough badly needed a replacement for Simpson yet it lacked the means to pay for one.

From October 1645 until March 1646 Scarborough parish had a temporary 'preaching minister' called Mr Boatman. When none of Stephen Thompson's sequestered estate could be secured from the North Riding Committee or any other source, the Common Hall had to ask for a voluntary contribution of the townspeople to raise Mr Boatman's half-year salary. Only one of the accounts of the collectors for the four Quarters has survived in the corporation records: it shows that St Mary's Quarter managed to raise £4 12s. 6d. for Mr Boatman's benefit. The two largest donations were from Mr Bailiff Thomas Gill and Captain John Lawson: they each gave ten shillings.[193]

Mr Wood of Whitby was Scarborough's first choice as its permanent vicar. An undated, unsigned, fragmentary testimonial recorded that he was sober and honest and 'in these tymes of tryall' had been 'very faithfull . . . in all his performance as regards the Parliament'.[194] The parishioners of Whitby wholeheartedly agreed however and were therefore unwilling to part with Mr Wood.[195] And Mr Wood was most reluctant to part from them. Considering the great affection that the people of Whitby had expressed towards him and his advanced age, he had no wish to move from there to Scarborough.[196] Perhaps also Mr Wood was not a little apprehensive about Mr Simpson. As Scarborough's bailiffs admitted, 'Mr Wood desiers Mr Simpson may be removed before he undertake the place.'[197]

In 1647 Mr Wood was eventually persuaded to transfer from Whitby to Scarborough, though doubts were expressed by the Committee of Plundered Ministers about his suitability. It was suggested to bailiffs Harrison and Nesfield that they ask Mr Prowd and Mr Bradley, the two clerical witnesses to Wood's certificate of worthiness, to examine him further about his 'opinions of familists or antinomians & other errors contrary to sound doctrine'. Consequently, on 1 April 1647, a certificate was produced to the effect that Mr Wood was indeed free of 'blasphemyes of the familists . . . [and] all other erronious opinions . . . and . ..that he [was] so sound & substantially orthodoxall in his doctrine, of such exceeding diligence, sober conversation & in his affections to the publick cause of the church & state of such approved integrity (as by his suffrings for the same to us knowne)' that the signatories were convinced that he was indeed perfectly suited to become Scarborough's minister.[198]

Perhaps Mr Wood regretted his move particularly when he soon learned that there was stlll no guaranteed revenue to pay his stipend. By the beginning of 1648 he was in such 'great necessity . . . for want of the sallarye' that the Common Hall agreed to lend him fifteen, ten and five shillings each from its members in the three Twelves until he received the arrears of his income.[199] However, this order does not seem to have been carried out and instead, the following October, the town fell back on voluntary contributions to support Mr Wood and his family.[200] Finally, towards the end of March 1649, the Committee for Plundered Ministers at last ruled that £50 a year should be taken out of the rectory of Skipsea in Holderness 'for the maintenance of such godly and orthodox divine as this committee shall approve of to preach a lecture in the parishe church of Scarborough'.[201]

Alas, for Mr Wood, the order came too late: he died before the arrears in his stipend could be made up. His widow, Dorothy, now resident in Harwood Dale, about seven miles inland from Scarborough, was compelled to write to the outgoing bailiffs, John Harrison and Matthew Fowler, in September 1649. Apparently, she had still not received her husband's last half-year salary. Sadly, Mrs Wood reminded the bailiffs 'with what willinge cherefullnesse and diligence' her late husband had laboured amongst them in the ministry of the gospel, and how during the time they lived in Scarborough her family 'were straitned for necessaries'. Now she had lost the chief comfort of her life and the only pillar of her livelihood and subsistence, and she pleaded with the bailiffs to bring her plight to the notice of the Committee for Plundered Ministers.[202] Of the widow Wood nothing more is mentioned in the corporation records.

Scarborough's burgesses were glad to be rid of William Simpson but many must have had mixed feelings about the absence of other leading royalists. As the bailiffs' memorandum on the borough's Civil-War losses put it: 'Those that were formerly the ablest men of their towne being now found delinquents & their estates sequestred to the publique use soe that they have wanted & still doe want their contribution towards these great charges'.[203] By 'ablest' Scarborough's new bailiffs meant 'richest', and though none of these well-to-do delinquents were named in the memorandum most of them were called Thompson.

Some of the ships in which Richard and Christopher Thompson had shares, such as the *Adventure*, the *Violet* and the *Welcome*, were soon back at sea, carrying coals from Sunderland. Others, however, such as the *Restore*, the *Margaret* and the *Ann of Whitby*, are not to be found in the customs book of July to December 1645. Perhaps they were amongst the many other Scarborough vessels which the bailiffs claimed were beached and rotting on Sandside. Alternatively, the Thompsons might well have decided to take their ships to a more friendly port, such as Bridlington.[204]

However, the Thompsons had many other investments and interests in Scarborough other than shipping from which the town had benefited. Richard's house and tenements were worth £72 a year;

besides the castle and part of the rectory, Stephen had leases in Northstead and Peasholm which were worth nearly £60 a year before the war; and Christopher's properties in the town, which included a mansion house, three cottages, a brewery and a shop, formerly had a rental value of at least £10.[205] As well as these freehold and long-term leases, the Thompsons also held numerous shorter leases from the town for which no rent could now be expected. Finally, the wealth of the Thompsons, which derived from their country estates at Kilham and Humbleton, as well as their properties and commerce in Scarborough, would be sorely missed when the town was taxed: it has already been noted that five Thompsons contributed nearly 8 per cent of a levy on householders in July 1643.[206]

In a vain attempt to recover some of these losses, past, present and anticipated, Scarborough's bailiffs petitioned the Commons through their two new Members, Sir Matthew Boynton and Luke Robinson. Since Boynton and Robinson had perfect Parliamentary credentials, perhaps bailiffs Harrison and Gill deluded themselves that London would be sympathetic to Scarborough's woes. Conscious of the value that the merchants and shipowners of the capital and the East coast placed on the port of Scarborough, the bailiffs first asked that 'the well affected of the city of London & the Eastern Association' should be invited to make a voluntary gift towards the relief of the town. Secondly, they requested that 'some faithful & honest members of this corporation' could be authorised 'to compound with delinquents for soe much of their estate reall & personall as lye within the liberties of this corporation'. In other words, if the Thompsons were to be mulcted then it should not be at the expense of Scarborough which was already damaged by their delinquency. Finally, as proof of their self-restraint and reasonableness, the petitioners limited their claim to a maximum of £500 in composition fines; any surplus above that figure could go to the treasurer of the North Riding Committee![207]

Eventually, the Thompsons paid about £500 in composition fines for all their estates, but Scarborough received not a penny of it. Nor was there any voluntary subscription raised in London or elsewhere to compensate the town for its many losses, actual or inflated. The House of Commons, the city of London and the mercantile leaders of the East coast ports had no reason to feel sorry for Scarborough.

On the contrary, if Scarborians had not consented so tamely to Cholmley's defection, then Parliament and its supporters would have been spared much blood and treasure. If Scarborough had suffered siege, bombardment, military occupation and martial law, then it had only itself to blame: it could have avoided such calamities by rejecting Cholmley long before the siege occurred.

Besides, there were many more innocent and deserving cases than Scarborough. Parliamentary towns that had been raped and ransacked by royalist troops were much more likely to engage Parliament's sympathy and support. Lancaster, for instance, was deliberately burnt down by a retreating royalist army. Its people were promised not only the proceeds of a public collection amongst Londoners but also compensation amounting to £8,000 raised by fines on the town's Catholics and delinquents.[208] After Leicester was plundered by Prince Rupert's Welshmen in May 1645, 709 burials were recorded in the parish register. Prisoners of war and women were butchered. As one eyewitness reported, there was 'scarce a cottage unplundered . . . and no quarter given to any'.[209] Parliament's response to this outrage was to sanction a house-to-house collection in London and throughout twenty counties.[210]

Compared with such appalling experiences Scarborough had come off lightly. Meldrum's Scots behaved themselves well when they took the town. Meldrum was too sternly professional to permit indiscriminate slaughter or pillage. Moreover, Cholmley's wise decision not to attempt a defence of the walls and ditches but to fall back to the castle at once saved the civilian population from revengeful rapine. At Leicester, thirty of the King's soldiers had been killed forcing a breach through a stubbornly defended town wall; at Scarborough, nothing like this happened to provoke the anger of the attackers.[211]

Above all else, Scarborough could hardly claim for damages against Parliament when it had succoured a royalist garrison and a pack of royalist pirates for the past two years. Indeed, Parliament and the country might with more justice have claimed damages from Scarborough. The cost to East coast ports, in voluntary contributions to Meldrum's siege and the loss of trade and shipping to such as Bushell and Denton, must have run to many thousands of pounds.

Finally, Parliament's expenditure of men, money and firepower on the reduction of Scarborough had been enormous. Perhaps as many as two thousand infantry had been employed in the storming of the town and the siege of the castle. Sixteen of Parliament's ships had been needed to maintain an effective blockade. Parliament's commitment of artillery had been extraordinary: Meldrum had been given the biggest and best cannon available. Some of Parliament's losses had been irreplaceable. The death of Sir John Meldrum was a great blow, and so was that of Vice-Admiral Zachary, killed on board one of the blockading ships by a cannon-shot from the castle. At least nine other Roundhead officers of the rank of captain and above had lost their lives in the siege. After such events it was not in the least surprising that, even though it was now represented in London by stout Parliamentarians Boynton, Robinson and John Lawson, Scarborough's cries for help were ignored. The only relief allowed to the town was remission of the king's fee-farm rent of £40 a year for the three years 1643, 1644 and 1645.[212]

CHAPTER FIVE

The Second Civil War, 1648

For more than two years, ever since Sir Hugh Cholmley changed sides and General John Hotham had been arrested for treason, Scarborough was without parliamentary representation. Not until August 1645, by which time Cholmley was a disenfranchised exile and Hotham was dead, did the House of Commons begin to issue writs to fill the two hundred or so vacancies caused since 1640 by death, withdrawal and disablement. Scarborough's writ was finally issued on 12 September 1645.[1]

Naturally, Parliament was careful to exclude royalists: its known enemies were declared ineligible for election or re-election and all new Members were required to sign the Solemn League and Covenant, a Presbyterian pledge. Though historians have failed to find any distinctive social differences between the new 'Recruiter' MPs and their predecessors elected in 1640, not surprisingly, however, the new men were generally much more radical in religion and politics.[2]

Scarborough's Members were no exception to the generality: here there seems to have been a sharply-fought contest for one of the two seats between the nominee of Ferdinando, Lord Fairfax, James Chaloner of Guisborough, and Luke Robinson of Thornton Risebo-rough, near Pickering. To what extent this was an ideological dispute, or merely a matter of personal rivalry and family pride, remains an open question. Confusingly, Lord Fairfax could be fairly classed as a moderate, whereas his candidate, a distant relative by marriage, was known to be an extreme enemy of the Crown. The Chaloners believed that they had been cheated of their rightful alum-mining rights and dues by King Charles and his father.[3]

Chaloner was strongly supported. More than a fortnight before the bailiffs received the election warrant from the sheriff at York, from Fairfax they had a written endorsement of Chaloner's 'wisdome, fidelity and fittnes'.[4] Then on Michaelmas day, on the morrow of his election as Scarborough's bailiff, John Harrison senior accepted from Chaloner himself another letter of recommendation written by Francis Pierrepont, son of the Earl of Kingston. According to Pierrepont, Chaloner was 'a gentleman without all exception'. Lord Fairfax had also written to the governor, Colonel Matthew Boynton, on Chaloner's behalf.[5]

When the newly-elected Common Hall next met on 8 October, Chaloner's return seemed certain. Not only was he allowed to present himself before his electors, but he was also permitted to bring two of his supporters, Mr Etherington and Captain Harrison, into the body of the Hall. The letters of endorsement from Lord Fairfax and Pierrepont were then read out and Captain Harrison reminded the assembly of 'the great services performed by my Lord & Sir Thomas [his son, General Sir Thomas Fairfax] & their tryed integrityes'.[6] At this moment, either by remarkable coincidence or, more likely, by well-managed timing, a messenger entered the chamber with a letter addressed to the bailiffs and burgesses. As the members soon learned when it was read out to them then and there, the letter was from Luke Robinson, and it was more like a hand grenade tossed into the Hall than any ordinary communication.[7]

First of all, Robinson implied that the presentation of the sheriff's warrant to hold a by-election in Scarborough had been deliberately delayed. Secondly, without naming anyone, he called upon the town's ruling body to exercise its freedom of choice and privilege and not be afraid of 'the displeasure of the greatest person'. 'If you bee biass't by the favour of great men', he continued, 'you will cast your selves into infinite inconveniences'. Finally, he exhorted them to 'Remember you chuse for Scarbrough and for Yorkeshire & the Lord bee att your choice.'[8]

The high sheriff of the county accused of holding back the warrant was Sir Matthew Boynton, himself a candidate for one of Scarborough's seats; and there was no need to refer to Lord Fairfax by name either: everyone present must have understood whom Robinson meant by 'the greatest person'. Chaloner's backers certainly regarded Robinson's remarks as a personal and direct attack on his lordship 'whom the Parliament was pleased to thanke for his extraordinary services.'[9] At this point, however, Captain Harrison, a blunt soldier not a politician, and no doubt unfamiliar with the pride and traditions of the Common Hall, made a series of errors which proved fatal for his candidate's chances. Two or three times he asked that the election of two burgesses should proceed forthwith. When the bailiffs told him that this would be premature, unwisely he demanded that the precept for the election should be handed over to him. Of all the many privileges enjoyed by Scarborough corporation during the past three and a half centuries the one they prized most highly was that of returning two Members of Parliament, and here was an outsider attempting to wrest this authority from the hands of the bailiffs. Nevertheless, foolishly, Harrison persisted. He now tried to appeal over the heads of the bailiffs to the whole assembly and demanded that a motion to hold the election should be put to the vote. Captain Harrison had overstepped the boundary of tolerable behaviour. Senior bailiff John Harrison told him politely but firmly that it was for the bailiffs only to determine when votes were taken in the Hall, and that right now he had other things to do. On that cold and curt retort 'the house was broken upp'.[10] There were to be no elections that day.

A week after this extraordinary meeting at Sandside, the bailiffs received another letter about the forthcoming election. This one had been written by John Darley of the Buttercrambe family and was brought from London by Captain John Lawson. Darley would not recommend any candidate by name, but he reminded the bailiffs that the county needed 'men of great understanding, courage & integritye' and advised them to choose burgesses 'such as by their birthing, cohabitation & subsistence amonge you are ingaged to advance the happines of that countye'. Since all the candidates were Yorkshiremen this was not very helpful. Darley concluded by saying that it would be dishonourable if they chose 'such who are onely hopefull, havinge never appeared publiquely during the firye triall', in preference to those who had been 'eminent for actinge & sufferinge in the common cause of religion & libertye both at home & abroad.'[11] Whatever subtlety of meaning the bailiffs were expected to read into Darley's letter the last three and a half centuries have completely erased it.

Perhaps Chaloner's goose was already cooked, but Robinson's next move made sure of it. A few days later, he addressed another letter 'to the bailiffs, burgesses and commons of Scarborough'. Again, he mentioned no names and yet the thrust was deadly. He pointed out that 'in the beginning of this parliament' the House of Commons had passed an order condemning the practice whereby peers tried to arrange the outcome of borough elections by writing persuasive letters to their electors. Just in case Scarborough's forty-four were unfamiliar with the order of 10 December 1641, Robinson kindly enclosed a copy of it! The House of Commons had indeed condemned such practices on the grounds that they tended 'to the violation of the priviledges of Parliament and the freedome of elections of the members that ought to serve.' Such letters, if received, should not be allowed to influence the minds of electors who ought to send or bring them to the Speaker of the House.[12]

In the meantime the bailiffs had received a terse note from Lord Fairfax who was in London; he had been told of Robinson's bombshell at the meeting of the Common Hall on 8 October and demanded a copy of this letter to be sent by return in the hands of his bearer. Clearly, whatever Robinson might say subsequently to excuse his action, it was regarded by Fairfax as hostile and insulting.[13]

The last act in this curious episode revealed that Luke Robinson's motives were self-advancing. Though he had been careful not to commit himself on paper, the truth was that he had blocked Chaloner's election in order to accomplish his own. When the Common Hall met to choose its two Members on 25 October, three candidates were named. According to one unsubstantiated claim, Sir Matthew Boynton got 28 votes, Luke Robinson 26 and Chaloner a derisory two![14] As far as the corporation's surviving records are concerned, there is only one tantalising hint of what had happened to produce this astonishing result. In their letter to Robinson, informing him of his successful return, the bailiffs concluded: ' Sir, this is the effect of the publique carriage of this busines, but what hath beene done and sollicited in private wee shall acquaint you with att our first meeting.'[15] In other words, then as now, the vital decisions had been made behind, and not in front of, the scenes.

In contrast, Boynton's return was inevitable. He had all the right qualifications for the time. Unlike Chaloner, he had no need of 'a great man' to endorse his candidature. Sir Matthew was a strong Calvinist who had once seriously considered emigration to the American colonies. To practise his faith freely between 1638 and 1641 he had lived with his family in Holland. He was rich: in October 1645 his personal estate included £2,600 in money and bonds. He was politically experienced: he had been justice of the peace, deputy lieutenant and twice high sheriff of the county.[16]

Above all, Sir Matthew had fought a good war. He was with Cholmley in 1643 when they beat the royalists at Guisborough; he had played a key role in Parliament's successful defence of Hull and the arrest of Sir John Hotham; and after Meldrum's death he had conducted the siege of Scarborough castle until its fall in July 1645. When he was made high sheriff of Yorkshire his second son, also called Matthew, was made governor of the town and colonel of its garrison. In all these ways he fitted Darley's description of a desirable new Member of Parliament and he was just the man to represent Scarborough's interests at Westminster.[17]

Luke Robinson's credentials were much less impressive. He was not from a long-established local family. His father, Sir Arthur Robinson of Deighton, north of Northallerton, did not acquire Thornton Riseborough Hall until 1632. In 1645 Luke was only thirty-five years old and lacked experience. His first and last recorded appearance on the North Riding justices bench was at Malton as recently as April 1645.[18] Unlike Chaloner, Robinson had no influential outside backer, unless Darley is counted as one. Nevertheless, his friends were where they counted most – inside the borough's new oligarchy. From subsequent correspondence between Robinson and the town's hierarchy it emerges that he had established good working personal relations with the men who now mattered most – principally the two John Harrisons, father and son, and the two captains, William Nesfield and John Lawson. It was to be Robinson, rather than Sir Matthew, who wrote frequently and at length from London to the bailiffs in Scarborough, and it was he who found a close rapport with another zealous Puritan, John Lawson. In June 1646, for instance, we find Robinson writing to Lawson, who was then in Scarborough, and apologising to him in a postscript for not having the time to send him books.[19]

If James Chaloner felt any resentment about his defeat at Scarborough it did not last long. Within a short time he was returned to the House of Commons as one of the new Members for Aldborough, while his elder brother, Thomas, secured one of Richmond's vacant seats. Both were to be involved in the trial of King Charles a few years later. Eventually James became governor of the Isle of Man and died there in 1660, whereas Thomas succeeded in becoming one of Scarborough's MPs in 1659 only to die in exile in 1661.[20]

Sir Matthew Boynton might have been better qualified than Luke Robinson but as Scarborough's representative the latter proved far more durable. In an undated letter to John Harrison, Robinson reported that his colleague had 'had some distemper in his health lately', and then, on 9 March 1647, from London he wrote: 'It pleased god to take Sir Mathew out of this sinful & troublesome world the last Friday night'.[21]

The election of John Anlaby as Boynton's successor on 19 May 1647 could not have been simpler. There were no other candidates and Anlaby, who had no previous known connections with the town, did not even bother to travel to Scarborough from his home at Etton, near Beverley, in the East Riding.[22] If the bailiffs received any letters of recommendation for this by-election none has survived in the corporation records.

The new Common Hall, elected the day after Michaelmas 1645 and marking the restoration of local civilian government, reflected Parliament's military victory at Scarborough. The local royalists were swept out and committed Parliamentarians took their places. The name of Thompson, which had been so dominant in Scarborough for the past half century, disappeared altogether, and so did that of Tristram Fysh and John Hickson. Other lesser royalists, elected in 1644, such as Francis Fawether, Francis Sollitt and William Cooper, were also missing from the new lists of elected burgesses.[23]

To fill these gaps there were some rapid promotions and a few new faces in the Common Hall. Thomas Gill had been no higher than the Second Twelve in July 1644 when he was permitted to leave royalist Scarborough, yet in September 1645 he was chosen junior bailiff. During the past year he must have done some exceptional service for Parliament: it was unknown for a mere master mariner to be given a bailiff's place without first rising up the ladder to the top of the First Twelve. Newcomers to the First Twelve in September 1645 included Captain William Nesfield, who still had a contract of service in Parliament's merchant navy. He too had never previously been higher than the Second Twelve. Peter Hodgson, Edward Hickson and Christopher Poskitt were three more men promoted from the Second to the First Twelve to occupy the seats once held by supporters of Cholmley. But the most significant and meteoric promotion to the First Twelve was that of Captain John Lawson: though a successful and respected master mariner, he was a complete outsider who had never held even the lowest position in the Common Hall.[24]

Though eventually he came to play a crucial role in national history, Lawson's origins and early life have never been clearly established: no one yet has been able to discover for certain when and where and in what circumstances he was born. Several authorities have stated that he was the son of poor parents who lived in Hull;[25] others have said that he came from near Scarborough;[26] but the majority view, endorsed by the author of his biography in the *Dictionary of National Biography*, is that he was 'a native of Scarborough'.[27] Without a record of his baptism, Hinderwell's conclusion, that 'it is highly probable that he was born at Scarborough', seems the safest.[28] Only one piece of documentary evidence has been found to establish his year of birth. At the end of 1639, ' John Lawson, nautam, 24 of Scarborough' was licensed to marry 'Isabel Jefferson, spinster, 23 of Lythe'.[29] Their wedding took place on 5 January 1640 in the bride's parish church at Lythe.[30]

As for John Lawson's early circumstances, they were neither so impoverished, nor so privileged, as some have suggested. Clarendon wrote that his father was 'a common sailor' and both Campbell and Hinderwell accepted this partisan view.[31] On the other hand, because later he used the arms of the Lawsons of Longhirst in Northumberland, others have assumed that he was a gentleman by birth.[32] Lawson, or Lowson, was and still is a very common surname in Scarborough;[33] but it is probable that John's father was the William Lawson whose name appears frequently in the records of Scarborough's Society of Owners, Masters and Mariners. In December 1636 William was elected to serve as one of the four wardens of the society. Between 1636 and 1639 he was master of a collier called the *Hopewell*; between 1639 and 1641 he was master of another Scarborough ship, the *John*; and finally, in 1643 and 1645, as master of the *Isabel*, he made successful return voyages to Rotterdam and Sunderland.[34]

It would be a remarkable coincidence if any other sea-going Scarborough Lawson had close relatives christened John and Isabel. Perhaps even more conclusive is that in the same records of the Society of Owners, Masters and Mariners the name of John Lawson, master of the *Adventurer*, first appears next to that of William Lawson in 1639, and again in 1641 and 1642. Only one voyage was entered against John's name and ship in 1639, presumably the year he qualified as master, but in 1641 he made 26 successful voyages and in 1642 five more.[35] So John Lawson was born in 1615, had become a master mariner by the age of 24 and an experienced merchant sea captain when the Civil War broke out in 1642.

By the time of his election to Scarborough's First Twelve three years later, Lawson had distinguished himself as a loyal and courageous servant of Parliament. Whereas most Scarborians were reluctant or refused to take sides, in his own words, 'in the year 1642 I voluntarily engaged in the Parliament's service'.[36] In recognition of his skill as a seaman and his political reliability, he was soon hired by Parliament as commander of the well-named *Covenant* of Hull, a merchantman of 140 tons with a crew of 42 and twelve cannon, in which he had a part share.[37] Under Lawson, the *Covenant* served in Parliament's summer guard of 1644 and 1645 and winter guard of 1645.[38]

There is an early glimpse of Lawson's Nelsonian dash and appetite for battle in a petition he addressed to the Committee of the Navy in December 1644. Near Scarborough he had taken an enemy ship, transferred four of its guns to his own vessel, and then, 'for better advantage in chasing a man of war cut off his own boat which was thereby lost'.[39] Merchantmen were not expected to engage, let alone pursue warships, but the *Covenant*, with Lawson in command, was no ordinary merchant ship.

When he was not chasing and capturing royalist ships Lawson was conveying vital military supplies. In March 1644 the *Covenant* carried lead out of Hull intended to be made into musket balls for the Scottish army.[40]

The one Lawson service which Parliament probably valued above all others was his part in the frustration of Sir John Hotham's plot to defect to the King and take Hull with him. The details of Lawson's intervention on this occasion are not recorded; his own comment on it was characteristically brief and modest: 'it pleased God to make me an instrument in discovering, and in some measure, preventing, the intended treachery of Sir John Hotham'.[41]

Lawson was honest enough to admit that he had made a good living out of his naval service to Parliament, or, as he put it, 'receiving my freight well, I had subsistence'.[42] However, there was one major penalty he incurred as a result of his loyalty to Parliament. When Sir Hugh Cholmley suddenly changed sides at the end of March 1643, rather then let his family live under a royalist regime, Lawson preferred exile in Hull. That he regarded Scarborough as his true home is confirmed by his own description of this event as 'my wife and children being banished two years to Hull'.[43] In December 1642, John Lawson, then living in 'Awdbrough' Quarter, probably paid the three shillings which was his assessment 'for raising £50 for making two pairs of gates and other works for the benefit and safety of the towne';[44] but by July 1643, when he was assessed at six shillings by a royalist Common Hall, he and his family had already moved to Hull.[45]

Lawson's return to Scarborough with his family in the autumn of 1645 was a welcome asset to the new rulers of the town. His Parliamentary credentials were perfect and as a representative of Scarborough it was hoped that his influence and advocacy would help to counterbalance the town's not entirely deserved reputation for royalism. It seems highly unlikely that he ever joined Parliament's winter guard in the North Sea: he was far too busy on land acting on behalf of individual townsmen and Scarborough as a whole. As early as October 1645 Lawson was in London representing the town's interests there. According to a letter written by John Darley to the bailiffs and brought to Scarborough from the capital, 'Captane Lawson' had 'beene very diligent in the puttinge on of your busines'.[46] A month later, along with the two bailiffs and John Harrison junior, Lawson was one of the four signatories of a letter to Yorkshire's MPs asking that Scarborough should soon be provided with artillery defences.[47] When bailiff John Harrison senior found himself in dispute with the town over his loss of profits from the pierage and his tenancy of St Thomas's fields and Wheatcroft's, he asked Lawson to act for him as an arbitrator. Harrison won his case. In compensation for his losses between 1643 and 1645, he was awarded the pierage profits for the next two years, a renewal of his lease on Wheatcroft, and financial recompense 'in full satisfaction of his losse for want of . . . St Thomas feilds'.[48] Lawson was a good man to have on your side.

In 1646 and 1647 Lawson spent almost as much time in London as in Scarborough. Though the borough had two capable and respected MPs, the Common Hall placed a high value on Lawson's additional support there. For instance, in April 1646, he was asked by the bailiffs 'to put our burgesses in mind' of the fact that King's Lynn was still charging 4*d*. a chalder on Scarborough coals.[49] Only a week later, he was being pressed again by the bailiffs to find a new source of stipend for the town's minister.[50] Though Lawson spent April and May 1646 in lodgings at the Three Cups in Holborn at the town's expense and Scarborough had still no satisfaction on either the King's Lynn imposition or their vicar's income, the bailiffs seemed well pleased with what they called the captain's 'extraordinary care in sollicitation of busines'.[51] The following September the Common Hall agreed that Lawson should have £10 'towardes his charges when he did solicite the townes busines att the Parliament'.[52] By November he was back in London. This time he stayed at The Unicorn at the lower end of King's Street in Westminster. By now the bailiffs had become desperate: the garrison at Scarborough was twenty weeks in arrears of pay and the town was having to provide free quarter. There had already been one mutiny and now there was danger of another.[53] With Robinson and Boynton to help him, it was hoped that Lawson could prevail upon Parliament to pay its soldiers and compensate the town.

In April 1646 Lawson had been commissioned captain of the 100 soldiers Parliament had ordered should be kept as a permanent garrison in Scarborough castle; but this extra responsibility seems not to have restricted his movements.[54] Just over a year later he was back in London when Luke Robinson reported the death of Sir Matthew Boynton. Until the burgesses elected John Anlaby as Boynton's replacement in May 1647, Lawson's efforts on behalf of his native town were even more appreciated there. In that month the chamberlains were authorised to pay £5 16*s*. 8*d*. to the captain 'which he had disbursed att London about severall businesses for the towne according to his bill of particulars'.[55]

Scarborough rewarded Lawson in other ways. In September 1646 and again a year later, 'Mr John Lawson', as the town clerk now preferred to write his name, was re-elected to his place in the First

Twelve. Captain William Nesfield had become junior bailiff then coroner at these elections, but presumably Lawson's military commission and his frequent absences in London disqualified him from such burdensome offices. Nevertheless, he was now one of Scarborough's propertied oligarchy. In June 1647 he bought a handsome house in West Sandgate, opposite the lower end of Merchant Row.[56] By that time he had already taken out a seven-year lease from the town on pastures known as the Garlands at a rent of £7 12s. per annum;[57] and early in 1648 he acquired another valuable seven-year lease of Butt Closes for a rent of £2 13s. 4d. and thirty shillings for an entry feast.[58] Both of these properties were much sought after by townsmen and held only by favoured leaseholders.

Even as late as 1648, however, John Lawson might still have thought of himself first as a master mariner and part owner of a merchant ship. He was still taking on apprentices. William Atmar, son of Martin, the late bailiff, was bound apprentice to him by his widowed mother 'to be taught the art and mystery of a mariner'.[59] Two of his other indentured apprentices, John Reeves and John Walker, completed their seven-year terms with him in October 1647. According to long-standing custom they were then admitted as freemen to the corporation on payment of four shillings each.[60]

Nevertheless, Lawson's radical politics and religion, his outstanding service for Parliament at Hull and at sea, his recent experience of politics and government in London and now his captain's commission at Scarborough castle set him well apart from his contemporary burgesses. He was in constant demand to fulfil new duties and take on extra responsibilities. He was one of the six auditors appointed for the town's affairs in the year ending October 1647; the following March he handed over £15 to Parliament's receiver-general in the North Riding at York as Scarborough's contribution to the current £60,000 assessment. At the end of the next month, April 1648, he was named with eight others as a permanent assessor of Scarborough's monthly tax bill of £5 5s. 7d.[61]

In these circumstances it is hardly surprising that Lawson's attendance record at Common Hall meetings would not have won him prizes. He was present 27 October 1647, 16 January and 28 April 1648, but absent 26 November 1647 and 25 January 1648. On the last occasion his absence was considered excusable, but for that on 26 November, along with five other members, he was fined a shilling.[62]

Having taken so much time and trouble to capture the castle at Scarborough, Parliament was now determined to keep a tight hold on it. A month after Cholmley's surrender, the appointment of Colonel Matthew Boynton, second son of Sir Matthew, as governor of the town and commander of the castle garrison, was approved by both Houses. Conscious of the vital importance of the castle and the harbour at Scarborough, Parliament also ruled that neither the Committee for the North Riding nor that for Military Affairs in the Northern Association had the authority to make such appointments.[63] They trusted neither committee of soldiers to choose a man who was utterly loyal to London; but they were satisfied, given young Matthew's parentage and record, that they could trust him. There were to be no more turncoat Cholmleys.

As early as 1 August 1645, the Commons asked the Committee of the Northern Association to consider 'the whole state of the case concerning Scarborough'.[64] Should the castle be re-built or demolished? Should a military garrison be maintained there permanently? Could the townsmen be trusted? If civilian self-government was re-established there how might its allegiance to Parliament be secured and strengthened? These were the questions the committee was expected to address.

The first action of the House of Commons was to restore Scarborough's parliamentary representation. The writ for a by-election was issued to Sir Matthew Boynton, high sheriff of Yorkshire, on 12 September.[65] However, some delay was unavoidable. Since there was no question of changing the electorate or allowing all those in the Common Hall of September 1644 to exercise the franchise, a new governing body had to be chosen first. Though a copy of 'the humble petition of the well-affected party of Scarborough' has not survived in the corporation archive, no doubt one of the requests made was for the re-election of a new Common Hall.[66]

Consequently, the annual tradition of electing a new Common

Hall on the day after Michaelmas was maintained in 1645, and it was this body which returned Sir Matthew Boynton and Luke Robinson to the Commons a month later. Though Scarborough's 'delinquents' were not officially and formally disenfranchised and disabled from holding office until the House of Commons order of April 1646, the town's 'well-affected party' had already made sure of their exclusion from Sandside.[67]

The Committee of the Northern Association took several months to decide what should be done at Scarborough; its detailed report was accepted by the Commons in April 1646. Scarborough castle was to be made tenable and permanently garrisoned. The establishment of one hundred soldiers was to have a chaplain paid four shillings a day. Soldiers billeted in the town were to be maintained by the Northern Association; there was to be no forced or free quarter. Colonel Boynton was confirmed as governor and John Lawson was commissioned army captain of the castle garrison.[68]

Of all Yorkshire's many castles, Pontefract was the only other besides Scarborough to be granted this protected privilege. Tickhill, Sheffield, Knaresborough, Cawood, Sandal, Bolton, Middleham, Helmsley, Mulgrave, Crayke, and later, Wressle, 'being inland castles [were] to be made untenable and no garrisons kept or maintained in them'. Skipton castle was to lose its outworks and be kept only as a home for the Earl of Pembroke, not as a military stronghold.[69] In February 1647, after some debate and a House of Commons division, even Pontefract castle lost its military status, though later that year £360 was voted for the relief of its garrison.[70]

Though the future of Pontefract castle might have divided the House of Commons, there was no difference of opinion or doubt about what should be done at Scarborough. The wrecked gateway and barbican had already been cleared of rubble and their walls repaired in 1645[71] when the House ordered that in addition to the garrison of one hundred 'the forts which command the harbour at Scarborough be kept up, with three score men in them'.[72] In May 1646 Luke Robinson had told the Commons that Scarborough lacked 'several sorts of ammunition'.[73] As a result, the following month, the Eastern Association's Committee was instructed to spare some of its ammunition in Cambridge castle and send it to Scarborough.[74] When Scarborough's military needs had still not been satisfied, the Commons ordered that sixty barrels of gunpowder and twelve tons of match should 'be forthwith supplied out of the public stores for the service of the castle'.[75] Just a year afterwards, in October 1647, the House authorised the payment of £540 a month for the 'present relief' of the garrison at Scarborough, the most northerly in England. By comparison, Hull's military garrison was allowed £2,400 a month.[76]

Parliament's particular anxiety to maintain 'the forts which command the harbour at Scarborough', by which it meant South Steel battery, indicates the reasons why it gave privilege and priority to the castle defences. Though the Scottish army had been paid off and had returned home early in 1647, though King Charles was now a prisoner, though the royalists were everywhere defeated and scattered, the North Sea was still infested with the King's privateers and Parliament still feared that its enemies might land troops on the Yorkshire coast. Whoever commanded Scarborough castle controlled the use of the harbour below it.

Captain Browne Bushell was still at large. Though he never returned to Scarborough, it was feared that he might. Only a few days before Cholmley surrendered, his cousin was operating in the English Channel when he had a narrow and dramatic escape. Off Portland, the *Cavendish*, his 750-ton warship, loaded with arms intended for Lord Goring at Exeter, was intercepted by one of Parliament's superior men-of-war. As the *Cavendish* was boarded on the seaward side its captain and a dozen or so of his crew dived through the port-holes on the landward side and then swam the 1½ miles to shore and safety. The 'old sea pirot', as *Parliament's Post* called him, had lost the ship Cholmley gave to him but saved his skin.[77]

Bushell seems to have made a full recovery from this setback. In 1647 he was at Boulogne, along with other privateer captains, when the news arrived that Cardinal Mazarin had ordered their expulsion. According to one account of their reaction, the captains first got themselves violently drunk, drove their crews back to their ships, weighed anchor, and then skilfully evaded Parliament's reception party waiting outside the harbour. Within a few days they were all back in their pirates' nest in Jersey.[78]

If, for the time being, Bushell preferred to prey on Channel vessels, there were many others of his kind at work in the North Sea. In

February 1646, Robinson and Boynton received a petition to the House of Commons from 'the inhabitants of Scarborough, Whitby, Bridlington and Bridlington Quay' complaining that they were suffering 'very great losses by the enemyes att sea'. One of their frigates had recently taken two merchant ships bound for Newcastle 'within sight of shore'. Altogether, they believed that six hostile ships were now patrolling the Yorkshire coast 'threatening to do worse mischeifes & to take some of your peticioners out of their bedds and their shipps out of the harbours'.[79]

Luke Robinson wasted no time: the following day he presented the petition to the Committee for the Admiralty. Within a matter of hours he was then able to write to the bailiffs at Scarborough to assure them that 'Capt Elison is gon out with five ships to your coasts'.[80] In fact, to prevent 'the king's frigates' from doing further damage off the north-east coast, the Admiralty had already dispatched Captain John Ellison in the *Harry* and two other armed merchantmen along with the frigate *Warwick* 'with all speed toward that coast'.[81]

If Ellison and his little squadron ever managed to sail as far north as Scarborough, they did not stay there for long or do much good. The bailiffs wrote again, this time to John Lawson, on 3 April 1646, to complain that 'the pyrates doe still continue their mischeifes upon these coasts'. Within the past eight days alone they had taken as many as nine ships, one of them from Scarborough belonging to John Headley. If 'some speedy & especiall care' were not taken it would mean the 'utter undoeing' of all their sea-going trade.[82] Soon afterwards, to underline the seriousness of the matter and their deep anxiety, bailiffs Harrison and Gill wrote yet another letter to their representatives at Westminster. Once again they deplored 'the intollerable greivances occasioned by the cruelty of the enemyes pyrates', and what they described as 'the absolute neglect of the guarding of our coasts'. In particular, they protested about a 22-gun frigate which only the previous day had seized three ships 'within our sight', and was said to have sunk or burned twenty-six others, twelve of them Yarmouth fishing boats.[83] In these circumstances it seemed that no unarmed ship, great or small, was safe in the North Sea.

The reaction of the Westminster Committee for the Admiralty suggests that Harrison and Gill had not exaggerated. Whatever Captain Ellison might be doing, he had failed conspicuously to protect

North Sea shipping as ordered. Henceforth the bailiffs were advised by the London Committee to prevent single or defenceless ships from putting to sea; instead merchantmen and fishing vessels should sail only in convoy or fleet. To guard such convoys the Admiralty appointed a number of first-class frigates under Captain Phineas Pett of the *Mary Rose*. The frigate *Cygnet* was given the particular responsibility of protecting North Sea fishermen. Clearly, the Admiralty regarded the situation as most critical: to provide more North Sea cover they transferred ships from the Irish and Western stations and instructed the four ships of the Scottish guard 'to ply sometimes as farr southwards as Yarmouth Roades'.[84]

This prompt and heavy response of the Admiralty seems to have been effective, at least for the remainder of 1646 and throughout 1647. Nothing more during these years is recorded in Scarborough's archive of 'the king's frigates' or 'sea rovers' until the end of 1647 when the bailiffs received a letter from Whitby. John Newton, William Wigginer and Thomas Bower, all well-to-do shipowners and merchants of that town, reported that Nicholas Wigginer's ship, loaded with butter and alum, had been captured by a pirate who was now in the Tees estuary. They asked the bailiffs if they could furnish a warship that might engage the pirate or at least rescue Wigginer and his extremely valuable cargo. Probably they felt that Scarborough had some responsibility for their loss since the pirate's name was Captain John Denton.[85]

When prompted and sufficiently alarmed, Parliament had provided Scarborough with naval protection; but its lack of financial resources inhibited all attempts to sustain the loyalty of its military garrison there. The allotment of £540 a month for at the most 160 men was generous enough, but the money was simply not forthcoming. By May 1648, when the Commons finally voted £500 to provide accommodation for Boynton's troops and the Excise Commissioners were told to pay it out of their revenue, it was too late: the damage done to the garrison's morale and allegiance was irreparable.[86]

The first indication that there was something seriously wrong at

Scarborough is to be found in a draft letter from bailiffs John Harrison junior and William Nesfield, dated 19 November 1646, and addressed to Sir Matthew and Luke Robinson at Westminster. The letter referred bluntly to 'the great wants of this garrison' and pointed out that its pay was 'about 20 weeks in arrears'. Since no money was forthcoming from York, contrary to the ruling of the House of Commons of April 1646, the town itself had been obliged to give the troops free quarter. Should Parliament fail to send relief to 'our poore towne', then they promised that 'a petition will be framed with 1000 hands to it to averr the truth of what is here expressed'. They warned that there had already been a mutiny of the soldiers for lack of pay which Boynton had 'pacifyed' by guaranteeing that Parliament would soon make good their deficiences, and they reminded their MPs that 'discontents in that sort' would be 'found to bee of soe ill consequence'. The town could not be expected to bear this burden for much longer: to add to the poverty caused by the recent war, four of its ships had been lost this last summer 'being cast away in the stormes'.[87]

This particular emergency seems to have been ended by an order of the Exchequer of 3 February 1647 waiving Scarborough's fee-farm rent of £91 15s. 8d. a year, unpaid for the years 1643, 1644 and 1645.[88] Some of this money had already been spent during these exceptional years, but the remainder, derived from town rents, was used to calm Boynton's soldiers.[89] Ironically, then, the King's rent kept a Parliamentary garrison from mutiny and forced, free billeting, one of the principal grievances against the crown, had become a principal grievance against Parliament. Though Parliament issued an ordinance on Christmas Eve 1647 specifically forbidding soldiers to enter private houses without the owner's consent or to take free victuals from civilians, until it demobilised or paid for its army such commands remained more wishful than effective.[90]

By July 1648 Boynton was again almost penniless and totally dependent on the generosity or fear of the people of Scarborough. For the past three months his garrison of 120 had been billeted in and on the town at a cost of £252.[91] When the colonel asked his superiors for money, General Fairfax at Hull was instructed to send only gunpowder and match to Scarborough. There were no funds available for accommodation; the troops would have to sleep out in the open. The Committee of Both Kingdoms concluded their reply to Boynton's desperate plea with the hope that camping out of doors would 'be no discouragement to the soldiers, being summer time'.[92] Clearly, they had no experience of summer night-time temperatures in Scarborough.

On 7 July realisation was beginning to dawn in London that perhaps Colonel Boynton was no longer trustworthy. Scarborough's two MPs, Anlaby and Robinson, were asked to explain to the Committee of Both Kingdoms 'what grounds there are for the discontent with the Governor of Scarborough and what they think should be done for the safety of that place'.[93] As far as Boynton was concerned, however, it was far too late.

According to the misleadingly named *The Moderate*, one of Parliament's mouthpieces, Colonel Boynton had been heavily bribed by the Prince of Wales to betray Scarborough castle: five months earlier he had accepted a gift of £3,000 from the royalists.[94] This story seems highly improbable, especially in the light of subsequent events. No doubt Boynton's attachment to Parliament was corroded by a chronic lack of funds, and no doubt he did receive promises of money from the Prince, but when he changed sides his motives were no more mercenary than those of Sir Hugh Cholmley. Indeed, Boynton's personal sacrifices for the royalist cause were to go much further than Cholmley's: eventually he gave his life for it.

When on Thursday, 27 July 1648 Colonel Matthew Boynton draped a red flag over the wall of Scarborough castle and declared for the imprisoned King and his eldest son, he was acting out a small, but key, part in an elaborate, ambitious and doomed strategy.[95] *The Moderate* was right about one thing: Boynton's defection was long considered and planned; it was not done on sudden impulse. He had been in correspondence with Prince Charles for some time. The Monday before he declared his change of loyalty 'in the face of the town by beat of drum', he had received another letter from the Prince informing him that he was now in Yarmouth roads with twelve warships. The assumption of Parliamentary officers, such as Captain Robert Wittie, who saw Boynton at the castle on the morning of the 27th, was that the Prince of Wales was about to sail north from Yarmouth and that he intended to come ashore at Scarborough.[96] This was probably also Boynton's understanding.

The royalist plan was to coordinate a Scottish invasion from the north with a seaborne landing from the continent. Sir Marmaduke Langdale with his Englishmen from the northern counties was to link up with the Duke of Hamilton's Scots. When together they had secured Lancashire, the Marquess of Newcastle would cross over from Holland, land at Scarborough and then raise another army for the King in Yorkshire. To protect Newcastle's crossing and his line of supply, the Prince of Wales was expected to bring his warships up the east coast and take station off Scarborough or come ashore there.[97]

Once again Scarborough had betrayed Parliament. For a second time its governor had turned coat and traitor, suborned the garrison and taken the town with him. No one there had offered resistance to him. Moreover, in some ways, Boynton now posed a greater threat to Parliament than Cholmley had done five years earlier. On this occasion there had also been a revolt in the navy and some crews and ships had gone over to the Prince. Parliament's control of the North Sea had never been complete, but now it was jeopardised. A royalist Scarborough would once more attract every privateer to use it for plundering the coal and other east coast trade. Even worse, Scarborough might become the only royalist port of entry for Scottish and continental troops and munitions. With some exaggeration perhaps, Sir William Strickland, writing from Hull to Speaker Lenthall on 28 July, pointed out 'the dangerous consequences of this losse' [of Scarborough]. 'The enemie', he continued, 'had no holds at sea untill nowe, this will give them all manner of accomodacion, and incorage their great partie here to declare themselves and to leave you nothinge . . .'.[98] A day after Boynton put out his symbolic red flag, the Committee of Both Houses asked Mr Anlaby and Richard Darley to treat with him at Scarborough, because, as they explained, 'we fear that place, which is of so great importance, may be in danger'.[99]

The first indication in the corporation records that something extraordinary had happened was the attendance figure for the meeting of the Common Hall on Friday, 28 July. That morning there was a very high number of absentees. Though the two bailiffs, Christopher Jarratt and Nicholas Saunders, were present, John Harrison junior and William Nesfield, the two coroners, were not in their places. Of the First Twelve, William Conyers, Peter Rosdale, Robert Salton,

Peter Hodgson and John Lawson were all missing. John Redhead, one of the four chamberlains, could not be found. Only five of the Second Twelve turned up, and only seven of the Third Twelve.[100]

Though no minutes of this meeting were kept, or have survived, presumably the Common Hall was formally notified of Boynton's change of allegiance the previous day. Nevertheless, for some members, this act alone was enough to keep them out of the Common Hall indefinitely and perhaps even drive them out of the town. John Harrison junior and William Nesfield did not reappear on Sandside, and, predictably, neither did John Lawson or Peter Hodgson. As long as Boyton remained governor, the Second and Third Twelves never exceeded the Second and Third sixes.[101]

Some more resolute, or foolhardy, councillors decided to attend the next meeting of the Common Hall and oppose Boynton there. William Conyers came back on 29 July and indeed was present at every subsequent assembly, but at first he refused to lend money to Boynton, as did Samuel Hodgson, Robert Salton and Matthew Fowler, who were also in the First Twelve. Besides the chronic absentees, there were others in the Second and Third Twelves who at first would not contribute to a new loan.[102]

Extraordinarily, the Common Hall met on Friday, Saturday and Sunday, 28, 29 and 30 July, on Tuesday, 1 August, and both morning and afternoon on 2 August. On 30 July it was agreed 'upon debate' to accept Boynton's 'demaund' that the town should, at its own expense, mount a guard of thirty-six men 'in neighbour row according to their former watch bills'.[103] However, in what might have been a manoeuvre to resist the colonel, it was also agreed that the bellman should give notice throughout the town that 'all housholders of what degree soever [were] to appear att St Maries church to morrow morneing att 6 a clocke there to meet the Governor about some busines concerneing the towne'.[104]

The 'generall meeting' of all Scarborough's householders that took place early in the morning of Monday, 31 July at St Mary's was probably only the second of its kind in the history of the town. Like Cholmley's, held on 23 November 1644, this public gathering also seems to have been a triumph for the military governor. The meeting consented to Boynton's request that the town should raise a company of eighty soldiers for its own defence and for their maintenance it should pay him £20 every week. On the following day there were twenty-five councillors present in the Common Hall to approve this order and appoint assessors for it. Amongst the assessors were two men, Thomas Moone and Tristram Fysh, who had supported Cholmley and been excluded from Sandside during the past three years.[105]

When the Common Hall re-assembled on the morning of 2 August, only twenty-five of its full membership of forty-four were present. Boynton now demanded a 'loan' of £80 in addition to the £20 weekly. The debate must have been lengthy and probably passionate. However, at the end of the morning, it was decided that 'in regard of the present great charges upon the town, the scarsity & dearnes of all manner of provisions & the want of all manner of trading, wee are not able to lend'.[106] The meeting then broke up.

What happened next can only be guessed. Boynton would not take 'no' for an answer. He insisted that the burgesses returned to the Hall in the afternoon. As a minor concession to their stubbornness he was willing to accept £70 instead of £80. All twenty-five resumed their places and all obediently voted in favour of the 'loan'. Obviously, Boynton had threatened them with something worse if they did not cooperate – probably the closure of the Hall and rule by martial law. For the time being, the threat was sufficient.[107]

In the event, the colonel must have been disappointed with the proceeds of the 'loan'. Instead of assessing only the twenty-five members present, all forty-four and the clerk, Richard Dighton, were assumed willing and able to pay. As a result, it seems improbable that the governor's forced loan yielded more than £40.[108]

The rump of the Common Hall's surrender in the face of Boynton's demands was no doubt determined by adequate proof of his determination and military muscle. Parliament's immediate response to the governor's defection was to try to bribe him back. Two delegations were sent from York and Hull to offer him money. They arrived at Scarborough on Saturday, 29 July. The men from York he would not even admit into the castle and their written proposals were rejected out of hand. Those from Hull were allowed into the castle and there they offered Boynton £4,000 if he would surrender it. When at the same time they promised him 'an ordinance for his indempnity, he replied, he durst not trust to that'. Having failed with Boynton, the commissioners next tried to turn his garrison; they shot into the castle yard a printed order promising the soldiers £1,000 if they opened the gates. At this time there were said to be only eighty rebel soldiers loyal to Boynton, but the next piece of news from Scarborough proved this to be a gross underestimate.[109]

Bribery had failed, force was next employed. The following day, Sunday, 30 July, at four o'clock in the morning, Colonel Bethell arrived at Scarborough from Hull with a regiment of cavalry. Boynton brought up eighty horsemen and the same number of infantry to meet them. In the battle that followed, probably on the road to the castle just outside Oldborough Bar, Bethell's men took seven prisoners and drove some of Boynton's foot soldiers over the North Cliff 'and broke their necks for hast to make away'. However, Bethell had not the strength to take and hold even the town: he had to retire to Falsgrave, half a mile way, and there wait for Colonel Legard to reinforce him with a regiment of infantry. Meanwhile, a final attempt had been made to treat with the rebels. With tears in his eyes, Mr Anlaby, who was Boynton's brother-in-law, pleaded with him to give up before he was overwhelmed; but the colonel would not heed his warnings.[110]

By 9 August Colonels Bethell and Legard felt strong enough to mount an assault on the town and harbour, if not the castle. Though there were Parliamentary press reports that the royalists were closely besieged in the castle and unable to receive relief by land or by sea, they were untrue.[111] Indeed, Parliament, despite its many promises to Bethell, never managed to provide him with the naval support given to Meldrum and Boynton in 1645. On the other hand, apart from three officer deserters from the other side, since his revolt Boynton had not been able to add to his numbers, other from Scarborough itself.[112]

According to an eye-witness description, subsequently published in London under the journalistic title 'A Great and Bloudy Fight at Scarborough Castle', the two sides clashed again, as before in the vicinity of Oldborough Bar, on the morning of Wednesday, 9 August.

After 'seven gallant charges were made by the Forlornes of Horse' and 'some blood was spilt', Bethell's cavalry were overpowered. However, when Boynton's cavalry pursued the retreating Roundheads they were met by a counterattack from Colonel Bethell's 'whole bodie'. As a result, Boynton was compelled to commit all of his men in a general engagement. Now the Roundheads had the advantage and drove the royalists back up High Tollergate as far as the main gate of the castle. Some of Boynton's stragglers were cut off, forced over the cliff and died on the rocks below. Bethell took about seventeen captives, and killed about twenty more; his own casualties were fifteen killed and wounded.[113]

But Boynton, described by Parliament's *Moderate Intelligencer* as 'the young Cole [who] hath plaid the old Foxe',[114] was still master of town, harbour and castle. Until he had 'a considerable partie',[115] Bethell lacked the numbers he needed to secure the town and lay close siege to the castle. As a result, Scarborians still had to endure Boynton's occupation. On Saturday, 12 August, the remaining twenty-five members of the Common Hall unanimously consented to continue the weekly gift of £20, paying £19 3s. 10d. to Major Freeman, Boynton's second in command, and keeping the rest to cover 'necessary charges'.[116]

Three days later, it was revealed that 'necessary charges' now included the cost of 'deales and wood, nailes and iron work which the Governor had demaunded . . . about baracadoeing the towne'. In addition to workmen's wages, the town was also paying for 'coales & candles for the guards'.[117]

The following day Boynton made a sally from the castle. His horse and foot took Bethell's forward watch by surprise and overran its guard. Again there was a fierce fight in the market-place outside Oldborough Bar. When Boynton ordered a retreat towards the castle gates, 'Parliament's forces following the pursuit with such eagernesse of spirit' failed to notice the concealed cannon ready loaded for them. One volley from the royalist guns was sufficient to make the Roundheads turn tail. Bethell lost several wounded and a captain and two or three private soldiers killed, but the royalists claimed a great victory. They set up 'a bloudy flag' on top of the keep, sounded their trumpets and beat their drums. They said that they had killed four hundred including Bethell himself! In fact, according to a first-hand Parliamentary report, the colonel had received only 'a small bruise on the left shoulder'.[118]

Still, the Roundheads had no cause for contentment with the situation at Scarborough. More than once Admiral Warwick had been instructed to blockade the harbour, yet there was still no sight of a Parliament warship off the coast.[119] At the same time, the Prince of Wales was soon expected to come north either to Scarborough or Newcastle.[120] On land, Hamilton's huge Scottish army was making its slow, plundering progress through Westmorland and into Lancashire. There was great alarm that the Scots might cross the Pennines and ravage Yorkshire. Parliament's Committee of the Militia at York appealed to all men in the county between the ages of sixteen and sixty to report for service at the nearest military quarters with their weapons and ten days' supply of food. The Scots were rumoured to be taking everything: they were raping wives in front of their husbands, ransoming children back to their parents, and carrying off all goods, including 'pothooks'. They made no distinction between 'papist and protestant, cavalier and saint'.[121] In the face of superior numbers, General Lambert had fallen back over the Pennines to Knaresborough. Cromwell had been summoned from the south, but he did not link up with Lambert until 12 August.

In these critical circumstances, Bethell had no hope of reinforcements for some time to come. He dare not try to occupy the town or the harbour for fear of being cut off by a sally from the castle; and he had no naval support. As far as he knew, Boynton had the townsmen on his side: the town gates, walls and embankments were manned with armed guards. Boynton had as many horsemen and infantry as he had, and more artillery. Bethell and Legard did not fancy their chances in street battles. For the time being, the safest course was to stay in Falsgrave and from there operate a loose and distant siege on the town and castle, or what the royalist *Mercurius Pragmaticus* called 'blocking up at a distance'.[122]

Cromwell's rout of the Scots at Preston and Winwick on the 17 and 19 August ended the crisis in the North for Parliament and meant that eventually Bethell would have the benefit of reinforcements; but before that happened it was Boynton who gained an addition in numbers and strength. In the last days of August a motley force of about three hundred royalist mercenaries came ashore at

Scarborough from the Prince's ships. Parliament's press called these men 'Walloons', French-speaking Catholics from the Spanish Netherlands, since this description was in itself sufficiently damning to excuse any ill-treatment of them. In fact, however, Boynton's new men were a very mixed assortment of English, Welsh, Scottish and Irish, as well as continental soldiers and sailors, some of whom had survived the recent sieges of Deal and Colchester. They were commanded by a certain Major Ashton.[123]

This considerable increase in strength, which raised the royalist garrison to about five hundred, would have been welcomed by Boynton; Scarborians, however, were not likely to greet three hundred foreign soldiers with open arms. On 4 September, with only nineteen councillors present, the Common Hall courageously decided that the town could no longer bear the charges imposed upon it by the garrison. The constables were told to collect only half of the weekly assessment of £20, and pay the governor only £9, instead of the previous £19 3s. 10d.[124] This act of defiance brought matters to a head. Boynton seems to have been willing to accept £9 the first week; but on 11 September, when the Common Hall refused to offer another £9 for the next week and threatened him with a petition 'to be signed by all housholders in the towne of the inabilities of the towne to pay more', his patience broke. The bailiffs were commanded to hand over the Hall door keys to Lieutenant Sollitt. From now on the hall chamber was to be used only 'to keepe provisions'; there were to be no more meetings of councillors there. On the following day, despite Boynton's manoeuvre, some of the town's leaders, supported by 'divers other of the housholders', drew up a petition of protest addressed to Colonel Boynton.[125]

The 'humble representation of the bailiffs, burgesses and other inhabitants of Scarborough' listed the numerous heavy charges borne by the town during the past six weeks: 'for quartring of soldiers, paying assessments, furnishing provisions of victualls and bedding for the castle, loane moneys, deales, timber, workemens wages for makeing works, coales and candles for the guards (as 38 pecks of coales on a night), eateing up our meadowes, taking and wasting our hay, the takeing away our kine and horses, daily common noats [forced unpaid labour] (now charged upon the persons of housholders), the decay of all tradeing . . .'[126]

Perhaps the townsmen were emboldened by the news that Bethell and Legard were now reinforced with a regiment under Francis Lascelles and a company of 160 musketeers under Captain Smith and Lieutenant Holt from Hull.[127] It must have seemed to them that their deliverance from Boynton was imminent. Parliament's 'Bloudy News from the North' reported a sortie led by Major Ashton against Legard's quarters on Sunday 11 September, which the 'renowned' Colonel Bethell had repulsed; but this was the last foray out of the castle from the royalists.[128] As Lascelles later reported to Cromwell, since 'the enemy grew in strength by sea daily', the Parliamentarians decided to storm the town at once.[129]

For the second time in three and a half years Scarborough town was taken by assault on the morning of 15 September 1648. On this occasion, however, there was no planned and efficiently executed withdrawal to the castle by the defenders. Captain John Buck, a deserter from Bethell's regiment, who commanded the royalist cavalry, and Major Ashton, who seems to have retained command if not control of the miscellaneous gang of foreign soldiers, were determined to hold the town; but they were soon overwhelmed in a series of one-sided street fights. The Roundheads lost no more than half a dozen dead and perhaps twice that number wounded, whereas Parliamentary estimates of royalists killed varied between 25 and 40. Amongst the royalist dead were Buck and Ashton.[130] The House of Commons was so pleased by the news of the fall of Scarborough that the messenger, Francis Armitage, was rewarded with a generous gift of £50.[131]

In his preliminary report of the battle to General Cromwell, Colonel Lascelles gave the names of 156 prisoners, who included three captains, six lieutenants, a quartermaster, a cannoneer, nine sergeants and two surgeons. Some of the captives named – James Headley, John Foord, William Wooddall and Thomas Wolfe – were probably natives of Scarborough; none of them had foreign names. If the '22 more wounded' and the '25 dead' he gave are added to the list of prisoners taken, they bring the total to just over 200. So what had happened to the 300 so-called Walloons who, according to several different sources, had landed at Scarborough about three weeks earlier?[132]

Mercurius Melancholicus, the royalist news-sheet, was convinced that 'the Pagan Saints', under the orders of Bethell and Lascelles, had put all 300 foreign prisoners to the sword, using the lame lie that they were unfortunately mistaken by their men for Irish, and added:

> But know ye monsters, next will be your Fate,
> The time is coming we'll retaliate.[133]

If this gross accusation had been exclusive to royalist accounts,[134] it might have been safely discounted as yet another calumny, but even Parliament's *Moderate Intelligencer*, normally a fairly accurate source, reported that 'prisoners, some Walloons, whom the souldiers took for Irishmen, [were] put to the sword, countreymen not knowing the difference of languages'.[135] Subsequently, Parliament's historians, Rushworth and Whitelocke, accepted this story and wrote it into their accounts.[136]

In October 1644 Parliament had passed an ordinance directing that any Irishman in arms, captured on land or at sea, should be put to death without mercy.[137] The assumption behind this barbarous order was that an Irishman fighting for the King was sure to be a Catholic and therefore guilty, directly or by association, of the massacre of Ulster protestants in 1641.

Whether the 'Walloons' who surrendered were honestly mistaken for Irishmen cannot be determined. However, men who spoke a foreign language, made the sign of the cross and perhaps wore crucifixes on neck chains would be taken for papists and as such could not expect mercy. Another reason for not giving quarter to the 'strangers' might have been revenge for their alleged brutality towards civilians. One of Parliament's news-sheets claimed that the 'English, Welsh, Scotch and Walloons' (not Irish) had used 'much cruelty' towards the people of Scarborough so that some had been forced to leave the town and 'their estates to their mercy'. Houses that they feared might be of value to Bethell they had burned down and the schoolhouse, which had been a guardhouse in the siege of 1645, they had levelled to the ground.[138]

The second Civil-War siege of Scarborough castle lasted just three months; compared with the first it seems to have been a minor and uneventful affair, though perhaps because we lack an eye-witness account of it. Cholmley had been shut in tightly by land and by sea; Boynton was never blockaded from the sea. The many repetitions of orders to the navy to guard Scarborough and the frequent complaints of Bethell that the enemy might be relieved or even rescued by sea testify to Parliament's failure to establish, let alone maintain, a naval siege.[139]

Also, in contrast to the situation in 1645, the besiegers were outgunned by the besieged. Bethell had no artillery of any weight, whereas the royalists had at least four pieces of ordnance and an abundance of powder and match.[140] One of Parliament's informants, writing from Helmsley, claimed that Boynton's guns had 'battered down the church steeple and much of the church' on 26 September and concluded that the enemy had 'so much powder that they are very prodigal of it'.[141]

Unlike Cholmley's garrison, Boynton's men were never without food or water. At the surrender, they still had half a year's supply of rye and butter, and a month's of fish. Between mid-September and mid-December the rainfall fed the well of Our Lady. There were no reports this time of scurvy or other diseases. As Bethell noted in his report to General Fairfax at the end of the siege, the castle might well have held out for another three months. The garrison lacked only shoes and stockings.[142]

Meldrum had tried to take the castle by heavy bombardment and direct infantry assault; Bethell had some difficulty even to keep Boynton's men inside it. From Beverley it was reported that on 16 October the besieged had sallied out, taken the forward guards unawares, killed five of them and taken thirty prisoners. Bethell had quickly counterattacked with a troop of horse, rescued his men and taken fourteen captives himself with the loss of only one man.[143] Even the harbour was not safe. The House of Commons was informed at the end of October that the royalist gunners had 'sunk a frigate early in the morning that came in with coals in the night for the town'.[144] If this report was true it suggests that Boynton was still holding South Steel battery.

Contrary to popular belief, General Oliver Cromwell never set foot in Scarborough at this time or any other,[145] but after his crushing victories over the Scots in Lancashire he did spend eight weeks in October and November 1648 conducting the siege of Pontefract castle. There he kept in touch with the situation at the other Yorkshire castle siege. According to a letter he wrote to the Commons on 15 November, he and Bethell were both seriously impeded by shortages of ammunition. In response, the House ordered that 250 barrels of gunpowder should be sent to the leaguers at Pontefract and Scarborough.[146] Clearly, Colonel Overton, the governor of Hull, had failed to supply Bethell with the powder, match and bullet he had requested for the siege.[147]

The first indication that Boynton's resistance was crumbling came in a report from Scarborough to the House of Commons on 4 December. On the night of Tuesday, 28 November, the castle boat, which had been used to ferry in supplies and messengers through the sally port, was captured by the besiegers.[148] This loss caused alarm and despondency amongst 'the common soldiers [who] fell into a mutiny'. Boynton seems to have pacified the mutineers, but some of his officers now began to desert, in particular his ensign and his harbinger-general. The latter's name was given as Lieutenant 'Sallet'; he had 'come in and submitted . . . upon mercy' to Bethell.[149]

Presumably, Lieutenant 'Sallet' was none other than Francis Sollitt, who has already made several earlier appearances in this story. As a fifteen-year-old servant to Francis Thompson in March 1634, Francis had stayed up all night to catch thieves in the act of stealing beans from his master's barn.[150] As a merchant and shipowner, in 1643 he had been importing a cargo of wine, prunes, Malaga raisins, Newfoundland train-oil, Swedish iron and tar from Rotterdam into Scarborough harbour.[151] As a known royalist, Francis Sollitt had left the town when it fell to Parliament in 1645. When he returned home in March 1647, John Lawson thought the matter was important enough to include it in a letter to Luke Robinson who was then in London. In turn, Robinson told the bailiffs that he presumed that since 'Francis Sollett' was a delinquent they had disenfranchised him and 'then hee has noe relaition to your towne'.[152] Finally, on 11 September 1648, Francis Sollitt was the royalist lieutenant to whom the bailiffs were ordered by Boynton to surrender the keys of the Common Hall.[153]

On Sunday, 17 December both sides sent out their treaty commissioners to negotiate the terms of surrender. Bethell was represented by Colonels Christopher Legard, William Spencer and Barrington Bourchier, and Captains Nicholas Conyers and John Lawson; and Boynton appointed Colonel Thomas Fairfax, Majors Edward Gower and Thomas Reston, and Captains Roger Newinson and Timothy Wilkins to speak for the garrison 'on behalf of His Majesty'. They agreed that the castle should surrender the following Tuesday at nine in the morning. At that appointed time the garrison would march out of the castle down the road to Scarborough Common, 'their colours flying, drums beating, muskets loaded, bandileers filled, matches lighted and bullet in mouth there to lay down their arms'.[154] The governor and his senior officers were allowed horses, servants and side arms; junior officers could keep a sword and a pistol each; and all other ranks were allowed swords. All 260 soldiers in the garrison were given freedom to return to their homes or given passes 'to go beyond sea'. They might travel to any part of the kingdom 'except besieged places' at a rate of eight miles a day, not staying above one night in any place, except on the sabbath day. Gentlewomen within the castle were allowed to pass out 'with their wearing apparel, money and necessaries'. For those who needed and could afford to hire them, horses were to be made available at 'the backside of St Mary's church' on the day of the surrender.[155]

These were most generous terms, particularly when compared with what had happened to the defenders of Colchester when they surrendered in August after a siege lasting ten weeks. Many of them were transported to the West Indies to work on plantations as virtual slaves and their two senior officers, Sir Charles Lucas and Sir George Lisle, were summarily executed by firing squad.[156] Indeed, Colonel Bethell was himself so conscious that the terms might appear excessively lenient that he felt it necessary to justify them to Lord Fairfax and to the government in London.

As early as 12 December, Bethell had been reliably informed that there was a Dunkirk ship at sea bringing 'men, money and store of provisions for the reliefe of the castle'. Since the wind was then blowing from the south and there was no way that this ship could be prevented from reaching Scarborough, he and his council of officers unanimously concluded that it would be wisest to treat with Boynton. General Lambert had also encouraged them to do so. They had asked repeatedly for Parliament's naval support, but 'we never had yet the happinesse to have one ship upon these coasts, neither any assurance thereof'. Until then God had been 'merciful by his providence in the winds' and thereby hindered any enemy vessel from approaching Scarborough from the south. Now this was no longer the case. Though the treaty might seem softer than Fairfax or London expected, 'in the present exigencies it could not be avoided'.[157]

Bethell and his officers need not have worried themselves: Major Peter Acklam, who brought the news of the fall of the castle to London, was voted a reward of £40 and both Houses approved the articles of surrender without qualification. Bethell himself was appointed governor of the town and castle and John Lawson reappointed captain of the castle guard.[158]

Demoralisation and the daunting prospect of a long, cold winter on the exposed coastal headland defeated Boynton. Despite the rout at Naseby, the royalist cause was still alive and the King still at liberty when Cholmley surrendered. By the end of 1648, however, the castle garrison had no real hope of relief or rescue, except perhaps by sea. Sir Hugh had withstood siege throughout the spring and early summer; Boynton's men had the misfortune to be shut up at the beginning of winter. They had plenty of food and water but only three weeks' supply of firewood and many were without shoes and warm clothing.[159] The final inducement was Bethell's humane terms: he might have believed the Prince's ships were 'expected every houre'[160], but the besieged did not. Once the 'Walloons' had been dispatched, the cruelty that characterised the second Civil War elsewhere was not evident at Scarborough.

Throughout the five-month long siege of the castle in 1645, the town's corporate government had been suspended: Scarborough was ruled by martial law. The Common Hall was closed and none of the borough's courts were allowed to sit. Even the town markets were transferred to Peasholm. In contrast, soon after Parliament's troops took the town and harbour on 15 September 1648, the Common Hall re-opened. As early as 19 September, the bailiffs, Christopher Jarratt and Nicholas Saunders, were asked by the councillors present to 'sollicite the comaunders in cheife of the Parliament forces now in the towne for an order that the soldjers shall not take away nor deface the pewes & seates in the church'.[161] Some things had not changed since 1645: St Mary's was too conveniently placed for a siege of the castle not to be used as a forward strongpoint and soldiers were no respecters of church furniture.

A week later, when the Common Hall again assembled on Sandside, its members, in the circumstances, showed remarkable independence of spirit. Though perhaps fewer than twenty men were present, they objected to the two months' assessment of £140, which Bethell, Legard and Bourchier had previously agreed with the bailiffs: they would pay no more than £100, which they regarded as a fair proportion. Amongst the assessors appointed by the Common Hall to levy this tax were two members of the First Twelve, William Foord and Thomas Gill.[162]

Though the town and harbour were under sporadic fire from cannon in the castle, though Parliament's forces seemed scarcely sufficient to maintain a close blockade, and there were rumours rife of the Prince's warships heading north with reinforcements and relief for Boynton, at Michaelmas 1648 the town's ruling body acted as though everything was normal. Twenty-six members of the Common Hall turned up for the annual elections on 30 September. Of the senior burgesses only the two Harrisons were marked as absentees; of the First Twelve, only William Batty, Samuel and Peter Hodgson were missing. Heaviest 'casualties' were lower down in the municipal order: only three of the Second Twelve were there and eight of the Third.

Nevertheless, the elections and appointments proceeded as usual. Considering what had happened during the past eight weeks and what was still happening only yards away, there was astonishing smoothness and continuity. Richard Dighton was still in his accustomed place as town clerk. Philip Benson's term as town gaoler, a post he had held for many years, was renewed yet again. The sub-bailiffs, churchwardens, constables, leather searchers, sealer and registrar, the overseers of the poor, overseers of the highways, pasture masters for Weaponness, alefyners, breadweighers, and pindar were all named for the year to come; so were bellman, pier master and netherd. Anthony Conell kept his place as town warrener. New leases on town land were given out. New freemen were admitted: Colonels Bethell, Lascelles and Legard did not swear and did not pay, but as a friendly gesture they were admitted as freemen of the borough just the same. On the other hand, apprentices who had completed their indentures were admitted as freemen for four shillings, while the sons of burgess freemen paid 3s. 4d. for the privilege.[163]

Since the last Common Hall had been elected in September 1647 under a Parliamentary regime, the new one a year later contained few changes and only one surprise. According to custom, the former bailiffs, Christopher Jarratt and Nicholas Saunders, stepped down and were transformed immediately into coroners. Amongst the First Twelve there was only one new face: Edward Hickson, the master mariner, was promoted from the top of the Second Twelve to the lowest rung of the First. There were only two promotions from the Third to the Second, and only four new admissions to the bottom of the Third, who included William Nesfield junior.[164]

The single surprise was the meteoric rise of Matthew Fowler. He was a tanner by trade who lived and worked in Newborough. He had been admitted burgess in 1623 when his apprenticeship was fulfilled. By the 1630s he was one of the two dozen Scarborough men who owned a musket. By then he had a pew in St Mary's in the area on the north-west side of the back alley occupied by lesser but up-and-coming townsmen.[165] He had the good fortune to marry Mary, one of the daughters of William Batty, and they had a son, born in 1626, called after his grandfather.[166] By October 1642, Matthew was half way up the Third Twelve; a year later he had ascended to the Second where he stayed in 1644 and 1645. In 1646–7 he served as one of the four chamberlains and in September 1647 he just squeezed into the last place in the First Twelve. Now, only a year on, he was suddenly chosen junior bailiff to John Harrison senior.[167]

Though he was hardly likely to be aware of it, Matthew Fowler was the founding father of a local dynasty, the first of many generations of Scarborough Fowlers who were to run the town's affairs for the next three centuries. In the course of time and in more normal circumstances, he might still have become one of Scarborough's bailiffs, but the Civil Wars appear to have accelerated his progress. He was elected junior bailiff again in 1652 and finally senior of the pair in 1658.[168]

When the sheriff's tourn took place on 4 October and the general sessions three days later, bailiff Harrison and coroner Jarratt were amongst those presented for not bringing in their measures; William Foord and John Hickson were two leading burgesses accused of not dressing their street frontages; and Anne Harwood had maintained her family's notorious reputation by buying in butter before it came into the open market. As though the bailiffs did not have enough anxieties, they were presented for not cleaning out the common sewer in Quay Street.[169] At the sessions, the bailiffs listened to familiar cases of blood and affray. William Robinson had assaulted Ralph Witty; Isabel Webster had drawn blood from the body of Alice West. William Ray had had the audacity to question the judgement of the bailiffs and was required to make a humiliating, public apology.[170] Despite the disorder of the times, the bailiffs still insisted on keeping the old rule that they should be informed by householders if they had 'enterteined strangers into their houses'; offenders who failed to attend the sessions to answer this charge were fined a swingeing ten shillings for their contempt.[171]

But below this surface of normality there were glimpses of extraordinary damage that had been done to people and property. All the money and skilled workmanship spent on repairing St Mary's after the devastation of 1645 had been wasted: the parish church was now more ruined than ever. The church of St Thomas the Martyr was beyond repair: part of it had already fallen, the rest was ready to fall, 'for as much as much of the timber and slates are stollen away by evil disposed persons'. To prevent 'further imbezlement' of the structure, the whole building was to be demolished and the materials either sold or 'imployed about the repaireing of St Maryes church'. In fact, four of the existing octagonal piers forming an arcade on the north side of the north aisle of St Mary's originally belonged to St Thomas's.[172] The revestry on the exposed north side of the parish church was also taken down at this time and its lead, timber and stone re-used by the churchwardens to patch up other parts of St Mary's.[173]

Colonel Boynton, not the 'Walloons', had pulled down the schoolhouse and former charnel chapel 'after he revolted'. Again, there was no question of re-building it. Instead, the chamberlains were required to raise money from the sale of 'the charnell stones' and use it to convert Farrer's Aisle, or the south transept of St Mary's, into a new schoolhouse.[174] The chamberlains' accounts which have survived for the year 1648–9 show that the town spent heavily in wages and materials to convert the south transept into the new grammar school. A new door was cut in the west wall to allow the boys access without having to come through the main body of the church. A new wall was put up to divide the transept from the nave. Upper and lower classrooms were made by dividing the transept into two floors connected by a wooden staircase. In the financial year ending Michaelmas 1649, the chamberlains disbursed £14 7s. 6d. on timber, lead, slates, glass and wages for the benefit of the 'schoulehouse'.[175] Work on the conversion continued for the next four years. Though this new home was originally intended as temporary and makeshift, it remained Scarborough's grammar school for two hundred years until the Victorian reconstruction of 1848–50.[176]

Repairs and alterations to St Mary's were the heaviest drain on the town's stretched resources, but the parish church was not the only building in need of attention. The Common Hall windows had to be mended; the conduit door had to be replaced; fences and gates on Weaponess had gone. The pinfold was another war victim: including 6d. spent on drink for the workmen, it cost 9s. 6d. to re-build it. The town prison had also suffered. The chamberlains gave Robert Atkinson, his son and his man three shillings for 'mending the prison' in one day; they spent half a crown on lime for re-pointing the walls, sixpence on drink for the workers, and another sixpence on two stones for a new hearth.[177]

Ralph Harrison was paid half a crown for his five days' work on the conduit pipes, but he got twice as much 'for buryeing dead men when the leagar was'. So the town had to pay the costs of burying soldiers killed in the castle siege as well as the costs of maintaining them in food and bedding when they were alive. Six men were 'slaine when they sallied out upon [Francis] Faweathers house', and the town paid £1 2s. 6d. for their winding sheets and graves. Whether Fawether himself was one of the dead is not recorded; as one of Scarborough's sea pirates who had gone abroad with Browne Bushell he might well have come home when Boynton changed sides.[178] Another expensive casualty of the second Civil War was the town bull. When the town bought itself a replacement in 1649, it cost an inflationary £3 12s. 2d.[179]

Despite all these extra and onerous charges, the Common Hall managed to fulfil its obligations to employees and dependants. Mr Penston, the schoolmaster, had to wait for his school to be built, but he received a full year's salary of £10 for the year 1648–9. The pindar and the bellman had new coats at half a crown each. The town waits [singers and musicians] got new coats and trimming which cost £1 18s.; and 'the power [poor] at Christenmass' 1648 received the customary gift of £2 10s. to be spent on their food, drink and entertainment. Meanwhile, the bailiffs themselves do not seem to have economised on their own civic pleasures: William Lawson's vintner's bill for the period from Michaelmas 1648 to Lady Day 1649 was £6 4s. 6d. and that of the other vintner, William Saunders, from Michaelmas 1648 to May Day 1649 came to £10 3s. 8d. More surprisingly, in this time of extreme want, the churchwardens continued to pay a shilling for every foxhead brought to them, whereas the corpses of foumerts [polecats] fetched only fourpence each.[180]

After the town was taken by Bethell's men, the guardhouse near the oilhouse in St Nicholas Gate, which had cost so much to build, was demolished.[181] Yet even after the fall of the castle, Parliament's depleted garrison was still billeted in the town at its expense, and Bethell's guards were still being supplied with free coal, candles and firewood.[182]

Free quarter and outstanding billeting bills were issues that caused the greatest grief to Scarborians in the months following Boynton's surrender. As early as 6 January 1649, Captain John Lawson and Lieutenant John Rudlee signed a petition 'in the behalfe of the inhabitants of this poore towne'. As officers who had previously served under Colonel Boynton until his defection, they certified that between 15 January and 27 July 1648 his company of 120 soldiers had run up a debt of £252 with the town. Since during these six months 'before his revolt' Boynton's soldiers were part of Lord Fairfax's army, Scarborough should be credited for the sum still unpaid against its liability for taxation. Allowance should also be made for 'the extreame suffrings of our towne since the revolt haveing almost utterly ruined it'.[183]

The following month, the Common Hall passed a motion that the bailiffs should 'acquaint Col. Bethell with the present poverty of this towne and remind him of its late & great sufferings and that the poore of this towne are so many and the towne so unable to maintain them, that many of them are ready to starve'. As a consequence of their 'insufficiency', the burgesses contended that they were 'not able to quarter soldjers'. The colonel was also to be reminded that Scarborough was as free as other garrison towns such as Hull, Boston and King's Lynn, and therefore should not be forced to give free lodgings and diet in its private houses to soldiers.[184]

In reply, Bethell said that he was 'sensible of the poverty and insufficiency of the towne' and declared that he would rather throw in his commission than see its inhabitants 'impoverished & ruined'. However, he had no choice but to ask for free quarter, particularly in winter-time, until he received more money for accommodation and sustenance. As a compromise settlement, it was therefore agreed by the Common Hall to lend three shillings a week for the next fortnight to each soldier requiring lodgings in the town. The governor pledged himself to pay all debts in full and promised there would be no forced billeting.[185]

Nevertheless, as fragments of surviving corporation accounts reveal, Bethell's men long continued to receive town billets on credit. Between 25 March and 9 June 1649, a period of eleven weeks, about fifty soldiers in Captain Lawson's company ran up a total debt of nearly £25 to private householders. For instance, bailiff Harrison accommodated a soldier called John Paul for three weeks at three shillings a week, which was the average charge for lodgings and meals. The highest bill, for thirty shillings, was owed to William Chapman. The householders were given vouchers which recorded the soldier's name, the length of quarter and the sum owing, and they were signed either by the soldier himself or his lieutenant, John Rudlee. However, from a later, but undated petition, it is clear that these surviving vouchers represented only a part of the total costs of billeting during this eleven week period. Quartering the companies of Bethell and Lawson altogether was said to have amounted to £64 5s. 11d. and of this claim the petitioners were still owed £36 7s. 11d.[186] Therefore, in October 1649, when Major Acklam, representing Bethell, asked for a further loan from the town, the Common Hall gave him a brief, firm answer: 'the towne is nott att present in a capacity to lend money'. Until the accumulated arrears for quarters were first paid, there was no question of more credit.[187]

For the time being this seems to have settled the matter. The town's impoverishment was certainly no fiction. On an assessment list of 1643, Scarborough had nineteen widowed householders; by 1649, on a comparable list, that number had grown to twenty-nine.[188] In 1647, the town was responsible for maintaining sixteen orphaned pauper children too young to be apprenticed out; by 1654, the figure had risen to thirty-six. On the other hand, according to the records of the poorhouse of St Thomas, the number of aged and impotent inmates there remained at fifty-six or fifty-seven between 1647 and 1651. Probably the house was full. The ages there ranged from the youngest, a fifty-five year old widow, to George Potter, who was said to be 104 in 1648, though he had been a mere 101 the previous year. Most of Scarborough's official paupers were elderly widows who received weekly doles from the better-off residents at rates which varied from two to ten pence.[189]

Secondly, the Council of State in London came round to recognising that if Scarborough was to continue as a garrison town it would have to be properly and regularly financed. For a time, in 1651, it seemed that Scarborough castle was to suffer the same slighting as all the others in Yorkshire. In May the decision was taken in London to demolish it altogether: it was too accessible and attractive to enemies landing from the sea and Scarborough town still had a bad reputation for disloyalty and untrustworthiness.[190] However, anticipating local resistance to such a drastic solution, the Council of State ordered that Bethell's two infantry companies should be marched out and a new company brought in from Hull.[191] Presumably, it was supposed in London that three years' residence in Scarborough had softened and corrupted Bethell's men. Consequently, Lt.-Col. Salmon, the governor of Hull, was told to send a hundred soldiers under a reliable officer to Scarborough 'in regard that place is of so great importance'.[192]

But the Council of State soon had second thoughts about the future of Scarborough castle. It had received warning of a plot to rescue the late King's third son, Prince Henry, from the Isle of Wight, and bring him by sea to Scarborough.[193] This report came soon after the Council had been told that Captain James Cholmley, a kinsman of Sir Hugh, was again at Whitby with an armed following of Frenchmen. Luke Robinson was ordered to investigate this story and arrest the foreigners if he considered them dangerous.[194] Sir Hugh Cholmley himself was then staying with his Twysden in-laws at East Peckham in Kent, but no risks were taken and he and other royalist suspects were arrested and imprisoned in Leeds castle for eight weeks until the crisis had passed.[195] Within little more than a month of issuing the demolition order, the Council now suspended it indefinitely. Captain Southeron was put in Bethell's place at Scarborough and his pay increased by four shillings a day 'during his continuance in that charge'.[196]

There was no more talk of slighting the castle. On the contrary, the military establishment at Scarborough castle was to be permanent. From 20 October 1651 the Council approved a monthly allowance of £10 5s. 4d. to pay for a gunner and his mate, two 'matrosses' [labourers], a storekeeper and fire and candles for the guard at South Steel battery.[197] When the First Dutch War began the following year, Lord Fairfax was ordered to bring his forces in Yorkshire 'towards Scarborough and the sea coasts, for the security thereof'.[198]

CHAPTER SIX

Interregnum, 1649–1660

No doubt Scarborians were reassured by the presence of a permanent garrison at the castle and more so by the government's recent success in paying it, but at sea the Civil War continued unabated. The corporation records contain numerous references to the activities of pirates, often thinly disguised as privateers. Armed with a commission from Prince Charles to 'sincke, fire or otherwise destroy all ships . . . of his majesties subiects in England in actuall rebellion against his majestie . . . and to take [their cargoes] to the island of Jersey', many royalist captains took a heavy toll of North Sea coastal traffic.[1]

A letter written by Scarborough's governor, Colonel Bethell, in November 1649 reveals how serious and alarming the situation had become: 'There hath been very much spoyl committed this week by pirats upon these coasts; divers taken within view; some running for shelter close under the castle so that we were forced to preserve them with our guns. Wee sent out a vessel with muskitters, but there were so many of them, that they could not deal with them. There was one ship taken belonging to this towne, by one Denton, a pirate, formerly belonging to Sir Hu Chumley. It were well that better cours were taken to preserve trading by sea. There are great store of ships at present in this harbour, and dare not stir without a strong convoy.'[2] Soon afterwards, all the members of the Common Hall signed a petition 'for a better guard of the coast', requesting that for this purpose Captains Nesfield and Lawson should each be provided with an armed frigate.[3]

That Captain John Lawson scored at least one success is confirmed by a letter from Hamburg written by Richard Bradshaw, the British agent there, to the Council of State in London. It seems that down the river Elbe from Hamburg, at the Danish port of Gluckstatt, there was a regular market in English prizes taken by pirates. In May 1649, for instance, Browne Thomas had taken a ship of about 100 tons carrying coals; it belonged to Harrison and Sanderson of Scarborough. In flat defiance of an agreement made in 1645 between Parliament and the king of Denmark, Thomas had sold the lot, collier and cargo, at Gluckstatt. Lawson must have found out about this illegal market in stolen ships and he paid a special visit to Gluckstatt in the autumn of 1650. Ignoring Danish claims that their port was free to all, even pirate prizes, and scorning the guns of their fort, Lawson seized a small ship in the harbour which he knew to be formerly of Scarborough, and returned it to its rightful owners.[4]

Another success against piracy recorded at Scarborough was God-given rather than man-made. In December 1649, Captain Nicholas Marriner of the royal frigate *St George* was forced by 'extremity of weather' on to Scarborough sands. The *St George* was found to carry the Prince's commission and a cargo of barley lately stolen from a King's Lynn hoy. Consequently, some of its mixed crew of English, Irish, Flemings and Danes were sent to York assizes to stand trial.[5]

Three months later, a remarkable encounter took place near the coast between Filey and Scarborough. Robert Colman, master of a Yarmouth fishing boat, had come into 'Scarborough peares' with his catch. However, when he was told that an enemy warship was then in Filey Bay, immediately he volunteered himself, his crew and his boat, on condition that Colonel Bethell contributed soldiers, arms and ammunition. Accordingly, Captain Thomas Lascelles brought two small cannon and thirty armed men to stiffen Colman's two dozen volunteers. That same evening they set sail southwards and soon saw a foreign ship.[6]

Joseph Constant, master of the *St Peter* of Jersey, had left Dunkirk on 27 March with about thirty-two men, carrying the Prince's privateers' commission. When five days later he sighted a Yarmouth fishing boat coming straight towards him it must have seemed a welcome, easy bonus. The fishing boat was hailed, commanded to 'strike, yea dogs, for King Charles', and then grappled. Before Constant realised his error it was too late. Lascelles's soldiers fired a musket volley and their light guns blasted away with hailshot. Immediately afterwards Colman and his seamen leapt aboard the *St Peter*. After 'a hot skirmish', in which Colman himself and three of his crew were 'sore wounded', Constant surrendered his ship. Five of the privateers had been killed or drowned and the rest, including the captain and a Scarborough seaman called Ralph Slee, were taken prisoner. The *St Peter* was brought triumphantly into Scarborough and the survivors of its crew escorted to the castle at York. What reward the gallant Colman received is not locally recorded but he won an accolade of praise from bailiffs Thomas Gill and William Saunders for his 'unparelled service for the Commonwealth'.[7]

The capture of Captains Marriner and Constant was welcomed in London, but the greatest prize of all everyone agreed was Browne Bushell. In early April 1648, the 'old sea pirot' was reported to be preying on Newcastle colliers at the mouth of the Tyne. Captain John Lawson knew Bushell well: he had been master of a ship he had commanded when in 1642–3 they were both employed in Parliament's service. It was therefore sensible and appropriate that Lawson should be ordered to put to sea in his armed merchantman, the *Covenant*, to apprehend the most notorious of all the North Sea pirates.[8]

Whether Lawson or some other captain brought in Browne Bushell cannot be determined. However, by 17 April the Committee of Both Houses ordered that Bushell and any other person reported to be dangerous should be examined. Despite a specific instruction to the marshall at Whitehall that he should be guarded well and closely, almost at once he escaped from the custody of an admiralty messenger.[9] But this time Browne Bushell's freedom was brief: two men who were rewarded with gifts of £10 each soon recaptured him. From now on the House of Commons ordered that he should be kept 'strictly and safely' in Windsor castle. If the castle governor allowed him to escape again he would answer at his peril. In the meantime the admiralty was to prepare evidence against him 'for his piracy and other crimes'.[10]

The governor of Windsor castle was so afraid of losing Bushell that he kept him in close confinement. The prisoner complained of ill-treatment to the Council of State. In reply, the Council conceded that 'for one of his quality and in his condition' he should be accommodated more comfortably. For as long as he remained at Windsor he was allowed five shillings a week for his subsistence.[11]

The Council's reference to Bushell's 'condition' perhaps indicated that his health was suffering from imprisonment; alternatively, the Council might have been mindful that one way or another he had not very long to live. After nearly a year of captivity, Browne Bushell, it was decided by a Commons vote of 26 to 17, was to be tried for high treason.[12] The Attorney-General ruled that the prosecution should be based, not on his piracy, but on his surrender of Scarborough to Sir Hugh Cholmley on 29 March 1643. Nevertheless, gathering evidence against Bushell was a long, drawn-out business. Luke Robinson was the man entrusted by the Council of State to find witnesses, record sworn testimonies, and in some cases send up to London men who might speak against the captain.[13]

By July 1650, with the active assistance of bailiffs Gill and Saunders, Robinson had collected a mountain of eye-witness evidence against Bushell. Nicholas Ducke, fisherman, Robert Lacy, sailor, John Barry, William Foord and the two John Harrisons of Scarborough all swore that he had taken the castle in the name of Parliament and then handed it over to his cousin Sir Hugh the following day without the least show of resistance. Afterwards, when Hotham's two catches came into the harbour, Bushell had helped Cholmley to deceive their captains and crews that they were still loyal to Parliament.[14] Robinson went up to Whitby to acquire more affidavits from Richard Thackray, Nicholas Wigginer, John Yeoman, Henry Becke and the Newton brothers, Isaac and John. Browne's sister Hester had married Isaac Newton, but he regarded his brother-in-law as the man who had dispossessed him of his rightful inheritance, Bagdale Old Hall, and the gentleman's estate that belonged to it. Browne had refused to live under his sister's roof or accept charity from the wealthy Newtons. Instead, he had left Whitby to seek his fortune abroad in the service of the King of Spain. Whereas Bushell had changed sides in the First Civil War his Newton in-laws had remained steadfastly and prominently Parliamentarian. Hester's husband became one of Parliament's new justices of the peace in the North Riding and took a captain's commission in its army. It was Isaac Newton who was made 'Governor of Whitby' after Cholmley's expulsion from there in 1644 and it was he who brought his company of soldiers and mariners down to Scarborough in February 1645 to help General Meldrum storm the town. In these circumstances, the evidence of the Newtons against Browne Bushell was likely to be as damning as that of any other of Robinson's witnesses.[15]

Browne Bushell's imprisonment had been lengthy, but his trial in

Westminster Hall could hardly have been shorter: it lasted only one day, 25 March 1651. Robinson had done well: the evidence against Bushell was overwhelming. Though he pleaded not guilty, he had no defence. The court sentenced him to die on the eighth anniversary of his treason, 29 March.[16]

A witness of the event that Saturday afternoon wrote a vivid account of the execution of Captain Browne Bushell. At five o'clock, Bushell emerged from the Tower of London wearing a scarlet cloak. There was a great crowd of people there to watch him die. The captain smiled at the spectators, saluted the lieutenant of the Tower, took off his hat, and addressed the gathering. He told them that he had served the King of Spain for ten years. Then, at the beginning of these late 'distractions', he had sailed from Dunkirk to offer himself to the King and Parliament. However, his conscience and judgement had soon convinced him of the unlawfulness of that rash engagement and he had deserted Parliament to join the King's cause. He regretted only that he had not been on the royalist side from the outset. He declared himself to be a loyal subject of his late majesty and his heirs and a true son of the Church of England. Bushell then turned to the executioner to ask him if the same block and axe had been used to dispatch King Charles two years earlier. When he was told 'yes' this seemed to please him. To the axeman he gave twenty shillings and said he wished it had been more; to a kinsman standing by he gave his scarlet cloak and doublet. Finally, he pulled out a white cap from his pocket, put it on his head and kneeled down before the block. Seconds later, Browne Bushell became another royalist martyr.[17]

If Browne Bushell and Matthew Boynton were two local losers, John Lawson was undoubtedly one of those who gained most from the Civil Wars. In the year before Bushell and Boynton met their deaths, Lawson was commissioned into the State's navy. By 1650 he had served his apprenticeship, first during peacetime in the hard school of North Sea commercial navigation, and then in Parliament's wartime service as master of an armed merchantman, the *Covenant*, in which he had a part share. Now, after his singular successes in both wars, which proved his courage, skill and political loyalty, along with several other reliable radicals from the mercantile service, he was recruited into Parliament's war fleet.

After a brief spell as captain of a merchant vessel, the *Trade's Increase*,[18] he was given command of a succession of warships – the *Lion*, the *Fairfax* and the *Centurion*. Early in September 1650 it was reported that he had scattered a large fleet of French fishing boats from the Newfoundland grounds.[19] Later that same month he was in the *Lion* convoying merchant ships up the east coast between the Downs and Yarmouth. Nevertheless, even as late as December 1650, his employment at sea was still regarded by the Council of State in London as temporary: General Cromwell was told that, though an absentee from Scarborough, Lawson was to continue in his commission as captain of a company of infantry in its garrison.[20] By that time he had assumed command of the *Centurion*, a newly-built frigate of over 500 tons, carrying about 40 guns and a crew of 150.[21] Under Lawson, the *Centurion* provided escort for transports conveying supplies to Cromwell's army in Scotland.[22] At the beginning of 1651 Lawson followed Admiral Penn southwards in the *Fairfax* and joined him at the Azores. For the next fourteen months he served in the Mediterranean squadron.[23] This was his first experience in these waters. Subsequently, he was rewarded with a gift of £60 from the government for his 'good service in his employment to the southward'.[24]

When Lawson returned home from the Mediterranean in April 1652 he had intended to retire from Parliament's naval service and resume his family life in Scarborough. Despite his recent long absence, he had been re-elected to the First Twelve and could expect to be chosen bailiff in the near future. However, fate, or God's providence, as Lawson would have called it, had a different destiny for him. In May 1652 the first of the wars with the United Provinces broke out, and Lawson could not allow himself to remain a mere onlooker. As he later wrote to Sir Henry Vane, his good friend and powerful patron at the admiralty:

> At my return from the Straits last summer I resolved to have left the sea employment and to have endeavoured some other way to provide for my family, but this difference breaking out betwixt the Dutch and us I could not satisfy my conscience to leave at this time, being

very well satisfied that this service is in order to the design of God in the exaltation of Jesus Christ, and therefore with much cheerfulness shall spend myself in this cause where the glory of God and the good of his people is so much concerned.[25]

In other words, fighting the Dutch, just like fighting royalists or corsairs, was no adventure for John Lawson. It was not even a way of earning a living and providing for his family. Before he could go back to sea, he had to convince himself that it was his bounden duty to respond to God's call, as well as his country's, and fulfil His divine purpose.

The First Dutch War (1652–4), an entirely naval conflict, brought Lawson to the top of the service: when it began he was only one of dozens of ships' captains; when it ended he was Vice-Admiral of the Fleet, the fourth highest ranking officer. Of the six major battles fought at sea, he had a decisive part in four of the five English victories. Lawson owed his outstanding success and rapid promotion to three advantages: unrivalled knowledge of the sea and ships; a close affinity with his crews; and extraordinary courage and boldness which sprang from his religious zeal. He was also very lucky.

Unlike their Dutch counterparts, English naval commanders had little or no previous seagoing experience. Before their appointments, none of Lawson's superiors, the three Generals-at-Sea, Blake, Deane and Monck, had even stepped on aboard a warship. All of them were soldier admirals. Lawson's knowledge and lengthy experience of the sea was exceptional. Secondly, though his lowly origins, rough manners and speech disqualified him from the highest post, at the same time they found favour with the common sailors under his command. Lawson was a true 'tarpaulin' admiral. There is a tradition that he first went to sea as a cabin-boy or apprentice at the age of seven, and the tradition lacks only documentation not plausibility. His handwriting was crude and clumsy. Clearly his education was in 'the art and mystery of a mariner', not in Latin grammar at Scarborough High School. As the editor of the letters and papers of the First Dutch War lamented, '[Lawson's] account does not come from the pen of a ready writer and is none too lucid'.[26]

There is ample evidence that Lawson, again unlike most of his contemporaries, took a personal and sympathetic interest in all his lower-deck seamen, and that they responded with admiration and loyalty. It was his enormous popularity with ordinary seamen, both volunteers and pressed men, which gave him unique authority over the fleet which even Cromwell was forced to respect.

Lawson is usually described as a baptist, yet he seems not to have belonged to any particular sect. He was an outspoken advocate of religious toleration and the only Anglican practice to which he took strong exception was compulsory church tithes. Religious conviction, however, was the mainspring of his career. Having survived the Dutch war without so much as a scratch, he was certain that God had deliberately spared him for His particular purposes. Luck, in the modern sense of the word, would have been meaningless, or even blasphemous to him. As he wrote after surviving 'very tempestuous weather' in the North Sea, 'I must and desire always to acknowledge godes great favour and providence . . . and I noe can butt walke worthy and answerable to such mercyes I douth nott he haith more in store for us'.[27] It was this unshakeable self-confidence that so irritated his critics and inspired his fellow captains and crews.

For John Lawson the First Dutch War was a steep, short ladder to fame and power; for Scarborough, his home town, it might have been a disaster. In the recent past, Dutch warships had lorded over the North Sea and Dutch fishermen had virtually monopolised the best fishing grounds there. However, since the 1630s, all that had changed: thanks to the building programmes of Charles I and the Commonwealth, by 1652 the English had the best battle fleet in the world. Moreover, Cromwell's Protectorate gave far greater consideration to its sea-faring citizens than that afforded to the long-suffering subjects of Charles. From 1652, for the first time, Navy captains were obliged by law to provide merchant vessels with free escort.[28] Also, again in contrast to the experience of the 1630s, the government in London gave vital advanced warning to all East coast ports as soon as Dutch warships approached home waters.[29] Finally, as a result of the Civil Wars, Scarborough town and castle had qualified for a permanent military garrison armed and ready to defend the harbour if necessary.

Scarborough now had its own artillery store. In September 1653, when Captain Thorpe sailed into the harbour in search of ammunition for his ship's demi-culverin, bailiff Matthew Fowler agreed to sell him twenty shots from the town's arsenal. Thorpe had to pay threepence a round. His five shillings were passed on by Fowler to the overseers of the poor of St Thomas's.[30]

As the correspondence during this time between William Foord in Scarborough and Peter Hodgson, his shipping partner in London, reveals, far from being the helpless victim of Dutch attacks, during the war Scarborough became a convenient port for treating sick and wounded sailors, for provisioning the state's warships, and for harbouring enemy prizes. The First Dutch War prompted new government measures for the care and maintenance of invalided mariners; and for the first time coastal communities were reimbursed for looking after them. Scarborough seems to have become a temporary hospital for war casualties. Some Scarborians, such as John Reeve, master of the *Employment of Scarborough*, developed a profitable business carrying supplies to ships of the fleet when they were stationed in coastal waters. Finally, Scarborough was chosen to be the location of an official 'prize office', and Richard Dighton, the long-serving town clerk, was appointed sub-commissioner for prize goods at Whitby and Bridlington as well as in his home town.[31] The new military governor of the town, Colonel Edward Salmon, was also one of the admiralty commissioners at a salary of £400 a year. As further recognition of the importance of Scarborough, he was allowed a grant of £150 to make necessary repairs to the castle and provide bedding there for his soldiers. Salmon's privileged position also meant that he was able to call up armed escorts for local merchant ships when he thought they might be endangered by Dutchmen or privateers.[32]

In addition to Scarborough's role as a convenient port for prizes and prisoners, its value as a harbour of refuge for the coal trade was never more sharply illustrated than during the First Dutch War. After the long, cold winter of 1652–3 fuel was exceptionally scarce in London and there the price of coal had trebled. There was even fear of a popular revolt in the streets of the capital if some relief was not soon forthcoming. Aware of the crucial nature of England's East coast coal traffic, Admiral de Witt had stationed himself with 18

Dutch warships off Flamborough Head, there to intercept the colliers as they came southwards. Sure enough on 3 April 1653, oblivious of the danger, an enormous fleet of 300 loaded colliers set sail from Tynemouth bound for the Thames. They were escorted by Captain Peter Motham in the *Bear* and eight other frigates. Fortunately for the coal fleet, the bailiffs of Scarborough were soon informed of de Witt's position and intentions, and passed a warning to Motham. The odds against them were too high and the Englishmen gratefully came into Scarborough. However, only half of the colliers could find room between the harbour piers; the other half had to anchor under the castle headland. Motham anchored his warships on the flanks of the exposed colliers, put some of his guns on the great pier, ordered the castle artillery forward to the edge of the sea cliff, and waited for de Witt to close in. Whether the Dutch were held back by contrary winds or deterred by Motham's cannon is not clear, but there was no attack. After a harmless exchange of long-distance shots and insults, de Witt hauled in his red battle flag and sailed away. In the circumstances it was probably a wise decision: Admirals Penn and Lawson were already on their way northwards to rescue the colliers and bring them all safely down to London.[33]

Admiral Lawson was never happy with Cromwell's Protectorate. He disliked soldiers and distrusted soldier politicians. During the war with the Dutch he remained loyal to the government, but after it was over he became 'a notable thorn in the Protector's side'.[34]

Under the Instrument of Government of December 1653, the new constitution which made Cromwell Lord Protector, Scarborough lost one of its two parliamentary seats. Since both Luke Robinson and John Anlaby, the borough's sitting Members, preferred to offer themselves for Yorkshire county places in the new Parliament, a single vacancy was created at Scarborough. Lawson was no longer one of the First Twelve after September 1653, but his decisive influence on the Common Hall's choice is plainly evident. In July 1654 John Wildman was elected to represent Scarborough.[35]

Wildman was a notorious Leveller radical and an outspoken critic of Cromwell and his government. He had no connection with Scarborough, except that he and Lawson were fellow, secret conspirators. Wildman had first stood for Westminster, an unusually democratic constituency, but Cromwell made sure he was defeated there. Though at Scarborough he seems to have been returned unopposed, soon afterwards the Council of State retaliated by declaring his election null and void on the grounds that he was not a person 'of known integrity, fearing God, and of good conversation' as required by the Instrument of Government.[36] Wildman responded defiantly by drawing up a petition which denounced the Protectorate as a tyranny and called for a new, free Parliament to restore the nation's liberties.[37] Lawson did not put his name to the petition but there is no doubt that he agreed wholeheartedly with it.[38] About the same time that Wildman's petition was published, another was drawn up by the sailors at Spithead. It demanded an end to impressment and improvement in pay and conditions of service. It was almost certainly drafted by Lawson who was now in sole command of the Channel fleet at Portsmouth. All that Cromwell could do was to pacify the sailors with pay and promises, which only raised Lawson's prestige in their eyes.[39]

Wildman was soon arrested and other fellow conspirators were driven out of the country, whereas Lawson was allowed to remain in command of the Channel fleet. Clearly, Cromwell was afraid of his power; he dare not force an open confrontation with him. The climax came after October 1655 when the Lord Protector declared war on Spain and announced plans to launch a naval expedition the following spring. This time Lawson was not to stay at home. Blake, the senior General-at-Sea, was to lead the expedition, but instead of making Lawson his second, Cromwell gave the honour to Edward Mountagu. Mountagu was still only thirty years old and another landsman totally without seagoing experience yet he was now to be made General-at-Sea above Vice-Admiral Lawson. Everyone knew that this extraordinary appointment was due entirely to Cromwell's favour. If this was a deliberate manoeuvre to neutralise and insult Lawson then it worked well. Without consulting anyone, in February 1656, the Vice-Admiral resigned his commission.[40]

Perhaps Lawson expected that his resignation would prompt a naval mutiny, but if so he was mistaken: only three other captains resigned in sympathy and there was no lower deck revolt.[41] Blake and Mountagu went off to Spain as planned. Nevertheless, Cromwell continued to show the former Vice-Admiral diplomatic respect. Lawson received his back pay in full, and even though there was now much damning evidence of his intrigues, he was neither arrested nor exiled.[42] However, instead of retiring quietly, foolishly Lawson continued to plot against the Protectorate with every kind of dissident – militant religious fanatics, admiralty officials, old naval colleagues, rebellious soldiers and even covert royalists. Finally, he was arrested, imprisoned in the Tower and then released only on condition that he left London and returned permanently to his native Scarborough.[43]

The only recorded connection between Scarborough and John Lawson's disaffection concerned the case of John Best, captain of the *Adventurer*. Though Best was not one of the frigate captains who resigned in sympathy with Lawson, at his court martial in September 1656 it became clear that he shared the former Vice-Admiral's political and professional prejudices. According to Jonas Palmer, the *Adventurer's* carpenter, who gave evidence at the trial, Captain Best had openly denounced the war with Spain, had tried to undermine the loyalty of his ship's crew, and was in possession of subversive literature. When the *Adventurer* was at Scarborough in June 1656 Best had gone ashore to visit his friends, the Harrisons. Palmer said that Mr John Harrison senior, who was then coroner and his son of the same name, who was a member of the First Twelve, had themselves produced a doubtful document entitled 'A letter from a friend out of the country to a Christian brother'. This 'book', as Palmer called it, contained the words, 'You know him whom some call the Protector, and what shifts he hath made; but now he hath made so many that his cloak has grown too threadbare that he hath nothing to cover him'.[44]

Best was also reported to have said that seamen should not be servants to soldiers, a sentiment also felt strongly by Lawson. However, other accusations against Bell at his trial indicate that he did not share Lawson's religious and professional ethics. When he returned to the

Adventurer from his visit to the Harrisons, the captain was drunk and violent. With him he had brought one of the gunners from the castle and when the lieutenant tried to rescue him Best put them both below in chains. At the court martial Best had nothing good to say about any of his crew, and none of them supported him. In reply to their evidence he had only personal slander. He condemned his boatswain as a slut, his carpenter as a drunkard, and claimed that his gunner had never scored a single hit.[45]

Though Oliver Cromwell's Instrument of Government had robbed Scarborough of its second parliamentary seat, Richard, his son and successor as Lord Protector, restored the borough's ancient right to return two burgesses to the new House of Commons. However, the election of January 1659 seems to have caused a contest, rather than the usual walk-over, in Scarborough. According to the only surviving corporation document concerning the election, there were no fewer than five candidates for the two places: Thomas Chaloner, Colonel Edward Salmon, Durand Hotham, Richard Etherington and John Lawson, the last still described respectfully, not accurately, as 'Vice-Admiral'. After Wildman's expulsion, the admiralty commissioner and town and castle governor, Colonel Salmon, had succeeded him as the borough's only MP in 1656. The Common Hall now re-elected him, and as his partner chose Thomas Chaloner of Guisborough.[46]

Richard Etherington could not have entertained realistic hopes of election, particularly in such a competitive field. He was a political nobody even outside Scarborough, and unknown in the town. However, the rejection of Durand Hotham, and especially Lawson, indicated how much the strength and direction of the political wind had changed. Durand was the youngest son of Sir John, the former governor of Hull, who had died on the scaffold in January 1645. When Sir John and his eldest son, 'Captain' Hotham, had changed sides and then been found guilty of treason, Durand had pleaded unsuccessfully for their lives and was with them to the end on Tower Hill. Since 1645 he had led a semi-retired life mainly at Fyling Old Hall. Not until the return of the King could he expect any public favour.[47] Though his waiting time proved to be shorter than Hotham's, John Lawson's candidature was also wishful as long as a Cromwell remained in power.

Though poorly documented, the election of January 1659 illustrates how greatly the relations between Scarborough's governing body and central government had altered during the past twenty years. In 1639 and 1640, in the elections to the Short and Long Parliaments, the Common Hall had defied the all-powerful Strafford and returned two of his political opponents. Even in 1645, after the wounding experience of Civil War, the forty-four had stood stubbornly on their tradition of proud independence and refused Lord Fairfax's nominee, James Chaloner. Despite unprecedented intimidation, they elected Luke Robinson, a local man without influential patronage. Now the mood was one of guarded deference. The town's most eminent and effective champion, John Lawson, had been stripped of his authority and 'exiled' to Scarborough; Luke Robinson preferred to sit for Malton; and the Harrisons had been expelled from the corporation for their association with Lawson and Cromwell's detractors. When Richard Cromwell succeeded his father, Scarborough sent the new Lord Protector a message of loyalty and urged him to rule according to the laws of God, and the warship then anchored in the harbour, the *Assurance*, also conveyed a similar message to London.[48] Salmon and Chaloner were the safest choices, and this was enough to secure their election.

The fall of Richard Cromwell, which marked the end of the Protectorate in April 1659, once again changed the balance of the political regime in Scarborough, as elsewhere in the Republic. When the new Common Hall was elected after Michaelmas that year the changes in personnel were few but highly significant.

Most notably, John Harrison, the younger, not only returned to the oligarchy he came back as senior bailiff. He had held the borough's premier post only once before in 1646–7 and since 1656, along with his father, he had been excluded from the Common Hall. John Harrison senior had been the town's bailiff no fewer than six times and had once represented it in the House of Commons; presumably, however, he was now considered too old, even for local government.[49] Nevertheless, despite their radical politics and religion, the Harrisons continued to prosper. When John the elder died in 1663 he left £600 in cash to his 'careful, lovinge and deare beloved wife' Ann and daughter Dorothy, and a considerable estate in goods, shipping and land to them and his only son John.[50]

The Batty family seems to have been less fortunate. The William Batty who sat in his St Mary's pew between Richard Thompson and John Harrison in 1635 had been rich, well-connected and highly esteemed. His father, Thomas, had been bailiff five times earlier in the century; he himself had held the position four times before the Civil War and had managed to keep his seat at the top of the First Twelve during Royalist and Roundhead regimes alike.[51] However, when he died in 1651, William's will indicated a recent decline in family possessions. His eldest son Thomas inherited the Batty residence in Cargate, but nothing more. His second son, William, got three closes of meadow; his daughter Mary, who had married Matthew Fowler, received only £3, and his other two surviving daughters only £2 each. William's three grandchildren had to make do with twelve pence each, whereas 'the preacher' received ten shillings and the town poor forty shillings.[52] There was no reference in the will to shares in ships or shop premises. Thomas Batty never sat in the Common Hall and it was left to his younger brother William to carry on the family's role in local politics. However, though William soon became 'Mr William' and in 1656 moved up into the First Twelve, this was as far as he ever reached. In the 1659 elections he was actually demoted to the Second Twelve, a rare humiliation for a gentleman, and afterwards, even during the Restoration, he never succeeded in climbing out of it.[53]

The Scarborian who undoubtedly gained most from the collapse of the Protectorate was John Lawson: in May 1659, after little more than a year in silent retirement at Scarborough, he was recalled to service in his previous rank of Vice-Admiral of the Fleet. As proof of their trust in him, the new Council of State and the old Rump Parliament approved his appointment as commander of the Channel fleet. Lawson was regarded as an utterly loyal republican and highly valued because of his known popularity with the seamen. Other captains who had previously sailed under him were also recalled and given ships under his command.[54]

However, in October 1659, an army junta, led by Generals Lambert and Fleetwood, calling itself a Committee of Safety, forced out the Rump. Lawson had once conspired against one military dictator, now he was faced with a group of them; but, like Cromwell before, the generals were too respectful of Lawson's standing with his captains and crews to dismiss him. Though they tried every measure and manoeuvre, Lawson could not be reconciled to their rule: he insisted on the restoration of the Parliament. Finally, in December 1659, Admiral Lawson moved the Channel fleet from the Downs up the Thames to Gravesend and from there threatened to blockade the capital. Particularly in the middle of a severe winter Lawson had the power to starve and freeze the City into surrender and on Christmas Eve General Fleetwood admitted defeat and abdicated: he sent the keys of the Parliament house to Speaker Lenthall. On Boxing day the Rump reassembled. As the historian of the Commonwealth navy has written: 'The second restoration of the Rump was Lawson's finest hour'.[55] For the time being, the tarpaulin admiral was master of both the fleet and the capital. On 9 January 1660 he stood at the Bar of the House of Commons while Lenthall extolled his 'great and eminent services' and his 'constant fidelity to the Parliament'. Lawson was made a member of the new Council of State, voted lands worth £500 a year, and awarded General Lambert's apartments in Whitehall.[56]

Lawson's triumph was temporary. The arrival of General Monck in London at the end of January 1660 marked a crucial turning-point on the road to the Restoration. Like many others, Lawson was completely deceived by Monck who professed his loyalty to the Commonwealth when in fact he was working for the return of King Charles. Lawson's position was soon undermined and by-passed. In March, Monck and Mountagu, another closet turncoat, were named as joint Generals-at-Sea over Lawson, who was dropped from the Council of State. One by one the captains who had backed Lawson when he drove out Lambert and Fleetwood were themselves replaced by men obedient to Monck and Mountagu. By the time Lawson realised what was happening he no longer had the means to prevent it. In any case, the once-unbending republican had come round reluctantly to accept that the Commonwealth was bankrupt, financially as well as politically. Since October 1659 no money had been received by the Navy from the Exchequer. Lawson's ships were running out of food and even fresh water.[57]

When Charles and his brother James, the Duke of York, sailed back to England from Holland in May 1660, the Duke, who had taken a particular liking to Lawson, chose to return on the Vice-Admiral's ship, the *London*.[58] Most royalists could not forgive Lawson for his republican past. Even his friends and admirers found it difficult to defend him against accusations of hypocrisy, sycophancy and moral cowardice; but fortunately for Lawson his fate rested with the two brothers who knew how much they owed to him. The King gave Lawson a knighthood, secured him his pension of £500 a year, and sent him off to the Mediterranean to intimidate the Barbary corsairs. The Duke of York showed his gratitude by authorising a free gift of a £1,000 from the sale of surplus navy stores.[59]

If Lawson had made a vital contribution to the decisive defeat of the Dutch in the war of 1652–4, that had been his deliberate purpose in fighting them. When, ten years later off Alicante, his old enemy Admiral de Ruijter struck his flag in salute, Lawson was delighted with the gesture.[60] But the Vice-Admiral's part in the Restoration of 1660 had been as unintentional as it was crucial. The notorious republican was the one who brought back the King and his brother. The baptist who tolerated Quakers but not tithes unwittingly helped to re-establish the Church of England and hundreds of clergymen like William Simpson whom he detested. Samuel Pepys had to admit that Lawson was modest and good-natured, but politically he found him as deferential as a spaniel dog.[61] Robert Blackborne, an admiralty official under the Protectorate, probably voiced the opinion of many when he described Lawson as a 'stout man but a false one . . . [who] appears the greatest hypocrite in the world'.[62] Blackborne, like Lawson, was a firm republican who changed his tune in 1660, but unlike Lawson he retained a sense of bitterness, shame and anger against those he believed had betrayed 'the good old cause'.[63]

The best that might be said in John Lawson's defence is that he suffered from an acute and chronic case of political naivety and that he reconciled himself to the Restoration only when it appeared to him that the only alternative was indefinite military rule by the generals, or worse still, anarchy. Ironically, it was a royalist, the Earl of Clarendon, who had only praise for Lawson. He wrote that the Vice-Admiral was 'incomparably the modestest and the wisest man, and the most worthy to be confided in'. When Lawson died in 1665, of a wound suffered in the battle of Lowestoft during the Second Dutch War, Clarendon described his loss to the nation and the Navy as 'almost irreparable'.[64]

CHAPTER SEVEN

Restoration

As General Mountagu and Vice-Admiral John Lawson led the Channel fleet out of the Thames and along the Kent coast to its station in the Downs, the election of a new Convention Parliament took place throughout the country. At Scarborough, on 4 April 1660, the forty-four members of the Common Hall exercised their ancient right to return two burgesses to the House of Commons.[1]

Lawson was a long way from home when the election took place, yet his influence is said to have been felt on Sandside.[2] On the other hand, it seems unlikely that Scarborough's ruling body could have been then aware of the admiral's very recent and covert conversion to the restoration of the monarchy. Indeed, their choice of representatives suggests that they were ignorant of Lawson's change and even unaware that the return of the King was imminent. After all, like Lawson, the majority of the forty-four councillors had come to the top locally during the past decade as a result of Parliament's victories over the late King, and they had nothing to gain and possibly much to lose by the restoration of his son. The senior bailiff was John Harrison, junior, a radical republican like his father and a friend and political ally of Lawson. Harrison's partner was John Cotterill, formerly a lieutenant-colonel and governor of the town as well as commandant of the castle. His election to the second office in the corporation had come as a surprise to him: though during the previous year while governor he had been honoured with a place in the First Twelve, by October 1659 he had retired to his home at Huggate on the Wolds and seemed reluctant to return to Scarborough for any reason.[3] As for the remainder of the Common Hall, no doubt there were some political hermaphrodites and not a few flexible republicans, but no known royalists.

There were three candidates for Scarborough's two seats – Luke Robinson, John Legard and William Thompson. Robinson was the strongest and most senior. He had represented the borough at Westminster from 1645 until 1653, held the office of senior bailiff in 1651–2, and sat in the Council of State before the Protectorate and was now reappointed to it. Like Lawson he was a committed republican and radical who had returned to favour and power with the downfall of the military junta and the restoration of the Rump. His most recent employment had been to keep a close watch on General Monck, whose allegiance to the republic was rightly doubted. In February 1660 he had reported to the Council of State information regarding the suspicious behaviour of Yorkshire gentry such as Sir Henry Cholmley, Colonel Hugh Bethell and Thomas Legard. In the uncertain circumstances of the spring of 1660, with a royal restoration far from assured, Robinson's return was predictable.[4]

John Legard's political position was ambiguous. His family had been deeply and tragically divided by the Civil Wars. He had been too young to fight in them. In 1660 he was still only twenty-nine years old. However, the Legards of Ganton, unlike their cousins of Anlaby, had leaned to the royalist side. John's uncle Richard had been one of Sir Hugh Cholmley's captains holding Scarborough castle for the King; his aunt Frances was the third wife of Sir John Hotham and the mother of General John Hotham, who had both been executed for treason to the Parliamentary cause. John's own credential was that recently he had helped the Fairfaxes to oust the junta's control from York.[5]

If Robinson was an extremist on one side and Legard somewhere near the middle, young William Thompson of Humbleton and Scarborough might have been seen as a potential, if not actual, royalist. He was the thirty-year-old son of Stephen Thompson and heir to his father's considerable, though now diminished, estate. All the Thompsons had had to compound for their property; some, like Christopher, William's uncle, had been active royalists; and the restoration of the monarchy could bring only benefits to the family. If the King came back, William would lay claim to both Scarborough castle and a large proportion of St Mary's income from tithe and land.[6]

What happened in the Common Hall on Wednesday, 4 April 1660 is not entirely clear: not surprisingly, there is no account of the election in the corporation records. However, it seems that Robinson was well ahead in the voting and the contest for the other seat was between Legard and Thompson. More votes were cast for Thompson, but then some of his supporters were persuaded to sign a document revoking their votes. Consequently, the bailiffs declared that Legard had won![7]

When the Convention Parliament first assembled in London three weeks later, Luke Robinson and John Legard were present to take their seats. By this time, however, Charles's conciliatory Declaration of Breda, promising a general pardon, religious freedom for 'tender consciences' and a parliamentary settlement of land titles and army pay arrears, had booked his return ticket.[8] On 11 June Robinson, 'all bathed in tears', delivered a recanting speech at the Bar of the House of Commons which lasted nearly half an hour. His submission was so humble and pathetic that he was merely disabled and not otherwise punished.[9] His last-minute conversion to royalism had saved his neck but not his place in Parliament.

The House of Commons accepted the verdict of the Committee of Privileges that the bailiffs of Scarborough had misconducted the election there. Thompson was declared elected, a writ was issued for the other seat, and bailiffs Harrison and Cotterill were summoned to the capital and imprisoned. On 11 July, after a salutary fortnight in the custody of the serjeant-at-arms, the two were released on their petition.[10] For the seat vacated by Robinson, the Duke of York recommended Hugh Cholmley, the younger son of the late Sir Hugh. Sir Thomas Gower of Stittenham, who had impeccable royalist qualifications, also seems to have entertained some hopes for his son Edward. Finally, however, on 25 July, John Legard was duly elected by a chastened Common Hall in preference to Cholmley.[11]

As elsewhere in the county and country, the transition from republic to monarchy took place in Scarborough almost imperceptibly and entirely without bloodshed. Captain Northend, governor of the castle, like most other officers in Yorkshire, fell in behind the Fairfaxes and accepted their alliance with General Monck against General Lambert.[12] As Colonel Fairfax reported to Monck from York on 18 February 1660:

> Captain Nordhend [sic] – Governor of Scarborough – came hither yesternight and goes back this morning. He gives this account of his

charge; that his men are faithful, but in great want of pay. They have thirty-eight double barrels of powder – most for great shot – four hundred and fifty serviceable pikes, a like number of muskets with firelocks, fourteen kegs of musket ball, and some shot for demi-cannon.[13]

Monck's advantage was that he had the money to pay garrisons whereas Lambert did not. According to another letter from Fairfax to Monck, dated 17 April, each of his soldiers stationed at Hull, Scarborough and Clifford's Tower, York, had the means to pay for his own accommodation 'what his landlord exacts'.[14]

The full impact of the return of the old political and religious regime was not felt immediately in Scarborough: there was a gradual transition, not an abrupt counter-revolution. When his year of office as bailiff expired at the end of September 1660 John Cotterill was probably relieved to quit the scene, yet his partner, John Harrison, stayed on as coroner for the next year, according to the time-honoured custom. Neither of the two new bailiffs, William Saunders and William Lawson, had royalist records. On the contrary, both seem to have prospered under the Commonwealth. Saunders was a woollen draper and a wine licensee who had been elected bailiff twice before, in 1649 and 1654. Lawson, who was no relation to the Admiral, had the other vintner's licence and a tavern on Sandside.[15] His exceptional promotion from the middle of the Second Twelve perhaps suggests that he was thought to be more royalist than republican. In his case it was probably significant that he made his first appearance in the Common Hall in October 1644 when the town was run by royalists and even at that early date was described as 'gent'.[16] Since his return as a councillor in 1655 he had remained in the Second Twelve yet, uniquely amongst that number, entitled 'Mister'.[17]

The most conspicuous changes in the composition of the First Twelve of September 1660 were the inclusion of Sir Jordan Crosland, William Wyvill and John Hickson. All three had been in arms against Parliament. Both Crosland and Wyvill were Catholics. Crosland's wife was an open papist and Wyvill had been educated abroad at the Catholic college at Douai. They were named as numbers one and two respectively. Hickson had been junior bailiff in 1643–4 in partnership with William's father, Roger Wyvill, and coroner the following year. He was probably in the castle with Cholmley in 1645 and perhaps there with Boynton in 1648. Though he is known to have lived in the town, throughout the 1650s he was excluded from its government. Neither Crosland nor Wyvill had previously sat in the Common Hall.[18]

Nevertheless, there was no royalist takeover at Michaelmas 1660. The other nine members of the First Twelve, William Foord, William Nesfield senior, Matthew Fowler, John Kay, William Robinson, William Walker, Robert Rogers, John Rosdale and Henry Nicholson, were all long-standing, veteran burgesses. Foord, Nesfield, Fowler, Kay, Robinson, Walker and Rogers had all served as bailiffs during the Interregnum, and only John Rosdale, the master baker, and Henry Nicholson, the master mariner, were not described by the clerk as 'Mr'. To make room for the royalist newcomers, Roger Boyes, the butcher, and John Redhead, a master mariner, had to drop down from the bottom of the First to the top of the Second Twelve. Surprisingly, not a single member of the Thompson family was elected.[19]

William Chapman, gentleman, was almost certainly Parliamentarian in sympathy: in November 1642 he had been chosen bailiff as junior partner to John Harrison, but after Cholmley turned coat he was a notable absentee from the Common Hall. From 1645 to 1649 inclusive he sat continuously in the First Twelve. When Luke Robinson should have been coroner in 1652–3, Chapman took his place. On the other hand, Chapman's absence from the First Twelve in 1660 might have had more to do with his age and health than his political record. He was buried in St Mary's on 11 May 1661. It also worth noting that he named John Hickson, 'my very good friend', as supervisor of his will and there referred to another royalist, Francis Sollitt, as a tenant of one of his houses in Merchant Row.[20] Another Parliamentarian missing from the lists at Michaelmas 1660, Christopher Jarratt, was also running out of time. He was buried in St Mary's on 30 March 1661. Jarratt had last been bailiff in 1655–6 and coroner the year following, but after 1657 his name disappeared from the First Twelve list.[21]

Further down the local hierarchy, in the Second and Third Twelves, the continuity was even more evident. Of the twenty-four members elected on 30 September 1660 all but three had served there or in the office of chamberlain during the past, momentous year. Coming into the Common Hall for the first time, though only at number ten in the Third Twelve, was Richard Bilbrough. He was one of only four men named by Captain Northend a year earlier as having 'beene in armes against the parliament'.[22] As a suitable reward for his services to the crown Bilbrough might have expected a higher place, but he had to wait until 1665 before he was promoted into even the Second Twelve.[23] Henry Swaine's re-entry to the Common Hall as the last of the last Twelve was also miserly compensation for his exclusion from it since 1645. It must have been a borough record for a burgess to find himself in exactly the same place he had occupied seventeen years earlier![24]

As for the third new entrant, Daniel Foord, he simply took his elder brother, Timothy's, position. The Foord family was one of Scarborough's most commercially successful and politically flexible. The 'godfather', William, had survived and even prospered through every regime since 1642. He had been bailiff five times. When he died in 1662 he was one of the town's richest residents. To his eldest son and heir, Timothy, he left land in Holderness and Cloughton and five closes in Scarborough and Falsgrave fields; and to his second son, Daniel, after his mother's death, the family mansion house and grounds in Friarage. All three inherited several eighth parts of Scarborough ships. All three of William's grandchildren, Cornelius Fysh, Thomas Ducke and Elizabeth Knowsley, were also well endowed. Cornelius got a close of meadow on the shore of Byward Wath, Thomas ten pounds in money, and Elizabeth a shop in Newborough.[25]

Among the corporation's officers there were no changes at all. Richard Dighton had been town clerk since 1645. He was appointed to this post every year from then until 1664 when his name appeared, for the first time, as one of the First Twelve. He was buried at St Mary's on 22 February 1666.[26] For lesser officials too there might never have been a revolution or a Restoration. Philip Benson was town gaoler from 1645 until 1664 and retained his place as sub-bailiff after that year, at least until 1667. Ralph Moxon, the mace-bearer, George Merry, the netherd, Ralph Harrison, the bellman, Thomas Hampton, the warrener, William Batty, the piermaster – all survived the upheavals of 1660 as though they had never happened in Scarborough. Most surprising was the endurance of John Taylor, the parish clerk. In 1658 the vicar had reported him for being drunk in the street, but Taylor retained his post until at least 1683, even though by 1677 he was seventy years of age and had become so weak and infirm that he could no longer 'teach a Latin schoole'. Yet for longevity and stamina no one could hold a candle to William Penston: he was Scarborough's schoolmaster from 1627 until old age, deafness and blindness forced his retirement in 1677. At appropriate times, he had sworn allegiance to Charles I, the Commonwealth, the Protectorate and Charles II.[27]

Sir Jordan Crosland was one of Scarborough's contributions to the new Cavalier Parliament of 1661. On 10 April that year the Common Hall voted again for William Thompson, but now preferred Sir Jordan to Legard.[28] The previous October Crosland had been made constable and keeper of Scarborough castle at a salary of £16 a year. The government was conscious of the strategic potential of Scarborough harbour and continued to maintain a garrison in the castle for its security. Moreover, the town itself was described as 'populous but factious' so that the presence of loyal soldiers there was thought necessary. Finally, since the position of the castle was believed to be strong, it was at this time suggested that a magazine for the North Riding and Durham should be kept there.[29]

Scarborough castle was also used as a prison for republicans. In July 1662 Crosland was sent a warrant to take Colonel Berry into his custody. The colonel was accused of, but not tried for, 'treasonable designs'.[30] When his wife petitioned for the release of her 'aged and peaceable' husband, the most the government conceded was that Berry, who had now been shut up for three years, was to have as much liberty of the castle 'as may conduce to the benefit of his health'.[31] During one of the frequent alarms about a republican rising, in January 1663, Colonel Lascelles and Captain Matthew Beckwith were arrested and put in Scarborough castle.[32] Luke Robinson was also accused of being one of the Yorkshire plotters, but no action was taken against him.[33] He died two years later.

Sir Jordan Crosland retained his place as number one in the First Twelve until 1665, though the honour was more nominal than functional. Perhaps it was meant to suggest a royalist leadership and control that did not really exist. Past Parliamentarians, such as John Harrison junior, William Nesfield senior and Matthew Fowler, were not ousted from the First Twelve immediately: again the changes came gradually and singly, not all at once. At Michaelmas 1662, another active royalist, Tristram Fysh, came back into the First Twelve. His last appearance in the Common Hall had been in 1643-4 when he rose from the Third Twelve to junior bailiff in one great leap. After only two years in the First Twelve, Tristram was elected senior bailiff in 1664, and served again in that office in 1670-1. However, he was the last of that prominent family name to figure in Scarborough's government: his son Cornelius was not even a member of the Common Council.[34]

Though the younger John Harrison lived on until 1673, for the last ten years of his life he was excluded from Scarborough's government. William Nesfield senior was elected to the First Twelve in 1661, but the following year his name disappeared from the Council. His son was head of the Third Twelve after Michaelmas 1662 then was dropped altogether the next year. Matthew Fowler was also ousted from the First Twelve after the year ending Michaelmas 1663. His son of the same name remained in the Second Twelve only to slip down to the bottom of it by 1665.[35]

As an employee of the Thompsons and an active supporter of Sir Hugh Cholmley and Matthew Boynton during their royalist rule, Francis Sollitt had committed himself as strongly as anyone in the town.[36] After 1645 and 1648 he continued his association with the Thompson interest and remained a resident of Scarborough, though denied a role in its government. However, at Michaelmas 1661, along with another who had fought for the King, Richard Bilbrough, Sollitt was placed in the Third Twelve. A year later he had left Bilbrough behind and reached the foot of the Second Twelve. During the year 1662-3 he was one of the four churchwardens of St Mary's. In September 1666 he finally reached the First Twelve and four years later he was chosen junior bailiff as partner of Tristram Fysh. When he died in 1683 he was described as a gentleman. His father, Anthony, had been a woollen draper and merchant, but Francis seems to have made a good living out of boiling down whale blubber. Perhaps he had a monopoly in the industry since 'Sollitt oyle' was a term in common use during the later part of his lifetime. In 1661 he lived in a house in Merchant Row rented from William Chapman. By 1673 he had a house of his own in Newborough with four hearths and a new pew in St Mary's. In April 1676, his son, Christopher Sollitt, was licensed to teach in Scarborough's grammar school.[37]

One local consequence of the Civil Wars and their aftermath had been to break the near-monopoly power of the Thompsons. Between 1600 and 1644, the family practically ran the Common Hall and during twenty of those years there was at least one Thompson serving as bailiff. After 1660, the family held the office of bailiff only three times, in 1661–2, 1663–4 and 1668–9. William and his son Francis were the last of the Thompsons to sit in the First Twelve.[38] On the other hand, their parliamentary success far surpassed that of their pre-war predecessors. William represented the borough throughout the reign of Charles II and was again a Member of William III's first Parliament when he died in 1691. Francis shared the seats with his father in 1679 and 1681 and was elected again in 1688 and 1689. Francis's son, another William, had the longest record of representation. He was first returned in 1701; sat in every Parliament until removed in 1722; came back in 1727, 1734 and 1741; and died, the third in his family to do so, as Scarborough's Member in 1744. The Thompsons were the founders of the Scarborough Whigs.[39]

In at least one other way the Thompsons profited from the Restoration. The crown accepted that they had acquired Scarborough castle legitimately from the Earl of Holderness and agreed to compensate them for its return to royal ownership. In April 1662, Stephen and William Thompson were granted a reduction of the fee-farm rent on their manor of Humbleton from £55 11s. 6d. to forty shillings on the calculation that their castle had been worth £50 a year.[40]

The most celebrated prisoner Scarborough castle ever had was George Fox, founder of the Society of Friends, the Quakers. Fox first visited Scarborough in the autumn of 1651. Though he had been forcibly ejected from York Minster, in other parts of Yorkshire he seems to have been tolerated and often warmly welcomed. At Pickering, for instance, he was received by Luke Robinson 'at his chamber door'. Even though Robinson's 'priest' was converted by Fox's passionate preaching, the justice listened politely and attentively to what he had to say and offered money to his companions.[41]

Fox did not report it in his *Journal*, but at Scarborough he probably stayed at the home of Peter Hodgson, his chief follower in the town. Hodgson was a master mariner who had become a wealthy merchant. In 1642 he had been ninth in the Second Twelve. When Sir Hugh Cholmley asked the men of the Common Hall to provide him with a squadron of dragoons, Hodgson's contribution was a generous thirty shillings. After Cholmley turned royalist, Hodgson remained in the Second Twelve, but by 1644 he was more often absent from than present in the Council chamber. Parliamentarian sympathies are suggested by his abrupt promotion to the First Twelve in September 1645. He retained his senior place until elected the junior of the two bailiffs in 1653 and coroner the year after. By this time he was a rich man. He had a substantial mansion house at the top of Cargate, which backed on to Blackfriargate, several apprentices under his wing, and a profitable commercial partnership with William Foord which frequently took him to London.[42] In 1635 he had bought one of the new pews in St Mary's on the south side of the 'great allee' for £1 18s.; after the destruction of the church furniture in 1648 he had another built for his family about the time Fox first passed through Scarborough.[43]

When Hodgson first entertained Fox as his guest neither suffered official persecution. Fox is said to have preached from the gallery inside Hodgson's home.[44] However, in 1655, Cromwell's government excepted Quakers and Ranters from toleration and allowed Jews back into the country. From now on Fox and his growing number of followers were to experience a richly varied but unsubtle range of punishments, physical and mental. Peter Hodgson was named in the First Twelve of 1655–6; thereafter he was excluded altogether from the Common Hall.[45] Though by the Restoration in 1660 most Quakers had given up politics and taken up pacifism, they were still regarded as seditious and even subversive. Their refusal to doff their hats to social superiors and their insistence on addressing everyone as 'thou' instead of 'you' caused great irritation and anger. Their refusal to conform even outwardly to the established church – to be baptised, married or be buried in it – to pay tithes to it, or to swear allegiance to Charles II cut them off from all official posts and commissions.[46]

At Scarborough, Fox's converts were soon in trouble. As early as January 1661, two illiterate corporals in the castle garrison, Christopher Walton and Samuel Aram, no doubt under instructions from Sir Jordan Crosland, their commanding officer, paid an uninvited and unwelcome visit one Sunday to Hodgson's house. The following Monday they told Scarborough's magistrate bailiffs that they had witnessed a gathering of about thirty men and women. A woman who was speaking to the meeting fell silent when the corporals walked in. What happened to the twelve men caught in Hodgson's house that particular Sunday is not recorded; but nine men were imprisoned in Scarborough castle soon afterwards for refusing to take oaths.[47]

If Hodgson and other Scarborough Friends were arrested and confined in 1661 they were soon released and continued to add to their congregation. At the end of November 1662, bailiffs John Hickson and John Kay ordered the town constables to levy fines on twenty men who, 'with divers others and many women', had been discovered 'mett together . . . upon pretence of joynge in a religious worshipp'. This time Scarborough Quakers had celebrated Sunday at the home of William Gradell and Ellinor 'said to be his wife'. The first name on the list of offenders was Mr Peter Hodgson. He was required to pay twenty shillings within a week or have his goods distrained.[48]

Fox did not come to Scarborough again until 1663. Thanks mainly to the courage and patronage of Peter Hodgson the Quakers there were now well established. Soon afterwards, however, Hodgson was locked up in York castle prison where he spent five and a half very unhappy years. Not surprisingly, therefore, some of his contemporaries left the Friends rather than suffer such extreme penalties. For example, another master mariner, Thomas Sedman, who had also been fined twenty shillings in November 1662, was elected to the Third Twelve and made a churchwarden of St Mary's within less than a year after. Eventually, he was elected bailiff three times, in 1672, 1677 and 1681. In 1684 he was empanelled on a jury to listen to the case against a group of Scarborough Quakers who included Peter Hodgson. Sedman had been one of Fox's earliest converts.[49] Another leading local Quaker who bent with the merciless gale was Francis Beswick of Hutton Buscel. He had been amongst the congregation at William Gradell's, but Scarborough's parish register shows that in 1671 he had his sixteen-year-old son John and his thirteen-year-old daughter Mary baptised.[50] On the other hand, the two Nesfields, William the elder and his son, were Quakers who were excluded from the corporation after 1662 for sticking to their convictions.

George Fox's third visit to Scarborough was the longest and best documented. This time, in May 1665, he came not as a free preacher and guest of Peter Hodgson but as a prisoner to the castle. At first Crosland put him in a room which had a hearth and a chimney, but instead of going up the chimney the smoke stayed in the room. He complained to the governor 'and he being a papist, I told him that was his Purgatory which they had put me into'. To unblock the chimney and make his room more habitable he was obliged to 'lay out a matter of fifty shillings'. Then he was moved to another place without fireplace or chimney which was much worse. It is generally believed that Fox's new quarters were in Charles's tower on the cliff overlooking the town and harbour.[51] Here there were no shutters to the windows and the rain came in drenching him and his bed. He had to bail out the water with a platter and was numb with the cold and damp. The soldiers stole his beer and even his bread. Friends were denied access to him. He was treated like some exotic caged animal yet amazed his hostile visitors with his fortitude, spirit and learning. A company of Catholics came to mock him and 'went away in a great rage'.[52]

One group of curious visitors included the governor of Tynemouth castle, Thomas Bellasis, Viscount Fauconberg, and Scarborough's spa-season physician, Dr Robert Wittie. The 'great doctor of physic', as Fox described him sarcastically in his *Journal*, asked him why he was in prison. Fox replied that he had lost his freedom because he would not break Christ's commandment by swearing an oath. Wittie then rebuked him for refusing to declare his allegiance to the King. Fox ended the exchange with a crushing reply. Since Wittie was 'a great Presbyterian' he must have sworn an oath renouncing the monarchy and the House of Lords and taken the Scottish Covenant yet subsequently taken more oaths swearing loyalty to King Charles and denying the Covenant. In other words, any hypocrite could swear an oath: true allegiance was expressed in deeds not empty words and false promises.[53]

A few days later, now in the company of 'sixteen or seventeen great persons', Wittie tried again. This time he argued theology with Fox and fared no better than before. When Fox told the gathered audience that Christ died for all, sinners especially, Wittie, the Calvinist, left in a boiling rage and never returned to the castle.[54]

Governor Crosland seems to have done his best to indoctrinate his distinguished prisoner. Catholics, Presbyterians, Anglicans and several different kinds of dissenters were tried in turn, yet all came away angry, defeated or both. Some may have been converted. None of them knew their Bible better than Fox. Though the deputy governor threatened to hang him over the castle walls 'to keep the people down', the governor himself gradually warmed to Fox. When Sir Jordan went up to London to take his seat in the Commons he met there several men who spoke well of Fox and wanted him to be set at liberty. Finally, after Fox had written directly to the King, Crosland was sent an order to discharge his prisoner which he did gladly on 1 September 1666.[55]

Fox had not wasted the sixteen months he spent in Scarborough castle. Though Crosland died a Catholic, for the next four years that remained of his life he refused to employ his soldiers against Friends' meetings in the town. When Fox paid his fourth and last visit to Scarborough in 1669, Sir Jordan invited him up to the castle for a social call. According to Fox, the governor on this occasion 'was very curteous and lovinge'.[56] Similarly, also according to Fox's *Journal*, the officers and soldiers in the castle garrison had 'mightily changed' and become respectful and even friendly towards him, saying, 'he is as stiffe as a tree & as pure as a bell, for wee could never stirr him'.[57] Soon after he left the castle in 1666, Fox had attended a meeting of Friends in the town at Peter Hodgson's house which went undisturbed by the borough's bailiffs.[58]

Nevertheless, when Peter Hodgson came back home to Scarborough in 1669 or 1670 from York castle gaol, he found that the town bailiffs had not grown in tolerance of his kind. Sir John Legard and William Lawson distrained his goods to the value of £26 14s. as a punishment for allowing his house to be used as a Friends' meeting place. On this occasion there were twenty-one other names on the black list.[59] However, whatever pain and loss Hodgson had suffered for his faith, he had not been bankrupted by it. It was he who gave the Scarborough Quakers their first burial ground alongside Bull Lane [now Westover Road] and he who made the biggest contribution to paying for their first purpose-built meeting house. The land and building in Low Conduit Street [now Princess Square] together cost £150 13s 4d. and the house was finished in 1676.[60]

Right up to the Toleration Act of 1689, Scarborough's Quakers felt the harshness of the laws passed against the Society. For instance, Richard Sellers, a native of Kilnsea, who earned his living by inshore fishing, was press-ganged for the Royal Navy in 1665 at the time of the Second Dutch War. Just as he was entering Scarborough harbour he was seized by force and taken on board his majesty's warship the *Royal Prince*. When he refused to work or even to accept 'the King's victuals', he was severely beaten and put in irons below deck. Only the personal intervention of Admiral Sir Edward Spragge saved Sellers from being hanged from the mizzen yard arm; and only after he had prevented the *Royal Prince* from running aground and colliding with a fire-ship was Sellers granted his freedom.[61] After his release he seems to have settled in Scarborough. His name, along with that of 'Prisseley Sellers', appeared on a list of Quakers accused of meeting illegally at the Scarborough Friends' House in 1684.[62]

How Scarborough's Quakers fared depended much on the attitude to them of the bailiffs of the time. When Timothy Foord and Nicholas Saunders were bailiffs in 1682–3 the Friends were locked out of their meeting house in Low Conduit Street and then violently dispersed by the constables when they tried to congregate outside. Afterwards several of them had their goods distrained.[63] In April 1684 six Quaker tradesmen were presented before the bailiffs' sessions for opening their shops the previous Christmas day.[64] Nevertheless, the number of Quakers in Scarborough continued to grow and in the month and year of the Act of Toleration forty of them signed a certificate indicating their presence as witnesses to a marriage in the meeting house of two of them, William Stonehouse and Sarah Breckon.[65]

The vast majority of Scarborough's residents were of course Anglicans, but St Mary's churchwardens' accounts, running from 1649 onwards, show that the repair and rebuilding of the town's only parish church were piecemeal, slow and ultimately too expensive to complete. Though interior fittings and furniture were gradually restored after 1660, it took more than a decade to rebuild a truncated central tower. The western front towers, the north transept and the choir were never replaced; the north aisle was not rebuilt until 1848–52; and the High School continued to occupy its 'temporary' quarters in Farrer's Aisle for the next two centuries!

St Mary's customary, almost stationary, income was quite inadequate to cover the colossal costs of rebuilding. During the 1650s and 1660s, when they were collected, rents from church grounds and houses brought in an average of only fifteen pounds a year. The most valuable rental was for the Common: in 1651 Christopher Jarratt paid £3 14s. for it; in 1667, Francis Sollitt, £6 5s. In the same years, John Harrison had to find £1 6s. 8d. for St Thomas's churchyard and William Fowler £2 for the same. The rent for two acres on Conduit Bank was £2 to William Nesfield and still only £2 9s. to Leonard Porter sixteen years later. The income from St Sepulchre's yard was fixed at a mere 6s. 8d. Most of the cottage rents were only 2d., 3d., 4d., or at the most 8d. a year. One unidentified item on the churchwardens' rentals, Quartridge groats, raised £3 10s. in 1651 but had fallen to £3 5s. by 1673.[66]

Burial fees were standardised: like some rents they remained unchanged for decades. A child's funeral cost 3s. 4d., that of an adult outside in the yard, 6s. 8d., and a special interment inside St Mary's 10s. These were the same mortuary fees in 1679 as they had been in 1622![67] What the vicar charged for baptisms and weddings is not recorded in the churchwardens' accounts so he probably pocketed these fees for himself.

Consequently, during the 1650s, the churchwardens had little to spend and rarely. In 1651–2, for instance, William Batty and William Fowler disbursed only £15 6s. 2d., most of it on the pulpit, pews, two new bells and rebuilding the low chamber in the steeple. Some payments were inescapable: the bellringers on 5 November expected ten shillings and a shilling's worth of beer; the bearers of fox heads still expected a shilling for each killing; and the vicarage had to be repaired.[68]

George Fox always referred disparagingly to parish churches as 'steeple houses', but after the stormy night of 10 October 1659 Scarborough's St Mary's ceased to meet this description.[69] The medieval bell tower over what had once been the crossing collapsed bringing down with it the remains of the choir and the north transept. St Mary's was now such a ruin that it must have been virtually useless.

Fortunately, the new government in London showed more sympathy than its predecessor would have done. In response to a petition from the town endorsed by several North and East Riding justices, on 5 December 1660 King Charles granted Scarborough 'liberty to crave and receive the benevolence of such well disposed people as God shall stir up to contribute to their assistance in rebuilding this House'. That the corporation now appeared safely in the hands of loyal subjects, that the Crown regarded Scarborough as a place of some importance, and that St Mary's had suffered twice because the town had been held for the King, no doubt contributed to this prompt and favourable response. As the preamble to the royal grant explained without benefit of sufficient punctuation:

> . . . during the late wars our Town of Scarborough was twice stormed, and the inhabitants disabled from following their ancient trade, whereby they are much impoverished, and almost ruined in their Estates; and that nothing might be wanting to make their condition most deplorable, their two very fair churches were by the violence of the cannon beaten down, and that in one day there were three score pieces of ordnance discharged against the steeple of the upper church, there called Saint Maries, and the Quire thereof quite beaten down, and the steeple thereof so shaken, that notwithstanding the endeavours of the said inhabitants to repair the same, the steeple and the bells . . . fell and brought down with it most part of the body of the same church . . .

Since Scarborough's only other church, 'called Saint Thomas', had been battered down to the ground, St Mary's had to be rebuilt at once, 'otherwise the said Inhabitants will remain destitute of a place wherein to assemble themselves for the publick worship of God'. This somewhat exaggerated and misleading account of what had happened to St Thomas's and St Mary's ended with the claim that it would cost £2,500 'at the least' to make good the latter.[70]

Richard Thompson, described in the patent as a confectioner of the parish of St Mary Woolchurch in London, was named as the official treasurer and receiver for the Home Counties. The other collectors mentioned there were William Thompson, Tristram Fysh, John Hickson, William Foord and William Walker, all gentlemen of Scarborough. Besides these five, accountants of the money spent and supervisors of the building work to be done were named as John Legard, Robert Rogers, John Kay, John Bambrough, Edward Porter, John Rosdale, Thomas Oliver, William Sedman, Daniel Foord, Henry Nicholson, William Shimmings and John Dodsworth, 'being common-council men of the said Corporation'. In fact, neither William Thompson nor Tristram Fysh were members of the Common Hall until elected to it the following September, though of course Thompson and Legard were the borough's burgesses at Westminster. Only four members of the First Twelve were not included in the list, two papists, Sir Jordan Crosland and William Wyvill, and two republican radicals, William Nesfield and Matthew Fowler.[71]

Despite this promising start, the net result of the national appeal preached from every parish pulpit the following Sunday, 9 December 1660, proved profoundly disappointing. Edmund Coale, one of the collectors for London and the southern counties, absconded with the £940 he had acquired, and consequently from the richest part of the kingdom Scarborough eventually received only £54. Altogether, the final sum raised came to £247 7s. 6½d.[72]

In October 1660 the Common Hall had approved a general assessment on the town 'towards repair of St Mary's church', yet this brought in only £21 14s. 1d.[73] In short, therefore, little more than 10% of what was needed was provided by public subscription and local levy, so that the rebuilding of St Mary's had to be postponed indefinitely. The most that could be achieved in the near future was to secure what remained of the structure and make it weather-proof: the magnificent medieval church was irrecoverable.

During the next decade spending on St Mary's was therefore necessarily restricted and selective. The two most expensive items on Richard Bilbrough's churchwardens' accounts for 1661 were £2 15s. spent on a church Bible and 13s. invested in a Common Prayer Book. Christopher Jilson, the plumber, was busy mending the windows and the masons plastered and patched up the damaged east end of the nave.[74] In 1661–2 the drawing, gilding and setting up of the King's arms, including the wooden frame and hinges, cost the parish at least £2 16s. 10d. Putting up the Ten Commandments on a board cost another 15s.; repairing the font, cost £1 10s.; mending the churchyard perimeter walls, another 5s. 4d.; planting a sundial and gilding it, another 5s.; and payment to John Taylor, the parish clerk, for his parchment and register and his writing in it came to 2s. 10d. But again, the principal outlay for that year went on repairs to the building to Jilson for lead, solder, stone and labour.[75] At sixpence a foot church window glass was costly; even a sheet of parchment for the parish register was then priced at one shilling. The great west window over the doorway was not reglazed until 1666–7. Also during that financial year the parish finally paid a labourer 1s. 8d. for the two days he spent clearing out rubbish and rubble from the ruined choir.[76]

William Simpson, the restored vicar, did not live long enough to see the tower restored. Not until a year after his death and his replacement by William Hodgson in 1668 were the first positive steps taken towards rebuilding the steeple. Thanks to Admiral Sir John Lawson, Scarborough received a gift of £100 after his death in 1665. At first, and for good reason as events proved, Lady Lawson was most reluctant to hand over her husband's bequest to the corporation: she needed to be convinced that the money would be used, as intended by the Admiral, solely for the benefit of the town's poor. In August 1667 the bailiffs and burgesses agreed to reassure Lawson's widow of their honest purposes by setting aside £6 a year out of the rent of Ramsdale for the inmates of St Thomas's poorhouse. Presumably, they regarded six per cent as a reasonable return in interest. The capital sum of £100 they decided to hold in reserve 'until such time as their can be a convenient piece of ground found out to be purchased' with it.[77]

Though Lady Lawson appears to have accepted this arrangement, from the patchy records of the Common Hall it gradually becomes clear that the burgesses intended to use the Admiral's welcome windfall to pay for St Mary's new steeple. In September 1669 it is revealed in the corporation minutes that bailiffs Francis Thompson and Thomas Oliver had made an agreement with Richard Wilkinson, a mason of Grimsby. However, it is also revealed here that Wilkinson had failed to finish the construction of a tower by the date set down. The work under another contractor dragged on until 1670 and the costs mounted.

A double assessment of £84 3s. was laid upon the town 'for the use of the church'. Even so, the bailiffs were empowered to borrow more money if they found that Lawson's gift and the special double rate were together not sufficient to cover the final costs. By 1672, when the work seems to have been at last finished, the charges had risen to nearly £200. In November 1671, the stone masons, William Husband and Matthew Etherington, had been paid £59 15s., and a year later they received £55 5s. more. In addition, it had cost the parish £6 4s. 10d. to carry 3,500 stones from the North Bay sands up to the church and another £12 1s. 6d. to bring six great loads of stones from Cloughton. Finally, Robert Minithorpe, the younger, charged £15 for laying 158 stone of lead at 19 pence a stone on the roof of the old nave and the new steeple. Two masts for 'the great ladder' and one for the crane he used were bought for just over £2.[78]

Above the lofty interior doorway entrance to the bell and clock tower a stone inserted in the wall still bears the inscription 'Francis Thompson, Thomas Oliver, Bayliffs, 1669'. Needless to say, there is no indication that it took three years to complete the work that they had originally contracted. Nor is there any mention of the fact that Admiral Sir John Lawson's generous gift had made it possible.

Scarborough Council finally fulfilled the terms of Lawson's will by buying a site on which the Society of Owners, Masters and Mariners was able to build a hospital or almshouse for their distressed members and their dependants. When Ralph Thoresby visited Scarborough briefly in 1682 he recorded that, in St Sepulchre Street, opposite where the church of the Holy Sepulchre had once stood, the Society had recently erected a fine building for poor seamen's widows on land which had cost just £100.[79] The first Trinity House, which originally had accommodation for twenty-seven aged seamen and widows of seamen, was rebuilt in 1832, but its lower massive stone courses can still be seen at its St Sepulchre Street frontage.

In the popular conception the Restoration is associated with the end of the rule of the Saints – not merely the return of King, Lords and bishops, but also of theatres, maypoles and bull-baiting.

Pleasure-seeking and pleasure-making came back into fashion from the Merry Monarch downwards. In an indirect yet substantial way Scarborough profited richly from this new turn of events: after 1660 it became increasingly famous as a health and holiday resort for the well-to-do.

About 1627 Mrs Thomasin Farrer is said to have discovered that the spring bubbling up from the base of the cliff at Driple Cotes in South Bay had special medicinal qualities,[80] but the reputation of Scarborough 'spaw' spread abroad only slowly at first. As Dr Robert Wittie, the spa's earliest and most effective publicist, wrote later of the water: 'it became the usual Physick of the Inhabitants of Scarbrough, and by degrees it came into use and reputation among those of the East-Riding near adjoyning'.[81] Reference has already been made above to the local belief that those unfortunates who came out of the besieged castle in July 1645 suffering from scurvy were soon cured by drinking the spa waters.[82] At this time Dr Wittie was a practising physician in Hull, but we know that he was at Scarborough in July 1648, and it seems likely that by that summer he was already checking the spa and visiting patients to whom he had recommended it.[83] According to his own account, he was 'usually wont every year to step to Scarbrough'.[84] When he came to write his first book on Scarborough spa in 1660 he was able to claim that it was then 'well known to the Citizens of York, and the Gentry of the County, who do constantly frequent it; yea and to severall persons of quallity in the Nation, who . . . have made triall of it, with whom it hath gained such credit that they come above an hundred miles to drink of it, preferring it above all other medicinal waters'.[85]

Two of Wittie's regular patients were William and Alice Thornton of East Newton, near Helmsley. Alice had married down: her father was Christopher Wandesford of Kirklington whose close association with Wentworth brought him the lucrative office of Master of the Rolls in Ireland. However, Christopher's early death, the Irish rebellion and then Strafford's fall reduced the Wandesford family to near poverty. Until 1660 Alice struggled heroically against anti-royalist prejudice as well as penury. Out of necessity she married William Thornton in 1651 and found him weak, careless and spendthrift. Worst of all, she suffered from a succession of difficult pregnancies, debilitating child-births and tragic losses. Between 1652 and 1667 she had nine children and only three of them survived. During all this time Alice and her sickly husband were attended by Dr Wittie. At first, Wittie bled her when she was ill and recommended St Mungo's well at Knaresborough for curing her children of rickets, but in August 1659 she was advised to journey to Scarborough to take the waters there. She stayed in the town for a month and believed that the spa had cured her haemorrhoids. From then on Alice and William went to Scarborough almost every year, usually in August for a whole month. When William died at Malton of the palsy in September 1668 he was on his way back to East Newton from Scarborough.[86]

The Thorntons were by no means the only Yorkshire gentry who regularly took the waters at Scarborough spa. Colonel Charles Fairfax, for instance, the 62-year-old uncle of General Lord Fairfax, who had recently taken command of the military garrison at Hull, on 11 May 1660, wrote to General Monck of his visit there. The purpose of his letter was to give proof of his conscientiousness: 'I . . . have never been a stonecast from the works here save for a journey at the season of the year to Scarborough Spaw', he wrote.[87] Going to Scarborough for the season was, apparently, already considered normal practice even before the Restoration.

The appearance of the first edition of Wittie's *Scarborough Spaw* in 1660 marked the next, most important stage in the history of the town as a resort. The book was printed in London by Charles Tyus at the Three Bibles on London Bridge and near the Minster in York by Richard Lambert. The author dated his work 'York, May 29 1660', adding later the words, 'being the very day & year of his Majesties most happy restauration'. By the first week in October the book was advertised by two London weeklies, the *Parliamentary Intelligencer* and *Mercurius Publicus*.[88] When John Ray, the itinerant botanist, passed through Scarborough the following summer he had read Wittie's book.[89]

From now on an increasing galaxy of rich, fashionable, idle, overfed, underexercised and unhealthy gentlemen and ladies became habitual Scarborough 'spawers'. The second edition of Wittie's work, published in 1667, contained a lengthy list of persons of honour, quality and reputation who had benefited from treatment at the spring. Lord John Roos, son and heir of the Earl of Rutland, for example, 'had long been troubled with Hypochondriack Wind'. However, after three consecutive summers in Scarborough he now enjoyed 'a constant state of health' and had 'become much more lively and fleshly than formerly'.[90] Another fully satisfied customer at the well was Sir John Anderson. This unfortunate gentleman, according to Wittie, suffered from chronic gout and scurvy 'and other indispositions'. Nevertheless, after drinking eight pints of spa water and then passing eleven pints of urine, 'the humours' of his body were permanently expelled. Even when bottled and transported, Scarborough spa water could still work miracles. Christopher Keld, a gentleman of nearby Newby, rid himself of several very painful stones 'besides much gravel' after consuming between four and six pints.[91]

In response to Wittie's pioneering propaganda, a growing number of claims were made for the curative powers of Scarborough spa by other 'doctors of physic'. William Simpson agreed with Wittie that the waters were good for 'Scurvy, Dropsie, Stone or Strangury, Jaundise, Hypocrondriack Melancholy, Cachexia's and Women's Diseases', but could not accept that they were a remedy for ' Pestilential Diseases, Plurisies, Prunella's, Poysons taken in or inbred . . . Leprosie, French Disease, Morphew, Cancer, Falling Sickness . . . Apoplexie, Palsie or Asthma'.[92] Taking a more detached and rational view than Wittie, Simpson suggested that, in many cures at Scarborough, fresh air and physical exercise had probably been more effective than drinking the spa waters.[93] A third doctor, George Tonstall of Newcastle, was soon adding his own professional wisdom to the debate. Before long the disagreements between Wittie, Simpson and Tonstall became more personal and vitriolic than scientific. Wittie denounced Simpson as a mountebank; Simpson made fun of Wittie's ignorance of basic chemistry; and Tonstall turned to vulgar insult by calling Wittie 'the Crackfart of Scarbrough Spaw'.[94] None of this did much to enhance the professional reputations of the doctors concerned, but their many books and pamphlets extended the fame of Scarborough spa ever wider amongst 'persons of quality'.

According to Simpson's testimony, the Marquess of Winchester had derived much relief at Scarborough from 'the oppressing symptoms of Hypochondriacal wind'; the daughter of Robert Rogers, one of Scarborough's oligarchy, was permanently cured of 'scorbutick Elephantiasis'; and,perhaps most encouraging of all, Mrs Thomas St Quintin of Flamborough conceived for the first time in over seven years of marriage after taking the waters for fourteen days. Four years later the spa well worked a second miracle for the St Quintins when they returned to Scarborough for the season. Even venereal disease succumbed to the therapy of the spa: two anonymous gentlemen were said to have been relieved of 'the reliques of a Clap'.[95]

But what made Scarborough's spa unique throughout the British Isles was not its waters: it was the only one at the seaside. In the second edition of his book in 1667, Wittie had recommended to his readers 'frequent bathing in Sea-water cold' against the common complaint, even of young men, of gout.[96] The North Sea, or German Ocean, as he called it, was as cold if not colder than any waters around the British Isles, and Wittie convinced himself and others that plunging naked into icy sea water followed by 'a sweat in a warm bed' was a sovereign cure.[97] Though it was some time yet before the sea-bathing machine was invented and used at Scarborough, from Wittie's time sea-bathing from hired cobles became an established ritual amongst seasonal and seasoned visitors.[98] There is no evidence that residents followed this practice in late September or early October when the sea was warmest.

If 'spawers' were too nervous or fragile to take the plunge they could exercise themselves by riding or walking over the flat, firm sands of South Bay. One later visitor described them as 'a beautiful Parterre . . . of two miles . . . as level as a Bowling-Green.'[99] Since the spa spring was at the foot of a perpendicular sea cliff the only sensible approach to it was by way of the sands at low tide. 'Spawers' could risk the shorter but steeper descent from St Nicholas Cliff or take the long way round by crossing the sands from the harbour. The more feeble and elderly complained of the inaccessibility of the spa well; the majority relished the fresh, salty air and the sharp, clear distant views of sea and coast. The boldest hired rowing boats for trips round the Bay.[100]

Not until the end of the century did the owners of the foreshore, Scarborough corporation, begin to reap a commercial profit from the spa, but long before then the town was a beneficiary of its growing reputation as a summer resort. Scarborough's seasonal visitors were invariably rich and they stayed not overnight but for weeks or perhaps months between June and September. Lodgers either stayed as paying guests in the private houses of friends and relatives, or they hired rooms or even a whole house. When Henry Newcome brought his sick wife back to Scarborough for a second time in June 1666 the innkeeper could provide accommodation only for their horses, so they rented 'two excellent rooms' on Dr Wittie's recommendation in a house that had been taken for the whole season.[101] Meals could be brought in or they could be eaten in one of the several 'ordinaries' in the town which served food at fixed prices. Extra charges were made for wines and spirits. Early in the next century visitors from near and far commented favourably on the high quality, wide variety and low cost of Scarborough's fare. No doubt visitors took advantage of the cheapness of commodities, especially tea, wine and liquors, which somehow had evaded excise duties. Those who had made the often long and sometimes perilous journey to Scarborough as a reward for their enterprise expected to find plenty of smuggled goods there. Another main attraction to many was the informality of the company: husbands did not always bring their wives; some wives and daughters left their husbands and fathers behind; gentlemen felt safe enough to walk abroad without their swords; and there was an easy familiarity amongst strangers regardless of rank. Social conventions and restrictions that applied elsewhere were relaxed at Scarborough. It was a place where you could misbehave yourself without the usual impunities.[102]

Nature had contrived to locate a mineral spring next to a firm, flat, sandy beach and this accidental juxtaposition was to make Scarborough into Britain's first, and for a long time only, seaside spa resort. When Ralph Thoresby passed through Scarborough in 1682 he noted that the castle was ruinous and remarkable only for its extent which afforded summer pasture for twenty cows, whereas the town was 'famous for the medicinal waters'.[103] If Scarborough was now less important to His Majesty, it was fast becoming a hospital and playground for his more privileged subjects.

Epilogue

Any Scarborian returning to his native town in the early 1660s after an absence of twenty years or more would have seen some striking changes – nearly all for the worse. First of all, the skyline had been altered. Looking up from the town street towards the castle, where Henry II's majestic keep had stood proudly for half a millennium, he would now have noticed a gaping hole in its western side. The tower had lost its roof, turrets, upper floors and interior newel staircase. Though still a landmark for many miles around, it now provided neither place of last refuge nor lookout point. The Civil Wars had rendered it a permanent ruin. On the other hand, since Scarborough castle was now back in the possession of the Crown, it was garrisoned with soldiers and its barbican, drawbridges, curtain walls and towers were being maintained and repaired better than at any time since the death of Richard III. Furthermore, Cholmley's South Steel battery had become a permanent artillery platform, armed and constantly manned to guard the harbour below it. From the end of 1660, Sir Jordan Crosland, 'Governor of His Majesty's castle of Scarborough', received £131 2s. 8d. a month from the excise commissioners of beer and ale to pay for his garrison.[1]

The most grievous and irreparable damage, however, had been suffered by Scarborough's religious buildings. The old charnel chapel near the main entrance to the castle had disappeared entirely; all that remained of the church of St Thomas the Martyr that once stood next to Newborough Bar was a street name and a few pillars and stones now incorporated into St Mary's church; and the parish church itself, once the finest medieval structure, had become a sad, shrunken, shattered remnant of its former glory.

Scarborough's perimeter landward defences – the two gateways at Oldborough and Newborough and ditches and earth banks between and beyond them – had been renovated and re-dug in 1642–3, but by 1660 they had reverted to their more familiar state of dilapidation and neglect. In vain, the bailiffs repeatedly tried to prevent townspeople from using the dykes as refuse dumps. Any traveller approaching Scarborough by land from the north or the west would have recognised the town by its odours long before he reached it: dunghills were piled high outside both Newborough and Oldborough Bars.[2] After 1660 it seemed no longer necessary to maintain the town's landward fortifications: instead the threat came from the sea. When the Second Dutch War began in 1665, Scarborough raised a home guard of thirty men and paid for their arms and ammunition. Captain Francis Thompson was placed in command of them.[3]

The townspeople would have been glad to see two of their buildings fall into disuse and decay – the pesthouses in Tintinholmes on the north side and on Driple Cotes overlooking South cliff. 'God in his mercy', preserved Scarborough from the pestilence of 1665, probably because the town authorities took sensible precautions to deny entrance to anyone who might have been in recent contact with infected people, property or places. A day and night watch was maintained in all four Quarters under the close supervision of members of the Common Hall. Residents who refused or failed to do their service were liable to a fine of one shilling; and councillors who tried to avoid their duties incurred a penalty of twice that amount.[4]

Scarborough was a smaller place by 1660 than it had been in 1640 also in the sense that fewer people now lived there. Two Civil Wars, two prolonged sieges and at least one visit of the plague in 1645 had all taken their toll of the town's population, as well as its buildings. Three different kinds of demographic evidence all point towards this same conclusion.

In the absence of a parish register until after 1682 and relying on only fragments of bishops' transcripts, estimates of population figures are necessarily provisional and approximate. Nevertheless, the transcripts indicate that whereas the average number of annual baptisms at St Mary's in the 1630s was 87; during the years 1661–6, it was only 48; in the years 1671–4, only 57; and even by 1681–3, still only 77.[5] Even after allowance has been made for the existence by 1660 of a small community of Quakers, who would have refused baptism in the parish church, the fall seems dramatic and possibly catastrophic. Moreover, whereas before 1640, with the exception of the plague year of 1635–6, there had always been a healthy surplus of baptisms over burials, during the reign of Charles II deficits were almost as frequent as surpluses. In short, population recovery was only slow and gradual, and perhaps owed more to immigration than to natural increase.

The most informative Hearth Tax return for Scarborough is that of Michaelmas 1673. Altogether, including those that were exempted as well as those charged, Scarborough then had 497 households. At an average of four persons to each household this number would yield a total of just under 2,000 inhabitants. Furthermore, like the bishops' transcripts, a run of Hearth Tax lists for the town suggests that recovery was long-term and undramatic: in 1660, 341 households were charged, in 1670, only 324, and in 1673, the figure was 366.[6]

Thirdly, the undated and incomplete list of inhabitants, which must have been drawn up sometime between 1674 and 1680, also indicates that by then the population of the town had passed the 2,000 mark. Newborough was shown to have had 502 residents and Undercliff 689, making 1,191 in the two Quarters. Since Newborough and Undercliff had fewer inhabitants than Oldborough but each more than St Mary's, the two of them together had about half the total number of residents.[7]

The Hearth Tax returns and the list of inhabitants also show that, despite Scarborough's recent development as a fashionable health and spa resort, a clear pattern of residential distribution had not yet occurred. All four Quarters contained the houses of the richest and the poorest alike, living side by side. Thirty per cent of St Mary's inhabitants were judged too needy to pay the Hearth Tax in 1673, yet within this same small district lived some of the community's wealthiest members – William Lawson, the vintner, two Thompsons, Richard and Francis, Captain John Robinson and John Knowsley – all of whom were at one time senior officers of the corporation.[8]

But not all the better-off residents had a view of South Bay from the top of the hill. Scarborough's grandest mansion with twelve hearths belonging to William Thompson, one of the borough's Members of Parliament, was in St Sepulchregate in the heart of Oldborough. Other prominent residents of that Quarter included Daniel Foord and William Robinson, who were the two bailiffs during the year 1673–4. Oldborough was the most populous part of the town with 182 households, yet only 30 per cent there were considered too poor to afford the Hearth Tax. With 131 households Newborough was the second most populous Quarter, and here 36 per cent of them with only one or two hearths each were exempted from the tax. Nevertheless, this same busy area with its street markets and workshops was the home of some of the most affluent burgesses, such as Thomas Sedman, Tristram Fysh, Timothy Foord, John Hickson, Francis Sollitt, Thomas Oliver and John Key – all First-Twelve men who served terms as bailiffs.[9]

Finally, Undercliff, which had a slightly lower proportion of poorer households than Newborough, was not without its own rich residents. Mrs Harrison, widow of John Harrison junior, had a house there with ten hearths; Thomas Southeron's home had the same number; and William Saunders, the vintner, had eleven fireplaces in what was probably his inn on Sandside. Other occupiers of valuable property in this seafront area, such as the Tindalls, Cockerills and Porritts, represented the new generation of shipbuilding families.[10]

The poorest community of all was Falsgrave village. No one there had more than three hearths and 42 per cent of the households were excused the tax.[11]

Master mariners and seamen might have been expected to live on or near the harbourside, yet according to a survey taken by the constables in 1665, of the 189 masters and men and apprentices who went to sea, 53 were residents of Newborough, 50 of Undercliff, 45 of Oldborough and 32 of St Mary's. The remaining nine, three masters, three seamen and three apprentices, all lived in Falsgrave.[12]

Nevertheless, major changes in the physical appearance of the town or even in the number of its inhabitants were probably of little significance as far as the lives of its ordinary people were concerned. For many of them the upheavals of the past twenty years might never have happened; or, if their world had been turned upside down, after 1660 it soon seemed right way up again.

The Elizabethan Acts imposing penalties on people who refused to attend their parish churches had been repealed in 1650, but Charles II's Cavalier Parliament restored and strengthened them. After an absence of fifteen years, William Simpson resumed his place in the vicarage and St Mary's pulpit. Once again the town's two vintners were kept busy and in profit supplying him with his favourite tipples –

canary wine and claret.[13] The only conspicuous and lasting result of the religious turmoils of the Interregnum was Scarborough's small but distinctive Quaker community.

The self-perpetuating, self-serving oligarchy of forty-four members of the Common Hall saw to it that life in Scarborough went on very much as it had done before the 'distractions' of the Civil Wars. Even during the Interregnum and the so-called rule of the major-generals, when most corporations lost their powers of self-government, apart from the aldermen of Richmond, the bailiffs of Scarborough were the only borough officers in the North Riding to retain their ancient right to assess and collect local taxes.[14] Just in case anyone might suppose that past events had diminished their dignity and importance, in October 1661 the newly-elected councillors agreed that henceforth they should always appear properly dressed in public. By Christmas of that year all the First Twelve, the bailiffs, coroners and town clerk were to provide themselves with distinctive gowns and wear them when attending Common Hall meetings and Sunday church services. Each failure to do so would incur a fine of forty pence. A similar order, but with lower penalties for infringement, was passed at the same time to apply to members of the Second and Third Twelves.[15]

At least two attempts were made to break the High School's monopoly of education in the town; but both of them failed. In April 1662 William Gradell, the schoolmaster, a leading Quaker, was presented before the bailiffs for teaching scholars without their authority and the archbishop's licence. Gradell's house, along with that of Peter Hodgson's, was one of the earliest meeting places of Scarborough's Quakers. Who John Carr was is not known, but he too was prevented from teaching in the town because he had neglected to win the authorisation of the corporation. Until he lost both his sight and his hearing, William Penston continued as Scarborough's only grammar schoolmaster.[16]

Perhaps Scarborough's waits, the town's company of official minstrels, had been victims of Puritan distaste for musical entertainment and singing; if so, then the company was revived soon after the Restoration. Since the middle of the fifteenth century, and probably much earlier, it had been the custom for the bailiffs to appoint three or four musicians and vocalists to serve the town usually for a year at a time. The waits were required to take an oath promising loyalty to the borough and were issued with official badges which they returned when their term expired at Michaelmas. This was one medieval tradition that would last for some time yet.[17]

After 1660, in Scarborough, as elsewhere, there might have been a more relaxed attitude to boisterous recreation, ale-house drinking and even Sunday church attendance, but in matters concerning private property and its public protection local law enforcement was as unforgiving as it had ever been. Just three days after bailiffs William Thompson and Timothy Foord had approved the order on what they and the other Common Hall burgesses should wear in public, in their role as justices of the peace they heard the case of Joseph Weatherill. He was a cordwainer and former constable presented to the court for stealing and carrying away a portmanteau, 'not haveing the fear of God before his eyes'. There was nothing unusual about this particular accusation except that the offence was alleged to have taken place in July 1644, more than seventeen years previously![18]

The first witness to be called, Thomas Boyes, said he had been taking a letter out of Scarborough very early in the morning of the 4 or 5 July 1644 when he saw the accused in the act of committing the robbery. Weatherill had taken the portmanteau from the back of a horse tethered in the street. Later that same day Boyes had been told by a servant of Lord Widdrington that his master had had a luggage trunk stolen.

Widdrington had complained about the loss to his host, Sir Hugh Cholmley, who had sent a body of musketeers to look for Weatherill, but by that time it was too late: the thief had left the town with the stolen goods. Soon afterwards, Lord Widdrington and the other royalist staff officers with the Marquess of Newcastle, who had just been defeated and disgraced at Marston Moor on 2 July, left by ship for exile in Hamburg.[19]

Another surviving witness, Mary Wright, was called next. She confirmed Boyes's story and added detail to it. She said that on the morning of Seamer Fair day, which meant it must have been 4 or 5 July, as a servant of Mr Roger Wyvill, she had got out of bed very early. Through a chamber window she looked down upon the street below. No one was stirring yet. Several men were asleep on the ground and some packhorses were standing by them. Then she saw her neighbour, Joseph Weatherill. He went up to a bay horse with two white feet and with a knife cut the thongs holding a portmanteau to its back. When Weatherill found the trunk too heavy, he rested it on his thigh and called for assistance. Several men then helped him to haul the trunk across the street and up a pair of stairs into Joseph's house.[20]

Unfortunately, the fate of Joseph Weatherill is not recorded in the reports of the bailiffs' sessions. For his grand larceny he was probably sent off to York to appear before the judges of the assizes. However, the case has been described at length because it illustrates more than one important historical point. Whatever irregularities and illegalities had occurred in Civil-War Scarborough, it is clear that, even after an interval of seventeen years, there was a determination that none should go unpunished and unavenged. That the stolen property belonged to a royalist nobleman and that one of the witnesses for the prosecution was a servant of a leading local royalist gave the case an especially sharp political significance.

The town of Scarborough had suffered exceptionally, though not uniquely, during and after the Civil Wars because of its strategical position, safe harbour and strong castle. It also suffered from the presence of first Sir Hugh Cholmley and then Colonel Matthew Boynton. When Sir Hugh deserted Parliament and went over to the king in March 1643 he saved the town from the grief of a certain royalist attack and occupation and possible plunder. However, when he continued to hold the town, even after Marston Moor, and the castle, even after he had lost the town and harbour, he sacrificed the people of Scarborough to unnecessary hardship and injury on the altar of his pride and honour. No wonder it was said that the women of the town had to be restrained from stoning him when he emerged last from the castle on 25 July 1645. No wonder after that day he never again set foot in Scarborough. Matthew Boynton had even greater reason to fear a stoning when he came out of the castle on 19 December 1648. His change of sides the previous July had done nothing but harm to Scarborough: it had subjected its diminished population to five months of street-fighting, forced billeting, mercenary looting and artillery bombardment. For those five months the port was closed and all commerce with the hinterland ceased. At least when Cholmley declared for the King some Scarborians were able to profit from privateering and make a new career out of it. Boynton's defection brought no such windfalls. Above all, Scarborough's greatest misfortune was that in both Civil Wars it suffered the consequences of association with a defeated cause simply because twice its military governor deserted Parliament.

Yet Scarborough's fate was not just the fault of Cholmley and Boynton. If King Charles had taken Hull in 1642 or 1643, neither he nor Parliament would have taken any interest in Scarborough. If the Queen had not come ashore at Bridlington Quay then Sir Hugh might never have quit Parliament. If Rupert had not been routed on Marston Moor, then Scarborough would have found itself in the hands of winners not losers. Events elsewhere determined the town's experience of Civil War.

Scarborough was never able to challenge first Bath and later Brighton as the country's foremost resort for the rich and idle because it was too far away from the South where most of them lived. Not even the world's earliest holiday advertisement lie of 1725, which claimed that Scarborough was only 160 miles from London, could bring them any closer together.[21] However, that same considerable distance from the capital probably saved Scarborough from even worse calamities during the Civil Wars. The further away from Parliament's London and the King's Oxford the less interest the two sides had in it and the less damage they could inflict upon it. The towns that were injured most, such as Pontefract, Newark, Leicester, Worcester and Gloucester, stood on main road routes and junctions in the middle parts of England that changed hands frequently. Scarborough's remote, coastal location, 'at an out-Angle', as Cholmley expressed it, provided it with protection from marauding armies on the march. Nevertheless, though Scarborough was to become a great shipping and shipbuilding port, a fashionable spa, and ultimately a popular seaside holiday resort, in military and strategical terms its national importance was never more significant than during the Civil Wars.

Notes on the Text

Introduction

1. W. D. Macray (ed.), *The History of the Rebellion and Civil Wars in England . . . by Edward, Earl of Clarendon*, 6 vols (1888), iii, p. 102.
2. G. W. Johnson (ed.), *The Fairfax Correspondence. Memoirs of the Reign of Charles the First*, 2 vols (1848), i, pp. 210–11.
3. J. W. Ord, *The History and Antiquities of Cleveland* (1846), pp. 601–2.
4. Suffolk County Record Office, Ipswich, HD 36, 2672/69: 3 March 1645.
5. J. C. Atkinson (ed.), *NRQSR*, North Riding Record Society, i–iv (1884–6), iv, p. 233.

Chapter One, Decline and Recovery

1. Leland, p. 59; J. Chandler (ed.), *John Leland's Itinerary. Travels in Tudor England* (Alan Sutton, Stroud, Glos., 1993), pp. xx, xxx.
2. Leland, p. 59.
3. Ibid., p. 60.
4. Ibid., p. 59. The engineer's plat (BL, Cottonian MSS, Aug. I, ii 1.) has been published previously in several works but wrongly dated as either *c.* 1485 (Baker, facing p. 194) or 'Elizabethan' (*VCH, YNR*, ii, p. 540; Rowntree, p. 212; and Edwards, p. 46), but not in C. Platt, *The English Medieval Town* (1976), p. 179. There now seems little doubt that the plat was drawn by one of Henry's military engineers in or about 1538. See J. Binns, 'The Oldest Map of Scarborough', in *The Transactions of the Scarborough Archaeological and Historical Society*, 25 (1983), pp. 13–15.
5. Leland, p. 60.
6. Rowntree, pp. 104, 105.
7. Edwards, pp. 34–5.
8. Ibid.
9. *CTSC*, p. 23.
10. Edwards, p. 35.
11. Hinderwell, pp. 160–1; Ashcroft, i, pp. v, 24, 319; ii, p. v.
12. Hinderwell, pp. 160–1.
13. R. Carroll, 'Yorkshire Parliamentary Boroughs in the Seventeenth Century', *NH*, iii (1968), p. 71; C. Cook and J. Wroughton, *English Historical Facts 1603–1688* (1980), pp. 83–4.
14. Baker, pp. 217–18; Ashcroft, i, p. 301.
15. Chapman, ii, p. 380.
16. Ashcroft, i, p. 311.
17. NYCRO, Scarborough Corporation Records (hereafter DC/SCB), MIC 1355, f. 122v.; MIC 1358, f. 3v.; MIC 2150/3404.
18. Leland, p. 60.

Notes to pages 16–29

19. *VCH, YNR*, ii, pp. 541–9; Rowntree, pp. 141–53; G. Port, *Scarborough Castle* (English Heritage, 1989), pp. 4–12.
20. Rowntree, pp. 159–64.
21. *APC*, 1556–8, p. 254.
22. Ibid., 1558–70, pp. 231, 233, 301; *CSPD, Addenda*, 1547–65, p. 567. In this last reference, the name 'Chamberlain' is given wrongly instead of 'Cholmley'.
23. Rowntree, p. 220.
24. Baker, p. 97.
25. Ashcroft, i, pp. 22, 23. A 'brat' is a turbot fish and a 'couger' probably a conger eel.
26. Baker, p. 97.
27. Ibid.
28. *VCH, YNR*, ii, p. 542. William Thompson seems to have had privileged access to the castle long before he acquired it legitimately. In 1597, when he was bailiff, the Common Hall allowed him to take stones from the 'new towre' to make up the stairs near his house. (NYCRO, DC/SCB, MIC 1358/356)
29. *VCH, YNR*, ii, p. 542.
30. In April 1597 there was a report of boys climbing the castle walls for their sport and pleasure. (NYCRO, DC/SCB, MIC 1358/340)
31. *CTSC*, p. 4.
32. Baker, pp. 351–2.
33. Leland, p. 60.
34. Baker, p. 352.
35. *Proceedings and Ordinances of the Privy Council*, viii (1837), p. 251; *APC*, 1547–50, p. 266; Ibid., 1550–2, p. 299.
36. *Scarborough Gazette*, 24 April 1902.
37. Chapman, iii, pp. 42, 65.
38. Rowntree, pp. 204–5.
39. Scarborough Central Library, Scarborough Room, pamphlet 518, Queen Elizabeth's letter, Greenwich, 6 March 1566.
40. Baker, pp. 357–8.
41. Ibid, p. 357.
42. Ashcroft, i, p. 36; Hinderwell, pp. 192–3; Rowntree, pp. 178–9.
43. Ashcroft, i, p. 36; Hinderwell, pp. 193–4; Rowntree, p. 179.
44. Chapman, i, pp. 45–8, 140.
45. Ashcroft, i, pp. 52–3.
46. Ibid., pp. 52–6.
47. T. S. Willan, *The English Coasting Trade 1600–1750* (Manchester, 1967), p. 14.
48. B. Hall, 'The Trade of Newcastle upon Tyne and the North East Coast, 1600–1640' (unpublished Ph.D. thesis, University of London, 1933), reviewed and summarised in *BIHR*, xii, 1934–5, p. 57; J. U. Nef, *The Rise of the British Coal Industry*, 2 vols (1932), ii, p. 26, n. 2.
49. *APC*, 1613–14, pp. 417–18; Ashcroft, i, pp. 53–4; *CTSC*, pp. 153–4.
50. Ashcroft, i, p. 336.
51. Ibid., pp. 127, 292; Chapman, iii, p. 20.
52. Ashcroft, i, pp. 242, 254; ii, p. 26; Chapman, ii, pp. 400, 401.
53. Leland, p. 60.
54. BL, Cotton Aug. I.ii.1.
55. J. Fawcett, *A Memorial of the Church of St Mary's, Scarboro'* (1850), pp. 54–69.
56. Ibid., pp. 53–4; Rowntree, 86–8.
57. Hinderwell, pp. 138–51.
58. Pearson, pp. 18, 20, 25–6.
59. Edwards, illustration 9 'Plan of Scarborough 1725' inset; L. S. Debenham, 'Scarborough's Water Supply', in *TSDAS*, 15 (1972), offprint, pp. 1–6.
60. *Yorkshire Inquisitions*, iii, YASRS xxxi (1902), p. 81.
61. For example, in 1538, Robert Edmunde left 3s. 4d. for 'mending and paveinge of wais' (BIHR, PW, V.11, f. 323).
62. Fawcett, p. 30.
63. Ibid., pp. 41–2; Pearson, p. 16.
64. Leland, p. 60.
65. BL, Cotton Aug. I.ii.1.
66. Ashcroft, i, pp. 56, 250, 292; ii, pp. 11, 12.

Notes to pages 30–42

67. BIHR, Archbishops' Visitation Court Book, part 2 (i), 1633.
68. Ashcroft, i, p. 242.
69. Ibid., p. 257.
70. Ibid., pp. 267, 269; HUCRO, Churchwardens' Accounts, PE 165/241, p. 6.
71. HUCRO, PE 165/241, p. 11; Ashcroft, i, pp. 203, 301.
72. Ashcroft, i, p. 278. For Scarborough's population at this time see pp. 52–3.
73. HUCRO, PE 165/241, p. 6.
74. Ibid.
75. Ibid.
76. BIHR, PW, V.31, f. 201; V.36, f. 584; V.41, f. 225; YASRS, x (1889), p. 185.
77. HUCRO, PE 165/241, p. 6. Information on occupations has been derived from wills, indentures and craft guild compositions or rules which are scattered indiscriminately through the corporation records.
78. HUCRO, PE 165/241, p. 6.
79. Jeayes, p. 83; Hinderwell, p. 161.
80. BIHR, PW, V.13, f. 497; V.17, f. 71; Jeayes, p. 83; P. W. Hasler (ed.), *The House of Commons 1558–1603* (1981), i, p. 291.
81. *Scarb. Wills*, iii, pp. 527–32.
82. Ibid.
83. Jeayes, 120B, 140A, 78B, 106A, 104B, 107B; Hinderwell, p. 161.
84. Hinderwell, p. 162; Rowntree, p. 398.
85. Ashcroft, ii, pp. 19, 28.
86. *Scarb. Wills*, iii, p. 767.
87. Ibid., p. 719; SRL, MIC 5582, Scarborough parish register, bishops' transcripts, 19 Feb. 1628; Ashcroft, ii, p. 82.
88. Hinderwell, pp. 161–2, 186–7.
89. Dugdale, iii, pp. 41–2; J. J. Sheahan and T. Whellan, *History and Topography of the City of York and the East Riding of Yorkshire*, ii, p. 369.
90. Dugdale, ii, pp. 438–9; *YAJ*, xviii (1905), pp. 233–40.
91. Jeayes, p. 83; Hinderwell, pp. 161–2; Dugdale, ii, p. 489.
92. Dugdale, iii, pp. 41–2; Sheahan and Whellan, ii, p. 369.
93. Jeayes, p. 83; Hinderwell, p. 161; Ashcroft, i, p. 72.
94. HUCRO, DDHO/55, 2, 5; T. S. Willan, 'The Parliamentary Surveys of the North Riding', *YAJ*, xxxi (1934), pp. 267–9.
95. Fawcett, p. 88; *Scarborough Evening News*, 4 Apr. 1985.
96. Ashcroft, i, pp. 70, 71; H. Aveling, *Northern Catholics: The Catholic Recusants of the North Riding of Yorkshire 1558–1790* (1966), p. 271.
97. *APC*, 1627, pp. 22–9.
98. Hinderwell, pp. 161–2; HUCRO, DDHO/55, 4, 5.
99. Dugdale, iii, p. 148; *YRCP*, i, YASRS xv (1893), pp. 10–15.
100. Hinderwell, pp. 161, 162; *YRCP*, i, pp. 3–9, 158–60.
101. J. Buckley, *The Outport of Scarborough* (1959), p. 9; Jeayes, p. 83; Hinderwell, pp. 161–2; *CTSC*, pp. 114–20.
102. Baker, p. 45.
103. *DNB*; G. C. F. Forster, 'Faction and County Government in Early Stuart Yorkshire', *NH*, xi (1976), pp. 70–86.
104. PRO, Star Chamber, 5/43/22.
105. YML, Add. MS 343, f.7v.
106. NYCRO, SCB/DC, B1, General Letters, 4, 30 Sept., 8 Oct. 1597; Ashcroft, i, pp. 28, 32; D. M. Meads (ed.), *Diary of Lady Margaret Hoby 1599–1605* (1930), p. 211.
107. J. T. Cliffe, *The Yorkshire Gentry from the Reformation to the Civil War* (1969), p. 88; Meads, *Diary of Lady Margaret Hoby*, p. 36.
108. Ashcroft, i, pp. 200, 202–3.
109. Ibid., p. 216; SCL, WWM, Strafford Papers, 12(d), f. 248.
110. Ashcroft, i, p. 217.
111. Carroll, *NH*, iii, p. 82, n. 46; Ashcroft, i, pp. 223, 225, 227, 230.
112. Ashcroft, i, p. 233.

Notes to pages 43–56

113. Ibid., p. 232.
114. Ibid., pp. 232–3.
115. Ibid., p. 240.
116. Ibid., p. 56.
117. Ibid., pp. 270–1.
118. Ibid., pp. 110, 206, 336, 318, 345.
119. Ibid., pp. 78, 159, 258, 274, 302.
120. Ibid., pp. 236, 110, 117.
121. Ibid., pp. 96–7, 118–19, 138–9; ii, p. 112.
122. Ibid., i, pp. 121, 188.
123. BIHR, Archbishop's Visitation Court Book, 1633, Pt 2 (1).
124. Ashcroft, i, p. 159; Aveling, *Northern Catholics*, p. 271.
125. Ashcroft, i, p. 69.
126. Ibid., pp. 107, 125, 135.
127. Ibid., p. 185.
128. Ibid., pp. 290–1.
129. Aveling, *Northern Catholics*, pp. 221, 272.
130. Ashcroft, i, p 293.
131. *Hackness Parish Register, 1557–1783*, Yorkshire Parish Register Society, xxv (1906), p. 65.
132. Hinderwell, p. 162; YML, Add. MS 343, f.24r.
133. W. G. Hoskins, *Local History in England* (2nd edn, 1972), p. 238.
134. Ibid., p. 239.
135. Platt, *English Medieval Town*, p. 176; J. Guy, 'The Tudor Age', in *The Oxford History of England*, iii (Oxford, 1992), p. 2.
136. Baker, pp. 319–20.
137. D. M. Palliser, 'Civic Mentality and the Environment in Tudor York', in J. Barry (ed.), *The Tudor and Stuart Town 1530–1688* (1990), pp. 218–19.
138. SRL, MIC 5582. For the reliable multipliers now available, see E. A. Wrigley and R. S. Schofield, *The Population History of England and Wales, 1541–1871* (1981).
139. Ashcroft, i, p. 278.
140. NYCRO, DC/SCB, K11, Lists of Inhabitants, n.d.
141. Mean household sizes in pre-industrial English urban communities ranged between seven and four, but the lower figure is more common than the higher. N. Goose, 'Household Size and Structure in Early-Stuart Cambridge' in Barry, *Tudor and Stuart Town*, p. 94, table 4.
142. PRO, Exchequer King's Remembrancer Port Books, 187/5, 310/9, 315/10, 317/14.
143. Ibid., 318/4.
144. Ibid., 317/8.
145. Hall, thesis, p. 208; PRO, E190/318/11, Scarborough Port Book, July–Dec. 1645.
146. Hall, thesis, pp. 225–6.
147. Ashcroft, ii, pp. 24–6.
148. *APC*, 1596–7, p. 426.
149. Ashcroft, i, pp. 11, 23, 214; Baker, pp. 343–4.
150. Chapman, ii, p. 380.
151. Ashcroft, i, pp. 65–6.
152. Ibid., p. 30.
153. Ibid., p. 264.
154. Hinderwell, pp. 368–70; Baker, pp. 317–24; Rowntree, pp. 222–4.
155. Rowntree, p. 205.
156. J. Schofield, *An Historical and Descriptive Guide to Scarborough and its Environs* (York, 1787), pp. 115–21.

Chapter 2, Defence and War, 1600–1642

1. Ashcroft, i, pp. 59–60.
2. Ibid., p. 60.
3. Ibid.
4. Ibid., pp. 68–9.
5. Ibid., pp. 70–1, 72, 73.
6. Ibid., p. 129.

Notes to pages 56–75

7. Ibid., pp. 127–8, 131, 134.
8. Ibid., pp. 141, 142, 145, 146.
9. *CSPD*, 1625–6, pp. 135, 275
10. *APC*, 1627, p. 14.
11. Ashcroft, i, pp. 151–2.
12. Ibid., pp. 152–3.
13. Ibid., pp. 155–6, 157.
14. Ibid., pp. 160–1.
15. Ibid., pp. 163–4, 173–4.
16. Ibid., pp. 184–5, 186, 188.
17. Ibid., pp. 236, 237.
18. Ibid., pp. 237, 233. See above, p. 38.
19. *CSPD*, 1633–4, p. 314; Ashcroft, i, pp. 247, 248, 249, 258, 260, 262.
20. Ashcroft, i, pp. 272, 273.
21. *CSPD*, 1634–5, p. 273; Scarborough Central Library, Scarborough parish register, MIC 5582.
22. *CSPD*, 1634–5, p. 273.
23. Ashcroft, i, pp. 274–6.
24. Ibid., pp. 276–8.
25. *CSPD*, 1635, p. 317; Ashcroft, i, pp. 279, 281.
26. *CSPD*, 1635, p. 294.
27. Ashcroft, i, p. 277.
28. *CSPD*, 1635, pp. 322–3, 326–7, 336, 339, 365, 372.
29. J. Rushworth, *Historical Collections*, Part II, i (1680), p. 322; C. V. Wedgwood, *Thomas Wentworth, First Earl of Strafford, 1593–1641, A Re-evaluation* (1964), p. 217.
30. *CSPD*, 1636–7, p. 96; K. R. Andrews, *Ships, Money and Politics: Seafaring and Enterprise in the Reign of Charles I* (Cambridge, 1991), p. 155.
31. Andrews, *Ships, Money and Politics*, p. 155.
32. Cliffe, *Yorks Gentry*, pp. 309–11; SCL, WWM, SP10 (214).
33. Ashcroft, i, pp. 327–9; *L&P*, xvii, p. 510.
34. Ashcroft, i, p. 330; Chapman, iii, p. 112.
35. YML, Add. MS 343, f. 24r.
36. Ibid.
37. Ashcroft, i, p. 335.
38. Ibid., pp. 335–6.
39. Chapman, iii, p. 112.
40. Cliffe, *Yorks Gentry*, pp. 317–18; *CSPD*, 1640, pp. 154–5.
41. *CSPD*, 1639, pp. 88, 99.
42. Ashcroft, i, p. 340.
43. Cliffe, *Yorks Gentry*, p. 313.
44. A. M. W. Stirling, *The Hothams*, 2 vols (1918), i, pp. 31–2; W. Knowler (ed.), *The Earl of Strafford's Letters and Despatches*, 2 vols (Dublin, 1739–40), ii, pp. 393, 408; PRO, SP16, 448/66.1.
45. Ashcroft, i, pp. 340, 341, 342.
46. Ibid., pp. 341, 343.
47. Ibid., pp. 343, 344.
48. E. S. Cope and W. H. Coates (eds), *Proceedings of the Short Parliament of 1640*, Camden, 4th series, xix (1977), pp. 161–2, 194.
49. *CSPD*, 1640, pp. 154–5; YML, Add. MS 343, ff. 24r–24v, 28v.
50. YML, Add. MS 343, f. 25r.
51. Ibid., f. 24v; *CSPD*, 1640, p. 586.
52. Cliffe, *Yorks Gentry*, pp. 323–5; Ashcroft, i, pp. 347, 349.
53. Ashcroft, ii, p. 7.
54. *CJ*, ii, p. 174; *CSPD*, 1641, pp. 474–5.
55. *CSPD*, 1641, p. 473; *CJ*, ii, p. 174.

Chapter Three, First Civil War, 1642–1645

1. Ashcroft, ii, p. 11.
2. See above, p. 63.
3. Ashcroft, ii, pp. 11, 12.
4. Ibid., p. 12.
5. Ibid., p. 14.
6. Baker, p. 361.
7. J. R. Powell, *The Navy in the English Civil War* (1962), p. 18; E. Gillett and

Notes to pages 75–87

K. A. MacMahon, *History of Hull* (1980), p. 170; *LJ*, v, p. 182.
8. *LJ*, v, p. 213.
9. J. R. Powell and E. K. Timings (eds), *Documents relating to the Civil War, 1642–1648* (1963), pp. 22–3.
10. E. B. G. Warburton, *Memoirs of Prince Rupert and the Cavaliers*, 2 vols (1849), i, pp. 461–2; C. Duffy, *Siege Warfare* (1979), p. 147.
11. Ashcroft, ii, p. 16.
12. *CSPD*, 1641–3, p. 515.
13. *LJ*, v, p. 314.
14. Ibid., pp. 224, 314.
15. Ashcroft, ii, p. 15.
16. Chapman, ii, p. 36.
17. *LJ*, v, p. 314. It is not certain from Trenchfield's letter whether by 'this town' he meant Scarborough or Bridlington, but his judgement might have applied equally to either.
18. Baker, pp. 255–6; Ashcroft, ii, pp. 15–16.
19. Ashcroft, ii, p. 14.
20. Clarendon, *History of the Rebellion*, ii, p. 226.
21. T. Hobbes, *Behemoth* in *The English Works of Thomas Hobbes* ed. W. Molesworth, 11 vols (1839–45), vi, p. 128.
22. C. Hill, *The Century of Revolution, 1603–1714* (1961), pp. 121-4; B. Manning, *The English People and the English Revolution* (Peregrine edn, 1978), pp. 258–65.
23. For example, see J. Kenyon, *The Civil Wars of England* (pbk edn, 1989), p. 38.
24. R. Howell, 'The Structure of Urban Politics in the English Civil War', *Albion*, vol. 2, no. 2 (1979), pp. 111–26; J. Morrill (ed.), *Reactions to the English Civil War, 1642–49* (1982), pp. 67–88.
25. E. A. Andriette, *Devon and Exeter in the Civil War* (Newton Abbot, 1971), pp. 82–4, 102–3; R. Howell, *Newcastle-upon-Tyne and the Puritan Revolution* (1967), pp. 117, 152, 166; Forster, *VCH Yorks. E.R.*, i, pp. 100–2.

26. *EHR*, xxxii, p. 569.
27. Ibid., p. 570.
28. Hinderwell, p. 162; Ashcroft, ii, pp. 5, 272-8.
29. Carroll, *NH*, iii, p. 83; *Scarb. Wills*, V.44, f. 55; Ashcroft, ii, pp. 18–19.
30. YML, Add. MS 343, f. 26v.
31. *CSPD*, 1642, pp. 366, 379, 387. Unfortunately, *CSPD* does not distinguish Sir Hugh from his brother Sir Henry, which explains why Sir Charles Firth at first failed to appreciate that Sir Henry, and not Sir Hugh, raised and led the regiment which 'fought' at Edgehill (*DNB*). Later Firth corrected his own error (*BIHR*, iii, no. 9 (1926), p. 189) by reference to E. Peacock, *The Army Lists of the Roundheads and Cavaliers* (1874), p. 38.
32. P. Young, *Edgehill 1642* (Kineton, 1970), pp. 116, 317–19.
33. Ibid., pp. 131, 253.
34. Ashcroft, ii, pp. 17–18.
35. HMC, *Bouverie MSS*, x, pt 6 (1886), pp. 90-1.
36. BL, *TT*, E85(17): *Two Letters from Cholmley to the Speaker*, 18 Jan. 1643; *CJ*, ii, p. 831.
37. HMC, *Bouverie*, x, pp. 90–1; BL, *TT*, 85(17): *Two Letters*.
38. Ibid.
39. Ibid.
40. Ashcroft, ii, pp. 18–19.
41. R. Bell (ed.) *Memorials of the Civil War*, 2 vols (1849), i, p. 25.
42. Ibid., pp. 26, 29.
43. BL, *TT*, E85(17): *Two Letters*.
44. *CJ*, ii, pp. 891, 893.
45. *CSPD*, 1625–49, pp. 644, 650; *CJ*, ii, p. 926.
46. Ashcroft, ii, pp. 19–20, 269–72.
47. Ibid., p. 20.
48. Ibid., p. 21.
49. Ibid.
50. Ibid., pp. 20–1.
51. Chapman, iii, p. 114.
52. HMC, *Portland*, i, 90-1; Rushworth, *Historical Collections*, v, p. 125.

Notes to pages 89–101

53. Ibid. In his chapter in Rowntree's *History*, Professor Grant transferred this battle at Guisborough to Guiseley, near Leeds: A. Rowntree (ed.), *A History of Scarborough*, p. 231.
54. HMC, *Fifth Report*, p. 69; *Portland*, i, p. 90.
55. BL, *TT*, E95(9): *Letter from John Hotham to Speaker*; *Mercurius Aulicus*, 8, 15 Feb. 1643, *ORN*, I, i, pp. 95, 105; HMC *Hastings*, ii, p. 92. In the last reference, writing from Oxford, the King's secretary, Sir Edward Nicholas, mistakenly located the battle at 'Burrow brig', instead of Yarm. Cholmley's men were imprisoned in Durham and there ill-treated.
56. Powell & Timings, *Documents*, pp. 60–7.
57. *Mercurius Aulicus*, 27 Feb., 10 Mar. 1643, *ORN*, I, i, pp. 131, 151.
58. D. Parsons (ed.), *Diary of Sir Henry Slingsby* (1836), pp. 87–8.
59. BL, *TT*, E95(9): *Letter from Hotham*; HMC, *Portland*, i, p. 104.
60. *EHR*, xxxii, pp. 570–1; Rushworth, *Historical Collections*, v, pp. 264–5.
61. *EHR*, xxxii, pp. 571–3; BL, *TT*, E95(9): *Letter from Hotham*; Rushworth, *Historical Collections*, v, p. 265.
62. *EHR*, xxxii, p. 572.
63. *DNB*; *CJ*, iii, p. 29; Ashcroft, ii, p. 166.
64. *EHR*, xxxii, p. 573.
65. BL, *TT*, E95(9): *Letter from Hotham*.
66. *EHR*, xxxii, p. 573.
67. BL, *TT*, E95(9): *Letter from Hotham*.
68. BL, *TT*, E97(3): *Certain Informations*, no. 13, was incorrect when it reported that Cholmley had retaken Scarborough with 1,500 troops. Sir Hugh's own version of these events was fully endorsed by the submissions of John Harrison, senior, Nicholas Ducke, seaman, John Barry and Robert Lacey, all of Scarborough, who were eyewitnesses and gave sworn testimonies at the trial of Captain Browne Bushell (Ashcroft, ii, pp. 165–8.
69. *EHR*, xxxii, p. 573.
70. BL, *TT*, E95(9): *Letter from Hotham*; Ashcroft, ii, p. 23.
71. BL, *TT*, E97(3): *Certain Informations*, 10 Mar.–1 Apr. 1643, no. 13.
72. Ashcroft, ii, pp. 28–9; Hinderwell, p. 162.
73. The Queen had nearly lost her life when Parliament's warships came right into the defenceless harbour and bombarded the quayside house where she was sleeping. BL, *TT*, E292(27), 296(1): *Letters from the Queen at York to King Charles*, 30 Mar. 1643.
74. *Mercurius Aulicus*, 26 Mar. 1643, *ORN*, I, i, pp. 177–8.
75. YML, Add. MS 343, f. 27r.
76. *CJ*, iii, p. 28.
77. *CSPV*, 10, 17 Apr. 1643, pp. 260, 263–4.
78. For example, BL, *TT*, E270(33): *Scottish Dove*, 21–28 Feb. 1645; Ibid., E258(327); *A Prefect Diurnall*, 17–24 Feb. 1645
79. *Mercurius Aulicus*, 31 Mar. 1643, *ORN*, I, i, p. 195; Hinderwell, p. 83; BL, *TT*, 292(27): *Letters from the Queen*, 30 Mar. 1643.
80. *Mercurius Aulicus*, 31 Mar., 16 Apr. 1643, *ORN*, I, i, pp. 189, 195; P. Young & R. Holmes, *The English Civil War* (1974), pp. 104–5.
81. *LJ*, vi, p. 70; *CJ*, iii, p. 111.
82. BL, *TT*, E60(4): *Two Letters between Cholmley and Capt. Gooderick*, 12 July 1643; *CJ*, iii, p. 160; T. T. Wildridge (ed.), *The Hull Letters, 1625–46* (Hull, 1887), pp. 158, 159.
83. Young & Holmes, *English Civil War*, pp. 111–13, 153–4.
84. *Mercurius Aulicus*, 7 July 1643, *ORN*, I, i, p. 382.
85. YML, Add. MS 343, f. 27v; BL, *TT*, E59(11): *Siege of Hull*, 11 Oct. 1643.
86. Parsons (ed.) *Slingsby Diary*, p. 103; J. Vicars, *England's Parliamentary*

Notes to pages 101–113

Chronicle 1640–46, 4 vols (1646), ii, pp. 154, 156–7; Ashcroft, ii, p. 75.
87. YML, Add. MS 343, f. 27v.
88. BL, TT, E50(30): *An Exact Relation*, 12 June 1644; *CSPD*, 1644, p. 203; *EHR*, xxxii, p. 575. Darley was sent off to London in August 1644 with Cholmley's nineteen propositions of surrender.
89. BL, TT, E53(12): *Exact and Certain Newes from the Siege at Yorke*, 3 July 1644.
90. *Mercurius Aulicus*, 11 Oct. 1643, *ORN*, I, ii, p. 293.
91. *EHR*, xxxii, p. 580.
92. BL, TT, E85(17): *Two Letters from Cholmley to the Speaker*, 18 Jan. 1643; Clarendon, *History of the Rebellion*, ii, p. 468.
93. *EHR*, xxxii, p. 573; HMC, *Portland*, i, pp. 113–14; *CJ*, iii, p. 86.
94. HMC, *Various Collections*, vii (1913), p. 59.
95. Ashcroft, ii, p. 32.
96. Ibid.
97. Ashcroft, ii, pp. 32–3.
98. Ibid., pp. 24–6.
99. Ibid., pp. 30–2, 34–5; PRO, E190/318/11.
100. Ashcroft, ii, pp. 29–30.
101. Ibid., p. 30.
102. *CSPD*, 1644, pp. 157–8, 159, 160.
103. Ibid., pp. 273–4.
104. *CSPV*, 1643–47, pp. 21, 115, 118.
105. T. H. Brooke, 'The Memoirs of Sir Hugh Cholmeley' (unpublished B. Litt. thesis, University of Oxford, 1937), p. 113; *CSPD*, 1644, p. 557.
106. Margaret, Duchess of Newcastle, *The Life of William Cavendish, Duke of Newcastle* (1667), p. 53; YML, Add. MS 343, f. 27v.
107. BL, Egerton MSS 2884, f. 41.
108. *EHR*, xxxii, p. 576; YML, Add. MS 343, f. 27v.
109. *CSPD*, 1644, p. 447.
110. *EHR*, xxxii, p. 575; YML, Add. MS 343, f. 27v.
111. Bell, *Memorials*, ii, pp. 121–2.
112. *CSPD*, 1644, pp. 450, 452, 531; *EHR*, xxxii, pp. 576–9.
113. *EHR*, xxxii, pp. 576–9. For the relationship between Cholmley and Remmington and the latter's religious record see J. Binns, 'Sir Hugh Cholmley of Whitby, 1600–1657: His Life and Works' (unpublished Ph.D. thesis, University of Leeds, 1992), pp. 347–9.
114. *CJ*, iii, p. 29.
115. *Mercurius Aulicus*, 30 June 1643, *ORN*, I, i, p. 365.
116. Ashcroft, ii, pp. 31-5.
117. J. Binns, 'Captain Browne Bushell: North Sea Adventurer and Pirate', *NH*, xxvii (1991), pp. 90–105.
118. HMC, *Portland*, i, p. 167; Powell & Timings, *Documents*, pp. 120–1.
119. HMC, *Sixth Report*, p. 434(a); Ashcroft, ii, pp. 31, 34, 35, 179.
120. J. U. Nef, *The Rise of the British Coal Industry*, 2 vols (1932), ii, p. 287.
121. BL, TT, E81(29), E90(17), E99(6): *Ordinances and Declarations of Parliament*, 13 Jan., Feb., 15 Apr. 1643; *CJ*, iii, pp. 46, 68.
122. *CSPV*, 1643–47, pp. 106, 116.
123. BL, TT, E86(20): *Sea Coale, Char-coale, and Small-Coale*, 27 Jan. 1643.
124. *CJ*, iii, p. 432.
125. BL, TT, E40(27): *Report from the English Commission at Sunderland*, 6 Apr. 1644.
126. *Mercurius Aulicus*, 11 Oct. 1644, *ORN*, I, iii, p. 293.
127. *CSPD*, 1644–5, p. 94.
128. B. Whitelocke, *Memorials of English Affairs* (1732), p. 107; BL, TT, E269(8): *The English Post*, no. 23, 3 Feb. 1645.
129. BL, TT, E269(14): *A Diary or An Exact Journal*, no. 39, 7 Feb. 1645.
130. BL, TT, E270(23): *Perfect Passages*, 19–25 Feb. 1645; Ibid., E270(29): *Mercurius Civicus*, 20–27 Feb. 1645.
131. *EHR*, xxxii, pp. 580, 581.

Notes to pages 113–131

132. YML, Add. MS 343, f. 28r.
133. Ashcroft, ii, p. 23.
134. Hinderwell, p. 115.
135. BL, TT, E270(23): *Perfect Passages*, 19–25 Feb. 1645.
136. J. Schofield, *An Historical and Descriptive Guide to Scarborough and its Environs* (York, 1787), pp. 88–9.
137. Ashcroft, ii, pp. 27-8.
138. Ibid., p. 41.
139. Ibid., p. 28.
140. Chapman, ii, p. 561.
141. NYCRO, DC/SCB, C2, Chamberlains' Accounts, 1644.
142. Ibid.
143. Ibid.
144. Ibid.
145. NYCRO, DC/SCB, H1, Assessment Lists, 1601–65.
146. Ashcroft, ii, pp. 18, 24, 26, 36.
147. Ibid., p. 26.
148. Ibid., p. 37.
149. Ibid., p. 39
150. *YRCP*, I, YASRS, xv (1893), pp. 35-8; Aveling, *Northern Catholics*, pp. 221, 271. According to one Yorkshire Catholic refugee, William Vavasour, even after Marston Moor, Cholmley was still refusing sanctuary at Scarborough to those of his religion. *CSPD*, 1644–5, pp. 197–8.
151. Hinderwell, p. 161; *Scarb. Wills*, V42, f. 559; Ashcroft, ii, pp. 18–19, 28–9.
152. Ashcroft, ii, p. 166; *EHR*, xxxii, p. 573.
153. Ashcroft, ii, p. 274.
154. Ibid., pp. 5, 18; *Scarb. Wills*, iii, p. 749.
155. Ashcroft, ii, pp. 28–9, 36, 258; Rowntree, p. 398.
156. *EHR*, xxxii, p. 575.
157. Ashcroft, ii, pp. 28, 29, 40.
158. Hinderwell, 161–2; *Scarb. Wills*, V45, f. 533.
159. Ashcroft, ii, pp. 3, 12, 40.
160. Ibid., p. 41.
161. NYCRO, DC/SCB, Book of Elections 1645–63; Hinderwell, p. 162.
162. Ashcroft, ii, p. 41.
163. *YRCP*, I, YASRS, xv, pp. 3–9, 9–10, 10–15, 158–60; Ashcroft, ii, p. 41; Dugdale, ii, p. 488; Ibid., iii, pp. 41, 148.
164. *CJ*, iv, p. 523.
165. Rowntree, pp. 360, 398; Ashcroft, ii, p. 258.
166. *YRCP*, I, YASRS, xv, pp. 35-8; Ashcroft, ii, p. 41.
167. Ashcroft, ii, p. 32.
168. Ibid., p. 31.
169. Ibid., p. 36.
170. *CJ*, iv, p. 523.
171. Ashcroft, ii, pp. 26, 41. Ann Cooper supplied hogsheads of beer to captain Denton's 'litle catch' in 1644 (Ashcroft, ii, p. 34).
172. Ashcroft, ii, p. 41.
173. Ashcroft, i, pp. 251–2.
174. Ashcroft, ii, p. 17.
175. Ibid., pp. 29–30.
176. Ibid., pp. 30, 31, 32.
177. Ibid., pp. 28–9, 87, 98, 112, 115, 131.
178. Hinderwell, p. 162.
179. Ashcroft, ii, p. 41.
180. Ibid., pp. 41–2.
181. NYCRO, DC/SCB, A20, Common Hall Memoranda 1499–1737, 23 Nov. 1644.
182. Ashcroft, ii, p. 39.
183. Ibid., p. 37.

Chapter Four, The Great Siege, 1645

1. BL, TT, E258(27): *A Perfect Diurnall*, 17–24 Feb. 1645; E258(28): *Perfect Occurrences*, 22 Feb. 1645; E270(2): *The London Post*, no. 24; E270(9):

Notes to pages 131–144

Mercurius Civicus, 13–20 Feb. 1645; E270 (15): Mercurius Britanicus, 17–24 Feb. 1645; E270(21): London Post, 25; E270(23): Perfect Passages, 19–25 Feb. 1645; E270(29): Mercurius Civicus, 20–27 Feb. 1645; E270(30): A Diary or An Exact Journal, 20–27 Feb. 1645; E270(33): The Scottish Dove, 21–28 Feb. 1645; E271(5): Mercurius Britanicus, 24 Feb.–3 Mar. 1645.

2. *EHR*, xxxii, p. 581; *CSPD*, 1644–5, p. 329.
3. *EHR*, xxxii, pp. 580–1; J. Vicars, *England's Parliamentary Chronicle*, iv (1646), p. 110.
4. *EHR* xxxii, pp. 580–1.
5. BL, *TT* E270(8): *A Diary or An Exact Journal*, no. 40.
6. Ibid., E270(5): *Perfect Passages*, 12–28 Feb. 1645.
7. *CSPD*, 1644–5, p. 323; *CSPD*, 1645–7, pp. 95, 110.
8. BL, *TT*, E270(23): *Perfect Passages*, 19–25 Feb. 1645.
9. *EHR*, xxxii, p. 581.
10. Brooke, thesis, pp. 143–4.
11. BL, *TT*, E270(21): *London Post*, no. 25.
12. YML, Add. MS 343, f. 28r; BL, *TT*, 258(27): *Perfect Diurnall*, 17–24 Feb. 1645; Whitelocke, *Memorials*, p. 133; Vicars, *Chronicle*, iv, p. 110.
13. *EHR*, xxxii, p. 581.
14. *CJ*, iv, p. 528.
15. *YRCP*, I, pp. 158–60.
16. Ashcroft, ii, p. 258.
17. *CJ*, iv, p. 528.
18. Ashcroft, ii, p. 258.
19. HUCRO, PE 165/241, p. 6.
20. Ashcroft, ii, p. 75.
21. BL, *TT*, E270(33): *Scottish Dove*, 21–28 Feb. 1645.
22. Ibid., E258(27): *Perfect Diurnall*, 17–24 Feb. 1645.
23. *CSPD*, 1644–5, p. 323; *CJ*, iv, pp. 59, 97, 149.
24. *Mercurius Aulicus*, 8 Mar. 1645, *ORN*, I, iii, p. 455. The other places on this list were Shrewsbury and Weymouth.
25. BL, *TT*, E270(21): *London Post*. no. 25.
26. Ibid., E270(23): *Perfect Passages*, 19–25 Feb. 1645.
27. *CSPD*, 1644–5, p. 304.
28. Ibid., p. 323.
29. HMC, *Braye MSS*, X, vi, p. 155.
30. Brooke, thesis, p. 146; Vicars, *Chronicle*, iv, p. 110.
31. Vicars, *Chronicle*, iv, p. 110.
32. HMC, *Braye*, X, vi, pp. 155–6.
33. Ibid.; C. Russell (ed.), *The Origins of the English Civil War* (1973), p. 16; C. Russell, *The Causes of the English Civil War* (1990), pp. 165–6.
34. HMC, *Braye*, X, vi, pp. 156–7.
35. Ibid.
36. T. S. Willan, 'The Parliamentary Surveys of the North Riding', *YAJ*, xxxi (1934), p. 255, n. 3.
37. R. B. Turton (ed.), 'A Survey of the Honour and Forest of Pickering, 1651', *NRRS*, I (1894), p. 65.
38. Ibid., p. 207.
39. Hinderwell, p. 87.
40. Wildridge, *Letters*, p. 151.
41. B. N. Reckitt, *Charles the First and Hull, 1639–1645* (Howden, 1988), pp. 117–18.
42. Rushworth, *Historical Collections*, v, p. 642.
43. *CSPD*, 1644, p. 241.
44. J. Torre, *The Antiquities of York City* (York, 1719), p. 109
45. J. Tucker & L. Winstock, *The English Civil War: A Military Handbook* (1972), p. 57.
46. *EHR*, xxxii, p. 582; Hinderwell, p. 86.
47. Whitelocke, *Memorials*, p. 142; Hinderwell, p. 87.
48. Powell & Timings, *Documents*, pp. 200–1.
49. Hinderwell, p. 89.
50. BL, *TT*, E258(27): *Perfect Diurnall*, 17–24 Feb. 1645.
51. Ibid., E285(5): *Exchange Intelligencer*, May 1645.

Notes to pages 144–157

52. Ibid., E292(8): *Mercurius Veridicus*, 28 June–5 July 1645.
53. Powell & Timings, *Documents*, pp. 203–4
54. *CJ*, iv, p. 528.
55. S(uffolk) C(ounty) R(ecord) O(ffice), Ipswich, HD 36, 2672/69.
56. Ibid., HD 36, 2672/77.
57. Ibid., HD 36, 2672/25.
58. *CSPD*, 1645–7, p. 31.
59. Ibid., p. 55.
60. Ashcroft, ii, p. 78.
61. *CSPD*, 1644–5, p. 447.
62. BL, *TT*, E258(28): *Perfect Occurrences*, 22 Feb. 1645.
63. Ibid., E260(36): *Perfect Passages*, 13 May 1645.
64. *Mercurius Aulicus*, 8 Mar. 1645, *ORN*, I. iii, p. 455.
65. Ibid., 11 Apr. 1645, *ORN*, I, iv, p. 14.
66. Hinderwell, p. 88.
67. All three manuscripts, or copies of them, are amongst the Clarendon Papers at the Bodleian Library in Oxford: 'Some Observations and Memorialls Tuching the Hothams' (MS 1809); 'Memorialls Tuching the Battle of Yorke' (MS 1764); and 'Memorialls Tuching Scarbrough' (MS 1669).
68. Clarendon, *History of the Rebellion*, ii, pp. 267, 468.
69. R. Scrope & T. Monkhouse (eds), *Clarendon State Papers*, 3 vols (Oxford, 1767–86), II (1773), p. 186.
70. Schofield, *Guide to Scarborough*, p. 86.
71. Hinderwell, p. 70; Baker, pp. 437–9.
72. YML, Add. MS 343, f. 27r.
73. Sir Hugh Cholmley, *The Memoirs of Sir Hugh Cholmley . . . in which he gives some account of his family, and the distresses they underwent in the Civil Wars* (1787).
74. *EHR*, xxxii (1917), pp. 568–87.
75. Rowntree, pp. 232–5.
76. *EHR*, xxxii, p. 582.
77. BL, *TT*, E260(5): *A Perfect Diurnall*, no. 87, 24 Mar. 1645; *Mercurius Aulicus*, 11 Apr. 1645; *ORN*, I, iv, p. 14.
78. *EHR*, xxxii, p. 582.
79. Ibid.
80. Ibid.
81. Ibid., p. 583.
82. Ibid.
83. Ibid., p. 587.
84. Ibid., pp. 583–4.
85. BL, *TT*, E284(7): *Mercurius Civicus*, 5–11 May 1645.
86. *EHR*, xxxii, p. 584.
87. BL, *TT*, E260(39): *Perfect Passages*, 17–19 May 1645; Ibid., E285(3): *Mercurius Civicus*, 17 May 1645.
88. *EHR*, xxxii, p. 584.
89. BL, *TT*, E260(41): *A Perfect Diurnall*, 19 May 1645; Ibid., 285(2): *Mercurius Civicus*, 17 May 1645.
90. BL, *TT*, E260(39): *Perfect Passages*, 19 May 1645.
91. Ibid.
92. *EHR*, xxxii, p. 584.
93. BL, *TT*, E260(41): *A Perfect Diurnall*, 19 May 1645.
94. BL, *TT*, 285(3): *Mercurius Civicus*, 17 May 1645.
95. BL, *TT*, E260(40), *Perfect Occurrences*, 16–23 May 1645.
96. BL, *TT*, E285(7): *The Moderate Intelligencer*, 16 May 1645.
97. BL, *TT*, E260(39): *Perfect Passages*, 19 May 1645; Ibid, E260(41): *A Perfect Diurnall*, 19 May 1645; Ibid., E284(23): *Weekly Intelligencer*, May 1645.
98. BL, *TT*, E285(12): *Mercurius Veridicus*, 17–24 May 1645.
99. *EHR*, xxxii, p. 584.
100. BL, *TT*, E286(12): *The True Informer*, 30 May 1645.
101. Cholmley wrote that the interval was 'above 12 weekes' (*EHR*, xxxii, p. 584), but if Meldrum died on 17 May, six days after receiving his wounds, and the surrender took place on 25 July, the interval was nine weeks and six days.

Notes to pages 157–168

102. *EHR*, xxxii, pp. 584–6.
103. BL, *TT*, E290(8): *Mercurius Veridicus*, 21–28 June 1645.
104. BL, *TT*, E293(24): *Mercurius Civicus*, 17–24 July 1645.
105. Ibid, E293(29): *The Scottish Dove*, 18–25 July 1645.
106. Ibid., E293(35): *The True Informer*, no. 14; E294(5): *Mercurius Britanicus*, 21–28 July 1645; E294(8): *The Weekly Account*, 29 July 1645; E294(11): *Parliament's Post*, 23–29 July 1645; E294(20): *The Scottish Dove*, 25 July–1 Aug. 1645.
107. BL, Egerton MS 2884, f. 41.
108. *EHR*, xxxii, pp. 585–6.
109. Ibid., p. 586.
110. Ibid.,, p. 587,
111. BL, *TT*, E294(15): *An Exact Relation of the Surrender of Scarborough Castle*, 25 July 1645.
112. Ibid., E294(11): *Parliament's Post*, 23–29 July 1645.
113. M. Whittaker, *The Book of Scarborough Spaw* (Buckingham, 1984), p. 24.
114. *EHR*, xxxii, p. 586.
115. Ibid.
116. BL, *TT*, E284(8): *A Diary, or an Exact Journal*, 14 May 1645.
117. *EHR*, xxxii, p. 584
118. Ibid., p. 586.
119. BL, *TT*, E294(17): *The Coppie of a Letter from Major Generall Poines*, 31 July 1645.
120. Ibid., E294(15): *An Exact Relation*, 25 July 1645; E294(18): *Mercurius Civicus*, 25 July–1 Aug. 1645.
121. Ibid., E294(8): *The Weekly Account*, 29 July 1645; E294(11): *Parliament's Post*, 23–29 July 1645.
122. Ibid., E294(5): *Mercurius Britanicus*, 21–28 July 1645.
123. Ibid., E294(20): *The Scottish Dove*, 25 July–1 Aug. 1645; Rushworth, *Historical Collections*, iv, pp. 118–19.
124. *EHR*, xxxii, p. 586.
125. Hinderwell, pp. 91–4; *EHR*, xxxii, p. 587.
126. BL, *TT*, E294(15): *An Exact Relation*, 25 July 1645; E294(17): *The Coppie of a Letter from Major General Poines*, 31 July 1645.
127. Ibid., E294(8): *The Weekly Account*, 29 July 1645.
128. In his 'Memorialls Tuching Scarbrough', Cholmley wrote that he went directly to France from Bridlington (*EHR*, xxxii, p. 587), but later in his Memoirs he remembered that he had sailed first to Holland and stayed there two or three weeks before travelling on to France (YML, Add. MS 343, f. 28v.).
129. YML, Add. MS 343, f. 28r.
130. Ibid., f. 28v.
131. Ibid.
132. Ibid., ff. 28v–29r.
133. Ibid., f. 33v.
134. Ibid.
135. *CJ*, iv, p. 245.
136. BL, *TT*, E294(15): one recent account states that Cholmley was stoned by the women of the town (C. Carlton, *Going to the Wars* (1992), pp. 157, 377), but this is a misreading of *An Exact Relation*, 25 July 1645.
137. BL, *TT*, E294(18): *Mercurius Civicus*, 25 July–1 Aug. 1645.
138. HUCRO, PE 165/241, p. 35.
139. Hinderwell, p. 86; Rowntree, p. 233.
140. *EHR*, xxxii, p. 582.
141. Ashcroft, ii, pp. 78, 80.
142. Ibid., p. 53.
143. HUCRO, PE 165/241, p. 35.
144. Hinderwell, p. 127.
145. Schofield, *Guide*, p. 85.
146. *EHR*, xxxii, p. 585; Rowntree, facing p. 234.
147. J. Fawcett, *A Memorial of the Church of St Mary's, Scarboro'* (1850), p. 88.
148. Ashcroft, ii, pp. 11–12.
149. NYCRO, DC/SCB, C2, Chamberlains' accounts, 1646–7.
150. Ashcroft, ii, pp. 53, 68.
151. Ibid., pp. 52–3; NYCRO, DC/SCB, C2.

Notes to pages 168–182

152. Ashcroft, ii, pp. 1, 45.
153. Ibid., p. 4.
154. Ibid., pp. 52, 53.
155. Ashcroft, i, pp. 126, 213, 319.
156. Ashcroft, ii, p. 57.
157. Ibid., p. 52.
158. Ibid., p. 57.
159. Ashcroft, i, p. 213; Ashcroft, ii, pp. 1, 57; NYCRO, DC/SCB, C35, Corporation leases.
160. NYCRO, DC/SCB, C34; Ashcroft, ii, p. 47.
161. Ashcroft, i, p. 226; Ashcroft, ii, p. 57.
162. NYCRO, DC/SCB, C34.
163. Ashcroft, i, p. 225; Ashcroft, ii, p. 57.
164. Ashcroft, i, pp. 85, 198, 286; HUCRO, PE 165/241, p. 9.
165. Ashcroft, ii, p. 47; HUCRO, PE 165/241, pp. 17, 25, 43, 48.
166. Ashcroft, ii, pp. 52, 101.
167. Ibid., pp. 49, 55.
168. Schofield, *Guide*, p. 85.
169. Hinderwell, p. 86.
170. Ibid.
171. Schofield, *Guide*, p. 85.
172. Ibid., p. 84.
173. Ashcroft, ii, p. 52.
174. PRO, Scarborough Port Book, July–Dec. 1645, E190/318/11.
175. Ashcroft, ii, pp. 57, 59, 60.
176. Ibid., p. 53.
177. Ibid.
178. Ibid., pp. 52, 53.
179. Ibid., p. 89.
180. NYCRO, DC/SCB, C2.
181. Ashcroft, ii, p. 91.
182. Hinderwell, p. 101.
183. NYCRO, DC/SCB, C2.
184. Ashcroft, ii, p. 91.
185. Ibid., pp. 51, 53–4.
186. Ibid., pp. 61, 62.
187. Ibid., p. 49.
188. Ibid., p. 48; Baker, p. 147.
189. Ashcroft, ii, pp. 101–2.
190. Ibid., p. 94.
191. Ibid., p. 101.
192. YRCP, I, p. 11; NYCRO, DC/SCB, J3, Clergy Papers, 1646–1659.
193. Ashcroft, ii, pp. 60, 278–9.
194. HUCRO, PE 165/241, p. 26.
195. Ashcroft, ii, p. 76.
196. Ibid., p. 77.
197. Ibid., p. 75.
198. Ibid., pp. 95–6.
199. Ibid., p. 111.
200. Ibid., p. 125.
201. Ibid., p. 130.
202. Ibid., p. 141.
203. Ibid., p. 52.
204. YRCP, I, pp. 13, 159–60; PRO, E190/318/11.
205. YRCP, I, pp. 3–9, 11–13, 158–60.
206. Ashcroft, ii, pp. 272–8.
207. Ibid., pp. 52–3.
208. *Tracts relating to . . . Lancashire during the Civil War* (Chetham Society, II, 1844), pp. 84–9; *CJ*, iii, p. 623, iv, p. 168.
209. C. Carlton, *Going to the Wars*, p. 177; J. Morrill (ed.), *The Impact of The Civil War* (1991), p. 31.
210. J. Morrill (ed.), *Reaction to the English Civil War 1642–49* (1982), p. 125.
211. C. V. Wedgwood, *The King's War 1641–47* (1958), pp. 446–8.
212. Hinderwell, p. 97.

Chapter Five, The Second Civil War, 1648

1. G. C. F. Forster, 'Elections at Scarborough for the Long Parliament, 1640–47', *Transactions of the Scarborough and District Archaeological Society*, 1960, pp. 4–5.
2. D. Brunton & D. H. Pennington, *Members of the Long Parliament* (1954),

Notes to pages 182–193

pp. 22–3, 25–9, 36–7; G. E. Aylmer, *Rebellion or Revolution?* (Oxford, 1987), p. 69.
3. J. T. Cliffe, *The Yorkshire Gentry from the Reformation to the Civil War* (1969), pp. 90–1, 350.
4. Ashcroft, ii, p. 42.
5. Ibid., p. 43.
6. Ibid., p. 49.
7. Ibid.
8. Ibid., pp. 44–5.
9. Ibid., p. 49.
10. Ibid., pp. 49–50.
11. Ibid., p. 46.
12. Ibid.
13. Ibid., pp. 45–6, 47–8.
14. Forster, *TSDAS*, 1960, p. 7.
15. Ashcroft, ii, p. 50.
16. Cliffe, *Yorkshire Gentry*, pp. 280, 307–8.
17. Reckitt, *Charles I and Hull*, pp. 79, 84, 92, 94.
18. *NRQSR*, iv, p. 237.
19. Ashcroft, ii, p. 75.
20. Dugdale, ii, pp. 231, 232; *DNB*; Ashcroft, ii, p. 251.
21. Ashcroft, ii, pp. 57, 94.
22. Ibid., pp. 98, 99.
23. NYCRO, DC/SCB, A2, Book of Elections, 1645–63.
24. Ibid.
25. J. Campbell, *Lives of the British Admirals*, ii (1750), p. 422; *Pepys' Diary* (Everyman edn, 1978), i, p. 1.
26. Hinderwell, p. 299; G. Young, *A History of Whitby* (Whitby, 1817), ii, p. 842.
27. *DNB*. See also R. L. Greaves & R. Zaller (eds), *Biographical Dictionary of British Radicals in the Seventeenth Century* (Brighton, 1983), ii, p. 178.
28. Hinderwell, p. 295.
29. *Paver's Marriage Licences*, YASRS, xl (1909), p. 154.
30. *Parish Register of Lythe, 1619–1768*, YASPR (1973), p. 32.
31. Hinderwell, pp. 295, 299; Campbell, *Lives*, ii, p. 422.
32. *DNB*; Greaves & Zaller, *Biographical Dictionary*, ii, p. 178.
33. Scarborough District telephone directory lists 72 of this name.
34. NYCRO, DC/SCB, F9, Marine Papers, 1606–94; Ibid., G11, Account Book, 1643; PRO, E190/318/11, Port Book 1645.
35. NYCRO, DC/SCB, F9.
36. *DNB*.
37. *CSPD*, 1641–3, p. 562. See also *CJ*, iii, p. 29.
38. *CSPD*, 1645, p. 629; *LJ*, vii, p. 594; Powell & Timings, *Documents*, pp. 9, 202, 219.
39. *CSPD*, 1644–5, p. 223.
40. C. S. Terry (ed.) *Papers relating to the Army of the Solemn League and Covenant, 1643–47* (Edinburgh, 1917), i, p. 18.
41. *DNB*.
42. Ibid.
43. Ibid.
44. Ashcroft, ii, p. 269.
45. Ibid., p. 275.
46. Ibid., p. 46.
47. Ibid., pp. 53–4.
48. Ibid., p. 55.
49. Ibid., p. 64.
50. Ibid., ii, pp. 66–7.
51. Ibid., p. 71.
52. Ibid., p. 83.
53. Ibid., p. 89.
54. *CJ*, iv, p. 528.
55. Ashcroft, ii, pp. 94, 98.
56. Hinderwell, p. 303.
57. Ashcroft, ii, p. 57.
58. Ibid., p. 112.
59. Ibid., p. 82.
60. Ibid., p. 103.
61. Ibid., pp. 107, 111, 114.
62. Ibid., pp. 105–6.
63. *CJ*, iv, pp. 226, 247, 248; *LJ*, vii, p. 548.
64. *CJ*, iv, p. 226.
65. Ibid., p. 272.
66. Ibid., pp. 283, 301; Ashcroft, ii, pp. 42–3.

Notes to pages 194–206

67. *CJ*, iv, p. 528.
68. Ibid.
69. Clifford's Tower was to be kept as a garrison with 60 men, but York city was to have its outworks slighted and lose its garrison.(*CJ*, v, p. 99)
70. *CJ*, v, pp. 99, 325.
71. Hinderwell, p. 101.
72. *CJ*, v, p. 99.
73. *CJ*, iv, p. 547.
74. *CSPD*, 1645–7, p. 444.
75. *CJ*, iv, p. 686.
76. *CJ*, v, p. 325.
77. Powell & Timings, *Documents*, p. 204; BL, *TT*, E293(2): *Parliament's Post*, 8–15 July 1645. The *Cavendish* was valued at £250 (PRO, Audit Office, AO1, 1812/443A.)
78. Powell, *The Navy in the English Civil War*, p. 136.
79. Ashcroft, ii, p. 58.
80. Ibid., pp. 58–9.
81. Powell & Timings, *Documents*, p. 231; *LJ*, viii, p. 140.
82. Ashcroft, ii, p. 64.
83. Ibid., pp. 67–8.
84. Ibid., p. 69; Powell & Timings, *Documents*, pp. 244–5.
85. Ashcroft, ii p. 109.
86. Hinderwell p. 101 says that £5,000 were voted, but this is wrong: *CJ*, v, p. 549; *LJ*, x, pp. 247, 248.
87. Ashcroft, ii, p. 89.
88. Ibid., p. 92.
89. Ibid., p. 90.
90. Ibid., pp. 109–10.
91. Ibid., p. 125; NYCRO, DC/SCB, H1, Assessment Lists, 1601–65.
92. *CSPD*, 1648–9, p. 69.
93. Ibid., pp. 170, 172.
94. BL, *TT*, E.457(21): *The Moderate*, 1–8 July 1648.
95. HMC, *Portland*, I, p. 490; Hull City Archives, BRL 503.
96. HMC, *Portland*, I, p. 491; Hull City Archives, BRL 503.
97. HMC, *Ormonde*, NS, II (1903), p. 396; HMC *Portland*, I, pp. 490–2; *Pepys* (1911), pp. 221, 283, 285, 293.
98. HMC, *Portland*, I, p. 491.
99. *CSPD*, 1648–9, p. 221.
100. Ashcroft, ii, pp. 105–6.
101. Ibid.
102. Ibid.
103. Ibid., p. 117.
104. Ibid.
105. Ashcroft, ii, pp. 117–18.
106. Ibid., p. 119.
107. Ibid.
108. Ibid., pp. 118–19.
109. BL, *TT*, E457(21): *The Moderate*, 1–8 Aug. 1648; Ibid., E457(24): *The Perfect Weekly Account*, 2–9 Aug. 1648.
110. Ibid., E457(28): *Packets of Letters from Scotland*, 7 Aug. 1648.
111. Ibid., E457(33): *The Moderate Intelligencer*, no. 177, 3–10 Aug. 1648.
112. Ibid., E457(28): *Packets of Letters*, 7 Aug. 1648; Ibid., E458(16): *A Great and Bloudy Fight at Scarbrough castle*, 14 Aug. 1648.
113. Ibid., E458(16). The letter was written at Falsgrave by Matthew Gibson and dated 11 August 1648. It is printed in Hinderwell as Appendix D, pp. 337–8.
114. BL, *TT*, E457(33): *The Moderate Intelligencer*, no. 177, 3–10 Aug. 1648.
115. Ibid., E458(16).
116. Ashcroft, ii, p. 119.
117. Ibid.
118. BL, *TT*, E460(10): *Fight between His Majesty's forces and Parliament's at Scarbrough*, 17 Aug. 1648.
119. *CJ*, v, p. 673.
120. *CSPD*, 1648–9, pp. 254–5.
121. BL, *TT*, E459(7): *Declaration of the Committee of the Militia for the County of York*, 2 Aug. 1648.
122. Ibid., E464(12): *Mercurius Pragmaticus*, no. 25, 12–19 Sept. 1648.
123. Ibid., E464(15): *Mercurius Anti-Mercurius*, no.1, 12–19 Sept. 1648; Ibid., E464(18): *The Kingdome's Weekly Intelligencer*, no. 277, 12–19

Notes to pages 206–215

Sept. 1648; Ibid., E464(20): *Packets of Letters*, no. 27, 18 Sept. 1648; Ibid., E464(27): *Bloudy News from the North*, 18 Sept. 1648.
124. Ashcroft, ii, pp. 119–20.
125. Ibid., p. 120.
126. Ibid.
127. Hinderwell, p. 104.
128. BL, *TT*, E464(27): *Bloudy News from the North*, 18 Sept. 1648.
129. Ibid., E465(2): *Packets of Letters*, 16 Sept. 1648.
130. Ibid., E464(25): *The Moderate Intelligencer*, no. 183, 14–21 Sept. 1648; Ibid., E464(31): *A Bloudy Fight in Yorkshire*, 18 Sept. 1648; Ibid., E465(6): *A Perfect Weekly Account*, no. 28, 20–28 Sept. 1648.
131. *CJ*, vi, p. 32.
132. BL, *TT*, E465(2): *Packets of Letters*, 16 Sept. 1648; Whitelocke, *Memorials*, p. 336.
133. BL, *TT*, E465(14): *Mercurius Melancholicus*, no. 58, 25 Sept.–2 Oct. 1648.
134. Ibid., E464(45): *Mercurius Pragmaticus*, no. 26, 22 Sept. 1648.
135. Ibid., E464(25): *The Moderate Intelligencer*, no. 183, 14–21 Sept. 1648.
136. Rushworth, *Historical Collections*, iv, p. 1265; Whitelocke, *Memorials*, p. 337.
137. *LJ*, vii, p. 34.
138. BL, *TT*, E464(20): *Packets of Letters*, no. 27, 18 Sept. 1648.
139. *CJ*, vi, pp. 6, 32; *CSPD*, 1648–9, p. 273; BL, *TT*, E477(29): *Col. Bethell's Letter to his Excellency the Lord Fairfax*, 19 Dec. 1648; HMC, *Stewart*, p. 98.
140. BL, *TT*, E460(10): *Fight at Scarbrough*, 17 Aug. 1648; Ibid., E477(29): *Bethell's Letter*.
141. Ibid., E465(35): *Packets of Letters*, no. 29, 30 Sept. 1648.
142. Ibid., E477(29): *Bethell's Letter*; *LJ*, x, p. 639.
143. BL, *TT*, E468(30): *A Bloudy Fight at Scarborough Castle*, 18 Oct. 1648.
144. Hinderwell, p. 106.
145. There is still a common assumption that Oliver's Mount, overlooking the south side of the town, was named after Cromwell. However, until the end of the eighteenth century, this hill and its slopes were called Weaponness; and the earliest reference found to 'Oliver's Hill' occurs on a map of Yorkshire by Thomas Jeffrey dated 1770.
146. *CJ*, vi, p. 77; Hinderwell, p. 106.
147. *CJ*, vi, p. 32.
148. One observer described the vessel as 'a pink or catch wherewith they go to sea from the back of the castle' HMC, *Stewart*, p. 98.
149. Rushworth, *Historical Collections*, iv, p. 1352; Hinderwell, p. 107.
150. Ashcroft, i, pp. 251–2.
151. Ibid., ii, pp. 29–30.
152. Ibid., p. 95.
153. Ibid., p. 120.
154. BL, *TT*, E477(29): *Bethell's Letter*. Musketeers wrapped a length of match, lit at both ends, round their left hands, and kept bullets in their mouths ready to be spat down the muzzle.
155. Ibid.; *LJ*, x, pp. 639–40.
156. Carlton, *Going to the Wars*, pp. 327–8.
157. *LJ*, x, p. 639; BL, *TT*, E477(29): *Bethell's Letter*.
158. *LJ*, x, p. 640; *CJ*, vi, pp. 104, 105.
159. Rushworth, *Historical Collections*, iv, p. 1352.
160. BL, *TT*, E477(29): *Bethell's Letter*.
161. Ashcroft, ii, p. 120.
162. Ibid., pp. 120, 121.
163. NYCRO, DC/SCB, A2; Ashcroft, ii, p. 121.
164. NYCRO, DC/SCB, A2.
165. Ashcroft, i, pp. 107, 113, 280; HUCRO, PE165/241, p. 6.
166. *Scarb. Wills*, iii, p. 753; Scarborough Parish Register, 1602–82, Scarborough Central Library, MIC 5582.
167. NYCRO, DC/SCB, A1, A2.
168. Hinderwell, pp. 162–6.

Notes to pages 215–226

169. Ashcroft, ii, p. 122.
170. Ibid., p. 126.
171. Ibid., p. 123.
172. H. Horspool, *The Stones of St Mary's* (Scarborough, 1982, 3rd edn), p. 8.
173. Ashcroft, ii, pp. 127, 140.
174. Ibid., p. 127.
175. NYCRO, DC/SCB, C2, Chamberlains' Accounts 1648–9.
176. Fawcett, *Memorial*, pp. 66, 80, 110.
177. NYCRO, DC/SCB, C2.
178. Ibid.
179. Ibid.
180. Ibid.; HUCRO, PE165/241, pp. 15, 17, 19.
181. Ashcroft, ii, pp. 91.
182. NYCRO, DC/SCB, C2.
183. Ashcroft, ii, pp. 125–6.
184. Ibid., pp. 127–8.
185. Ashcroft, ii, p. 128.
186. Ibid., pp. 138–9, 145, 146.
187. Ibid., p. 146.
188. Ibid., pp. 272–8, 293–301.
189. NYCRO, DC/SCB, I5, Assessment and Payment (Poor Law) Book 1647–51.
190. *CSPD*, 1651, p. 187.
191. Ibid., p. 188.
192. Ibid., p. 206.
193. Ibid., pp. 209, 212.
194. Ibid., pp. 194–5.
195. YML, Add. MS 343, f. 30v.
196. *CSPD*, 1651, pp. 249, 287.
197. *CSPD*, 1651–2, pp. 46–7; *CJ*, vii, p. 47.
198. *CSPD*, 1651–2, p. 336.

Chapter Six, Interregnum, 1649–1660

1. Ashcroft, ii, pp. 149, 157.
2. *Scarborough Mercury*, 1 Sept. 1973.
3. Ashcroft, ii, p. 152.
4. HMC, *Sixth Report* (1877), pp. 433(b), 434 (a,b).
5. Ashcroft, ii, pp. 149, 150, 154, 156.
6. Ibid., p. 157.
7. Ibid., pp. 157–8; Hinderwell, p. 341; Baker, p. 113.
8. Powell, *Navy*, p. 150; Ashcroft, ii, p. 167.
9. *CSPD, 1648–9*, pp. 47, 49, 50.
10. Rushworth, *Historical Collections*, iv, pp. 1069–70; *CJ*, v, p. 545.
11. *CSPD, 1649–50*, p. 455; Ibid., *1650*, p. 13.
12. *CJ*, vi, p. 165.
13. *CSPD, 1650*, pp. 248, 332, 455; Ibid., 1651, p. 5; Ashcroft, ii, p. 165, 169.
14. Ashcroft, ii, pp. 165–9.
15. Whitby LPS, Bagdale Old Hall MSS, 3, 4, 5, 6; 'Paver's Marriage Licences', ed. J. W. Clay, *YAJ*, xvi (1902), p. 35; BL, *TT*, E270(21): *The London Post*, no. 25; Ashcroft, ii, p. 168.
16. BL, *TT*, E262(14): *The Speech of Capt. Brown-Bushel at the place of execution 29 Mar. 1651*.
17. Ibid. Colonel Matthew Boynton soon joined him: he was killed at the battle of Wigan in August 1651 after he had been proscribed and his estate confiscated by Parliament for his continued resistance. Hinderwell, p. 111; C. H. Firth & R. S. Rait (eds), *Acts and Ordinances of the Interregnum, 1642–1660*, 3 vols (1911), ii, p. 520.
18. G. Penn, *Memorials of the Professional Life and Times of Sir William Penn*, 2 vols (1833), i, p. 297.
19. B. Capp, *Cromwell's Navy: the Fleet and the English Revolution, 1648–1660* (Oxford, 1989), p. 71.
20. *CSPD, 1650*, pp. 347, 448.
21. S. R. Gardiner & C. T. Atkinson (eds), *Letters and Papers Relating to the First Dutch War, 1652–54*, 6 vols,

Notes to pages 226–237

Navy Records Society (1899–1930), i, p. 67.
22. Penn, *Memorials*, i, p. 303.
23. Ibid., pp. 311–12, 317, 319.
24. *CSPD*, 1651–2, p. 618.
25. *First Dutch War*, iv, p. 46.
26. Ibid., vi, p. 1. Lawson's only rival in sea-going experience and seamanship was William Penn, who became the third General-at-sea in place of Deane, after he was killed at the battle of the Gabbard in June 1653. See L. Street, *An Uncommon Sailor* (The Kensol Press, Bourne End, Bucks., 1986).
27. Greaves & Zaller, p. 178; *DNB*; Capp, *Cromwell's Navy*, pp. 302–3; PRO, SP46/115, f. 89.
28. M. Oppenheim, *A History of the Administration of the Royal Navy, 1509–1660* (1988 edn), pp. 311–13.
29. Ashcroft, ii, p. 204.
30. Ibid., pp. 209–10.
31. Ibid., pp. 212, 218; *CSPD*, 1653–4, pp. 220, 289, 442, 475, 554; Oppenheim, *Administration of the Royal Navy*, p. 321.
32. *CSPD*, 1656–7, pp. 98, 169, 301, 407.
33. *CSPD*, 1652–3, pp. 257, 264, 272, 287; Hinderwell, pp. 342–5.
34. Capp, *Cromwell's Navy*, pp. 123, 128.
35. Ashcroft, ii, p. 219.
36. M. Ashley, *John Wildman, Plotter and Postmaster* (1947), pp. 84–8.
37. Ibid.
38. S. R. Gardiner, *A History of the Commonwealth and Protectorate, 1649–60*, 3 vols (1894–1903), iii, p. 57; T. Birch (ed.), *A Collection of State Papers of John Thurloe*, 7 vols (1742), iii, p. 147.
39. Capp, *Cromwell's Navy*, p. 136; Gardiner, *Commonwealth and Protectorate*, iii, p. 57; J. R. Powell, 'The Expedition of Blake and Mountagu in 1655' [sic], *Mariner's Mirror*, 52 (1966), p. 344.
40. *CSPD*, 1655–6, pp. 137–8, 141; Ibid., 1656–7, p. 17; Gardiner, *Commonwealth and Protectorate*, iii, pp. 464–7.

41. M. Baumber, *General-at-Sea: Robert Blake and the Seventeenth-Century Revolution in Naval Warfare* (1989), pp. 212–13.
42. *CSPD*, 1656–7, p. 420; HMC, *Fifth Report*, p.1488b; J. R. Powell (ed.), *The Letters of Robert Blake*, Navy Records Society, 76 (1937), pp. 393–6.
43. C. H. Firth, *The Last Years of the Protectorate, 1656–58* (1909), pp. 207, 209, 217; Birch, *Thurloe Papers*, iv, pp. 321, 589–90, 650; v, pp. 60, 197; vi, pp. 185–6. In Thurloe's correspondence, Lawson is referred to by the code number 607.
44. *CSPD*, 1655–6, pp. 546, 570; Ibid., 1656–7, p. 52; Ibid., 1657–8, p. 244; Capp, *Cromwell's Navy*, pp. 134–5, 146–7.
45. Capp, *Cromwell's Navy*, p. 226.
46. Ashcroft, ii, p. 251; Hinderwell, p. 187.
47. Stirling, *The Hothams*, i, pp. 89, 94.
48. NYCRO, DC/SCB, Book of Elections 1645–63; G. Davies, *The Restoration of Charles II* (Oxford, 1955), p. 10; Oppenheim, *Administration of the Navy*, p. 320.
49. NYCRO, DC/SCB, Book of Elections, 1645–63.
50. BIHR, *PW*, V46, f. 419.
51. Hinderwell, pp. 161–2; Ashcroft, ii, pp. 18, 28; NYCRO, DC/SCB, Book of Elections, 1645–63.
52. *Scarb. Wills*, iii, p. 753.
53. NYCRO, DC/SCB, Book of Elections, 1645–63.
54. *CSPD*, 1658–9, pp. 355, 357; *CJ*, vii, p. 676.
55. Capp, *Cromwell's Navy*, pp. 348–50.
56. *CJ*, vii, pp. 797, 799, 801, 806, 818.
57. Oppenheim, *Administration of the Navy*, pp. 320, 327–8; *CSPD*, 1659–60, pp. 380, 385, 391–2, 531, 550; Capp, *Cromwell's Navy*, pp. 364–5.
58. Capp, *Cromwell's Navy*, pp. 359, 376.
59. *CJ*, viii, p. 214; R. Latham & W. Matthews (eds), *The Diary of Samuel*

Notes to pages 237–248

Pepys, 10 vols (1983), i, p. 254; CSPD, 1661–2, pp. 43, 605; HMC, Heathcote MSS (1899), p. 51.
60. HMC, Heathcote, p. 155.
61. Diary of Pepys, i, pp. 106, 159.
62. Ibid., iv, p. 376.
63. Capp, Cromwell's Navy, pp. 363–4.
64. Hinderwell, pp. 298–9.

Chapter Seven, Restoration

1. CJ, viii, p. 86.
2. B. D. Henning (ed.), The House of Commons 1660–1690, 3 vols (1983), i, p. 486.
3. Ashcroft, ii, p. 259; NYCRO, DC/SCB, Book of Elections, 1645–63, MIC 2150.
4. CSPD, 1659–60, pp. 370–1; Henning, House of Commons, i, pp. 485–6, iii, p. 344.
5. J. D. Legard, The Legards of Anlaby and Ganton (1926), pp. 94–6; A. H. Woolrych, 'Yorkshire and the Restoration', YAJ, xxxix (1958), pp. 502, 504.
6. YRCP, I, YASRS xv, pp. 3–9, 9–10, 10–15, 158–60.
7. CJ, viii, p. 70.
8. LJ, xi, pp. 7–8
9. Henning, House of Commons, iii, p. 344.
10. CJ, viii, pp. 70, 86.
11. Henning, House of Commons, i, pp. 485–6; HMC, Fifth Report (1876), p. 194(b).
12. Woolrych, YAJ, xxxix, pp. 483–507.
13. HMC, Leyborne-Popham MSS (1899), p. 153.
14. Ibid., p. 175.
15. Ashcroft, ii, pp. 131, 140.
16. Ibid., p. 41.
17. NYCRO. DC/SCB, MIC 2150.
18. Ibid.; Ashcroft, ii, p. 258.
19. NYCRO, DC/SCB, MIC 2150.
20. Ibid.; SRL, Bishops' transcripts, MIC 5582; BIHR, PW, V44 f. 55.
21. SRL, MIC 5582; NYCRO, DC/SCB, MIC 2150.
22. Ashcroft, ii, p. 258.
23. NYCRO, DC/SCB, MIC 2150.
24. Ashcroft, ii, p. 29.
25. BIHR, PW, V45, f. 533.
26. NYCRO, DC/SCB. MIC 2150; SRL, MIC 5582.
27. Ashcroft, i, p. 185; Ibid., ii, pp. 171, 250; NYCRO, DC/SCB, B2, General Letters, 1643–1781; K8, Grammar School, 1619–1843; MIC 2150.
28. CSPD, 1660–1, p. 327.
29. CSPD, 1661–2, p. 21.
30. Ibid., p. 446.
31. CSPD, 1662–3, p. 110.
32. Ibid., p. 16.
33. Henning, House of Commons, iii, p. 344; CSPD, 1663–4, p. 18.
34. Ashcroft, ii, pp. 29, 41; NYCRO, DC/SCB, MIC 2150.
35. NYCRO, DC/SCB, MIC 2150.
36. See above, pp. 128, 187, 210–11.
37. Ashcroft, i, pp. 51, 101; Ibid., II, pp. 252, 258; NYCRO, DC/SCB, MIC 2150, K8; BIHR, PW, V44, f. 55; PRO, E179/216/462.
38. Hinderwell, pp. 161–2.
39. Ibid., pp. 185–6.
40. CSPD, 1661–2, pp. 329, 378.
41. N. Penney (ed.), The Journal of George Fox (Everyman, Dent, 1924), pp. 44, 50–1.
42. Ashcroft, ii, pp. 19, 29, 149, 154, 208, 218–19.
43. HUCRO, PE 165/241, pp. 6, 19.
44. J. S. Fletcher, Yorkshiremen of the Restoration (1921), p. 204.
45. NYCRO, DC/SCB, MIC 2150.

Notes to pages 248–261

46. C. Hill, *The World Turned Upside Down* (Penguin edn, 1975), pp. 246–7; R. Hutton, *The Restoration* (Oxford, 1985), pp. 11, 169–71.
47. NYCRO, DC/SCB, J11, Quakers' Papers; Baker, p. 492 (Baker's version of the names of the accused is inaccurate).
48. NYCRO, DC/SCB, J11; Baker, p. 493.
49. NYCRO, DC/SCB, MIC 2150; Hinderwell, p. 162; Rowntree, p. 321.
50. SRL, MIC 5582.
51. This curtain-wall tower, called Cockhill before the Civil War, no longer exists. By 1746 it was already perilously close to the edge of the eroded sea cliff. To prevent it collapsing down on to the South Steel battery below, it was demolished as part of the 'improvements' prompted by the Jacobite rising of 1745–6 (Schofield, *Guide*, p. 104).
52. *Fox Journal*, pp. 237–9.
53. Ibid., pp. 239–40.
54. Ibid., p. 240.
55. Ibid., p. 245.
56. Rowntree, p. 323.
57. Ibid., p. 322; *Fox Journal*, p. 245.
58. Rowntree, p. 323.
59. Ibid., p. 324.
60. Ibid., p. 326.
61. Baker, pp. 442–4.
62. Rowntree, p. 325.
63. Ibid., p. 324.
64. NYCRO, DC/SCB, J11.
65. Rowntree, p. 327.
66. HUCRO, PE 165/241, pp. 25, 51, 60.
67. Ibid., pp. 2, 64.
68. Ibid., pp. 19–20.
69. The royal grant of 5 December 1660 refers to the fall 'upon the tenth day of October last', but all the secondary authorities say that the fall occurred a year earlier: Hinderwell, p. 124; Fawcett, p. 50; Baker, p. 152; M. Horspool, *The Stones of St Mary's* (1972), pp. 7, 30.
70. PRO, Chancery, C7/480/64. A copy is in HUCRO, PE 165/241, pp. 35–6, but the brief is most accessible in Hinderwell, pp. 126–7.
71. Ibid.
72. P. J. Nash, 'Doncaster, Ripon and Scarborough, circa 1640 to 1750' (unpublished Ph.D. thesis, Leeds University, 1983), p. 427.
73. HUCRO, PE 165/241, pp. 38–40.
74. Ibid., p. 41.
75. Ibid., p. 47.
76. Ibid., p. 50.
77. NYCRO, DC/SCB, MIC 2150.
78. HUCRO, PE 165/241, pp. 54, 56, 57; NYCRO, DC/SCB, MIC 2150.
79. J. Hunter (ed.), *The Diary of Ralph Thoresby*, 2 vols (1830), i, p. 147; J. Buckley, *The Outport of Scarborough* (1953), pp. 17–19.
80. See above, p. 32.
81. R. Wittie, *Scarbrough Spaw* (2nd edn, 1667), p. 5.
82. Whittaker, *The Book of Scarborough Spaw*, p. 24.
83. HMC, *Portland*, I, p. 490.
84. Wittie (2nd edn), p. 5.
85. Wittie, *Scarbrough Spaw* (1st edn, 1660), pp. 7–8.
86. C. Jackson (ed.), 'The Autobiography of Alice Thornton', *Surtees Society*, lxii (1875), pp. 81–296.
87. HMC, *Leyborne-Popham*, p. 182.
88. Whittaker, p. 30.
89. Ibid.
90. Ibid.
91. Ibid.
92. W. Simpson, *Hydrologia Chemica* (1669), pp. 83–4, 115.
93. Whittaker, p. 31.
94. Ibid., p. 34.
95. Ibid., pp. 35–6.
96. Ibid., p. 76.
97. Ibid.
98. The first recorded bathing-machine is to be found on John Setterington's view of Scarborough South Bay drawn in 1735.

Notes to pages 261–270

99. C. Ward & R. Chandler, *A Journey from London to Scarborough in Several Letters from a Gentleman there* (1st edn, 1734), p. 30
100. Celia Fiennes hired 'a little boate' when she came to Scarborough in 1697, 'but found it very rough even just in the harbour' (D. Woodward (ed.), *Descriptions of East Yorkshire: Leland to Defoe* (1985), p. 52.).
101. Whittaker, p. 65.
102. Ward & Chandler, pp. 38–44; 'A Letter from Edmund Withers,' Scarborough, 1733, *YAJ*, xii (1893), pp. 134–5.
103. *Thoresby Diary*, i, p. 147.

Notes, Epilogue

1. SRL, Scarborough pamphlets: receipt dated 28 Feb. 1661.
2. NYCRO, DC/SCB, A20, Common Hall Memoranda 1499–1737.
3. Ibid., A3, Book of Elections, 1664–96.
4. Ibid.
5. SRL, MIC 5582.
6. PRO, E179/215/451; E179/216/461; E179/216/462.
7. NYCRO, DC/SCB, Kll. Though this list is dated 1663 in the *Descriptive Catalogue*, internal evidence indicates that it post-dates the Hearth Tax return of Michaelmas 1673 and pre-dates the death of Francis Sollitt in 1680.
8. PRO, E179/216/462.
9. Ibid. For the location of the Thompson mansion house see 'A New and Exact Plan of the Town of Scarborough', drawn by John Cossins in 1725, which was reproduced in Edwards, *Scarborough 966–1966*, p. 58.
10. PRO, E179/216/462.
11. Ibid.
12. NYCRO, DC/SCB, F6, Marine Papers 1606–94.
13. HUCRO, PE 165/241, p. 45.
14. Firth & Rait, *Acts and Ordinances*, ii, pp. 1368, 1446.
15. Baker, p. 201.
16. NYCRO, DC/SCB, vi(i), General Sessions, 9 Apr. 1662.
17. NYCRO, DC/SCS, MIC 1355, 1358, 2150.
18. Ibid., vi(ii), General Sessions, 12 Oct. 1661.
19. Ibid.
20. Ibid.
21. Below Cossins's 'New and Exact Plan' a commentary described Scarborough in glowing and exaggerated terms: its 'air' was 'Serene & Healthfull'; it had '2000 familys'; it afforded 'Extraordinary Accommodation to all Strangers'; and it was a mere 30 miles from York and Hull. In fact, the population of the town was then about 4,000 and the shortest road distances between Scarborough and London and between Scarborough and York and Hull were 217 and 40 miles respectively.

Bibliography

Primary Sources

1. Manuscript

Bodleian Library, Oxford (Bod.Lib.)
Clarendon MSS 22, 23
Firth MSS

Borthwick Institute of Historical Research (BIHR)
Archbishops' Visitation Books
Probate Wills in the York Registry

British Library (BL)
Egerton MSS 2884
Cottonian MSS

Hull University Library (HUL)
DCY Cholmley of Howsham MSS

Humberside County Record Office (HUCRO)
PE 165/241 Accounts and Papers relating to St Mary's, Scarborough 1607–98
DDHO Horthstead MSS

North Yorkshire County Record Office (NYCRO)
DC/SCB Scarborough Borough Corporation records
ZPK Cholmley estate papers
ZCG Cholmley miscellaneous MSS
ZF Hackness estate papers

Public Record Office (PRO)
Audit Office, AO1–3 Declared accounts
Exchequer, Hearth Tax, Lay Subsidy Rolls (E.179); Port Books 187, 190, 310, 315
Admiralty High Court, HCA
Star Chamber, StaC 5–8
State Paper Office, State Papers Domestic, SP 16, 18, 20, 21, 22.

Scarborough Central Library, Reference, Scarborough Room (SRL)
Chapman MSS
Scarborough Wills
MIC 5582 Bishop's transcript: Scarborough St Mary's register 1602–1682

Sheffield City Library (SCL)
WWM Wentworth Woodhouse MSS: Strafford papers

Skipton Library
Petyt collection

Suffolk County Record Office, Ipswich
HD 36: 2672 Meldrum correspondence

Whitby Literary and Philosophical Society (Whitby LPS)
Bagdale Old Hall MSS
Farside MSS
Percy Burnett MSS
Shaw Jeffrey MSS

York Minster Library (YML)
Add. MS 343 Memoirs of Sir Hugh Chomley

2. Printed

Acts of the Privy Council
Ashcroft, M. Y. (ed.), *Scarborough Records 1600–1660*, 2 vols (Northallerton, 1991)
Atkinson, J. C. (ed.), *North Riding Quarter Sessions Records*, North Riding Record Society, 5 vols (1884–7)
Bell, R. (ed.), *Memorials of the Civil War*, 2 vols (1849)
Birch, T. (ed.), *A Collection of the State Papers of John Thurloe*, 7 vols (1742)
Brigg, W. (ed.), *Yorkshire Fines for the Stuart Period*, Yorkshire Archaeological Society Record Series, liii, lviii (1915, 1917)
Calendar of State Papers, Domestic
Calendar of State Papers, Venetian
Calendar of the Proceedings of the Committee for the Advance of Money, 1642–56, ed. M. A. E. Green, 3 vols (1888)
Calendar of the Proceedings of the Committee for Compounding, 1643–60, ed. M. A. E. Green, 5 vols (1889–92)
Camden, E., *Britannia* (1695 edn)
Cartwright, J. J. (ed.), *Chapters in the History of Yorkshire* (Wakefield, 1872)
Chapman, J. (ed.), *Scarborough Records*, 3 vols (Scarborough, 1909)
Cholmley, Sir Hugh, *The Memoirs of Sir Hugh Cholmley* (1787)
—— *The Memoirs of Sir Hugh Cholmley* (Malton, 1870)
Clarendon, Edward, Earl of, *History of the Rebellion and Civil Wars in England*, ed. W. D. Macray, 6 vols (Oxford, 1888)
Clay, J. W. (ed.), *Yorkshire Royalist Composition Papers*, Yorkshire Archaeological Society Record Series, xv, xviii, xx (1893, 1895, 1896)
—— *Dugdale's Visitation of Yorkshire*, 3 vols (Exeter, 1899–1917)
Coates, W. H. (ed.) *The Journal of Sir Simonds D'Ewes, 12 October 1641 – 10 January 1642* (New Haven, 1942)
Coates, W. H., Young, A. S,. Snow, V. F. (eds), *The Private Journals of the Long Parliament, 3 January–5 March 1642* (New Haven, 1982)
Commons Journals, II–V

Cope, E. S. and Coates, W. H. (eds) *Proceedings of the Short Parliament of 1640* Camden Society, 4th series, 19 (1977)
Dugdale, Sir William (ed.) *The Visitation of Yorkshire 1665–66*, Surtees Society, xxii (1848)
Fairfax, T., 'A Short Memoriall of the Northern Actions . . . 1642 till 1644', *Yorkshire Archaeological Journal*, viii (1883–4)
Firth, C. H. (ed.) *The Life of William Cavendish, Duke of Newcastle* (1886)
—— 'Memorials touching the Battle of York', by Sir Hugh Cholmley, in *English Historical Review (EHR)*, v (1890)
—— 'Memorialls tuching Scarbrough', by Sir Hugh Cholmley, in *EHR* xxxii (1917)
Foster, J. (ed.), *The Visitation of Yorkshire in 1584–85 and 1612* (1875)
Gardiner, S. R. and Atkinson, C. T. (eds), *Letters and Papers Relating to the First Dutch War 1652–54*, 6 vols, Navy Records Society (1899–1930)
Gough, R., *The History of Myddle*, ed. D. Hey (1981)
Historical Manuscripts Commission:
  Fifth Report, House of Lords MSS (1876)
  Tenth Report, appendix VI, Bouverie MSS (1887)
  Tenth Report, appendix VI, Braye MSS (1887)
  Eleventh Report, appendix III, Corporation of King's Lynn MSS (1887)
  Thirteenth Report, Portland MSS, I (1891)
  Heathcote MSS (1899)
  Leyborne-Popham MSS (1899)
  Salisbury MSS, IX (1902)
  Various Collections, II (1903)
  Ormonde MSS, New Series, II (1903)
  Pepys MSS (1911)
  Various Collections, VIII (1913)
Hunter, J. (ed.), *The Diary of Ralph Thoresby*, 2 vols (1830)
Hutchinson, J. (ed.), *Memoirs of the Life of Colonel Hutchinson* (1905)
Jackson, C. (ed.), *The Autobiography of Mrs*

Alice Thornton of East Newton, Co. York, Surtees Society, lxii (1873)

Kenyon, J. P. (ed.), *The Stuart Constitution 1603–1688* (1966)

Knowler, W. (ed.), *The Earl of Strafford's Letters and Despatches*, 2 vols (Dublin, 1739–40)

Latham, R. and Matthews, W. (eds), *The Diary of Samuel Pepys*, 10 vols (1983)

Lords Journals, v–vi

Maltby, J. D. (ed.), *The Short Parliament (1640) Diary of Sir Thomas Aston* Camden Society, 4th series, 35 (1988)

Meads, D. M. (ed.), *The Diary of Lady Margaret Hoby 1599–1605* (1930)

Newcastle, Margaret, Duchess of, *The Life of William Cavendish, Duke of Newcastle* (1667)

Newsbooks, I, Oxford Royalist (ORN), i–iv (1971)

Notestein,. W. (ed.), *The Journal of Sir Simonds D'Ewes, from the beginning of the Long Parliament to the Trial of the Earl of Strafford* (New Haven, 1923)

Parsons, D. (ed.), *The Diary of Sir Henry Slingsby of Scriven, Bart.* (1836)

Peacock, E. (ed.), *The Army Lists of the Roundheads and Cavaliers* (1974)

Penny, N. (ed.), *The Journal of George Fox* (1924)

Powell, J. R. (ed.), *The Letters of Robert Blake*, Navy Records Society (1937)

Powell, J. R. and Timings, E. K. (eds), *Documents Relating to the Civil War*, Navy Records Society, 105 (1963)

Rushworth, J., *Historical Collections*, 7 vols (1659–1701)

Scrope, R. and Monkhouse, T. (eds), *Clarendon State Papers*, 3 vols (Oxford, 1767–86)

Simpson, W., *Hydrologica Chemica* (1669)

Smith, L. T. (ed.), *The Itinerary of John Leland 1535–1543*, 5 vols (1906–08)

Snow, V. F. and Young, A. S. (eds), *The Private Journals of the Long Parliament, 7 March to 1 June 1642* (New Haven, 1987)

Sutherland, J. (ed.), *Memoirs of the Life of Colonel Hutchinson* (Oxford, 1973)

Terry, C. S. (ed.), *Papers Relating to the Army of the Solemn League and Covenant 1643–47* (Edinburgh, 1917)

Thomason Tracts (TT): microfilm edition

Tibbutt, H. G. (ed.), *The Letter Books of Sir Samuel Luke 1644–45* (1963)

Vicars, J., *England's Parliamentary Chronicle 1640–46*, 4 vols (1646)

Ward, C. and Chandler, R., *A Journey from London to Scarborough* (1734)

Whitelocke, B., *Memorials of English Affairs* (1732)

Wildridge, T. T. (ed.), *The Hull Letters 1625–46* (Hull, 1887)

Wittie, R., *Scarborough Spaw* (1660, 1667)

Woodward, D. (ed.), *Descriptions of East Yorkshire: Leland to Defoe* (1985)

Yorkshire Parish Register Society, *Registers of Hackness, Thornton Dale and Whitby*.

Secondary Sources

1. General

(a) Books

Andrews, K. R., *Ships, Money and Politics: Seafaring and Enterprise in the Reign of Charles I* (Cambridge, 1991)

Ashley, M., *John Wildman, Plotter and Postmaster* (1947)

Aylmer, G. E., *Rebellion or Revolution? England 1640–1660* (Oxford, 1966)

BIBLIOGRAPHY

Barry, J. (ed.), *The Tudor and Stuart Town 1530–1688* (1990)
Baumber, M., *General-at-Sea: Robert Blake and the Seventeenth-Century Revolution in Naval Warfare* (1989)
Bence Jones, M., *The Cavaliers* (1976)
Borsay, P., *The English Urban Renaissance: Culture and Society in the Provinicial Town 1660–1779* (Oxford, 1989)
Brunton, D. and Pennington, D. H., *Members of the Long Parliament* (1954)
Capp, B., *Cromwell's Navy: the Fleet and the English Revolution 1648–1660* (Oxford, 1989)
Carlton, C., *Going to the Wars: the Experience of the British Civil Wars 1638–51* (1992)
Chandler, J., *John Leland's Itinerary: Travels in Tudor England* (Stroud, 1993)
Clark, P. and Slack, P., *English Towns in Transition 1500–1700* (1976)
Clark, P. (ed.), *The Transformation of English Privincial Towns 1600–1800* (1984)
Cliffe, J. T., *the Puritan Gentry* (1984)
Cook, C. and Wroughton, J., *English Historical Facts 1603–1688* (1980)
Coward, B., *The Stuart Age* (1980)
―― *Social Change and Continuity in Early Modern England 1550–1750* (1988)
Davies, G., *The Restoration of Charles II* (Oxford, 1955)
Dictionary of National Biography
Duffy, C., *Siege Warfare* (1979)
Firth, C. H., *The Last Years of the Protectorate 1656–58* (1909)
Fletcher, A., *The Outbreak of the English Civil War* (1981)
Fraser, A., *The Weaker Vessel: Woman's Lot in Seventeenth-Century England* (1984)
Gardiner, S. R., *History of the Great Civil War 1642–1649*, 3 vols (1886–91)
―― *History of the Commonwealth and Protectorate 1649–1660*, 3 vols (1894–1903)
Greaves, R. L. and Zaller, R. (eds), *Biographical Dictionary of British Radicals in the Seventeenth Century* (Brighton, 1983)
Gruenfelder, J. K., *Influence in Earl Stuart Elections 1604–1640* (Columbus, Ohio, 1981)

Hasler, P. W. (ed.), *The House of Commons 1558–1603*, 3 vols (1981)
Henning, B. D. (ed.), *The House of Commons 1660–1690*, 3 vols (1983)
Hill, C., *The Century of Revolution 1603–1714* (rev. edn, 1980)
―― *The World Turned Upside Down* (Penguin edn, 1975)
Houlbrooke, R., *The English Family 1450–1700* (1984)
Hoskins, W. G., *Local History in England* (2nd edn, 1972)
Hutton, R., *The Royalist War Effort, 1642–46* (1982)
―― *The Restoration* (Oxford, 1985)
Ives, E. W. (ed.), *The English Revolution* (1968)
Keeler, M. F., *The Long Parliament, 1640–41. A Biographical Study of its Members* (Philadelphia, 1954)
Kenyon, J., *The Civil Wars of England* (1988)
Manning, B., *The English People and the English Revolution 1640–49* (1976)
Morrill, J., *The Revolt of the Privinces* (1980)
―― (ed.), *Reactions to the English Civil War 1642–1649* (1982)
―― (ed.), *The Impact of the Civil War* (1991)
―― *The Nature of the English Revolution* (1993)
―― Slack, P., Woolf, D. (eds), *Public Duty and Private Conscience in Seventeenth-Century England* (Oxford, 1993)
Nef, J. U., *The Rise of the British Coal Industry*, 2 vols (1932)
Oppenheim, M., *A History of the Administration of the Royal Navy 1509–1660* (1988)
Penn, G., *Memorials of the Professional Life and Times of Sir William Penn*, 2 vols (1833)
Platt, C., *The English Medieval Town* (1976)
Porter, S., *Destruction in the English Civil War* (1994)
Powell, J. R., *The Navy in the English Civil War* (1962)
Richardson, R. C. (ed.), *Town and*

Countryside in the English Revolution (Manchester, 1992)
Ridley, J., *The Roundheads* (1976)
Sharpe, J. A., *Early Modern England: A Social History 1550–1760* (1987)
Slack, P., *The Impact of Plague in Tudor and Stuart England* (1985)
Timmis, J. H., *Thine is the Kingdom: the Trial for Treason of Thomas Wentworth* (Alabama Univ., 1974)
Tucker, J. and Winstock, L., *The English Civil War: A Military Handbook* (1972)
Underdown, D., *Fire from Heaven: Life in an English Town in the Seventeenth Century* (1992)
Warburton, B. E. G., *Memoirs of Prince Rupert and the Cavaliers*, 3 vols (1849)
Wedgwood, C. V., *The King's Peace, 1637–1641* (1955)
____ *The King's War, 1641–1647* (1958)
____ *Thomas Wentworth, First Earl of Strafford 1593–1641, A Revaluation* (1964)
Willan, T. S., *The English Coasting Trade, 1600–1750* (Manchester, 1967)
Wilson, J., *Fairfax* (New York, 1985)
Woolrych, A., *Battles of the English Civil War* (1961)
Wrightson, K., *English Society 1580–1680* (1982)
Wrigley, E. A. and Schofield, R. S., *The Population History of England and Wales 1541–1871* (1981)
Young, P. and Emberton, W., *Sieges of the Great Civil War, 1642–46* (1978)
Young, P. and Holmes, R., *The English Civil War 1642–1651* (1974)

(b) Articles and Pamphlets

Aylmer, G. E., 'Collective Mentalities in Mid-Seventeenth-Century England', *TRHS*, 5th series, 36, 1–25; 37, 1–30; 38, 1–25; 39, 1–22 (1986–89)
Aylmer, G. E. and Morrill, J. S., *The Civil War and Interregnum, Sources for Local Historians* (1979)
Dacre, Lord, 'The Continuity of the English Revolution'. *TRHS*, 6th series, 1 (1991), 121–33
Donagan, B., 'Codes and Conduct in the English Civil War', *Past and Present*, 118 (1988), 65–95
Firth, C. H., 'Clarendon's Rebellion', *EHR* xix (1904), 26–54
Howell, R., 'The Structure of Urban Politics in the English Civil War', *Albion*, II, no. 2 (1979), 111–26
Hughes, A. L., 'The King, the Parliament and the Localities during the English Civil War', *Journal of British Studies*, XXIV (1985), 236–63
Pennington, D. H., 'The Cost of the Civil War', *History Today* (Feb. 1958), 126–33
Porter, S., 'Destruction in the Civil Wars', *History Today* (Aug. 1986), 36–41
Routh, E., 'The English Occupation of Tangier 1661–1683', *TRHS*, 2nd series, 19 (1905), 61–78

2. Local

(a) Books

Aveling, H., *Northern Catholics: the Catholic Recusants of the North Riding of Yorkshire 1558–1790* (1966)
Baker, J. B., *The History of Scarbrough* (1882)
Buckley, J., *The Outport of Scarborough* (1959)
Cliffe, J. T., *The Yorkshire Gentry from the Reformation to the Civil War* (1969)
Fawcett, J., *A Memorial of the Church of St Mary's, Scarboro'* (1850)
Fletcher, J. S., *Yorkshiremen of the Restoration* (1921)
Foster, J. (ed.), *Pedigrees of the County Families of Yorkshire*, 4 vols (1874–5)
Gaskin, R. T., *The Old Seaport of Whitby* (Whitby, 1909)

Gent, T., *History of Hull* (Hull, 1735)
Gooder, A., *The Parliamentary Representation of the County of York 1258–1832*, II, YASRS, xcvi (1938)
Hey, D., *Yorkshire from AD 1000* (1986)
Hinderwell, T., *The History and Antiquities of Scarborough* (3rd edn, 1832)
Jeffrey, P. S., *Whitby Lore and Legend* (3rd edn, 1952)
Legard, J. D., *The Legards of Anlaby and Ganton* (1926)
Marchant, R. A., *The Puritans and the Church Courts in the Diocese of York 1560–1642* (1960)
Newman, P. R., *The Battle of Marston Moor 1644* (Chichester, 1981)
Pearson, T., *An Archaeological Survey of Scarborough* (Birmingham, 1987)
Port, G., *Scarborough Castle* (1989)
Reckitt, B. N., *Charles the First and Hull, 1639–1645* (Howden, 1988)
Roebuck, P., *Yorkshire Baronets 1640–1760* (Oxford, 1980)
Rowntree, A. (ed.), *The History of Scarborough* (1931)
Schofield, J., *An Historical and Descriptive Guide to Scarborough and its Environs* (York, 1787)
Smith, G. R., *Without Touch of Dishonour: the Life and Death of Sir Henry Slingsby 1602–1658* (Kineton, 1968)
Stirling, A. M. W., *The Hothams* 2 vols (19180
Tickell, J., *History of Kingston upon Hull* (1796)
Victoria County History:
  A History of Yorkshire: North Riding, 2 vols (1914, 1923)
  A History of Yorkshire: the City of York (1961)
  A History of Yorkshire: East Riding, 6 vols (1969–89)
Wenham, P., *The Great and Close Siege of York 1644* (Kineton, 1970)
Whellan, T., *History and Topography of the City of York and the North Riding of Yorkshire*, 2 vols (1857)
Whittaker, M., *The Book of Scarborough Spaw* (Buckingham, 1984)
Young, G., *A History of Whitby*, 2 vols (Whitby, 1817)
Young, P., *Marston Moor 1644: The Campaign and the Battle* (Kineton, 1970)

(b) Articles and Pamphlets

Binns, J., 'Scarborough in the 1640s', *Transactions of the Scarborough Archaeological and Historical Society*, 24 (1982), 11–19
―― 'The Oldest Map of Scarborough', *Transactions of the Scarborough Archaeological and Historical Society*, 25 (1983), 13–18
―― 'Scarborough and the Civil Wars, 1642–51', *NH* xxii (1986), 95–122
―― 'Captain Browne Bushell: North Sea Adventurer and Pirate', *NH* xxvii (1991), 90–105
Carroll, R., 'Yorkshire Parliamentary Boroughs in the Seventeenth Century', *NH* iii (1968), 70–104
Firth, C. H., 'Marston Moor', *TRHS*, 2nd series, 12 (1898), 17–79
―― 'Cholmley, Sir Hugh (1600–1657)', *BIHR*, III, 9 (1926), 189
Forster, G. C. F., 'Elections at Scarborough for the Long Parliament 1640–47', *Transactions of the Scarborough Archaeological and Historical Society*, 3 (1960), 3–8
―― *The East Riding Justices of the Peace in the Seventeenth Century*, East Yorkshire Local History Society, 30 (1973)
―― 'The North Riding Justices and their Sessions, 1603–1625', *NH* x (1975), 102–25
―― 'Faction and County Government in Early Stuart Yorkshire', *NH* xi (1976), 70–86
―― 'County Government in Yorkshire during the Interregnum', *NH* xii (1976), 84–104
Gruenfelder, J. K., 'Yorkshire Borough Elections, 1603–40', *YAJ* 49 (1976), 101–14

Horspool, M., *The Stones of St Mary's* (Scarborough, 1982)

Morrill, J. S., 'the Northern Gentry and the Great Rebellion', *NH* xv (1979), 66–87

Newman, P. R., *Marston Moor, 2 July 1644: The Sources and the Site*, University of York, Borthwick Paper 53 (1978)

Pickles, R. L., 'A Brief History of the Alum Industry in North Yorkshire, 1600–1875', *The Cleveland Industrial Archaeologist*, 2 (1975), 1–7

Ryder, I. E., 'The Seizure of Hull and its Magazine, January 1642', *YAJ*, 61 (1989), 139–48

Wenham, P., *The Siege of York and Battle of Marston Moor 1644* (Skipton, 1969)

Willan, T. S., 'The Parliamentary Surveys of the North Riding', *YAJ*, 31 (1934), 224–89

Woolrych, A. H., 'Yorkshire's Treaty of Neutrality', *History Today* (October 1956), 696–704

____ 'Yorkshire and the Restoration', *YAJ*, 39 (1958), 483–507

(c) Unpublished Theses

Binns, J., 'Sir Hugh Cholmley of Whitby 1600–1657: His Life and Works', Ph.D, Leeds Univ., 1992

Brooke, T. H., 'The Memoirs of Sir Hugh Cholmeley', B.Litt., Oxford Univ., 1937

Hall, B., 'The Trade of Newcastle and the North-East Coast, 1600–1640', Ph.D., London Univ., 1933

Kennedy, D. E., 'Parliament and the Navy, 1642–1648', Ph.D., Cambridge Univ., 1959

McIntyre, S. C., 'Towns as Health and Pleasure Resorts', D. Phil., Oxford Univ., 1973

Nash, P. G., 'Doncaster, Ripon and Scarborough, c.1640–1750', Ph.D., Leeds Univ., 1983

Newman, P. R., 'The Royalist Armies in Northern England 1642–45', D.Phil., York Univ., 1978

Townsend, D. A., 'Scarborough in the Civil War 1642–45', B.A., Manchester Univ., 1966

Index

Entries in bold refer to illustrations

Acklam, Major Peter 212, 219
Adwalton Moor, Battle of 100, 128
Agostini 106, 112
Aldborough 14, 186
Alured, Captain Launcelot 60, 61, 63, 65, 82, 83, 86, 94, 95, 100
Anderson, Peter 110
Anlaby, John 187, 191, 199, 200, 230
Aram, Sergeant 249
Ashton, Captain 206, 207
Atmar, Martin 37, 49, 61, 62, 65, 74
Atmar, William 31, 192
Ayton 71

Bambrough John 255
Batty, family 35, 214, 235
Batty, Mary 214
Batty, William 31, 56, 60, 74, 84, 96, 124, 128, 170, 213, 244, 253
Becke, Henry 224
Beckwith, Captain Matthew 245
Bellasis, Henry 77
Bellasis, Sir John 101, 138
Bellasis, Thomas 250
Benson, Philip 119, 171, 213, 244
Berry, Colonel 245
Berwick 65
  Truce of 69
Best, Captain John 232–3
Beswick, Francis 249
Bethell, Colonel 203–12, 213, 214, 218, 219, 221, 222, 240
Beverley 4, 5, 14, 30, 56, 69, 74–5, 77, 100, 209
Bilbrough, Richard 136–7, 244, 246, 255
Blackborne, Robert 237
Blackfriargate 28
Blake, Admiral 231

Boatman, Mr 176
Boroughbridge 14
Bourchier, Barrington 211, 213
Boyes, George 86
Boyes, Roger 243
Boyes, Thomas 268
Boynton, Sir Matthew 5, 58, 84, 85, 102, 157–62, 167, 175, 179, 181, 183–6, 191, 193, 194, 198
Boynton, Colonel Matthew 193, 194, 196, 197–212, 213, 216, 217, 225, 243, 269–70
Bradford 2, 79, 100
Bradshaw, Richard 221
Bridgnorth 146
Bridgwater, Lord 175
Bridlington 5, 24, 25, 101, 146, 162, 178, 229
  Bay 91
  Priory 26
  Quay 56, 96
Brompton 12
Buck, Captain John 207
Buckingham, Duke of 56, 59
Burghley, Thomas Lord 23
Burton, Sam 119
Burtondale 7, 12, 29
Bushell, Captain Browne 86, 87, **88**, 91, 94, 95, 100, 111, 114, 131, 136, 143–4, 195–6, 217, 223–5
Bushell, Henry 95
Bushell's battery 117, 119, 141–2, 148, 153, 155, 167
Butler, George 68
Byward Wath (Scarborough Mere) 7, 8, 244

Cargate 28, 33
Carnarvon, Lord 71

Chaloner, James of Guisborough 182–7
Chaloner, Thomas 233
Chapman, William 32, 81, 84, 123, 127, 218, 243
Charles I, King *passim*, 6, **54**, 64, 66, 68, 70, 71, 73–5, 77, 78, 84, 85–6, 96, 99, 107, **135**, 139, 158, 163, 186, 195, 199, 212, 270
Charles II, King 237, 254
  as Prince Charles 199, 205, 206, 212, 213, 221
Cholmley, Ann 163
Cholmley, Elizabeth 163
Cholmley, family of Whitby 41, 46
Cholmley, Henry 70, 71, 81–2, 109, 158, 163, 240
Cholmley, Hugh 163, 241
Cholmley, Sir Hugh 5, 41, 46, 56, 58, 59, 64, 65, 66, 70, 180, 182, 190, 193, 199, 202, 209, 212, 220, 224, 240, 242, 247, 268, 269–70
  changes allegiance 93–6
  and First Civil War 79–130
  and Great Siege 131–63
  and Long Parliament 71–8
  and Short Parliament 67–9
Cholmley, James 95, 127, 220
Cholmley, Nathaniel 149–50
Cholmley, Sir Richard 19
Cholmley, William 163
Cleveland 103
Cloughton 175, 244, 257
coal trade 23, 24, 49–51, 80, 111–13, 121, 145, 178, 230
Coale, Edmund 255
Cockerman, Colonel 156
Cockhill Tower 17, 114
Conell, Anthony 214
Constable, Sir John 19, 59
Constable, Sir William 101, 137
Constant, Joseph 222–3
Conyers, Ellinor 32
Conyers, Sir John 71–2
Conyers, Captain Nicholas 211
Conyers, William 32, 39, 74, 96, 128, 200, 201
Cooper, William 127, 136, 144, 187
Cotterill, John 239, 241, 242
Coward, Henry 32, 128
Craven, Lord 106

Crompton, Major 102, 155, 163
Cromwell, Oliver 108, 205, 207, 210, 226, 228, 231
Cromwell, Richard 233
Crosland, Sir Jordan 131, 242–3, 245, 251, 255, 263

Damgeth (stream) 28
Darley 102
Darley, Henry 45, 102
Darley, John 184, 186, 190
Darley, Richard 200
de Gomme, Bernard 75
de la Roche, Bartholomew 75
de Witt, Admiral 229, 230
Dent, Major 156
Denton, Captain John 111, 129, 136, 143, 197
Dickenson, Gregory 45
Digby, Lord 146
Dighton, Richard 145, 202, 213, 229, 244
Dodsworth, John 255
Doncaster 5
Ducke, Thomas 244
Durham 65

Edgehill, Battle of 82
Ellis, James 174
Ellison, Captain John 196
Essex, Earl of 79, 81, 83
Etherington, Matthew 257
Etherington, Richard 233
Eure, Francis 41
Everley 101

Fairfax, Sir Ferdinando 65, 182–3
Fairfax, Thomas Lord 85, 86, 87, 108, 112, 131, 138, 147, 183, 198, 209, 220
Falsgrave 12, 28, 65–6, 68, 95, 113, 125, 132, 136, 138, 166, 167, 244, 266
  Moor 12
Farrer, John 39, 51, 59
Farrer ('Farroe'), Thomasin 32, 39, 52, 258
Farthing, Richard 170
Fawether, Francis 32, 84, 104, 125, 127, 129, 136, 144, 187, 217
Fielding, Colonel 71
Filey 12, 101, 222
fishing 22, 48, 52, 53–6, 63
Flamborough 12, 91, 230

INDEX

Fleetwood, General 236
Foord, Daniel 125, 244, 255, 265
Foord, family 244
Foord, Thomas 31, 39, 56, 57, 74, 84, 86, 169
Foord, Timothy 125, 244, 252, 266, 268
Foord, William 32, 35, 42, 45, 71, 74, 96, 124, 125, 169, 213, 215, 224, 229, 243, 244, 247, 255
Fowler, Matthew 32, 73, 96, 169, 178, 201, 214–15, 243, 245, 246
Fowler, William 253
Fox, George 247–52, 253–4
Freeman, Major 204
Fysh, Cornelius 244, 246
Fysh, family 33–5, **34**, 77, 95, 127
Fysh, Gregory 30, 31, 37, 39, 43, 58, 60, 127, 169
Fysh, Robert 32, 39, 44
Fysh, Tristram 84, 124, 125, 126, 127, 136, 187, 202, 246, 255, 266
Fysh, William 30, 31, 74, 81, 84, 123, 127

Gate, family of Seamer 19–20, 40
Gate, Sir Henry 19, 47, 51, 53, 55
Gibson, Ralph 168
Gildshuscliff 28
Gill, Thomas 30, 32, 73, 125–6, 175, 176, 179, 187, 196, 213, 223, 224
Gilson, Christopher 118, 119, 168
Goodricke, Captain William 99
Goring, Lord 89, 91
Gower, Edward 241
Gower, Lieutenant John 156
Gower, Sir Thomas 156, 241
Gradell, William 267
Guisborough 87
  Battle of 89, 186

Hackness 101
Hamilton, Duke of 200, 205
Hamilton Marquess of 66, 71
Hampden, John 67
Hampton, Thomas 244
Harrison, Captain 183–4
Harrison, John Snr 31–2, 42, 43, 49, 59, 62, 74, 81, 84, 96, 123, 172, 175, 176, 177, 178, 179, 182–3, 190, 196, 213, 214, 215, 218, 224, 232–3, 234, 239
Harrison, John Jnr 190, 198, 200, 201, 213, 224, 234, 239, 241, 242, 245, 246, 253, 266
Harrison, Mrs 266
Harrison, Ralph 244
Harthropp, Robert 169, 170
Harwood, Anne 215
Headley, family 35, 123–4
Headley, John 196
Headley, William 31, 39, 81, 123, 129, 130
Hearth Tax 265
Hedon 5, 14
Helmsley 108, 109, 131, 194, 209
Henrietta Maria, Queen 75–6, 89, 91, **92**, 94, 95, 96–7, 99, 100, 140, 146, 270
Henry, Prince 220
Hickson, Edward 122–3, 188, 214
Hickson, family 122–3
Hickson, John 95, 118, 122–3, 127, 136, 169, 187, 215, 242, 243, 249, 255, 266
Hickson, William 76, 122, 129
Hoby, Sir Thomas Posthumous 29, 40–7, 58, 60, 64, 65
Hodgson, Peter 32, 129, 188, 201, 213, 229, 247–51, 267
Hodgson, Samuel 32, 128, 201, 213
Hodgson, William 256
Hogg, Ralph 111
Holderness 244
Holderness, Earl of, *see* Ramsay
Holt, Lieutenant 207
Holy Sepulchre, Church of 21, 29, 257
Hotham, Durand 233
Hotham, Captain John 68, 84, 98, 233
Hotham, Sir John 64, 65, 66, 67, 69, 71, 79, 81, 83, 91, 98, 99, 134, 148, 182, 186, 189, 224, 233, 240
Howe 140
Howebridge 91
Hull 2, 5, 24, 33, 47, 76, 79, 94, 99, 100, 101, 105, 111, 126, 128, 131, 142, 151, 159, 162, 186, 189, 195, 202, 203, 210, 219
Husband, William 257
Hutchinson, Edward 36
Hutchinson, Isabel 36, 39
Hutchinson, Stephen 36, 39, 58, 59, 78
Hutton Buscel 60, 65, 71
Hyde, Sir Edward, Earl of Clarendon 148

Ingram, Sir Thomas 138

James, Duke of York 237, 241
Jarratt, Christopher 170, 200, 213, 214, 215, 243, 253
Jermyn, (Lord) Henry 103, 146
Jilson, Christopher 255, 256

Kay, John 243, 249, 255
Key, John 266
Keyingham 75
King's Cliff 34
Kingston-upon-Hull 23
Knaresborough 14, 108, 110, 194, 205, 259
Knowsley, Elizabeth 244
Knowsley, John 265

Lambert, General John 205, 212, 236, 241
Lancashire 205, 210
Lancaster 180
Langdale, Sir Marmaduke 200
Langton, Sir Thomas 60
Lascelles, Colonel Francis 162, 207, 214, 245
Lascelles, Captain Thomas 222
Lawson, Captain John 35, **90**, 94, 96, 110, 126, 176, 184, 186, 188–93, 194, 196, 201, 210, 211, 212, 217, 218, 221–2, 223, 225–8, 230–4, 235–8, 239, 256, 257
Lawson, William 105, 124, 129, 130, 172, 181, 188, 217, 242, 251, 265
Leeds 5, 98
Legard, Colonel Christopher 203–5, 211, 213, 214
Legard, John of Ganton 77, 87, 94–5, 110, 239–40, 245, 251, 255
Legard, Captain Richard 121, 240
Legard, Thomas 240
Legge, Captain William 67
Leicester 6, 180
Leland, John 7, 26, 29, 33, 47, 167
Lenthall, Speaker 89, 200, 236
Leslie, General 101
Leven, Earl of 101, 108
Lindsey, Earl of 74, 77
London 24, 33, 47, 50, 70, 105, 112, 179, 190, 191, 270
Lothwithiel, Battle of 109
Lythe 176, 188

Mackworth, General 91, 93

Malton 7, 14, 59, 60, 81, 87, 91
Manchester, Earl of 101, 108, 142
Market Weighton 99
Marley, Sir John 111
Marriner, Captain Nicholas 222–3
Marston Moor, Battle of 2, 101–2, 106, 107, 124, 128, 130, 142, 148, 268
Maurice, Prince 75
Medley, Captain 89
Meldrum, Sir John 2, 99, 113, 114, 131–57, 160, 161, 165, 167, 170, 180, 181, 209
Melton, Sir John 67
Merry, George 119, 244
Metham, Sir Thomas 65
Mildmay, Captain 83
Millbeck 8
Minithrop, Robert 119
Minithrope, Robert Jnr 257
Monck, General 236, 240, 241
Monkman, William 129, 130
Moone, Thomas 118, 128, 202
Motham, Captain Peter 230
Mountagu, Edward 231, 236
Moxon, Ralph 244
Mucknell, Captain 143
Mulgrave, Earl of 99
Muston 65

Naseby, Battle of 96, 158, 212
Needham, Colonel Simon 162
Neighall, Paul 119
Neile, Archbishop 26, 29
Nesfield, William Snr 32, 110, 124, 126, 176, 177, 186, 187, 192, 198, 200, 201, 221, 243, 245, 246, 250, 253
Nesfield, William Jnr 214, 250
Nevile, Francis of Chevet 69
Newark 5, 140, 142, 159, 162
New Dyke Bank 8, 34
Newborough 8–9, 28, 34, 49, 65, 214, 263–4, 266
 Bar 73, 82, 95, 118, 169, 174
 Prison 86
 Gate 28, 29, 34, 51, 121
Newburn, Battle of 70
Newcastle 3, 23, 24, 50, 79, 85, 89, 91, 99, 101, 105, 108, 110, 111–12, 121, 128, 172, 196, 205
Newcastle, Earl of 4, 84, 85, 91, 94, 95,

99, 100, 101, 102, 106, 107, 124, 128, 130, 142, 146, 268
New Malton 71
Newport, Earl of 87
Newton, Captain Isaac 131, 224
Newton, John 224
Nicholson, Henry 32, 243, 255
Nightingale, Roger 32
Northallerton 14, 70
Northend, Captain 241, 244
Northstead 19
Northumberland, Earl of 64, 67–8, 70, 72
Norway 50
Norwich 3
Nottingham 75, 77, 78
Nottingham, Earl of 23, 84

Ogle, Mr 45
Oldborough 8–9, 28, 65, 86, 263–4, 265–6
 Bar 82, 174, 203–4
Oliver, Thomas 255, 256, 257, 266
Orange, Prince of 76
Osborne, Sir Edward 61, 63, 67–8, 73
Overton, Colonel 210
Oxford 100, 139, 270

Palmer, Jonas 232
Parliament *passim*, 66, 69
 Cavalier 245
 Convention 240–1
 Short 67–9
 Long *passim*, 70, 71, 73, 76, 77, 84–5, 182–7, 193, 198, 207, 236
Peacock, Elizabeth 32
Peacock, Paul 39, 56, 57
Peacock, Richard 39, 59
Pearson, George 32, 170
Penn, Admiral 226, 230
Pennington, Sir John 77
Penston, William 45, 118, 120, 217, 245, 267
Percy, Captain 106
Pett, Phineas 197
Pickering 51, 91, 247
 Castle 91, 141
 Forest of 21
Piercebridge 84
Piercie, Captain 156
Pierrepont, Francis 183
piracy 24, 55, 110–13

Pontefract 2, 5, 14, 108, 110, 147, 194, 210
Porter, Edward 255
Porter, Leonard 253
Poskitt, Christopher 128, 188
Poskitt, William 128
Potter Brompton 101
Potter, George 219
Powell, John 73
Poyntz, Major General 160–1
Preston, Battle of 205
Pym, John 83–4, 85

Rainsborough, Colonel Thomas 100
Ramsay, John, Earl of Holderness 20, 56, 247
Ramsdale 8, 12, 14, 86, 168
Ramshill 98
Ravenscar 12
Readhead, James 32
Redhead, John 201, 243
Reeve, John 229
Remmington, Robert 109
Richmond 5, 14, 267
Ripon 5, 14, 41, 71
 Treaty of 70
Robinson, Captain John 265
Robinson, Luke 175, 176, 179, 182–7, 191, 194, 196, 198, 199, 210, 224, 225, 230, 239–40, 243, 245, 247
Robinson, William 65, 68, 172, 243, 265
Rogers, Robert 124, 128, 129, 243, 255
Rosdale, John 30, 128, 170, 242, 255
Rosdale, Peter 32, 96, 169, 200
Ross, Sergeant Major 103
Ruddock, Captain 119, 121
Roxby 93
Rudlee, Lieutenant John 217, 218
Rupert, Prince 2, 75, 76, 101, 102, 106, 107, 123, 124, 128. 142, 180, 270

St Mary Magdalene (mortuary chapel) 29
St Mary's Church 9, 13, 14, 25, **27**, 29–33, 37, 41, 43–4, 48, 60, 118, 130, 131, 137, 140, 142, **143**, 143, 165–8, 176, 201, 213, 214, 215–16, 240, 243, 244, 247, 248, 253–7, 263, 264–5, 266
 churchwardens 14, 43, 73, 252–3, 255
 rectory 80
St Mary's Quarter 9, 65, 86, 170, 176

St Thomas the Martyr 14, 21, 29, 73, 167, 215, 254, 263
poorhouse 14, 120, 219, 229, 256
Salmon, Edward 233
Salmon, Lieutenant Colonel 219, 229, 233
Salton, Robert 73, 171, 175, 200, 201
Sandal 110, 147, 194
Sanderson, William 119
Sandside 22, 46, 51, 60, 71, 111, 118, 127, 178, 201, 213, 242
Sandys, Sir William 105, 106
Saunders, Nicholas 96, 170, 200, 213, 214, 224, 252
Saunders, William 223, 242, 266
Scalla Moor 66
Scarborough *passim*
  bailiffs 13, 28–9, 173
  bars 8, 28
  borough 8
  burgesses 13, 21–2, 26, 41, 61
  and the parish church 26
  Castle 15–21, **16**, **17**, **18**, 48, 60, 63, 76, 79, **152**, **154**, 186, 193, 194, 195, 199, 202–3, 228, 240, 245, 250, 263
    in First Civil War 82–3, 84, 104, 108, 117
    during Great Siege 131–62, 186
    in Second Civil War 202–4, 209, 213
    Stafford's coup 19
  chamberlains 13, 173–4, 216
  coastal defences 53–64
  Common 170
  Common Hall *passim*, 4–5, 13, 14, 31–2, 41–2, 43, 44, 45, 46, 55, 58, 59, 60, 67, 68, 73, 74, 77, 80, 82, 84, 87, 96, 104, 114, 117, 118, 120, 121, 122, 129, 165, 167, 168, 169, 170, 174, 176, 177, 183, 187, 191, 192–3, 200, 201, 202, 206, 213, 214, 216, 217, 219, 239–41, 242, 243, 245, 246
  coroners 13, 123
  economy and commerce 12, 47–52
  fairs 12
  geography 8–9, **10–11**
  government 12–15
  harbour 20–5, 52, 53, 73, 76, 110, 132, 143, 145, 148, 173
    foreign skirmishes in 61–2
  market 172
  market place 28

mills 168
Mere 8, 13
monastic establishments 27–9
parliamentary representation 13–14, 67–8, 182–7, 193–4, 233–4, 239–41, 245
pier 20–5, 53, 73
pinfold 216
'plat' **xii**, 8
population 48–50, **49**
prison 216
school 45, 47, 118, 167, 216, 247, 267
spa 48, 52, 258–62
Schofield, James 117, 148–9, 166, 171
Scotland, 50, 52, 64–70, 195
  and First Civil War 99, 101, 103, 105, 108, 112
  and Great Siege 131–5
  and Second Civil War 200–
Seacroft Moor, Battle of 98
Seamer 7, 12, 51, 72, 169, 175
  market 47, 51–2
  Moor 65
Sedman, Thomas 249, 266
Sedman, William 255
Selby 98, 101, 162–3
Sellers, Richard 252
Sharps, Matthew 119
Sheffield 142, 194
Sheffield, Lord 56, 71
Sherburn 7, 12
Shimmings, William 255
Ship Money 62, 66, 67, 68, 120
Simpson, William 31, 60, 109, 137, 159, 166, 175–6, 177, 178, 237, 256, 266
Skipton 2, 5, 110, 147
Slingsby, Sir Guilford 56, 87–9
Smith, Captain 207
Sollitt, Francis 128–9, 136, 170, 187, 206, 210–11, 243, 246, 253, 266
South Cliff 52, 125
South Steel battery 114, **115**, **116**, **117**, 134, 148, 151, 195, 210, 263
Southeron, Captain 220, 266
Spencer, William 211
Stafford, Sir Thomas 19
Stamford Bridge 83, 85, 140
Stanley, Lieutenant Colonel 156
Steward, Colonel 132
Strickland, Robert 87–9

INDEX

Strickland, Sir William 200
Sunderland 24, 50, 105, 111–12, 121, 172, 178
Swaine, Henry 119, 127, 244

Tadcaster 85, 86
Taylor, John 244–5, 256
Tennant, William 60
Thackray, Richard 224
Thirsk 14
Thirty Years War 53–64
Thomas, Browne 111, 136, 143, 221–2
Thompson, Christopher 30, 31, 36, 39, 55, 58, 74, 80, 83, 84, 86, 124, 126, 136, 178, 179, 240
Thompson, family 20, 31, 35–40, **36**, 77, 80–1, 95, 126, 178–9, 187, 243, 247
Thompson, Francis 31, 37, 39, 41–2, 46, 51, 55–6, 58, 71, 74, 80, 83, 84, 86, 124, 128, 169, 175, 210, 247, 256, 257, 264, 265
Thompson, Richard 31, 37, 39, 42, 46, 74, 80, 84, 86, 124, 125, 129, 169, 178, 265
Thompson, Richard of London 254–5
Thompson, Stephen 30, 31, 42, 80, 84, 86, 126, 176, 179, 240, 247
Thompson, Timothy 30, 31, 32, 37, 39, 42, 60, 65, 74, 80, 84, 124, 126
Thompson, William 31, 35, 39, 42, 43, 56, 58, 80, 167, 239–41, 245, 247, 255, 265, 268
Thoresby, Ralph 257, 262
Thornton 93
Thornton, family 258–9
Trenchfield, Captain 76–7
Tromp, Admiral 106

Undercliff 9, 49, 65, 266

Vane, Sir Henry 142, 226
Vavasour, Colonel William 71

Walker, Steven 137
Walker, William 243, 255
Walkington 109
Walton, Christopher 249
Warwick, Earl of 75, 205

Washbeck 7
Weaponness (Oliver's Mount) 8, 12, 13, 14, 119, 169, 216
Weatherill, Joseph 268–9
Webster, John 106
Wentworth, Colonel 71
Wentworth, Sir George of Woolley 70
Wentworth, Thomas, Earl of Strafford 42–3, 60, 67–8, 69, 70, 71, 79
Wetherby 71
Whitby 5, 24, 50, 69, 80, 87, 101, 109, 111, 131, 137, 145, 146, 176–7, 197, 220, 224, 229
  pier 58
Wickham, Captain 151
Widdrington, Lord 268
Wigginer, Giles of Whitby 106
Wigginer, Nicholas 197, 224
Wildman, John 230–1, 233
Wilkinson, Richard 256
Williamson, Jacob 104, 105, 110
Windmill Hill 134
Wittie, Captain Robert 199
Wittie, Dr Robert 250–1, 258–62
Wood, Mr of Whitby 176–7
Wood, Mrs 177–8
Woodall, John 124
Woodall, Thomas 169
Woolf, Mr 104
Wressle Castle 99
Wright, Mary 268
Wyvill, Roger of Osgodby 45, 68, 71–2, 77, 118, 122, 127, 242, 268
Wyvill, William 74, 77, 81, 83, 122, 242–3, 255

Yarm, Battle of 89, 91
Yedingham 140
Yeoman, John 224
York 2, 3, 5, 7, 9, 12, 25, 60, 61, 68, 70, 73, 76, 77, 79, 84, 85, 87, 91, 94, 100, 102, 103, 104, 106, 107, 108, 123, 124, 128, 142, 151, 160, 198, 202, 222, 223, 240, 259

Zachary, Vice-Admiral 143, 144, 157, 160, 181